THE GREAT HISTORIES is a new series designed to introduce modern readers to the works of the most important historical writers from Herodotus to the present day. The works chosen are notable both as literature, to be read for pleasure, and as significant contributions to the philosophy and study of history. Each volume has been edited by a distinguished scholar, expert in the particular field, and is devised to be easily readable, intelligible, and enjoyable for the interested layman.

In **THE GREAT HISTORIES** series, each historian is presented in the compass of one volume which includes the best of his work and illustrates his full range. The introductions will enable the reader to appreciate the contribution which each historian has made to the continuous process and changing philosophy of history.

GIBBON was edited by Hugh R. Trevor-Roper, distinguished Regius Professor of Modern History at Oxford University, who is also general editor of the series.

THE GREAT HISTORIES

A series under the general editorship of Hugh R. Trevor-Roper, Regius Professor of Modern History, Oxford University.

GIBBON

THE DECLINE AND FALL OF THE ROMAN EMPIRE and Other Selections from the Writings of Edward Gibbon

Edited and Abridged with an Introduction by Hugh R. Trevor-Roper. ▐▬▬▬▬

WASHINGTON SQUARE PRESS, INC. • NEW YORK

GIBBON

A *Washington Square Press* edition
1st printing......................September, 1963

The Decline and Fall of the Roman Empire was first
published in England between 1776 and 1788 by W.
Strahan and T. Cadell. The map of the Roman World
is used by permission of the copyright holders Har-
court, Brace and World and Chatto and Windus, Ltd.

L

Published by
Washington Square Press, Inc., 630 Fifth Avenue, New York, N.Y.

WASHINGTON SQUARE PRESS editions are distributed in
the U.S. by Affiliated Publishers, a division of Pocket
Books, Inc., 630 Fifth Avenue, New York 20, N.Y.

Contents

Edward Gibbon: Introduction

[a] PHILOSOPHICAL HISTORY

Edward Gibbon is the greatest of the historians of the
Enlightenment, the only one of them who is still read
not only as a stylist, but also as a historian. Two centuries of massive scholarship and constant intellectual evo-
lution have inevitably left many marks on Roman, Byzantine and, even more, on medieval European history;
but it remains a remarkable fact that anyone who wishes
to study the later Roman or Byzantine empire will still
find Gibbon's *Decline and Fall of the Roman Empire* the
best, as well as the most readable narrative of it. The
earlier historians whom we still read were nearly always
historians of their own times, whose authority springs
partly from their own direct observation. Gibbon is the
first great historian of a remote past whom the work of
later centuries has not driven from the field.

This unique phenomenon requires explanation. The explanation, like all explanations of individual genius, lies
partly in the times. The mid-eighteenth century was a
remarkable period in European intellectual history. It
was an age of great confidence in which new sciences
were being developed; and these new sciences encouraged
historians (and others) to unify and reinterpret the enormous, but still manageable data which had been accumulated by their predecessors. Gibbon and his contemporaries—Montesquieu, Voltaire, Robertson, Hume, Adam
Smith—were not content to be mere traditional historians
—local chroniclers, political partisans, or contemporary
memoir writers. They sought to answer more profound
questions, and about a far wider field. They called themselves "universal historians" or "philosophic historians."
And this "philosophic history" was peculiar to their generation. Neither the century before them, with its vast,
but ill-digested erudition, nor the century after them, with

its renewed national fragmentation, was so perfectly adapted to it.

But of all those who professed to study "universal history," Gibbon was the greatest. He was the greatest because he combined, as no other man did, beneath a majestic style and the appearance of ease, an equal mastery of the new "philosophy" and the old "erudition." In order to appreciate his achievement, we may begin by glancing briefly at the two processes which were fused in his work: the processes of historical scholarship and historical interpretation. In doing so, we shall refer particularly to those writers to whom Gibbon himself acknowledged the greatest debt.

Historical interpretation, or at least the secular interpretation of history, began, in the modern world, at the Renaissance with the great Florentines Machiavelli and Guicciardini. But the dawn was not followed immediately by day. With the rise of religious controversy in the sixteenth century, the new science was condemned as heretical by Catholics and Protestants alike. The greatest interpreters of history between the Renaissance and the Enlightenment were the Frenchman J. A. de Thou (Gibbon's "grave Thuanus") and the Venetian Fra Paolo Sarpi, or "Father Paul," "that incomparable historian" as Gibbon called him, who both wrote at the beginning of the seventeenth century. They were Catholics disliked at Rome—indeed, till the eighteenth century, Sarpi's work was only published in the freedom of Protestant countries. The great historical critics of the end of the seventeenth century who were not historians, though they did much to change historical attitudes, were similarly heretical. For Gibbon, the most significant of these "moderns"—the conquerors of the "Ancients" in the famous "Battle of the Books"—were two French Protestant émigrés, the Arminian scholar Jean Leclerc and the Huguenot encyclopædist Pierre Bayle. Turning the light of a new scepticism upon the past, they invited their successors to continue the process which religious orthodoxy had cut short, and still opposed.

But if interpretation was perilous for two centuries before Gibbon, the accumulation of fact was not only

viii

safe—it could be positively meritorious. Facts were missiles in the ideological war, and behind both fronts, successive scholars piled them up for ultimate use. In the sixteenth century the two great armouries of historical controversialists were the Protestant history of the so-called "Centuriators of Magdeburg" (1559-74) and, in planned opposition to it, the gigantic *Ecclesiastical Annals* of the Roman cardinal Cæsar Baronius (1588-93). In the seventeenth century the work continued. The Franciscan friar Antoine Pagi (1624-99) perfected Baronius' *Annals,* and the hardly less bigoted Jansenist, le Nain de Tillemont (1637-98) rivalled them with his compilations of imperial and church history. Baronius, "firm and hard as the rock of Peter," and Tillemont, "the surefooted mule of the Alps," are constant sources of Gibbon's facts—and butts of his wit. Other scholars, especially after 1650, were less polemical in their purpose. Gibbon acknowledged a great debt to the French Byzantinist Charles du Fresne du Cange, whose glossaries and works of reference would spread "a steady light over the darkness of the Lower Empire," and an even greater to what was undoubtedly the most magnificent enterprise of collective scholarship yet known: what he called "the Benedictine workshop of St. Germain-les-Prés" in Paris. This was the monastery of the reformed Benedictines of St. Maur, whose greatest figures were their third and fourth abbots, dom Jean Mabillon (1632-1707) and dom Bernard Montfaucon (1655-1741). Between them, Mabillon and Montfaucon laid a new base for medieval studies, collecting, elucidating and publishing the manuscripts, coins and other sources of European history. Their greatest disciple was the Italian archivist Ludovico Muratori (1672-1750) who edited and published thirty-four folio volumes of medieval Italian sources. Gibbon accepted Muratori as "my guide and master in the history of Italy," and in his last paper, "a sketch interrupted by death" (as Lord Sheffield called it) he lamented that there was still no "English Muratori."

Thus, by Gibbon's time the materials of history, and especially of Church history, were available as never before, and the great critics had prepared the way for a "philosophical" church historian. Already some attempts had been made. Two men in particular had ventured to handle Church history in a secular spirit, to see the Church not as a repository of truth (or error), but as a human society subject to the same social laws as other societies. One of these was J. L. von Mosheim, a Lutheran theologian who, in 1726, published a critical and impartial study of the early Church. In Protestant Hanover, he could do this safely. The other was Pietro Giannone, a Neapolitan lawyer, who, in 1723, analysed the institutional and social consequences of the Catholic Church in the history of Naples. He was soon taught another consequence. Excommunicated by the clergy, driven from Naples by the monks and from Vienna by the Jesuits, he took refuge in Protestant countries, but was ultimately lured into Catholic Savoy and died in prison in Turin. Fortunately, in France the Catholic Church was a little less powerful, and it was in France that two men, in the generation separating Giannone and Mosheim from Gibbon, laid the basis of a new universal "philosophic history." Both of them were of great importance in Gibbon's life and work. They were Montesquieu and Voltaire.

Montesquieu and Voltaire had much in common. Both were inspired by visits to England and by the example of the English constitution. Both took all human history for their material and used, in particular, the evidence of Antiquity and of modern China to the interpretation of Europe. Both applied purely secular criteria to religious history. Both were condemned at Rome and published their work in Protestant countries. But there were also great differences between them, differences which, as we shall see, caused Gibbon to reject Voltaire and identify himself exclusively with Montesquieu. For this reason we may postpone discussion of Voltaire and say a few words on Montesquieu, without whom (it is not too much to say), the *Decline and Fall* would never have been written.

In retrospect, we can say that Montesquieu was the father of sociology. Where other philosophers had confined their study of social cause and effect within relatively narrow compartments, he first regarded all human activities as basically comparable and sought to explain political and religious forms by geographical and social causes. By so doing he created a new science and brought the particular studies of men like Giannone and Mosheim into a generalised picture. Montesquieu's first essay in this direction was his exciting but somewhat naïve *Considérations sur les causes de la grandeur des Romains et de leur décadence* (Amsterdam 1734). It achieved its full form in his masterpiece, *De l'Esprit des Lois* (Geneva 1748). General enough not to lay down any cramping orthodoxy, clear enough to inspire fresh work, Montesquieu's principles gave a new impetus to "philosophic history." If they had little influence in France, increasingly dominated by the genius of Voltaire, they inspired notable work elsewhere. Their most immediate effect was not in England, where intellectual life was stagnant after the Whig triumph of 1715: it was in Scotland, where the mental discipline of a Calvinist society suddenly found itself—in consequence of the Union of 1707—in fertile contact with a maturer world.

The Scottish Enlightenment was particularly remarkable in historical and social studies, and it owed much to the stimulus of Montesquieu. The first to enter the field was the philosopher David Hume, the first volume of whose *History of England* appeared in 1754. Meanwhile Hume's friend, William Robertson, a clergyman of the Church of Scotland, was at work on his *History of Scotland,* which was published in 1759. Ten years later Robertson published his *History of Charles V,* whose long and brilliant first chapter remains one of the finest examples of the "universal history" inspired by Montesquieu. The climax of the Scottish Enlightenment was reached in 1776, with the publication of Adam Smith's *Wealth of Nations.* As Smith's disciple, John Millar, wrote of their subject, "the great Montesquieu pointed out the road. He was the Lord Bacon of this branch of science. Dr. Smith is the Newton."

Such was the position of historical studies in Gibbon's student years. A series of great scholars, from Baronius to Muratori, had accumulated the material. An old "heretical" tradition of secular interpretation had been revived by men like Bayle and Leclerc and applied to history by Giannone and Mosheim. And a new and exciting science of social causation had been expounded by Montesquieu and already applied with success to limited fields by Hume and Robertson. In one of his footnotes, Gibbon himself summarised the course of "philosophical history" before his time. "Guicciardini and Machiavel," he wrote, "with their worthy successors Fra Paolo and Davila, were justly esteemed the first historians of modern languages till, in the present age, Scotland arose to dispute the prize with Italy herself." For England itself, in Gibbon's time, still had no share in the movement. Its intellectual life was dominated by the high-church Tory bigot, Dr. Johnson. Hume, in his letters, continually referred to England as irretrievably sunk in philistinism and factionalism. Gibbon always regarded it as his great good fortune that an early misadventure caused him to be removed from Oxford and to discover his way, in a cosmopolitan country and a Calvinist society, into this modern European philosophy.

[b] EDWARD GIBBON

Of Gibbon's personal life we need say little here: he has recounted all that we need to know in his *Autobiography*—perhaps the most perfect of all autobiographies—of which portions are printed in this volume. "A puny child, neglected by my mother, starved by my nurse, and of whose being very little care or expectation was entertained," he was brought up by a devoted aunt and received, owing to his frail health, only a spasmodic education, culminating in the brief, inglorious episode of his premature year at Oxford University. But from the first moment of ambition he was resolved to be a historian and he always had a passion for reading. Even at Oxford he read; at least we know that he read one author, whose effect on him was to be immediately disastrous, ultimately salutary. This author was Conyers Middleton.

Conyers Middleton was a Cambridge clergyman, famous and controversial in his day for learning, scepticism and elegancy of style. Three of his works won him immediate fame. In what Gibbon called "his agreeable *Letter from Rome*" (1729), he showed the extent to which pagan beliefs and ceremonies had been incorporated in Roman Catholicism. His *Life of Cicero* (1741), compiled from Cicero's own writings, was a highly successful biography, even if it was largely plagiarised from another, very rare book. But his most famous work was his *Free Inquiry into the Miraculous Powers which are supposed to have subsisted in the Christian Church* (1749). In this work, Middleton effectively demolished the convenient Protestant compromise whereby the miracles of the first centuries after Christ were allowed to be genuine while those of the Church after its "corruption" by monasticism, the cult of relics and other "pagan" ceremonies, were rejected as fraudulent. The excitement and scandal caused by this work were immense. David Hume, returning from Italy in 1749, was mortified to find his own work totally eclipsed by it, and the young Gibbon, at Oxford, drew from it one logically possible conclusion, *viz*: that since (as Middleton wrote) "the earlier miracles rest on no better foundation, nor are supported by any better evidence, than the later," the later "popish" miracles must be regarded as genuine and must in turn guarantee the authenticity of the Catholic Church. So Middleton, who afterwards became the guarantor of Gibbon's mature scepticism, began by leading him, at the age of sixteen, into the Church of Rome. The immediate result was a public scandal, and hasty removal from Oxford to the custody of a sound Calvinist tutor in Lausanne.

In Lausanne, Gibbon soon recovered from his religious errors. He also embarked, under his tutor M. Pavilliard, on a systematic course of classical and modern reading which he continued after his return to England in 1758. In England he lived partly in London, partly with his father and new stepmother (to whom he became devoted) at Buriton in Hampshire. His studies were often interrupted by social life, and from 1760 they were seriously dislocated by two years of service with the Hampshire militia; but they were never altogether suspended and his journals, in these years, are a record of astonishingly wide reading. There we see Gibbon at work, adding to his vast knowledge, reducing it to order as he added, and at the same time always infusing into the scholarship of the past, which he so respected, the new philosophy of "the Moderns."

For Gibbon himself was essentially a "modern." Indeed, his modernity is one of the most attractive and most stimulating features of his writing. However remote or recondite his subject, he never forgot that he was a man of the world, and of the eighteenth century world too. He loved polite conversation, society, the theater; his house in London was elegantly furnished and decorated; his attitude towards the pedants of the past or future was one of rational condescension. His private letters charm by their irrepressible gaiety and humour, their zest for life and social pleasure, and make it easy to believe, as Lord Sheffield wrote, that "his conversation was still more captivating than his writings." And yet, behind this modernity, this gaiety, and often concealed by it, there lay a gigantic scholarship and a serious passion for scholarship. Between the two it was inevitable that there should sometimes be a tension. Indeed, the tension created an intellectual crisis in the heart of the Enlightenment. This tension evoked Gibbon's first work, his *Essay on the Study of Literature*, which he wrote in French in Lausanne, and published in 1761, after his return to England.

The tension can be summarised, too summarily no doubt, as the tension between Montesquieu and Voltaire, which was to develop into the tension between English Whigs and French revolutionaries. It sprang from a different intellectual attitude towards society. For whatever Voltaire and Montesquieu had in common, they were ultimately very different. Montesquieu was a reformer, but since he believed in the organic complexity of society, underlying and conditioning all political forms, he could only conceive of gradual and limited change. Even ideas, he believed, were subject to tenacious social forces. On the other hand Voltaire and his allies, the Encyclopædists, were far more radical. They saw themselves as practical reformers, even revolutionaries; in their supreme confidence in their own analysis and their haste to change society in accordance with it, they easily regarded the social structure which resisted them, not as a living organism, but as mere dead tissue and the ideas of their opponents as mere interested error and prejudice. This fundamental difference entailed, ultimately, a deep political difference. The Encyclopædists, supporters of revolutionary royalism in their own day, looked forward to the Jacobins of the French Revolution, while the disciples of Montesquieu looked forward to the anti-revolutionary Whig philosophy of Burke. Immediately, it entailed a different attitude in scholarship. Subordinating other considerations to politics, impatient of objectors and objections, the Encyclopædists could be ruthless to humanity and indifferent to truth.

This new attitude of the Encyclopædists was felt by Gibbon as a serious challenge. At Lausanne, he had been captivated by Montesquieu, but he had also admired Voltaire and courted him personally at Ferney. But as the new attitude was made clear, Gibbon's own attitude became clear too. He was particularly provoked by a suggestion of D'Alembert, that at the end of each century a selection be made of such knowledge as was worth preserving—i.e., such as was judged worth preserving by the advanced "philosophers" of the moment—and the rest destroyed. It was to defend the erudition of the past against such arrogant modernity that Gibbon wrote his *Essay*. All facts, he insisted, deserve respect: "a Montesquieu, from the meanest of them, will deduce consequences undreamed by ordinary men." If the blind cult of facts is pedantry, the opposite extreme, contempt of them, is fatal. "All sciences are founded on reasoning and facts. Without the latter, our studies would be chimerical; deprived of the former, they are blind." So Gibbon placed himself firmly on the side of Montesquieu —afterwards he would say that even the style of his *Essay* was vitiated by the imitation of Montesquieu—and firmly against the excesses of Voltaire; and all his writing afterwards illustrated this conscious choice. Throughout the *Decline and Fall* we can detect an underlying hostility to Voltaire, who is often cited;[1] and when the French Revolution came, we are not surprised to find Gibbon, in spite of many reasons for dissent, placing himself clearly on the side of the anti-Jacobin Burke.

Gibbon's *Essay* was provoked by the Encyclopædists, and it is interesting as showing his reaction against them. It is a defence of the "Ancients" and their erudition by one of the ablest of the "Moderns." But that is not its only interest. It is also the manifesto of a man who believes in the unity of knowledge, the fusion of "philosophy" and "erudition," and the possibility of general explanation. In it, Gibbon gives a particular illustration of his idea of "philosophic history." Comparing the two great Roman historians Livy and Tacitus, he remarks that Livy is an admirable narrator, but he is ultimately unsatisfactory because he ignores the connexion between the laws of the Roman republic and the genius of the Romans—in other words, Montesquieu's *esprit des lois*. From Tacitus, on the other hand, a reader can learn how it was that "these laws, made for a small, poor, half-civilised republic, overturned it when the power of its institutions had carried it to the highest pitch of grandeur." For this reason, he adds, "I know of no one except Tacitus who has quite come up to my idea of a philosophic historian."

In his *Essay*, Gibbon stated his philosophy. For the rest of his life he matured and applied it. It was a philosophy which tied him to no historical period or subject, and for all his classical training and vast knowledge of Antiquity, he might as easily as Hume or Macaulay, who were similarly trained, have become a modern historian. In fact, between his return to England and his final choice of subject, he considered a series of subjects, none of

---

[1] Gibbon's strictures on Voltaire as a historian, always on Gibbon's own ground, are not always fair. In spite of occasional superficiality, Voltaire made a great contribution to "philosophical history" as was recognised by Gibbon's friend, William Robertson. Indeed the panegyric of the infidel Voltaire by the greatest of Scottish historians—a Presbyterian clergyman and Moderator of the General Assembly of the Church of Scotland—is perhaps the most telling, because the least expected, tribute to his historical work.

them ancient. He considered medieval England, the French invasion of Renaissance Italy, the life of Sir Walter Ralegh, the history of Swiss liberty, Medicean Florence. But in the end he rejected all these subjects, and we must be glad of his rejection. Although anything written by Gibbon would no doubt have become a classic, the increase of merely factual knowledge would inevitably have caused an eighteenth-century work on such topics to date quickly. By a singular good fortune, before he had committed himself to any of them, Gibbon found an opportunity to travel which inspired him with a far happier idea: an idea truly worthy of a disciple of Montesquieu and "philosophic history."

For in January 1763, with the return of peace and the disbanding of the militia, Gibbon, like so many of his countrymen, seized the opportunity of foreign travel. He went first to Paris, where he frequented the salons and shared the company of the great, then back to Lausanne where he avoided the mean housekeeping of Mme. Pavilliard and stayed for a year at a fashionable *pension*. There he met two other young Englishmen who, in different ways, had a great influence on his life. One was John Baker Holroyd, afterwards first Earl of Sheffield, the friend of his lifetime to whom all his admirers are deeply in debt; the other, William Guise, the son of a Gloucestershire baronet, became his companion on the next stage of his travels—his famous visit to Rome.

Gibbon's Italian journey was a great success, for the two friends had many tastes in common. They travelled over the Alps to Turin and so through Milan, Genoa and Florence to Rome. They were presented at courts, studied antiquities, observed nature and art. Both of them kept diaries. But the importance of the journey is, of course, the inspiration which came to Gibbon in Rome when, as he afterwards wrote, "as I sat musing amidst the ruins of the Capitol, while the barefooted friars were singing vespers in the Temple of Jupiter . . . the idea of writing the decline and fall of the city first started to my mind." At first it was only the city of Rome whose fortunes he intended to trace. Later the idea developed in his mind and he envisaged nothing less than the decline and fall of the Roman Empire.

Back in England there were delays and distractions, but once Gibbon had begun to work, he worked systematically. With his powerful memory, his full command of the sources, and his marvellous organising capacity, he was able both to plan his huge work and to execute his plan. Neither social life in London, which he enjoyed, nor the entanglements of his property after his father's death in 1770, nor attendance in parliament, to which he was elected by a kinsman's influence in 1774, nor his (not very arduous) duties at the Board of Trade, of which he was a commissioner from 1779, seriously interrupted his work, and the first volume was published in 1776. It was an immediate success. Hume and Robertson themselves, the Tacitus and the Livy of Scotland, as Gibbon called them, wrote enthusiastically in praise of it; and Gibbon proudly told his stepmother that it had been "very well received by men of letters, men of the world, and even by fine-feathered ladies—in short, by every set of men except perhaps by the clergy who seem (I know not why) to show their teeth on the occasion."

The rage of the clergy, which seems genuinely to have surprised Gibbon, caused a slight interruption in his work. At first he treated with silent disdain the noise of parsons "sharpening their goose-quills" against him. Divinity professor after divinity professor rose up against him, Oxford followed Cambridge in the lists, but still Gibbon kept silent. It was not till a fifth antagonist, a young man from Balliol College, Oxford, one Davis, rushed into the fray and presumed, with the appearance of learning, to accuse him of dishonesty and plagiarism, that he decided to reply, and reply finally to all his critics. So he composed and published one of the most brilliant, most crushing rejoinders that has ever settled a literary dispute, his *Vindication*. This is a work which, as Lytton Strachey wrote, deserves to be better known than it is, for it shows Gibbon "really letting himself go." "Gibbon," as Dean Milman wrote, "with a single discharge from his ponderous artillery of learning and sarcasm, laid prostrate the whole disorderly squadron";

having done so, he returned quietly to his constructive work. By 1783, three volumes had been published, and a fourth was almost complete, when his whole plan of life suffered a much greater interruption. This was his migration from London back to Lausanne.

The immediate cause of the move was financial. Gibbon wished, and needed, to live less expensively than in London. But his need also coincided with an opportunity. In 1783, George Deyverdun, a Swiss friend of Gibbon since his first visit to Lausanne, found himself unable to maintain alone the large house, la Grotte, which he had inherited. Gibbon and he thereupon agreed to share the house and its expenses. Gibbon's English friends were astonished: how, they asked, could he ever live in "such an obscure nook in Switzerland" after tasting the society of Paris and London? The project, said Lord Sheffield, was "little short of insanity." But Gibbon was firm, and in fact, he never regretted his decision. He was charmed by the scenery; he lived in elegance and comfort; the social life of Lausanne was refreshed by visitors from England and France; and he was able to study. "I have health, friends, an amusing society and perfect freedom," he wrote. "A Commissioner of the Excise! The idea makes me sick!" It was in Lausanne, he declared, that he would finish the *Decline and Fall* and he would not return to England till the fourth year when the last volume, he confidently predicted, would be ready for the press.

He kept his word. In 1787, he completed his great work and immediately carried it to London. From Lord Sheffield's London house, in Downing Street, or his country house, Sheffield Place in Sussex, he supervised the printing and publishing of the last three volumes. Then he basked in the applause. The work had been far greater than he had expected: "I look back," he wrote, "with amazement on the road which I have travelled, but which I would never have entered had I been previously apprized of its length"; but it was done; he was assured of fame, and he never contemplated another major historical work. In 1788, he returned to Lausanne, and although the death of Deyverdun next year reduced the charms of his house, it did not deprive him of it; for

Deyverdun, by his will, left him a life-interest in it and the option of buying it from his legal heir. Gibbon secured his title for life, set about altering the house to suit his convenience, entertained his friends there and prepared to end his days in it. Meanwhile, he amused himself by writing his *Autobiography*, or rather (as he himself more accurately called it), his *Memoirs of my Life and Writing*. For essentially the *Autobiography* is not the personal life of Gibbon: it is the account of the making of a historian and of a great work of "philosophic history," the *Decline and Fall of the Roman Empire*.

Gibbon never completed the *Autobiography*. Nor did he die in Lausanne. In 1793, he had planned to visit England. When the time came, there were reasons for hesitation. The French Revolution was now in full swing; refugees from the Terror were pouring into Switzerland; and the revolutionary armies, having occupied Savoy, were preparing to attack Geneva. Moreover, Gibbon was himself unwell and movement was painful to him. But in April, 1793, a sudden event decided him. He learned that Lady Sheffield had died of pleurisy contracted while caring for French refugees in England. In spite of every difficulty, Gibbon resolved to visit Lord Sheffield at once, and passing within earshot of the French guns on the Rhine, he reached London in June. He spent the summer at Sheffield Place and then went for a round of visits. But in November, a long neglected glandular swelling necessitated a series of minor operations. Gibbon himself seems never to have taken the matter seriously. To the end he enjoyed society and on January 15, 1794, he remarked that "he thought himself a good life for ten, twelve or perhaps twenty years." The next day he died. Lord Sheffield, who had left him two days before, on the assurance that all was well, hurried back, but arrived too late. He caused Gibbon's body to be buried in his parish church in Sussex and, as his executor, secured his literary remains, which he afterwards published, including the *Autobiography*, which he reconstructed from six autograph drafts. Gibbon's papers remained in Lord Sheffield's family till 1896, when they were acquired by the British Museum.

[c] THE DECLINE AND FALL

The *Decline and Fall* is probably the most majestic work of history ever written. It covers 1,300 years of time; in space it ranges over Europe, Asia and North Africa; it includes the history of the most civilised and of the most barbarous nations; it describes the rise of two world religions; and its philosophical content rests on a yet wider observation, both in space and time. And yet this tremendous work is wonderfully coherent. Its structure is massive, but orderly. It was planned as a unit, and executed according to plan, single-handed. As Gibbon wrote, "my first rough manuscript, without any intermediate copy, has been sent to the press," and "not a sheet has been seen by any human eyes, excepting those of the author and the printer." In spite of this, errors of fact in it are infinitesimal. And the whole is presented in a style perfectly adapted for the material: a majestic, architectural style, and yet constantly alleviated by elegance in detail, flashes of wit and that most famous, most Gibbonian quality, the "grave and temperate irony" which he claimed to have learned from Pascal.

Of course Gibbon has not lacked critics. Writers from Horace Walpole to Lytton Strachey have said that he was essentially a "literary" or "classical" historian. The implication is that he confined himself to literary sources, ignoring the evidence of coins, inscriptions, archæology, etc., which provide so much essential matter to his successors and that his achievement consisted in reducing to ordered, "classical," narrative form the material presented to him by previous historians and scholars. Ironically, this is the charge which Gibbon himself made against Voltaire—or at least against Voltaire as a writer on the Middle Ages. Of Voltaire's *Siècle de Louis XIV*, Gibbon wrote in his diary, "I believe that Voltaire had for this work an advantage he has seldom enjoyed. When he treats of a distant period, he is not a man to turn over musty monkish writers to instruct himself. He follows some compilation, varnishes it over with the magic of his style, and produces a most agreeable, superficial, inaccurate performance. . . ." Much the same—except for the charge of inaccuracy, which no one has dared to make since the *Vindication*—has been said, by his detractors, of Gibbon.

From what has already been said here, it must be clear that this judgment upon Gibbon is very shallow. In all his writings, implicitly and explicitly, Gibbon continually revealed a clear, positive aim. He set out to be not a "classical" nor a "literary" but a "philosophic historian," a historian who, following Montesquieu, would use the new human and social philosophy of the Enlightenment to give meaning and depth to the historical data supplied by the erudition of his predecessors and accurately understood by himself. To Gibbon, history was never merely narrative—it was always explanation. It was never merely political—it was always social too. Even his style was not exclusively "classical." He was trained in classical studies and he believed strongly in the dignity of history, "the majesty of the great historians"; but beneath the balanced, polished sentences it is easy to discover, in his accounts of wild scenery or barbarous societies, the expression—the highly disciplined expression—of a naturally romantic temper. Moreover, it is simply not true that Gibbon ignored non-literary evidence; he used it more, probably, than any of his "literary" predecessors.

Of course there are certain admissions to be made. Gibbon did not practice what is now called "field-work." He did not travel or collect, at first hand, "local colour." Though his great work was largely a history of the Byzantine Empire, he never thought of visiting Constantinople or indeed, any part of that empire. Nor did he visit such archaeological sites as were being discovered in his time. Nor did he study manuscripts. He himself says, speaking of the *De Re Diplomatica* of Mabillon and the *Palæographia* of Montfaucon, "I studied the theory without attaining the practice of the art; nor should I complain of the intricacy of Greek abbreviations and Gothic alphabets, since every day, in a familiar language, I am at a loss to decipher the hieroglyphics of a female note." But he did study all these subjects through books, and it was because the *érudits* of the last century, by their labours, had enabled him to do this that he particularly resented the condescension of "lively philosophers," like Voltaire, towards them. The great scholars of the past might not have been philosophic historians themselves, but they had made philosophic history possible: they had enabled a Gibbon to examine sites, coins, inscriptions without leaving his study.

For instance, geography: To a social historian, a knowledge of geography, the physical matrix of human societies, is essential, and Gibbon was passionately interested in it. If he did not himself travel beyond Switzerland and Italy, he was an indefatigable mental traveller. His journals and notes bear constant witness to this. We there see that he has read all the works of early travellers, and is familiar with all geographical commentaries and controversies. He has mastered details of sites and can correct superficial travellers who have seen, but not understood them. Every town which he considers has been examined in minute topographical detail—Verona in the Marchese Maffei's *Verona Illustrata,* Jerusalem in "a rare and curious treatise of M. d'Anville"—and a single paragraph on the city of Ravenna rests on eight authorities, "yet," adds Gibbon regretfully, "I still want a local antiquarian and a good topographical map."

After physical geography comes climate, to which Montesquieu at first attached such social importance. Gibbon made a careful study of ancient climate and from the distribution of the reindeer, as well as from literary evidence of frozen rivers, deduced that Germany was colder in Antiquity than in his own time. Then there was human geography: the population which could be sustained by the Roman Empire and by the barbarous North. On this subject, Gibbon agreed with Hume and disagreed with Montesquieu and the scholars of the seventeenth century. He believed—and modern scholarship supports him—that the ancient world was not more, but far less, populous than the same areas in the eighteenth century. He also made a careful study of communications. On his Italian journey he took a number of works on Roman land and sea-routes, which he studied on the spot. By the time he came to write his great work,

Gibbon had travelled in imagination along all the routes of Antiquity: the sea-voyages of the Carthaginians in the West and of the Greeks and Arabs in the East, the caravan-routes of central Asia, the channels of invasion and migration from the Baltic to the Mediterranean, from China to Spain.

Nor was this study of human geography based only on literary sources. Just as Gibbon, sedentary in London or Lausanne, used his erudition to range over the whole world, so through the same medium of books, he contrived to marshal the evidence of excavations, inscriptions and coins, which he also used to construct his history. Gibbon's use of these non-literary sources is evident to anyone who looks below the surface, or into the footnotes, of his work. He studied ancient coins and medals in the "noble work" of the Swiss scholar-diplomat Ezechiel von Spanheim (1664) and his followers, and himself wrote a treatise on ancient weights, measures and coins. Inscriptions he studied in the useful old compilation of the Dutch scholar Janus Gruter (1602-3). The footnotes to his great work bear constant witness to his use of such evidence, from which he demonstrates (for instance) the travels of Hadrian, the paternity of Antoninus Pius and the provincial activity of Septimius Severus. He also kept abreast of the archaeological work done in his time by subscribing to the *Mémoires de l'Académie des Beaux Arts*, to the *Bibliothèque des Sciences et des Beaux Arts*, and to the *Journal des Savants*, all of which were regularly delivered to him in England. Altogether the suggestion that Gibbon overlooked non-literary sources, that he was merely a "literary," not a scientific historian, can be dismissed as absurd.

Even more interesting than his use of non-literary sources of history, is Gibbon's use of non-historical material for historical explanation. One instance of this is supplied by his study of social and legal institutions, in which—like Giannone and Montesquieu—he was always profoundly interested. We have seen how, in his *Essai,* he regarded the laws of the Roman Republic as a key to a "philosophic history" of the Roman Republic;

in his *Autobiography* he has described the fascination exercised upon his mind by the Theodosian Code, which he saw "as a full and capacious repository of the political state of the empire in the fourth and fifth centuries." How much he used it is clear to anyone who reads his chapters on the social revolution caused by the legal establishment of Christianity; and the same observation could be made about his use of other, later legal and institutional sources: the Pandects of Justinian, which he used as a social document for the sixth century; the Basilics of the "Macedonian" Emperors, from which he described the society of tenth century Byzantium; and "the immense labyrinth of the *Jus publicum* of Germany" from which he portrayed the society of medieval Europe. Gibbon's systematic use of these documents gives an added flavour to his contemptuous treatment, in the *Vindication*, of Mr. Davis, who, having applauded "with an agreeable irony, his own labours in turning over a few pages of the Theodosian Code," and having misunderstood even the scope of its contents, lightly accused Gibbon of not having read it.

But of course the most famous example of Gibbon's sociological approach to history is his treatment of Christianity. It was this which caused his work to seem novel, even shocking, in his own day; this which aroused the attacks upon him and elicited his *Vindication* in reply; this which, even today, gives unity and simplicity —often a misleading simplicity—to his wonderfully various work. Many a critic who has never read so far quotes (and misapplies) the remark in Gibbon's final chapter, that "in the preceding volumes of this History I have described the triumph of barbarism and religion." We may therefore take more extended notice of Gibbon's interpretation of religion as a force in history.

Gibbon was converted to Roman Catholicism at Oxford by intellectual arguments—or, as he would afterwards maintain, sophistries. At Lausanne, his tutor, M. Pavilliard, afterwards remembered him standing before him, "a thin little figure with a large head, disputing and urging, with the greatest ability, all the best arguments that had ever been used in favour of popery." But as logic and scepticism undermined these arguments at their base, Gibbon came to be interested in religion, and to judge it, largely as a social force. Impatient of all dogma, he saw the Church as a purely human institution, subject to the same general social laws as other human bodies, and meriting the praise or blame of the philosopher according to the service or disservice which it performed for the intellectual, moral or material improvement of humanity. For this reason Gibbon always hated clerical power which, he was convinced, had historically retarded the advancement of society, and he was a merciless critic of the deceptions and self-deceptions whereby that power was continued. For the same reason he hated monasticism, whose institutions, he wrote, "have counterbalanced all the temporal advantages of Christianity." How genuine that hatred was is clear from a passage in an early diary describing a visit, at the age of eighteen, to the great Catholic monastery at Einsiedeln in Switzerland. When Gibbon came to write his autobiography, he had mislaid that early diary, but the spectacle of Einsiedeln, he wrote, had made "a deep and lasting impression on my memory," and once again he describes how the "profuse ostentation of riches in the poorest corner of Europe . . . suggested to me, as in the same spot it had done to Zwinglius, the most pressing argument for the reformation of the Church." Another Swiss abbey elicited from him another such comparison. "Within the ancient walls of Vindonissa," he wrote in a footnote to the *Decline and Fall*, "the castle of Hapsburg, the abbey of Königsfeld and the town of Bruck have successively arisen. The philosophic traveller may compare the monuments of Roman conquest, of feudal or Austrian tyranny, of monkish superstition and of industrious freedom. If he be truly a philosopher, he will applaud the merit and happiness of his own time."

These passages sufficiently show the character and limits of Gibbon's anti-clericalism. Himself a deist in religion, he allowed certain "temporal advantages of Christianity" and he had no objection to the clergy so long as they did not, by their politics or their social organisation, seek for themselves a special status or

impede the progress of "industrious freedom." He regarded the subjection of the Church to the State as "a
salutary maxim," and allowed that a Church which had
been absorbed and digested by society, could be harmless and might even forward human progress. In a rational modern society even monasticism might be tamed:
one had only to look at the Benedictines of St. Germain-
les-Prés. Basically Gibbon was a Protestant, because
Protestants believed in human reason, liberty and progress and required their Church to forward these things;
but even Catholicism, he thought, could be civilised
more easily than replaced, and it was better to laicise and
liberalise an established religion than to mobilise a new
fanaticism against it. At the end of his life, when he
witnessed from Switzerland the excesses of the French
Revolution, he wrote to Lord Sheffield expressing his
admiration for Burke's *Reflexions:* "I admire his eloquence, I approve his politics, I adore his chivalry, and
I can even forgive his superstition." And he added, casting his mind back from the French Jacobins to the
early Christians, "the primitive Church, which I have
treated with some freedom, was itself at that time an innovation, and I was attached to the old Pagan establishment." In his *Autobiography*, repeating some of these
sentiments, he wrote "I have sometimes thought of writing a Dialogue of the Dead, in which Lucian, Erasmus
and Voltaire should mutually acknowledge the danger of
exposing an old superstition to the contempt of the blind
and fanatic multitude." To Gibbon, religious truth was
unimportant or at least unattainable; the Church was a
purely social organism which must be judged by its
works; and now that, in England, it was established,
subjected to the state and tamed by the laity, he agreed
with the view which Montesquieu expressed to Bishop
Warburton, that an attack on its doctrine, "even if its
reasons were correct, would only destroy a great deal of
practical good in order to establish a purely speculative
truth."

Gibbon's sociological approach to religion can be illustrated again and again from the *Decline and Fall*.
There, at every point, he shows an almost ostentatious

disinterest in dogma. It is fortunately not the duty of an historian, he remarks on one occasion, to interpose his private judgment in the nice and important controversy concerning the miracles of the early church; "perhaps it may not be necessary," he says, when dealing with the theological dispute which split the Eastern from the Western Church, "to boast on this subject of my own impartial indifference"; in the same genial spirit he describes the transmission of the pure doctrine of the Incarnation in the Church of England from the seventh-century archbishop of Canterbury, Theodore of Tarsus, "to the modern primates, whose sound understanding is perhaps seldom engaged with that abstruse mystery." On the other hand, the social character of the Church is to him all-important. The "jurisdiction, wealth and immunities" of the Church he describes as "perhaps the most essential part of episcopal religion"; when dealing with Priscillian, the heretical fourth-century bishop of Avila in Spain, he remarks that "the bishopric is now worth twenty thousand ducats a year, and is therefore much less likely to produce the author of a new heresy"; and he consistently treats early Christianity, as modern scholars treat it, as one of the many mystery-religions, with common features, any one of which might have prevailed and absorbed the others. Gibbon's whole approach to the rise of Christianity is in fact an essay in sociology, and this approach is continued throughout his work. "All religions are to a large extent local," he writes in his diary, when considering the interesting question why the barbarians rejected Christianity outside the Roman Empire but accepted it within. In the *Decline and Fall*, he represents the rise of Mohammedanism, and its sudden conquests at the expense of the Persian and Byzantine empires, as a social revolution like the rise of Christianity. In dealing with the medieval Church, he sees the fundamental importance of the growth of church patronage and pays a memorable tribute to that "golden book," Fra Paolo Sarpi's treatise *Of Benefices;* and, though he differed from them in detail, he agreed with Hume, Robertson and Adam Smith in seeing the Crusades as a crucial turning-point, not in the religious, but in the social and economic history of Europe.

Thus, Gibbon's great *History* is not merely a narrative, cast in a majestic eighteenth-century style, flavoured with pungent epigram, grave irony and distinguished by constant scepticism. It is a great work of complex social explanation. As a philosopher of history, Gibbon believed strongly in the unity of history, as in all human activities. It is one of his complaints against Voltaire that, in his *Siècle de Louis XIV*, he sought to divide history into compartments whereas, in fact, it was indivisible. But running through this complexity, animating it and giving it purpose and meaning, he saw a continuous thread. He believed in human progress by means of lay science, applied to human needs. But he also recognised that the course of such progress was never certain; it was conditioned by social facts—geography, climate, population, resources, tradition—and often, at the mercy of human folly. "The history of empires," he wrote in his *Essai*, "is the record of human misery; the history of the sciences is that of the greatness and happiness of mankind," and the interplay of these two forces provides the constant theme of the *Decline and Fall*. After describing the collapse of the Western Empire, Gibbon nevertheless concludes that scientific discoveries can never be lost and that therefore, "every age of the world has increased and still increases the real wealth, the happiness, the knowledge and perhaps the virtue of the human race"; but elsewhere he will admit, without inconsistency, that history is, in general, "little more than the register of the crimes, follies and misfortunes of mankind." Among the fundamental causes of the decline of ancient civilisation he did, indeed, include the rise of Christianity: the contrast between refined, but useless theological speculation and humble but beneficent mechanical arts forms a regular undercurrent to his work; but the connexion which he detected between these two movements was never dogmatically assumed or crudely expressed. As an *érudit*, master of all the learning of his predecessors, Gibbon was exempt from mere factual error; as a philosopher, who could congratulate himself on being born "in a free and civilised country, in an age of science and philosophy," he was able to manage his vast material, draw deductions, make comparisons, test theories; and the confidence that he had succeeded in combining these two faculties enabled him to adopt that tone of olympian condescension which has often maddened his frustrated adversaries. He could dismiss many of his "philosophical" but superficial French contemporaries as "fanciful," and despatch many of his erudite but unthinking predecessors with elegant disdain: "the dull mass"—850 folio pages—of the contemporary *Life of Mahomet*, he tells us, "is not quickened a spark of philosophy or taste" and when Dr. Johnson praised Knolles' *General History of the Turks* (1603), Gibbon could reply, in the true spirit of the Enlightenment, "I very much doubt whether a partial and verbose compilation from Latin writers, 1,300 folio pages of speeches and battles, can either instruct or amuse an enlightened age, which requires from the historian some tincture of philosophy and criticism."

Gibbon certainly set out both to instruct and to amuse. He spoke to an enlightened age in its own language; every page of his work contains philosophy and criticism. To glance at his footnotes, which reveal so much of his intellectual method, is to see not only the array of his ancient sources, but also the whole thought and experience of the eighteenth century applied to their interpretation. This indeed is what makes him seem so permanently modern. It was because he had read John Howard's *State of Prisons* that he could judge the inadequacy of monastic diet; because he had read the history of modern India and Siam, that he could calculate the number of elephants used in ancient warfare. From the statistics of modern Paris he could conjecture the number of slaves or servants in ancient Rome; from the incidence of taxation in modern France he could make social deductions about ancient Gaul. He would estimate the state of agriculture in Roman Britain from the number of Roman ships which sailed thither to fetch corn in the time of the emperor Julian, and the agricultural methods which would be required to fill them. He would draw conclusions from comparison with newly found Otaheite or the habits of the modern Samoyeds, compare the Roman Empire under the military emperors of the third century with the military republic of the Egyptian Mamelukes and the social effect of the establishment of the new Parthian court at Ctesiphon with that of the movement of the Mogul Court of Aurungzebe from Delhi to Kashmir. He would compare the military tactics of Julian with those of Agathocles of Syracuse, six centuries before, or of Hernán Cortés in Mexico, twelve centuries afterwards, and those of Mohammed II against Constantinople in 1453 with those of the British against the American colonies in his own day. He would show how the early Christians could be formidable without being numerous by analogies with the French Huguenots or the English Catholics in the early seventeenth century. To understand Antiquity he would appeal not only to classical commentators but also to contemporary works on contemporary subjects: to Winckelmann's *History of Art*, Hume's *Natural History of Religion*, Adam Smith's *Wealth of Nations*, Buffon's *Natural History*. But above all, his debt, for his whole method, now as always, is to Montesquieu; Montesquieu in whose hands, as he had written in 1761, "the theory of general causes would form a philosophic history of mankind"; Montesquieu, whose *De l'Esprit des Lois*, as he now wrote in his last volume, had been more read and criticised than any work in the last forty years, "and the spirit of enquiry which it has excited is not the least of our obligations to the author."

With Montesquieu, Gibbon also shared another quality which should not be overlooked: his humanity. Believing firmly, even passionately, in the possibility of progress by the application of reason, Gibbon detested bigotry and persecution of any kind. For that reason he disliked Dr. Johnson, whose writings showed him "the workings of a bigoted though vigorous mind, greedy of every pretence to hate and persecute those who dissent from his creed." He also hated all forms of social injustice, or affronts to human dignity, to which his contemporaries were often far less sensitive. On his famous journey to Rome he deeply resented (as Alexander von Humboldt did in South America) the necessity of being carried over dangerous mountain roads by human porters; he was horrified by the *corvées* imposed on the peasants of Savoy; and at the court of Turin he was disgusted by the empty splendor which needed such fiscal oppression to sustain it. "The servility of the courtiers," he wrote in his diary, "revolts me, and I look with horror on the magnificence of palaces, cemented with the blood of the people. In every gilded moulding I think I see a village of Savoyards ready to perish of hunger, cold and poverty." He felt as strongly as Montesquieu about the slave-trade. In the *Decline and Fall* he describes the tenth-century trade in eunuchs as "the last abomination of the abominable slave-trade"; and when Lord Sheffield, as member of parliament for the slaving city of Bristol, published a pamphlet supporting the trade, Gibbon protested in the name of "justice and humanity. Do you not expect," he asked, "to work at Beelzebub's sugar-plantations in the infernal regions under the tender government of a Negro driver?"

This constant humanity warms and enlivens the *Decline and Fall*, but it is also essential to its substance. It was because Gibbon had observed, as a social fact, that it was always laymen who had defended the rights of toleration and that clerical power insensibly led to clerical tyranny—to "the Catholic Inquisitors of Europe who defended nonsense by cruelty"—that he distrusted "the austere and dangerous virtues" of the greatest of medieval popes, and regarded the vices of the clergy, which made them akin to the laity, as less harmful to humanity. And it was because he was rationally convinced that human happiness was fostered by trade and industry and the free circulation of ideas that he resented the immobilisation of wealth in clerical mortmain or courtly magnificence and recorded, with sardonic pleasure, those occasions when conquest or reform caused it to be "sacrilegiously converted to the uses of mankind." This belief in productive industry (not merely trade) as the real motor of progress, distinguished Gibbon from some other historians of the Enlightenment. Robertson, for instance, believed that the Crusades, by capturing the trade of the east, hastened the growth of Europe. Gibbon did not. He saw them as the diversion into wasteful wars of resources which might have been "more profitably employed in the improvement of their native country." The only advantage of the Crusades, he insisted, was incidental: the ruin of the crusading lords led to the bankruptcy of an oppressive system and the emancipation of "the most numerous and useful part of the community." In his practical politics Gibbon was a loyal placeman of Lord North. In his general philosophy, he described himself firmly as a "Whig." In his economic interpretation of history he was more than a Whig. Humanity and reason combined to make him a radical.

❦ ❦ ❦

To abridge Gibbon's work is not easy. It was conceived as a whole, and every part of it has its function. To omit is to do injustice to its enormous range, but to compress is even more difficult. Gibbon wrote in paragraphs, and every paragraph is a necessary link in his argument. To cut out a paragraph is therefore, to violate a logical sequence. On the other hand, within each paragraph the sentences are carefully balanced, and to reduce them is to upset the balance. In these circumstances I have thought it best to give a series of extracts connected by brief summaries. The extracts which I have chosen are designed to illustrate Gibbon's historical philosophy, but they are related to the continuous history of the two capitals of the Roman Empire, Rome and Constantinople. Any abridgement which reduces a great work to less than a tenth of its full length inevitably entails heavy sacrifices, and it is with great difficulty that I have persuaded myself to omit (for instance) the reigns of Commodus and Elagabalus and the chapters on the career and religion of Mahomet. But I hope that the selections I have made will at least give a representative sample of Gibbon's work and some illustration of his philosophy.

I have also had to consider how to treat Gibbon's extensive footnotes, which not only show his historical sources and method but also contain a great deal of sense and learning, irony and wit. Heavily pressed for space, I have here settled for a policy of drastic selection. I have excluded all notes, or parts of notes, which merely refer to sources. I have also excluded all notes which do not seem to me necessary to explain or illustrate the information in the text. But I have printed a number of notes which, in my opinion, illustrate Gibbon's method or his philosophy, or deserve inclusion for their particular Gibbonian flavour; on one or two occasions I have even gone so far, for the sake of that flavour, to print a few words "in the decent obscurity of a learned language." On rare occasions, I have added explanatory notes of my own. These are always distinguishable from Gibbon's own notes, being in brackets [ ].

In his lifetime, apart from articles in journals and one government manifesto (in French), Gibbon only published his *Essai sur l'Etude de la Littérature*, *The Decline and Fall of the Roman Empire* and the *Vindication*. After his death, Lord Sheffield published Gibbon's *Miscellaneous Works*, which included his reconstruction of the *Autobiography*, an English translation of the *Essai*, and selections from his diaries and correspondence. The best editions of Gibbon's writings are:

Bury, J. B. (ed.). *The Decline and Fall of the Roman Empire*. 7 vols. London, 1897-.

Murray, Sir John. (ed.). *The Autobiographies of Edward Gibbon*. London, 1896. This gives the text of all six drafts, but Lord Sheffield's reconstruction remains the ideal text. The best edition of it is *The World Classics* (Oxford).

Norton, J. E. (ed.) *The Letters of Edward Gibbon*. 3 vols. London, 1956. This replaces the earlier, less complete *Private Letters of Edward Gibbon*. (ed.). Prothero, R. E., Lord Ernle. London, 1896.

Gibbon's Journal, written partly in English, partly in French, has been published in separate sections, in *Miscellanea Gibboniana*. (Lausanne, 1952); *Gibbon's Journal*. (ed.). Low, D. M. (London, 1929); *Le Journal de Gibbon à Lausanne*. (ed.). Bonnard, Georges. (Lausanne, 1945); *Gibbon's Journey from Geneva to Rome*. (ed.). Bonnard, Georges. (London, 1961).

The rest of Gibbon's writings must still be sought in his *Miscellaneous Works*, of which the best edition is that of 1814.

There are two excellent biographies of Gibbon: Young, G. M. *Gibbon.* (London, 1932) and Low, D. M. *Edward Gibbon.* (London, 1937). Norton, J. E. *A Bibliography of the Works of Edward Gibbon.* (Oxford, 1940), is complete and valuable. Keynes, G. *The Library of Edward Gibbon.* (London, 1940) is a reconstructed catalogue of the books owned by Gibbon.

DATES IN GIBBON'S LIFE

1737	May 8, Gibbon born at Putney.
1747	Death of his mother.
1748	G. enters Westminster School.
1748	Montesquieu's *De L'Esprit des Lois* published.
1749	Middleton's *Free Enquiry* published.
1752-3	G. at Magdalen College, Oxford.
1753-8	At Lausanne, under tuition of M. Pavilliard.
1754	Hume's *History of England,* vol. I, published.
1758-60	G. in England, at Buriton (Hants.), and in London.
1759	Robertson's *History of Scotland* published.
1760-62	G. serves with Hampshire Militia.
1761	Publishes *Essai sur l'Etude de la Littérature.*
1763	Peace of Paris ends Seven Years War with France.
1763-5	G. travels to Paris, Lausanne, Italy.
1765-72	At Buriton and in London.
1770	Death of his Father.
1773	Moves to Bentinck Street, London.
1773	Boston Tea Party.
1774-80	G. member of Parliament for Liskeard, (for Lymington, 1781-4), 1779 appointed Commissioner of the Board of Trade.
1776	*Decline and Fall,* vol. I. published.
1779	*Vindication* published.
1781	*Decline and Fall,* vols. II and III published.
1781	Cornwallis surrenders to Americans at Yorktown.

1782   Commission of Board of Trade abolished.

1783   G. leaves for Lausanne. Settles there with J. G. Deyverdun.

1783   Peace of Versailles: Britain recognises U.S.A.

1784   March 25, Dissolution of Parliament.

1787   G. visits England. *Decline and Fall,* vols. IV, V, VI published.

1789   Death of Deyverdun. Outbreak of French Revolution.

1793   G. visits England.

1794   January 16, Death in London.

1796   Lord Sheffield publishes Gibbon's *Miscellaneous Works,* including his *Autobiography.*

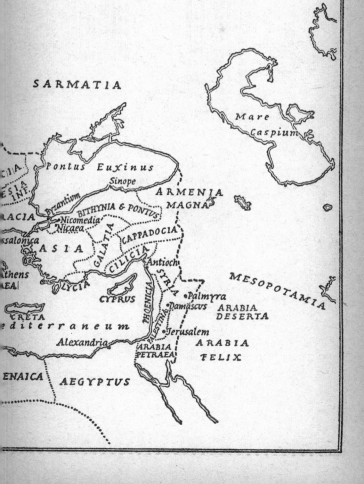

THE ROMAN EMPIRE
IN THE TIME
OF THE ANTONINES

SARMATIA

Mare Caspium

CIA
ESIA
INF.

Pontus Euxinus

Sinope

ARMENIA
MAGNA

RACIA

Byzantium

BITHYNIA & PONTUS

Nicomedia
Nicaea

ssalonica

ASIA

GALATIA

CAPPADOCIA

MESOPOTAMIA

CILICIA

Antioch

thens
EA

LYCIA

CYPRUS

PHOENICIA

SYRIA

• Palmyra

• Damascus

ARABIA
DESERTA

CRETA

editerraneum

Alexandria

PALESTINA

• Jerusalem

ARABIA
FELIX

ENAICA

AEGYPTUS

ARABIA
PETRAEA

PART I
Gibbon's Autobiography

[The Manuscript which Gibbon entitled Memoirs of my Life and Writings was left by him, at his death, in the form of several drafts, and was published as his Autobiography by his friend and executor, Lord Sheffield. Gibbon's own title is in fact more exact, since the book is only incidentally a personal autobiography: essentially it is a history of the making of his great work, The Decline and Fall of the Roman Empire.]

1. Gibbon at Oxford

[Gibbon's childhood was divided between repeated illness and "vague and multifarious reading." "From the ancients," he says "I leaped to the modern world; many crude lumps of Speed, Rapin, Mézéray, Davila, Machiavel, Father Paul, Bower, etc., I devoured like so many novels; and I swallowed with the same voracious appetite the descriptions of India and China, Mexico and Peru." But all systematic plans of instruction were upset by his delicate health and, after several educational experiments, in 1752, "my father's perplexity rather than his prudence was urged to embrace a singular and desperate measure. Without preparation or delay, he carried me to Oxford; and I was matriculated in the university as a gentleman-commoner of Magdalen College before I had accomplished my fifteenth year." He arrived there, he says, "with a stock of erudition that would have puzzled a doctor, and a degree of ig-

norance of which a schoolboy would have been ashamed." The following passages describe his brief, disastrous residence at Oxford.]

A traveller who visits Oxford or Cambridge is surprised and edified by the apparent order and tranquillity that prevail in the seats of the English muses. In the most celebrated Universities of Holland, Germany, and Italy, the students, who swarm from different countries, are loosely dispersed in private lodgings at the houses of the burghers: they dress according to their fancy and fortune; and in the intemperate quarrels of youth and wine, their *swords*, though less frequently than of old, are sometimes stained with each other's blood. The use of arms is banished from our English Universities; the uniform habit of the academics, the square cap and black gown, is adapted to the civil and even clerical professions; and from the doctor in divinity to the undergraduate, the degrees of learning and age are externally distinguished. Instead of being scattered in a town, the students of Oxford and Cambridge are united in colleges; their maintenance is provided at their own expense, or that of the founders; and the stated hours of the hall and chapel represent the discipline of a regular, and, as it were, a religious community. The eyes of the traveller are attracted by the size or beauty of the public edifices; and the principal colleges appear to be so many palaces, which a liberal nation has erected and endowed for the habitation of science. My own introduction to the University of Oxford forms a new era in my life; and at the distance of forty years I still remember my first emotions of surprise and satisfaction. In my fifteenth year I felt myself suddenly raised from a boy to a man: the persons, whom I respected as my superiors in age and academical rank, entertained me with every mark of attention and civility; and my vanity was flattered by the velvet cap and silk gown, which distinguish a gentleman-commoner from a plebeian student. A decent allowance, more money than a schoolboy had ever seen, was at my own disposal; and I might command, among the tradesmen of Oxford, an indefinite and dangerous latitude of credit. A key was delivered into my hands, which gave me the free use of a numerous and learned library: my apartment consisted of three elegant and well-furnished rooms in the new building, a stately pile, of Magdalen College; and the adjacent walks, had they been frequented by Plato's disciples, might have been compared to the Attic shade on the banks of the Ilissus. Such was the fair prospect of my entrance (April 3, 1752,) into the University of Oxford.

A venerable prelate, whose taste and erudition must reflect honour on the society in which they were formed, has drawn a very interesting picture of his academical life:—"I was educated (says Bishop Lowth) in the University of Oxford. I enjoyed all the advantages, both public and private, which that famous seat of learning so largely affords. I spent many years in that illustrious society, in a well-regulated course of useful discipline and studies, and in the agreeable and improving commerce of gentlemen and of scholars; in a society where emulation without envy, ambition without jealousy, contention without animosity, incited industry and awakened genius; where a liberal pursuit of knowledge and a genuine freedom of thought was raised, encouraged, and pushed forward by example, by commendation, and by authority. I breathed the same atmosphere that the Hookers, the Chillingworths, and the Lockes had breathed before; whose benevolence and humanity were as extensive as their vast genius and comprehensive knowledge; who always treated their adversaries with civility and respect; who made candour, moderation, and liberal judgement as much the rule and law as the subject of their discourse. And do you reproach me with my education in this place, and with my relation to this most respectable body, which I shall always esteem my greatest advantage and my highest honour?" I transcribe with pleasure this eloquent passage, without examining what benefits or what rewards were derived by Hooker, or Chillingworth, or Locke, from their academical institution; without inquiring, whether in this angry controversy the spirit of Lowth himself is purified from the intolerant zeal which War-

3

burton had ascribed to the genius of the place. It may indeed be observed that the atmosphere of Oxford did not agree with Mr. Locke's constitution, and that the philosopher justly despised the academical bigots, who expelled his person and condemned his principles. The expression of gratitude is a virtue and a pleasure: a liberal mind will delight to cherish and celebrate the memory of its parents; and the teachers of science are the parents of the mind. I applaud the filial piety, which it is impossible for me to imitate; since I must not confess an imaginary debt, to assume the merit of a just or generous retribution. To the University of Oxford I acknowledge no obligation; and she will as cheerfully renounce me for a son, as I am willing to disclaim her for a mother. I spent fourteen months at Magdalen College; they proved the fourteen months the most idle and unprofitable of my whole life: the reader will pronounce between the school and the scholar: but I cannot affect to believe that nature had disqualified me for all literary pursuits. The specious and ready excuse of my tender age, imperfect preparation, and hasty departure, may doubtless be alleged; nor do I wish to defraud such excuses of their proper weight. Yet in my sixteenth year I was not devoid of capacity or application; even my childish reading had displayed an early though blind propensity for books; and the shallow flood might have been taught to flow in a deep channel and a clear stream. In the discipline of a well-constituted academy, under the guidance of skilful and vigilant professors, I should gradually have risen from translations to originals, from the Latin to the Greek classics, from dead languages to living science: my hours would have been occupied by useful and agreeable studies, the wanderings of fancy would have been restrained, and I should have escaped the temptations of idleness, which finally precipitated my departure from Oxford.

Perhaps in a separate annotation I may coolly examine the fabulous and real antiquities of our sister universities, a question which has kindled such fierce and foolish disputes among their fanatic sons. In the meanwhile it will be acknowledged that these venerable bodies are sufficiently old to partake of all the prejudices and in-

firmities of age. The schools of Oxford and Cambridge
were founded in a dark age of false and barbarous science; and they are still tainted with the vices of their
origin. Their primitive discipline was adapted to the education of priests and monks; and the government still
remains in the hands of the clergy, an order of men
whose manners are remote from the present world, and
whose eyes are dazzled by the light of philosophy. The
legal incorporation of these societies by the charters of
popes and kings had given them a monopoly of the public instruction; and the spirit of monopolists is narrow,
lazy, and oppressive: their work is more costly and less
productive than that of independent artists; and the new
improvements so eagerly grasped by the competition of
freedom, are admitted with slow and sullen reluctance
in those proud corporations, above the fear of a rival,
and below the confession of an error. We may scarcely
hope that any reformation will be a voluntary act; and
so deeply are they rooted in law and prejudice, that even
the omnipotence of Parliament would shrink from an inquiry into the state and abuses of the two Universities.

The use of academical degrees, as old as the thirteenth
century, is visibly borrowed from the mechanic corporations; in which an apprentice, after serving his time, ob-
tains a testimonial of his skill, and a licence to practise
his trade and mystery. It is not my design to depreciate
those honours, which could never gratify or disappoint
my ambition; and I should applaud the institution, if the
degrees of bachelor or licentiate were bestowed as the reward of manly and successful study: if the name and
rank of doctor or master were strictly reserved for the
professors of science, who have approved their title to
the public esteem.

In all the Universities of Europe, excepting our own,
the languages and sciences are distributed among a numerous list of effective professors: the students, according to their taste, their calling, and their diligence, apply themselves to the proper masters; and in the annual
repetition of public and private lectures, these masters
are assiduously employed. Our curiosity may inquire
what number of professors has been instituted at Oxford

(for I shall now confine myself to my own University)?
by whom are they appointed, and what may be the probable chances of merit or incapacity? how many are stationed to the three faculties, and how many are left for
the liberal arts? what is the form, and what the substance, of their lessons? But all these questions are silenced by one short and singular answer. "That in the
University of Oxford, the greater part of the public professors have for these many years given up altogether
even the pretence of teaching." Incredible as the fact
may appear, I must rest my belief on the positive and
impartial evidence of a master of moral and political
wisdom, who had himself resided at Oxford. Dr. Adam
Smith assigns as the cause of their indolence, that, instead of being paid by voluntary contributions, which
would urge them to increase the number, and to deserve
the gratitude of their pupils, the Oxford professors are
secure in the enjoyment of a fixed stipend, without the
necessity of labour, or the apprehension of control. It has
indeed been observed, nor is the observation absurd, that
excepting in experimental sciences, which demand a
costly apparatus and a dexterous hand, the many valuable treatises that have been published on every subject
of learning may now supersede the ancient mode of oral
instruction. Were this principle true in its utmost latitude, I should only infer that the offices and salaries,
which are become useless, ought without delay to be
abolished. But there still remains a material difference
between a book and a professor; the hour of the lecture
enforces attendance; attention is fixed by the presence,
the voice, and the occasional questions of the teacher;
the most idle will carry something away; and the more
diligent will compare the instructions which they have
heard in the school, with the volumes which they peruse
in their chamber. The advice of a skilful professor will
adapt a course of reading to every mind and every situation; his authority will discover, admonish, and at last
chastise the negligence of his disciples; and his vigilant
inquiries will ascertain the steps of their literary progress. Whatever science he professes he may illustrate in
a series of discourses, composed in the leisure of his

6

closet, pronounced on public occasions, and finally delivered to the press. I observe with pleasure that in the University of Oxford Dr. Lowth, with equal eloquence and erudition, has executed this task in his incomparable *Prælectiones* on the Poetry of the Hebrews.

The College of St. Mary Magdalen was founded in the fifteenth century by Wainfleet, Bishop of Winchester; and now consists of a president, forty fellows, and a number of inferior students. It is esteemed one of the largest and most wealthy of our academical corporations, which may be compared to the Benedictine abbeys of Catholic countries; and I have loosely heard that the estates belonging to Magdalen College, which are leased by those indulgent landlords at small quit-rents and occasional fines, might be raised, in the hands of private avarice, to an annual revenue of nearly thirty thousand pounds. Our colleges are supposed to be schools of science, as well as of education; nor is it unreasonable to expect that a body of literary men, devoted to a life of celibacy, exempt from the care of their own subsistence, and amply provided with books, should devote their leisure to the prosecution of study, and that some effects of their studies should be manifested to the world. The shelves of their library groan under the weight of the Benedictine folios, of the editions of the fathers, and the collections of the middle ages, which have issued from the single abbey of St. Germain-des-Prés at Paris.[1] A composition of genius must be the offspring of one mind; but such works of industry, as may be divided among many hands, and must be continued during many years, are the peculiar province of a laborious community. If I inquire into the manufactures of the monks of Magdalen, if I extend the inquiry to the other colleges of Oxford and Cambridge, a silent blush, or a scornful frown, will be the only reply. The fellows or monks of my time were decent easy men, who supinely enjoyed the gifts of the founder; their days were filled by a series of uniform employments; the chapel and the hall, the coffee-house and the common room, till they retired, weary and well

---

[1] [i.e., The Congregation of St. Maur, see above, Introduction, p. ix]

satisfied, to a long slumber. From the toil of reading, or thinking, or writing, they had absolved their conscience; and the first shoots of learning and ingenuity withered on the ground, without yielding any fruits to the owners or the public. As a gentleman-commoner, I was admitted to the society of the fellows, and fondly expected that some questions of literature would be the amusing and instructive topics of their discourse. Their conversation stagnated in a round of college business, Tory politics, personal anecdotes, and private scandal: their dull and deep potations excused the brisk intemperance of youth: and their constitutional toasts were not expressive of the most lively loyalty for the house of Hanover. A general election was now approaching: the great Oxfordshire contest already blazed with all the malevolence of party zeal. Magdalen College was devoutly attached to the old interest; and the names of Wenman and Dashwood were more frequently pronounced than those of Cicero and Chrysostom. The example of the senior fellows could not inspire the undergraduates with a liberal spirit or studious emulation; and I cannot describe, as I never knew, the discipline of college. Some duties may possibly have been imposed on the poor scholars, whose ambition aspired to the peaceful honours of a fellowship; but no independent members were admitted below the rank of a gentleman-commoner, and our velvet cap was the cap of liberty. A tradition prevailed that some of our predecessors had spoken Latin declamations in the hall; but of this ancient custom no vestige remained: the obvious methods of public exercises and examinations were totally unknown; and I have never heard that either the president or the society interfered in the private economy of the tutors and their pupils.

The silence of the Oxford professors, which deprives the youth of public instruction, is imperfectly supplied by the tutors, as they are styled, of the several colleges. Instead of confining themselves to a single science, which had satisfied the ambition of Burman or Bernoulli, they teach, or promise to teach, either history or mathematics, or ancient literature, or moral philosophy; and as it is possible that they may be defective in all, it is highly

probable that of some they will be ignorant. They are
paid, indeed, by private contributions; but their appointment depends on the head of the house: their diligence
is voluntary, and will consequently be languid, while the
pupils themselves, or their parents, are not indulged in
the liberty of choice or change. The first tutor into whose
hands I was resigned appears to have been one of the
best of the tribe: Dr. Waldegrave was a learned and
pious man, of a mild disposition, strict morals, and abstemious life, who seldom mingled in the politics or the
jollity of the college. But his knowledge of the world
was confined to the University; his learning was of the
last, rather than of the present age; his temper was indolent; his faculties, which were not of the first rate,
had been relaxed by the climate, and he was satisfied,
like his fellows, with the slight and superficial discharge
of an important trust. As soon as my tutor had sounded
the insufficiency of his disciple in school-learning, he
proposed that we should read every morning from ten to
eleven the comedies of Terence. The sum of my improvement in the University of Oxford is confined to three or
four Latin plays; and even the study of an elegant
classic, which might have been illustrated by a comparison of ancient and modern theatres, was reduced to a
dry and literal interpretation of the author's text. During
the first weeks I constantly attended these lessons in my
tutor's room; but as they appeared equally devoid of
profit and pleasure, I was once tempted to try the experiment of a formal apology. The apology was accepted
with a smile. I repeated the offence with less ceremony;
the excuse was admitted with the same indulgence: the
slightest motive of laziness or indisposition, the most
trifling avocation at home or abroad, was allowed as a
worthy impediment; nor did my tutor appear conscious
of my absence or neglect. Had the hour of lecture been
constantly filled, a single hour was a small portion of my
academic leisure. No plan of study was recommended for
my use; no exercises were prescribed for his inspection;
and, at the most precious season of youth, whole days
and weeks were suffered to elapse without labour or
amusement, without advice or account. I should have

listened to the voice of reason and of my tutor; his mild behaviour had gained my confidence. I preferred his society to that of the younger students; and in our evening walks to the top of Headington Hill, we freely conversed on a variety of subjects. Since the days of Pocock and Hyde, oriental learning has always been the pride of Oxford, and I once expressed an inclination to study Arabic. His prudence discouraged this childish fancy; but he neglected the fair occasion of directing the ardour of a curious mind. During my absence in the summer vacation, Dr. Waldegrave accepted a college living at Washington in Sussex, and on my return I no longer found him at Oxford. From that time I have lost sight of my first tutor; but at the end of thirty years (1781) he was still alive; and the practice of exercise and temperance had entitled him to a healthy old age. . . .

After the departure of Dr. Waldegrave, I was transferred, with his other pupils, to his academical heir, whose literary character did not command the respect of the college. Dr. **** well remembered that he had a salary to receive, and only forgot that he had a duty to perform. Instead of guiding the studies, and watching over the behaviour of his disciple, I was never summoned to attend even the ceremony of a lecture; and, excepting one voluntary visit to his rooms, during the eight months of his titular office, the tutor and pupil lived in the same college as strangers to each other. The want of experience, of advice, and of occupation, soon betrayed me into some improprieties of conduct, ill-chosen company, late hours, and inconsiderate expense. My growing debts might be secret; but my frequent absence was visible and scandalous: and a tour to Bath, a visit into Buckinghamshire, and four excursions to London in the same winter, were costly and dangerous frolics. They were, indeed, without a meaning, as without an excuse. The irksomeness of a cloistered life repeatedly tempted me to wander; but my chief pleasure was that of travelling; and I was too young and bashful to enjoy, like a manly Oxonian in town, the pleasures of London. In all these excursions I eloped from Oxford; I returned to college; in a few days I eloped again, as if I had been an independent stranger in a hired lodging, without once hearing the voice of admonition, without once feeling the hand of control. Yet my time was lost, my expenses were multiplied, my behaviour abroad was unknown; folly as well as vice should have awakened the attention of my superiors, and my tender years would have justified a more than ordinary degree of restraint and discipline.

It might at least be expected that an ecclesiastical school should inculcate the orthodox principles of religion. But our venerable mother had contrived to unite the opposite extremes of bigotry and indifference: an heretic, or unbeliever, was a monster in her eyes; but she was always, or often, or sometimes, remiss in the spiritual education of her own children. According to the statutes of the University, every student, before he is matriculated, must subscribe his assent to the thirty-nine articles of the Church of England, which are signed by more than read, and read by more than believe them. My insufficient age excused me, however, from the immediate performance of this legal ceremony; and the Vice-Chancellor directed me to return, as soon as I should have accomplished my fifteenth year; recommending me, in the meanwhile, to the instruction of my college. My college forgot to instruct: I forgot to return, and was myself forgotten by the first magistrate of the University. Without a single lecture, either public or private, either Christian or Protestant, without any academical subscription, without any episcopal confirmation, I was left by the dim light of my catechism to grope my way to the chapel and communion-table, where I was admitted, without a question, how far, or by what means, I might be qualified to receive the Sacrament. Such almost incredible neglect was productive of the worst mischiefs. From my childhood I had been fond of religious disputation: my poor aunt has been often puzzled by the mysteries which she strove to believe; nor had the elastic spring been totally broken by the weight of the atmosphere of Oxford. The blind activity of idleness urged me to advance without armour into the dangerous mazes of controversy; and at the age of sixteen, I bewildered myself in the errors of the Church of Rome.

The progress of my conversion may tend to illustrate, at least, the history of my own mind. It was not long since Dr. Middleton's *Free Inquiry*[2] had sounded an alarm in the theological world; much ink and much gall had been spilt in the defence of the primitive miracles; and the two dullest of their champions were crowned with academic honours by the University of Oxford. The name of Middleton was unpopular; and his proscription very naturally led me to peruse his writings, and those of his antagonists. His bold criticism, which approaches the precipice of infidelity, produced on my mind a singular effect; and had I persevered in the communion of Rome, I should now apply to my own fortune the prediction of the Sibyl,

—— Via prima salutis,
Quod minimè reris, Graiâ pandetur ab urbe.[3]

The elegance of style and freedom of argument were repelled by the shield of prejudice. I still revered the character, or rather the names, of the saints and fathers whom Dr. Middleton exposes; nor could he destroy my implicit belief, that the gift of miraculous powers was continued in the Church during the first four or five centuries of Christianity. But I was unable to resist the weight of historical evidence, that within the same period most of the leading doctrines of Popery were already introduced in theory and practice: nor was my conclusion absurd, that miracles are the test of truth, and that the Church must be orthodox and pure, which was so often approved by the visible interposition of the Deity. The marvellous tales which are so boldly attested by the Basils and Chrysostoms, the Austins and Jeroms, compelled me to embrace the superior merits of celibacy, the institution of the monastic life, the use of the sign of the cross, of holy oil, and even of images, the invocation

---

2 [Conyers Middleton's *Free Inquiry*, see above, Introduction, p. xii-xiii]

3 ["The first way of safety will be opened, where you least expect, by a Greek city."

Vergil *Aeneid* vi. 96]

of saints, the worship of relics, the rudiments of purgatory in prayers for the dead, and the tremendous mystery of the sacrifice of the body and blood of Christ, which insensibly swelled into the prodigy of transubstantiation. In these dispositions, and already more than half a convert, I formed an unlucky intimacy with a young gentleman of our college. With a character less resolute, Mr. Molesworth had imbibed the same religious opinions; and some Popish books, I know not through what channel, were conveyed into his possession. I read, I applauded, I believed: the English translations of two famous works of Bossuet, Bishop of Meaux, the *Exposition of the Catholic Doctrine*, and the *History of the Protestant Variations*, achieved my conversion, and I surely fell by a noble hand. I have since examined the originals with a more discerning eye, and shall not hesitate to pronounce, that Bossuet is indeed a master of all the weapons of controversy. In the *Exposition*, a specious apology, the orator assumes, with consummate art, the tone of candour and simplicity; and the ten-horned monster is transformed, at his magic touch, into the milk-white hind, who must be loved as soon as she is seen. In the *History*, a bold and well-aimed attack, he displays, with a happy mixture of narrative and argument, the faults and follies, the changes and contradictions of our first reformers; whose variations (as he dextrously contends) are the mark of historical error, while the perpetual unity of the Catholic Church is the sign and test of infallible truth. To my present feelings it seems incredible that I should ever believe that I believed in transubstantiation. But my conqueror oppressed me with the sacramental words, "Hoc est corpus meum," and dashed against each other the figurative half-meanings of the Protestant sects: every objection was resolved into omnipotence; and after repeating, at St. Mary's, the Athanasian creed, I humbly acquiesced in the mystery of the real presence.

> To take up half on trust, and half to try,
> Name it not faith, but bungling bigotry.
> Both knave and fool, the merchant we may call,

To pay great sums, and to compound the small,
For who would break with Heaven, and would not
break for all?

No sooner had I settled my new religion than I resolved
to profess myself a Catholic. Youth is sincere and impetuous; and a momentary glow of enthusiasm had
raised me above all temporal considerations.

By the keen Protestants, who would gladly retaliate
the example of persecution, a clamour is raised of the
increase of Popery: and they are always loud to declaim
against the toleration of priests and jesuits, who pervert
so many of his majesty's subjects from their religion and
allegiance. On the present occasion, the fall of one or
more of her sons directed this clamour against the University; and it was confidently affirmed that Popish missionaries were suffered, under various disguises, to introduce themselves into the colleges of Oxford. But justice
obliges me to declare that, as far as relates to myself,
this assertion is false; and that I never conversed with
a priest, or even with a Papist, till my resolution from
books was absolutely fixed. In my last excursion to London, I addressed myself to Mr. Lewis, a Roman Catholic
bookseller in Russell Street, Covent Garden, who recommended me to a priest, of whose name and order I am at
present ignorant. In our first interview he soon discovered that persuasion was needless. After sounding the
motives and merits of my conversion, he consented to
admit me into the pale of the Church; and at his feet, on
the 8th of June, 1753, I solemnly, though privately, abjured the errors of heresy. The seduction of an English
youth of family and fortune was an act of as much danger as glory; but he bravely overlooked the danger, of
which I was not then sufficiently informed. "Where a
person is reconciled to the See of Rome, or procures
others to be reconciled, the offence (says Blackstone)
amounts to be high treason." And if the humanity of the
age would prevent the execution of this sanguinary stat-
ute, there were other laws of a less odious cast, which
condemned the priest to perpetual imprisonment, and
transformed the proselyte's estate to his nearest rela-

tion. An elaborate controversial epistle, approved by my director, and addressed to my father, announced and justified the step which I had taken. My father was neither a bigot nor a philosopher; but his affection deplored the loss of an only son; and his good sense was astonished at my strange departure from the religion of my country. In the first sally of passion he divulged a secret which prudence might have suppressed, and the gates of Magdalen College were for ever shut against my return. Many years afterwards, when the name of Gibbon was become as notorious as that of Middleton, it was industriously whispered at Oxford, that the historian had formerly "turned Papist": my character stood exposed to the reproach of inconstancy; and this invidious topic would have been handled without mercy by my opponents, could they have separated my cause from that of the University. For my own part, I am proud of an honest sacrifice of interest to conscience. I can never blush, if my tender mind was entangled in the sophistry that seduced the acute and manly understandings of Chillingworth and Bayle, who afterwards emerged from superstition to scepticism.

2. Gibbon at Lausanne

[*After the Oxford fiasco, Gibbon's father devised a new plan for his education, discipline and spiritual recovery. He sent him to Switzerland to be brought up in the house of a Calvinist minister in Lausanne, M. Pavilliard.*]

The first marks of my father's displeasure rather astonished than afflicted me: when he threatened to banish, and disown, and disinherit, a rebellious son, I cherished a secret hope that he would not be able or willing to effect his menaces; and the pride of conscience encouraged me to sustain the honourable and important part which I was now acting. My spirits were raised and kept alive by the rapid motion of my journey, the new and various scenes of the Continent, and the civility of Mr. Frey, a man of sense, who was not ignorant of books or the world. But after he had resigned me into Pavilliard's hands, and I was fixed in my new habitation, I had leisure to contemplate the strange and melancholy prospect before me. My first complaint arose from my ignorance of the language. In my childhood I had once studied the French grammar, and I could imperfectly understand the easy prose of a familiar subject. But when I was thus suddenly cast on a foreign land, I found myself deprived of the use of speech and of hearing; and, during some weeks, incapable not only of enjoying the pleasures of conversation, but even of asking or answering a question in the common intercourse of life. To a home-bred Englishman every object, every custom was offensive; but the native of any country might have been disgusted with the general aspect of his lodging and en-

tertainment. I had now exchanged my elegant apartment
in Magdalen College for a narrow, gloomy street, the
most unfrequented of an unhandsome town, for an old
inconvenient house, and for a small chamber ill-con-
trived and ill-furnished, which, on the approach of winter, instead of a companionable fire, must be warmed by
the dull, invisible heat of a stove. From a man I was
again degraded to the dependence of a schoolboy. Mr.
Pavilliard managed my expenses, which had been reduced to a diminutive state: I received a small monthly
allowance for my pocket-money; and helpless and awkward as I have ever been, I no longer enjoyed the indispensable comfort of a servant. My condition seemed as
destitute of hope as it was devoid of pleasure: I was
separated for an indefinite, which appeared an infinite
term from my native country; and I had lost all connexion with my Catholic friends. I have since reflected
with surprise, that as the Romish clergy of every part of
Europe maintain a close correspondence with each other,
they never attempted, by letters or messages, to rescue
me from the hands of the heretics, or at least to confirm
my zeal and constancy in the profession of the faith.
Such was my first introduction to Lausanne; a place
where I spent nearly five years with pleasure and profit,
which I afterwards revisited without compulsion, and
which I have finally selected as the most grateful retreat
for the decline of my life.

But it is the peculiar felicity of youth that the most
unpleasing objects and events seldom make a deep or
lasting impression; it forgets the past, enjoys the present,
and anticipates the future. At the flexible age of sixteen
I soon learned to endure, and gradually to adopt, the new
forms of arbitrary manners: the real hardships of my
situation were alienated by time. Had I been sent abroad
in a more splendid style, such as the fortune and bounty
of my father might have supplied, I might have returned
home with the same stock of language and science which
our countrymen usually import from the Continent. An
exile and a prisoner as I was, their example betrayed me
into some irregularities of wine, of play, and of idle excursions: but I soon felt the impossibility of associating

17

with them on equal terms; and after the departure of
my first acquaintance, I held a cold and civil correspondence with their successors. This seclusion from
English society was attended with the most solid benefits.
In the *Pays de Vaud*, the French language is used with
less imperfection than in most of the distant provinces
of France: in Pavilliard's family, necessity compelled me
to listen and to speak; and if I was at first disheartened
by the apparent slowness, in a few months I was astonished by the rapidity of my progress. My pronunciation was formed by the constant repetition of the same
sounds; the variety of words and idioms, the rules of
grammar, and distinctions of genders, were impressed in
my memory: ease and freedom were obtained by practice; correctness and elegance by labour; and before I
was recalled home, French, in which I spontaneously
thought, was more familiar than English to my ear, my
tongue, and my pen. The first effect of this opening
knowledge was the revival of my love of reading, which
had been chilled at Oxford; and I soon turned over, without much choice, almost all the French books in my
tutor's library. Even these amusements were productive
of real advantage: my taste and judgement were now
somewhat riper. I was introduced to a new mode of style
and literature: by the comparison of manners and opinions, my views were enlarged, my prejudices were corrected, and a copious voluntary abstract of the *Histoire
de l'Eglise et de l'Empire*, by le Sueur, may be placed in
a middle line between my childish and my manly studies.
As soon as I was able to converse with the natives, I began to feel some satisfaction in their company: my awkward timidity was polished and emboldened; and I frequented, for the first time, assemblies of men and wom-
en. The acquaintance of the Pavilliards prepared me by
degrees for more elegant society. I was received with
kindness and indulgence in the best families of Lausanne; and it was in one of these that I formed an intimate and lasting connexion with Mr. Deyverdun, a
young man of an amiable temper and excellent understanding. In the arts of fencing and dancing, small indeed was my proficiency; and some months were idly

wasted in the riding-school. My unfitness to bodily exercise reconciled me to a sedentary life, and the horse, the favourite of my countrymen, never contributed to the pleasures of my youth.

My obligations to the lessons of Mr. Pavilliard, gratitude will not suffer me to forget: he was endowed with a clear head and a warm heart; his innate benevolence had assuaged the spirit of the Church; he was rational, because he was moderate: in the course of his studies he had acquired a just though superficial knowledge of most branches of literature; by long practice, he was skilled in the arts of teaching; and he laboured with assiduous patience to know the character, gain the affection, and open the mind of his English pupil. As soon as we began to understand each other, he gently led me, from a blind and undistinguishing love of reading, into the path of instruction. I consented with pleasure that a portion of the morning hours should be consecrated to a plan of modern history and geography, and to the critical perusal of the French and Latin classics; and at each step I felt myself invigorated by the habits of application and method. His prudence repressed and dissembled some youthful sallies; and as soon as I was confirmed in the habits of industry and temperance, he gave the reins into my own hands. His favourable report of my behaviour and progress gradually obtained some latitude of action and expense; and he wished to alleviate the hardships of my lodging and entertainment. The principles of philosophy were associated with the examples of taste; and by a singular chance, the book, as well as the man, which contributed the most effectually to my education, has a stronger claim on my gratitude than on my admiration. Mr. De Crousaz, the adversary of Bayle and Pope, is not distinguished by lively fancy or profound reflection; and even in his own country, at the end of a few years, his name and writings are almost obliterated. But his philosophy had been formed in the school of Locke, his divinity in that of Limborch and Le Clerc; in a long and laborious life, several generations of pupils were taught to think, and even to write; his lessons rescued the academy of Lausanne from Calvinistic prejudice; and he had the

rare merit of diffusing a more liberal spirit among the
clergy and people of the Pays de Vaud. His system of
logic, which in the last editions has swelled to six tedious
and prolix volumes, may be praised as a clear and
methodical abridgement of the art of reasoning, from our
simple ideas to the most complex operations of the human understanding. This system I studied, and meditated, and abstracted, till I obtained the free command of
an universal instrument, which I soon presumed to exercise on my Catholic opinions. Pavilliard was not unmindful that his first task, his most important duty, was to reclaim me from the errors of Popery. The intermixture of
sects has rendered the Swiss clergy acute and learned
on the topics of controversy; and I have some of his letters in which he celebrates the dexterity of his attack,
and my gradual concessions, after a firm and well-man-
aged defence. I was willing, and I am now willing, to
allow him a handsome share of the honour of my conversion: yet I must observe that it was principally effected by my private reflections; and I still remember
my solitary transport at the discovery of a philosophical
argument against the doctrine of transubstantiation: *that*
the text of Scripture, which seem to inculcate the real
presence, is attested only by a single sense—our sight;
while the real presence itself is disproved by three of our
senses—the sight, the touch, and the taste. The various
articles of the Romish creed disappeared like a dream;
and after a full conviction, on Christmas Day, 1754, I
received the sacrament in the church of Lausanne. It
was here that I suspended my religious inquiries, acqui-
escing with implicit belief in the tenets and mysteries
which are adopted by the general consent of Catholics
and Protestants.

Such, from my arrival at Lausanne, during the first
eighteen or twenty months (July 1753—March 1755),
were my useful studies, the foundation of all my future
improvements. But every man who rises above the common level has received two educations: the first from
his teachers; the second, more personal and important,
from himself. He will not, like the fanatics of the last
age, define the moment of grace; but he cannot forget

the era of his life in which his mind has expanded to its proper form and dimensions. My worthy tutor had the good sense and modesty to discern how far he could be useful: as soon as he felt that I advanced beyond his speed and measure, he wisely left me to my genius; and the hours of lesson were soon lost in the voluntary labour of the whole morning, and sometimes of the whole day. The desire of prolonging my time gradually confirmed the salutary habit of early rising, to which I have always adhered, with some regard to seasons and situations; but it is happy for my eyes and my health, that my temperate ardour has never been seduced to trespass on the hours of the night. During the last three years of my residence at Lausanne, I may assume the merit of serious and solid application; but I am tempted to distinguish the last eight months of the year 1755 as the period of the most extraordinary diligence and rapid progress. In my French and Latin translations I adopted an excellent method, which, from my own success, I would recommend to the imitation of students. I chose some classic writer, such as Cicero and Vertot, the most approved for purity and elegance of style. I translated, for instance, an epistle of Cicero into French; and after throwing it aside, till the words and phrases were obliterated from my memory, I re-translated my French into such Latin as I could find; and then compared each sentence of my imperfect version with the ease, the grace, the propriety of the Roman orator. A similar experiment was made on several pages of the Revolutions of Vertot; I turned them into Latin, returned them after a sufficient interval into my own French, and again scrutinized the resemblance or dissimilitude of the copy and the original. By degrees I was less ashamed, by degrees I was more satisfied with myself; and I persevered in the practice of these double translations, which filled several books, till I had acquired the knowledge of both idioms, and the command at least of a correct style. This useful exercise of writing was accompanied and succeeded by the more pleasing occupation of reading the best authors. The perusal of the Roman classics was at once my exercise and reward. Dr. Middleton's *History,*

which I then appreciated above its true value, naturally
directed me to the writings of Cicero. The most perfect
editions, that of Olivet, which may adorn the shelves of
the rich, that of Ernesti, which should lie on the table
of the learned, were not within my reach. For the familiar epistles I used the text and English commentary
of Bishop Ross; but my general edition was that of Ver-
burgius, published at Amsterdam in two large volumes
in folio, with an indifferent choice of various notes. I
read, with application and pleasure, *all* the epistles, *all*
the orations, and most important treatises of rhetoric
and philosophy; and as I read, I applauded the observation of Quintilian, that every student may judge of his
own proficiency, by the satisfaction which he receives
from the Roman orator. I tasted the beauties of language,
I breathed the spirit of freedom, and I imbibed from his
precepts and examples the public and private sense of
a man. Cicero in Latin, and Xenophon in Greek, are indeed the two ancients whom I would first propose to a
liberal scholar; not only for the merit of their style and
sentiments, but for the admirable lessons, which may
be applied almost to every situation of public and private life. Cicero's *Epistles* may in particular afford the
models of every form of correspondence, from the careless effusions of tenderness and friendship, to the well-
guarded declaration of discreet and dignified resentment.
After finishing this great author, a library of eloquence
and reason, I formed a more extensive plan of reviewing
the Latin classics, under the four divisions of—(1) historians, (2) poets, (3) orators, and (4) philosophers, in
a chronological series, from the days of Plautus and Sal-
lust, to the decline of the language and empire of Rome:
and this plan, in the last twenty-seven months of my
residence at Lausanne (January, 1756—April, 1758), I
nearly accomplished. Nor was this review, however rapid,
either hasty or superficial. I indulged myself in a second
and even a third perusal of Terence, Virgil, Horace, Tacitus, &c., and studied to imbibe the sense and spirit most
congenial to my own. I never suffered a difficult or corrupt passage to escape, till I had viewed it in every light
of which it was susceptible: though often disappointed,

I always consulted the most learned or ingenious commentators, Torrentius and Dacier on Horace, Catrou and Servius on Virgil, Lipsius on Tacitus, Meziriac on Ovid, &c.; and in the ardour of my inquiries, I embraced a large circle of historical and critical erudition. My abstracts of each book were made in the French language: my observations often branched into particular essays; and I can still read, without contempt, a dissertation of eight folio pages on eight lines (287-294) of the fourth *Georgic* of Virgil. Mr. Deyverdun, my friend, whose name will be frequently repeated, had joined with equal zeal, though not with equal perseverance, in the same undertaking. To him every thought, every composition, was instantly communicated; with him I enjoyed the benefits of a free conversation on the topics of our common studies.

But it is scarcely possible for a mind endowed with any active curiosity to be long conversant with the Latin classics without aspiring to know the Greek originals, whom they celebrate as their masters, and of whom they so warmly recommend the study and imitation;

—— Vos exemplaria Græca
Nocturnâ versate manu, versate diurnâ.[1]

It was now that I regretted the early years which had been wasted in sickness or idleness, or mere idle reading; that I condemned the perverse method of our schoolmasters, who, by first teaching the mother language, might descend with so much ease and perspicuity to the origin and etymology of a derivative idiom. In the nineteenth year of my age I determined to supply this defect; and the lessons of Pavilliard again contributed to smooth the entrance of the way, the Greek alphabet, the grammar, and the pronunciation according to the French accent. At my earnest request we presumed to open the *Iliad;* and I had the pleasure of beholding, though darkly and through a glass, the true image of Homer, whom

---

[1] ["Night and day you must turn over the pages of the Greek models."]

Horace *Ars Pœtica* 2.68]

23

I had long since admired in an English dress. After my
tutor had left me to myself, I worked my way through
about half the *Iliad,* and afterwards interpreted alone a
large portion of Xenophon and Herodotus. But my ardour, destitute of aid and emulation, was gradually
cooled, and, from the barren task of searching words in
a lexicon, I withdrew to the free and familiar conversation of Virgil and Tacitus. Yet in my residence at Lausanne I had laid a solid foundation, which enabled me,
in a more propitious season, to prosecute the study of
Grecian literature.

From a blind idea of the usefulness of such abstract
science, my father had been desirous, and even pressing,
that I should devote some time to the mathematics; nor
could I refuse to comply with so reasonable a wish.
During two winters I attended the private lectures of
Monsieur de Traytorrens, who explained the elements of
algebra and geometry, as far as the conic sections of the
Marquis de l'Hôpital, and appeared satisfied with my
diligence and improvement. But as my childish propensity for numbers and calculations was totally extinct, I
was content to receive the passive impression of my professor's lectures, without any active exercise of my own
powers. As soon as I understood the principles, I relinquished for ever the pursuit of the mathematics; nor
can I lament that I desisted, before my mind was hardened by the habit of rigid demonstration, so destructive
of the finer feelings of moral evidence, which must, however, determine the actions and opinions of our lives. I
listened with more pleasure to the proposal of studying
the law of nature and nations, which was taught in
the academy of Lausanne by Mr. Vicat, a professor of
some learning and reputation. But, instead of attending
his public or private course, I preferred in my closet the
lessons of his masters, and my own reason. Without being disgusted by Grotius or Puffendorf, I studied in their
writings the duties of a man, the rights of a citizen, the
theory of justice (it is, alas! a theory), and the laws of
peace and war, which have had some influence on the
practice of modern Europe. My fatigues were alleviated
by the good sense of their commentator, Barbeyrac.

Locke's *Treatise of Government* instructed me in the knowledge of Whig principles, which are rather founded in reason than experience; but my delight was in the frequent perusal of Montesquieu, whose energy of style, and boldness of hypothesis, were powerful to awaken and stimulate the genius of the age. The logic of De Crousaz had prepared me to engage with his master Locke, and his antagonist Bayle; of whom the former may be used as a bridle, and the latter as a spur, to the curiosity of a young philosopher. According to the nature of their respective works, the schools of argument and objection, I carefully went through the *Essay on Human Understanding*, and occasionally consulted the most interesting articles of the *Philosophic Dictionary*. In the infancy of my reason I turned over, as an idle amusement, the most serious and important treatise: in its maturity, the most trifling performance could exercise my taste or judgement; and more than once I have been led by a novel into a deep and instructive train of thinking. But I canot forbear to mention three particular books, since they may have remotely contributed to form the historian of the Roman empire. (1) From the *Provincial Letters* of Pascal, which almost every year I have perused with new pleasures, I learned to manage the weapon of grave and temperate irony, even on subjects of ecclesiastical solemnity. (2) *The Life of Julian*, by the Abbé de la Bleterie, first introduced me to the man and the times; and I should be glad to recover my first essay on the truth of the miracle which stopped the rebuilding of the Temple of Jerusalem. (3) In Giannone's *Civil History of Naples* I observed with a critical eye the progress and abuse of sacerdotal power, and the revolutions of Italy in the darker ages. This various reading, which I now conducted with discretion, was digested, according to the precept and model of Mr. Locke, into a large commonplace book; a practice, however, which I do not strenuously recommend. The action of the pen will doubtless imprint an idea on the mind as well as on the paper: but I much question whether the benefits of this laborious method are adequate to the waste of time; and I must agree with Dr. Johnson (*Idler,* No. 74), "that what is twice read is commonly better remembered than what is transcribed."

During two years, if I forget some boyish excursions of a day or a week, I was fixed at Lausanne; but at the end of the third summer, my father consented that I should make the tour of Switzerland with Pavilliard: and our short absence of one month ((September 21— October 20, 1755) was a reward and relaxation of my assiduous studies. The fashion of climbing the mountains and reviewing the *Glaciers* had not yet been introduced by foreign travellers, who seek the sublime beauties of nature. But the political face of the country is not less diversified by the forms and spirit of so many various republics, from the jealous government of the *few* to the licentious freedom of the *many*. I contemplated with pleasure the new prospects of men and manners; though my conversation with the natives would have been more free and instructive had I possessed the German, as well as the French language. We passed through most of the principal towns in Switzerland; Neufchâtel, Bienne, Soleurre, Arau, Baden, Zurich, Basil, and Bern. In every place we visited the churches, arsenals, libraries, and all the most eminent persons; and after my return, I digested my notes in fourteen or fifteen sheets of a French journal, which I dispatched to my father, as a proof that my time and his money had not been misspent. Had I found this journal among his papers, I might be tempted to select some passages; but I will not transcribe the printed accounts, and it may be sufficient to notice a remarkable spot, which left a deep and lasting impression on my memory. From Zurich we proceeded to the Benedictine Abbey of Einsiedlen, more commonly styled Our Lady of the Hermits. I was astonished by the profuse ostentation of riches in the poorest corner of Europe; amidst a savage scene of woods and mountains a palace appears to have been erected by magic; and it was erected by the potent magic of religion. A crowd of palmers and votaries was prostrate before the altar. The title and worship of the Mother of God provoked my indignation; and the lively naked image of superstition suggested to me, as in the same place it had done to Zwinglius, the most pressing argument for the reformation of the Church. About two years after this tour, I passed at Geneva a useful and agreeable month; but this excursion, and some short visits in the Pays de Vaud, did not materially interrupt my studious and sedentary life at Lausanne. . . .

Before I was recalled from Switzerland, I had the satisfaction of seeing the most extraordinary man of the age; a poet, an historian, a philosopher, who has filled thirty quartos, of prose and verse, with his various productions, often excellent, and always entertaining. Need I add the name of Voltaire? After forfeiting, by his own misconduct, the friendship of the first of kings, he retired, at the age of sixty, with a plentiful fortune, to a free and beautiful country, and resided two winters (1757 and 1758) in the town or neighbourhood of Lausanne. My desire of beholding Voltaire, whom I then rated above his real magnitude, was easily gratified. He received me with civility as an English youth; but I cannot boast of any peculiar notice or distinction, *Virgilium vidi tantum.*[2]

The ode which he composed on his first arrival on the banks of the Leman Lake, *O Maison d'Aristippe! O Jardin d'Epicure*, &c., had been imparted as a secret to the gentleman by whom I was introduced. He allowed me to read it twice; I knew it by heart; and as my discretion was not equal to my memory, the author was soon displeased by the circulation of a copy. In writing this trivial anecdote, I wished to observe whether my memory was impaired, and I have the comfort of finding that every line of the poem is still engraved in fresh and indelible characters. The highest gratification which I derived from Voltaire's residence at Lausanne was the uncommon circumstance of hearing a great poet declaim his own productions on the stage. He had formed a company of gentlemen and ladies, some of whom were not destitute of talents. A decent theatre was framed at Monrepos, a country-house at the end of a suburb; dresses and scenes were provided at the expense of the actors;

---

2 ["Virgil, I merely saw" *Ovid Tristia iii.* x. 51.]

and the author directed the rehearsals with the zeal and attention of paternal love. In two successive winters his tragedies of *Zayre, Alzire, Zulime,* and his sentimental comedy of the *Enfant Prodigue,* were played at the theatre of Monrepos. Voltaire represented the characters best adapted to his years, Lusignan, Alvaréz, Benassar, Euphemon. His declamation was fashioned to the pomp and cadence of the old stage; and he expressed the enthusiasm of poetry, rather than the feelings of nature. My ardour, which soon became conspicuous, seldom failed of procuring me a ticket. The habits of pleasure fortified my taste for the French theatre, and that taste has perhaps abated my idolatry for the gigantic genius of Shakespeare, which is inculcated from our infancy as the first duty of an Englishman. The wit and philosophy of Voltaire, his table and theatre, refined, in a visible degree, the manners of Lausanne; and, however addicted to study, I enjoyed my share of the amusements of society. After the representation of Monrepos I sometimes supped with the actors. I was now familiar in some, and acquainted in many houses; and my evenings were generally devoted to cards and conversation, either in private parties or numerous assemblies. . . .

Whatsoever have been the fruits of my education, they must be ascribed to the fortunate banishment which placed me at Lausanne. I have sometimes applied to my own fate the verses of Pindar, which remind an Olympic champion that his victory was the consequence of his exile; and that at home, like a domestic fowl, his days might have rolled away inactive or inglorious. . . .

If my childish revolt against the religion of my country had not stripped me in time of my academic gown, the five important years, so liberally improved in the studies and conversation of Lausanne, would have been steeped in port and prejudice among the monks of Oxford. Had the fatigue of idleness compelled me to read, the path of learning would not have been enlightened by a ray of philosophic freedom. I should have grown to manhood ignorant of the life and language of Europe, and my knowledge of the world would have been confined to an English cloister. But my religious error fixed me at Lausanne, in a state of banishment and disgrace. The rigid course of discipline and abstinence, to which I was condemned, invigorated the constitution of my mind and body; poverty and pride estranged me from my countrymen. One mischief, however, and in their eyes a serious and irreparable mischief, was derived from the success of my Swiss education: I had ceased to be an Englishman. At the flexible period of youth, from the age of sixteen to twenty-one, my opinions, habits, and sentiments were cast in a foreign mould; the faint and distant remembrance of England was almost obliterated; my native language was grown less familiar; and I should have cheerfully accepted the offer of a moderate independence on the terms of perpetual exile. By the good sense and temper of Pavilliard my yoke was insensibly lightened: he left me master of my time and actions; but he could neither change my situation, nor increase my allowance, and with the progress of my years and reason I impatiently sighed for the moment of my deliverance. At length, in the spring of the year 1758, my father signified his permission and his pleasure that I should immediately return home.

3. The Years of Gestation

[*On his return to England in 1758, Gibbon lived mainly with his father at Buriton in Hampshire. Here he devoted himself to private study, but his study was interrupted by two years' service with the Hampshire militia. Gibbon much regretted the inconvenience of these tedious "exercises of the field and battle," but he published his first work, his Essay on the* Study of Literature, *written in French, in 1761 and he contrived to read a great deal of history. He also proposed to write history. "The old reproach," he says, "that no British altars had been raised to the Muse of History was recently disproved by the first performances of Robertson and Hume, the histories of Scotland and the Stuarts," and "without engaging in a metaphysical, or rather verbal dispute, I know by experience that from my early youth I had always aspired to the character of an historian." After considering several subjects, he almost settled on a history of Florence under the Medici, but in 1763, an opportunity of visiting Italy provided him with a new inspiration. On the way he stopped first at Paris, then once again at Lausanne. At both places, and while travelling, he never ceased to study.*]

If my studies at Paris had been confined to the study of the world, three or four months would not have been unprofitably spent. My visits, however superficial, to the Academy of Medals and the public libraries, opened a new field of inquiry; and the view of so many manuscripts of different ages and characters induced me to consult the two great Benedictine works, the *Diplomatica* of Mabillon, and the *Palæographia* of Montfaucon. I studied the theory without attaining the practice of the art: nor should I complain of the intricacy of Greek abbreviations and Gothic alphabets, since every day, in a familiar language, I am at a loss to decipher the hieroglyphics of a female note. In a tranquil scene, which revived the memory of my first studies, idleness would have been less pardonable: the public libraries of Lausanne and Geneva liberally supplied me with books; and if many hours were lost in dissipation, many more were employed in literary labour. In the country, Horace and Virgil, Juvenal and Ovid, were my assiduous companions: but in town, I formed and executed a plan of study for the use of my Transalpine expedition: the topography of old Rome, the ancient geography of Italy, and the science of medals. (1) I diligently read, almost always with a pen in my hand, the elaborate treatises of Nardini, Donatus, &c., which fill the fourth volume of the Roman Antiquities of Grævius. (2) I next undertook and finished the *Italia Antiqua* of Cluverius, a learned native of Prussia, who had measured, on foot, every spot, and has compiled and digested every passage of the ancient writers. These passages in Greek or Latin authors I perused in the text of Cluverius, in two folio volumes: but I separately read the descriptions of Italy by Strabo, Pliny, and Pomponius Mela, the Catalogues of the epic poets, the Itineraries of Wesseling's Antoninus, and the coasting Voyage of Rutilius Namatianus; and I studied two kindred subjects in the *Mesures Itinéraires* of d'Anville, and the copious work of Bergier, *Histoire des grands Chemins de l'Empire Romain*. From these materials I formed a table of roads and distances reduced to our English measure; filled a folio commonplace book with my collections and remarks on the geography of Italy; and inserted in my journal many long and learned notes on the insulæ[1] and populousness of Rome, the social war, the passage of the Alps by Hannibal, &c. (3) After glancing my eye over Addison's agreeable dialogues, I more seriously read the great work of Ezechiel Span-

---

[1] [blocks of apartments]

heim, *de Præstantia et Usu Numismatum,* and applied with him the medals of the kings and emperors, the families and colonies, to the illustration of ancient history. And thus was I armed for my Italian journey.

I shall advance with rapid brevity in the narrative of this tour, in which somewhat more than a year (April, 1764—May, 1765) was agreeably employed. Content with tracing my line of march, and slightly touching on my personal feelings, I shall waive the minute investigation of the scenes which have been viewed by thousands, and described by hundreds of our modern travellers. Rome is the great object of our pilgrimage: and first, the journey; second, the residence; and third, the return, will form the most proper and perspicuous division. (1) I climbed Mount Cenis, and descended into the plain of Piedmont, not on the back of an elephant, but on a light osier seat, in the hands of the dexterous and intrepid chairmen of the Alps. The architecture and government of Turin presented the same aspect of tame and tiresome uniformity; but the court was regulated with decent and splendid economy; and I was introduced to his Sardinian majesty, Charles Emanuel, who, after the incomparable Frederic, held the second rank (*proximus longo tamen intervallo*)[2] among the kings of Europe. The size and populousness of Milan could not surprise an inhabitant of London; but the fancy is amused by a visit to the Boromean Islands, an enchanted palace, a work of the fairies in the midst of a lake encompassed with mountains, and far removed from the haunts of men. I was less amused by the marble palaces of Genoa, than by the recent memorials of her deliverance (in December, 1746) from the Austrian tyranny; and I took a military survey of every scene of action within the enclosure of her double walls. My steps were detained at Parma and Modena, by the precious relics of the Farnese and Este collections: but, alas! the far greater part had been already transported, by inheritance or purchase, to Naples and Dresden. By the road of Bologna and the Apennine I at last reached Florence, where I reposed from

---

2 ["but second after a long gap." Virgil, *Aeneid.* v. 320.]

June to September, during the heat of the summer months. In the Gallery, and especially in the Tribune, I first acknowledged, at the feet of the Venus of Medicis, that the chisel may dispute the pre-eminence with the pencil, a truth in the fine arts which cannot on this side of the Alps be felt or understood. At home I had taken some lessons of Italian; on the spot I read, with a learned native, the classics of the Tuscan idiom; but the shortness of my time, and the use of the French language, prevented my acquiring any facility of speaking; and I was a silent spectator in the conversations of our envoy, Sir Horace Mann, whose most serious business was that of entertaining the English at his hospitable table. After leaving Florence I compared the solitude of Pisa with the industry of Lucca and Leghorn, and continued my journey through Sienna to Rome, where I arrived in the beginning of October. (2) My temper is not very susceptible of enthusiasm, and the enthusiasm which I do not feel I have ever scorned to affect. But, at the distance of twenty-five years, I can neither forget nor express the strong emotions which agitated my mind as I first approached and entered the *eternal city*. After a sleepless night, I trod, with a lofty step, the ruins of the Forum; each memorable spot where Romulus *stood,* or Tully spoke, or Cæsar fell, was at once present to my eye; and several days of intoxication were lost or enjoyed before I could descend to a cool and minute investigation. My guide was Mr. Byers, a Scotch antiquary of experience and taste; but, in the daily labour of eighteen weeks, the powers of attention were sometimes fatigued, till I was myself qualified, in a last review, to select and study the capital works of ancient and modern art. Six weeks were borrowed for my tour of Naples, the most populous of cities, relative to its size, whose luxurious inhabitants seem to dwell on the confines of paradise and hell-fire. I was presented to the boy-king by our new envoy, Sir William Hamilton; who, wisely diverting his correspondence from the Secretary of State to the Royal Society and British Museum, has elucidated a country of such inestimable value to the naturalist and antiquarian. On my return, I fondly embraced, for the last time, the miracles of Rome; but I departed without kissing the foot of Rezzonico (Clement XIII), who neither possessed the wit of his predecessor Lambertini, nor the virtues of his successor Ganganelli. (3) In my pilgrimage from Rome to Loretto I again crossed the Apennine; from the coast of the Adriatic I traversed a fruitful and populous country, which could alone disprove the paradox of Montesquieu, that modern Italy is a desert. Without adopting the exclusive prejudice of the natives, I sincerely admire the paintings of the Bologna school. I hastened to escape from the sad solitude of Ferrara, which in the age of Cæsar was still more desolate. The spectacle of Venice afforded some hours of astonishment; the University of Padua is a dying taper; but Verona still boasts her amphitheatre, and his native Vicenza is adorned by the classic architecture of Palladio: the road of Lombardy and Piedmont (did Montesquieu find them without inhabitants?) led me back to Milan, Turin, and the passage of Mount Cenis, where I again crossed the Alps in my way to Lyons.

The use of foreign travel has been often debated as a general question; but the conclusion must be finally applied to the character and circumstances of each individual. With the education of boys, *where* or *how* they may pass over some juvenile years with the least mischief to themselves or others, I have no concern. But after supposing the previous and indispensable requisites of age, judgement, a competent knowledge of men and books, and a freedom from domestic prejudices, I will briefly describe the qualifications which I deem most essential to a traveller. He should be endowed with an active, indefatigable vigour of mind and body, which can seize every mode of conveyance, and support, with a careless smile, every hardship of the road, the weather, or the inn. The benefits of foreign travel will correspond with the degrees of these qualifications; but, in this sketch, those to whom I am known will not accuse me of framing my own panegyric. It was at Rome, on the 15th of October, 1764, as I sat musing amidst the ruins of the Capitol, while the barefooted friars were singing vespers in the Temple of Jupiter, that the idea of writing the decline and fall of the city first started to my mind. But my original plan was circumscribed to the decay of the city rather than of the empire: and, though my reading and reflections began to point towards that object, some years elapsed, and several avocations intervened, before I was seriously engaged in the execution of that laborious work.

4. The Decline and Fall

[It was some years before Gibbon set himself to realise his great design. He wrote occasional critical articles. Old projects—Medicean Florence, the history of Swiss freedom—still haunted him. He was distracted by his father's death in 1770, and by the necessary, but difficult disposal of his encumbered estate. But finally he was able to settle in London and concentrate on his work. The following passages describe his gradual concentration, the completion of his first volume, and the response to it.]

In the fifteen years between my *Essay on the Study of Literature* and the first volume of the *Decline and Fall* (1761-1776), this criticism on Warburton, and some articles in the Journal, were my sole publications. It is more especially incumbent on me to mark the employment, or to confess the waste of time, from my travels to my father's death, an interval in which I was not diverted by any professional duties from the labours and pleasures of a studious life. (1) As soon as I was released from the fruitless task of the Swiss revolutions (1768), I began gradually to advance from the wish to the hope, from the hope to the design, from the design to the execution, of my historical work, of whose limits and extent I had yet a very inadequate notion. The Classics, as low as Tacitus, the younger Pliny, and Juvenal, were my old and familiar companions. I insensibly plunged into the ocean of the Augustan history; and in the descending series I investigated, with my pen almost always in my hand, the original records, both Greek and Latin, from Dion Cassius to Ammianus Marcellinus, from the reign of Trajan to the last age of the Western Cæsars. The subsidiary rays of medals, and inscriptions of geography and chronology, were thrown on their proper objects; and I applied the collections of Tillemont, whose inimitable accuracy almost assumes the character of genius, to fix and arrange within my reach the loose and scattered atoms of historical information. Through the darkness of the middle ages I explored my way in the Annals and Antiquities of Italy of the learned Muratori; and diligently compared them with the parallel or transverse lines of Sigonius and Maffei, Baronius and Pagi, till I almost grasped the ruins of Rome in the fourteenth century, without suspecting that this final chapter must be attained by the labour of six quartos and twenty years. Among the books which I purchased, the Theodosian Code, with the commentary of James Godefroy, must be gratefully remembered; I used it (and much I used it) as a work of history, rather than of jurisprudence: but in every light it may be considered as a full and capacious repository of the political state of the empire in the fourth and fifth centuries. As I believed, and as I still believe, that the propagation of the Gospel, and the triumph of the Church, are inseparably connected with the decline of the Roman monarchy, I weighed the causes and effects of the revolution, and contrasted the narratives and apologies of the Christians themselves, with the glances of candour or enmity which the Pagans have cast on the rising sects. The Jewish and heathen testimonies, as they are collected and illustrated by Dr. Lardner, directed, without superseding, my search of the originals; and in an ample dissertation on the miraculous darkness of the passion, I privately drew my conclusions from the silence of an unbelieving age. I have assembled the preparatory studies, directly or indirectly relative to my history; but, in strict equity, they must be spread beyond this period of my life, over the two summers (1771 and 1772) that elapsed between my father's death and my settlement in London. (2) In a free conversation with books and men, it would be endless to enumerate the names and characters of all who are introduced to our acquaintance; but in this general acquaintance we may select the degrees of friendship and esteem. According to the wise maxim, *Multum legere potius quam multa*,[1] I reviewed, again and again, the immortal works of the French and English, the Latin and Italian classics. My Greek studies (though less assiduous than I designed) maintained and extended my knowledge of that incomparable idiom. Homer and Xenophon were still my favourite authors; and I had almost prepared for the press an *Essay on the Cyropædia*, which, in my own judgement, is not unhappily laboured. After a certain age, the new publications of merit are the sole food of the many; and the most austere student will often be tempted to break the line, for the sake of indulging his own curiosity, and of providing the topics of fashionable currency. A more respectable motive may be assigned for the third perusal of Blackstone's *Commentaries*, and a copious and critical abstract of that English work was my first serious production in my native language. (3) My literary leisure was much less complete and independent than it might appear to the eye of a stranger. In the hurry of London I was destitute of books; in the solitude of Hampshire I was not master of my time. My quiet was gradually disturbed by our domestic anxiety, and I should be ashamed of my unfeeling philosophy had I found much time to waste for study in the last fatal summer (1770) of my father's decay and dissolution. . . .

As soon as I had paid the last solemn duties to my father, and obtained, from time and reason, a tolerable composure of mind, I began to form a plan of an independent life, most adapted to my circumstances and inclination. Yet so intricate was the net, my efforts were so awkward and feeble, that nearly two years (November, 1770—October, 1772) were suffered to elapse before I could disentangle myself from the management of the farm, and transfer my residence from Buriton to a house in London. During this interval I continued to divide my year between town and the country; but my new situation was brightened by hope; my stay in London was pro-

---

[1] [To read the same book often rather than many books.]

longed into the summer; and the uniformity of the summer was occasionally broken by visits and excursions at a distance from home. The gratification of my desires (they were not immoderate) has been seldom disappointed by the want of money or credit; my pride was never insulted by the visit of an importunate tradesman; and my transient anxiety for the past or future has been dispelled by the studious or social occupation of the present hour. My conscience does not accuse me of any act of extravagance or injustice, and the remnant of my estate affords an ample and honourable provision for my declining age. I shall not expatiate on my economical affairs, which cannot be instructive or amusing to the reader. It is a rule of prudence, as well as of politeness, to reserve such confidence for the ear of a private friend, without exposing our situation to the envy or pity of strangers; for envy is productive of hatred, and pity borders too nearly on contempt. Yet I may believe, and even assert, that in circumstances more indigent or more wealthy, I should never have accomplished the task, or acquired the fame, of an historian; that my spirit would have been broken by poverty and contempt, and that my industry might have been relaxed in the labour and luxury of a superfluous fortune.

I had now attained the first of earthly blessings, independence: I was the absolute master of my hours and actions: nor was I deceived in the hope that the establishment of my library in town would allow me to divide the day between study and society. Each year the circle of my acquaintance, the number of my dead and living companions, was enlarged. To a lover of books, the shops and sales of London present irresistible temptations; and the manufacture of my History required a various and growing stock of materials. The militia, my travels, the House of Commons, the fame of an author contributed to multiply my connexions: I was chosen a member of the fashionable clubs; and, before I left England in 1783, there were few persons of any eminence in the literary or political world to whom I was a stranger. It would most assuredly be in my power to amuse the reader with a gallery of portraits and a collection of anecdotes. But I have always condemned the practice of transforming a private memorial into a vehicle of satire or praise. By my own choice I passed in town the greatest part of the year; but whenever I was desirous of breathing the air of the country, I possessed an hospitable retreat at Sheffield Place in Sussex, in the family of my valuable friend Mr. Holroyd, whose character, under the name of Lord Sheffield, has since been more conspicuous to the public.

No sooner was I settled in my house and library, than I undertook the composition of the first volume of my *History*. At the outset all was dark and doubtful; even the title of the work, the true era of the *Decline and Fall of the Empire*, the limits of the introduction, the division of the chapters, and the order of the narrative; and I was often tempted to cast away the labour of seven years. The style of an author should be the image of his mind, but the choice and command of language is the fruit of exercise. Many experiments were made before I could hit the middle tone between a dull chronicle and a rhetorical declamation: three times did I compose the first chapter, and twice the second and third, before I was tolerably satisfied with their effect. In the remainder of the way I advanced with a more equal and easy pace; but the fifteenth and sixteenth chapters have been reduced by three successive revisals from a large volume to their present size; and they might still be compressed, without any loss of facts or sentiments. An opposite fault may be imputed to the concise and superficial narrative of the first reigns from Commodus to Alexander; a fault of which I have never heard, except from Mr. Hume in his last journey to London. Such an oracle might have been consulted and obeyed with rational devotion; but I was soon disgusted with the modest practice of reading the manuscript to my friends. Of such friends some will praise from politeness, and some will criticize from vanity. The author himself is the best judge of his own performance; no one has so deeply meditated on the subject; no one is so sincerely interested in the event.

By the friendship of Mr. (now Lord) Eliot, who had married my first cousin, I was returned at the general election for the borough of Leskeard. I took my seat at the beginning of the memorable contest between Great Britain and America, and supported, with many a sincere and silent vote, the rights, though not, perhaps, the interest, of the mother-country. After a fleeting illusive hope, prudence condemned me to acquiesce in the humble station of a mute. I was not armed by nature and education with the intrepid energy of mind and voice,

Vincentem strepitus, et natum rebus agendis.[2]

Timidity was fortified by pride, and even the success of my pen discouraged the trial of my voice. But I assisted at the debates of a free assembly; I listened to the attack and defence of eloquence and reason; I had a near prospect of the characters, views, and passions of the first men of the age. The cause of government was ably vindicated by Lord North, a statesman of spotless integrity, a consummate master of debate, who could wield, with equal dexterity, the arms of reason and of ridicule. He was seated on the Treasury Bench between his Attorney and Solicitor-General, the two pillars of the law and state, *magis pares quam similes;*[3] and the minister might indulge in a short slumber, whilst he was upholden on either hand by the majestic sense of Thurlow, and the skilful eloquence of Wedderburne. From the adverse side of the house an ardent and powerful opposition was supported by the lively declamation of Barré, the legal acuteness of Dunning, the profuse and philosophic fancy of Burke, and the argumentative vehemence of Fox, who, in the conduct of a party, approved himself equal to the conduct of an empire. By such men every operation of peace and war, every principle of justice or policy, every question of authority and freedom, was attacked and defended; and the subject of the momentous contest was the union or separation of Great Britain and America. The eight sessions that I sat in parliament were a school of civil prudence, the first and most essential virtue of an historian.

---

[2] ["Born for action, loud above the din" Horace *de Arte Poetica* 82.]

[3] [equal rather than alike]

The volume of my *History*, which had been somewhat delayed by the novelty and tumult of a first session, was now ready for the press. After the perilous adventure had been declined by my friend Mr. Elmsley, I agreed, upon easy terms, with Mr. Thomas Cadell, a respectable bookseller, and Mr. William Strahan, an eminent printer; and they undertook the care and risk of the publication, which derived more credit from the name of the shop than from that of the author. The last revisal of the proofs was submitted to my vigilance; and many blemishes of style, which had been invisible in the manuscript, were discovered and corrected in the printed sheet. So moderate were our hopes, that the original impression had been stinted to five hundred, till the number was doubled by the prophetic taste of Mr. Strahan. During this awful interval I was neither elated by the ambition of fame, nor depressed by the apprehension of contempt. My diligence and accuracy were attested by my own conscience. History is the most popular species of writing, since it can adapt itself to the highest or the lowest capacity. I had chosen an illustrious subject. Rome is familiar to the schoolboy and the statesman; and my narrative was deduced from the last period of classical reading. I had likewise flattered myself, that an age of light and liberty would receive, without scandal, an inquiry into the human *causes* of the progress and establishment of Christianity.

I am at a loss how to describe the success of the work, without betraying the vanity of the writer. The first impression was exhausted in a few days; a second and third edition were scarcely adequate to the demand; and the bookseller's property was twice invaded by the pirates of Dublin. My book was on every table, and almost on every toilette; the historian was crowned by the taste of fashion of the day; nor was the general voice disturbed by the barking of any *profane* critic. The favour of mankind is most freely bestowed on a new acquaintance or any original merit; and the mutual surprise of the public and their favourite is productive of those warm sensibilities, which at a second meeting can no longer be rekindled. If I listened to the music of praise, I was more seriously satisfied with the approbation of my judges. The candour of Dr. Robertson embraced his disciple. A letter from Mr. Hume overpaid the labour of ten years; but I have never presumed to accept a place in the triumvirate of British historians.

That curious and original letter will amuse the reader, and his gratitude should shield my free communication from the reproach of vanity.

"Edinburgh, March 18, 1776.

"DEAR SIR,

"As I ran through your volume of history with great avidity and impatience, I cannot forbear discovering somewhat of the same impatience in returning you thanks for your agreeable present, and expressing the satisfaction which the performance has given me. Whether I consider the dignity of your style, the depth of your matter, or the extensiveness of your learning, I must regard the work as equally the object of esteem; and I own that if I had not previously had the happiness of your personal acquaintance, such a performance from an Englishman in our age would have given me some surprise. You may smile at this sentiment, but as it seems to me that your countrymen, for almost a whole generation, have given themselves up to barbarous and absurd faction, and have totally neglected all polite letters, I no longer expected any valuable production ever to come from them. I know it will give you pleasure (as it did me) to find that all the men of letters in this place concur in their admiration of your work, and in their anxious desire of your continuing it.

"When I heard of your undertaking (which was some time ago), I own I was a little curious to see how you would extricate yourself from the subject of your two last chapters. I think you have observed a very prudent temperament; but it was impossible to treat the subject so as not to give grounds of suspicion against you, and you may expect that a clamour will arise. This, if anything, will retard your success with the public; for in every other respect your work is calculated to be popular. But among many other marks of decline, the prevalence

43

of superstition in England prognosticates the fall of philosophy and decay of taste; and though nobody be more capable than you to revive them, you will probably find a struggle in your first advances.

"I see you entertain a great doubt with regard to the authenticity of the poems of Ossian. You are certainly right in so doing. It is indeed strange that any men of sense could have imagined it possible, that above twenty thousand verses, along with numberless historical facts, could have been preserved by oral tradition during fifty generations, by the rudest, perhaps, of all the European nations, the most necessitous, the most turbulent, and the most unsettled. Where a supposition is so contrary to common sense, any positive evidence of it ought never to be regarded. Men run with great avidity to give their evidence in favour of what flatters their passions and their national prejudices. You are therefore over and above indulgent to us in speaking of the matter with hesitation.

"I must inform you that we are all very anxious to hear that you have fully collected the materials for your second volume, and that you are even considerably advanced in the composition of it. I speak this more in the name of my friends than in my own, as I cannot expect to live so long as to see the publication of it. Your ensuing volume will be more delicate than the preceding, but I trust in your prudence for extricating you from the difficulties; and, in all events, you have courage to despise the clamour of bigots.

I am, with great regard,
Dear Sir,
Your most obedient, and most humble Servant,
DAVID HUME."

Some weeks afterwards, I had the melancholy pleasure of seeing Mr. Hume in his passage through London; his body feeble, his mind firm. On the 25th of August of the same year (1776) he died, at Edinburgh, the death of a philosopher. . . .

Nearly two years had elapsed between the publication of my first and the commencement of my second volume;

and the causes must be assigned of this long delay. (1) After a short holiday, I indulged my curiosity in some studies of a very different nature, a course of anatomy, which was demonstrated by Doctor Hunter, and some lessons of chemistry, which were delivered by Mr. Higgins. The principles of these sciences, and a taste for books of natural history, contributed to multiply my ideas and images; and the anatomist and chemist may sometimes track me in their own snow. (2) I dived, perhaps too deeply, into the mud of the Arian controversy; and many days of reading, thinking, and writing were consumed in the pursuit of a phantom. (3) It is difficult to arrange, with order and perspicuity, the various transactions of the age of Constantine; and so much was I displeased with the first essay, that I committed to the flames above fifty sheets. (4) The six months of Paris and pleasure must be deducted from the account. But when I resumed my task I felt my improvement; I was now master of my style and subject, and while the measure of my daily performance was enlarged, I discovered less reason to cancel or correct. It has always been my practice to cast a long paragraph in a single mould, to try it by my ear, to deposit it in my memory, but to suspend the action of the pen till I had given the last polish to my work. Shall I add, that I never found my mind more vigorous, nor my composition more happy, than in the winter hurry of society and parliament?

Had I believed that the majority of English readers were so fondly attached even to the name and shadow of Christianity; had I foreseen that the pious, the timid, and the prudent, would feel, or affect to feel, with such exquisite sensibility, I might, perhaps, have softened the two invidious chapters, which would create many enemies, and conciliate few friends. But the shaft was shot, the alarm was sounded, and I could only rejoice, that if the voice of our priests was clamorous and bitter, their hands were disarmed from the powers of persecution. I adhered to the wise resolution of trusting myself and my writings to the candour of the public, till Mr. Davies of Oxford presumed to attack, not the faith, but the fidelity, of the historian. My *Vindication*, expressive of less anger than contempt, amused for a moment the busy and idle metropolis; and the most rational part of the laity, and even of the clergy, appear to have been satisfied of my innocence and accuracy. I would not print this Vindication in quarto, lest it should be bound and preserved with the history itself. At the distance of twelve years, I calmly affirm my judgement of Davies, Chelsum, &c. A victory over such antagonists was a sufficient humiliation. They, however, were rewarded in this world. Poor Chelsum was indeed neglected; and I dare not boast the making Dr. Watson a bishop; he is a prelate of a large mind and liberal spirit: but I enjoyed the pleasure of giving a royal pension to Mr. Davies, and of collating Dr. Apthorpe to an archiepiscopal living. Their success encouraged the zeal of Taylor the Arian,[4] and Milner the Methodist,[5] with many others, whom it would be difficult to remember, and tedious to rehearse. The list of my adversaries, however, was graced with the more respectable names of Dr. Priestley, Sir David Dalrymple, and Dr. White; and every polemic, of either University, discharged his sermon or pamphlet against the impenetrable silence of the Roman historian. In his *History of the Corruptions of Christianity*, Dr. Priestley threw down his two gauntlets to Bishop Hurd and Mr. Gibbon. I declined the challenge in a letter, exhorting my opponent to enlighten the world by his philosophical discoveries, and to remember that the merit of his predecessor Servetus is now reduced to a single passage, which indicates the smaller circulation of the blood through the lungs, from and to the heart. Instead of listening to this friendly advice, the dauntless philosopher of Birmingham con-

---

[4] The stupendous title, *Thoughts on the Causes of the grand Apostasy*, at first agitated my nerves, till I discovered that it was the apostasy of the whole Church, since the Council of Nice, from Mr. Taylor's private religion. His book is a thorough mixture of *high* enthusiasm and *low* buffoonery, and the Millennium is a fundamental article of his creed.

[5] From his grammar school at Kingston-upon-Hull, Mr. Joseph Milner pronounces an anathema against all rational religion. *His* faith is a divine taste, a spiritual inspiration; *his* church is a mystic and invisible body; the *natural* Christians, such as Mr. Locke, who believe and interpret the Scriptures, are, in his judgement, no better than profane infidels.

tinued to fire away his double battery against those who believed too little, and those who believed too much. From *my* replies he has nothing to hope or fear: but his Socinian shield has repeatedly been pierced by the mighty spear of Horsley, and his trumpet of sedition may at length awaken the magistrates of a free country.[6]

The profession and rank of Sir David Dalrymple (now a Lord of Session) has given a more decent colour to his style. But he scrutinized each separate passage of the two chapters with the dry minuteness of a special pleader; and as he was always solicitous to make, he may have succeeded sometimes in finding, a flaw. In his *Annals of Scotland,* he has shown himself a diligent collector and an accurate critic.

I have praised, and I still praise, the eloquent sermons which were preached in St. Mary's pulpit at Oxford by Dr. White. If he assaulted me with some degree of illiberal acrimony, in such a place, and before such an audience, he was obliged to speak the language of the country. I smiled at a passage in one of his private letters to Mr. Badcock: "The part where we encounter Gibbon must be brilliant and striking."

In a sermon preached before the University of Cambridge, Dr. Edwards complimented a work, "which can only perish with the language itself"; and esteems the author a formidable enemy. He is, indeed, astonished that more learning and ingenuity has not been shown in the defence of Israel; that the prelates and dignitaries of the Church (alas, good man!) did not vie with each other whose stone should sink the deepest in the forehead of this Goliath.

"But the force of truth will oblige us to confess, that in the attacks which have been levelled against our sceptical historian, we can discover but slender traces of profound and exquisite erudition, of solid criticism and accurate investigation; but we are too frequently disgusted by vague and inconclusive reasoning; by unseasonable banter and senseless witticisms; by embittered

---

6 [In fact, it aroused the "Church and King" mob, which burnt down Priestley's house in July, 1791. *Ed.*]

bigotry and enthusiastic jargon; by futile cavils and illiberal invectives. Proud and elated by the weakness of his antagonists, he condescends not to handle the sword of controversy."

Let me frankly own that I was startled at the first discharge of ecclesiastical ordnance; but as soon as I found that this empty noise was mischievous only in the intention, my fear was converted into indignation; and every feeling of indignation or curiosity has long since subsided in pure and placid indifference.

5. The Completion of a Life's Work

[*Gibbon wrote the first four volumes of the* Decline and Fall, *and published the first three of them, while living in London. In 1783, having "always cherished a secret wish that the school of my youth might become the retreat of my declining age," he migrated to Lausanne, and it was there that he wrote his last two volumes, there that he composed the drafts of his* Autobiography.]

Since my establishment at Lausanne, more than seven years have elapsed; and if every day has not been equally soft and serene, not a day, not a moment, has occurred in which I have repented of my choice. During my absence, a long portion of human life, many changes had happened; my elder acquaintance had left the stage; virgins were ripened into matrons, and children were grown to the age of manhood. But the same manners were transmitted from one generation to another: my friend alone was an inestimable treasure; my name was not totally forgotten, and all were ambitious to welcome the arrival of a stranger and the return of a fellow-citizen. The first winter was given to a general embrace, without any nice discrimination of persons and characters. After a more regular settlement, a more accurate survey, I discovered three solid and permanent benefits of my new situation. (1) My personal freedom had been somewhat impaired by the House of Commons and the Board of Trade; but I was now delivered from the chain of duty and dependence, from the hopes and fears of political adventure; my sober mind was no longer intoxicated by the fumes of party, and I rejoiced in my escape, as often as I read

49

of the midnight debates which preceded the dissolution of parliament. (2) My English economy had been that of a solitary bachelor, who might afford some occasional dinners. In Switzerland I enjoyed at every meal, at every hour, the free and pleasant conversation of the friend of my youth; and my daily table was always provided for the reception of one or two extraordinary guests. Our importance in society is less a positive than a relative weight: in London I was lost in the crowd; I ranked with the first families of Lausanne, and my style of prudent expense enabled me to maintain a fair balance of reciprocal civilities. (3) Instead of a small house between a street and a stable-yard, I began to occupy a spacious and convenient mansion, connected on the north side with the city, and open on the south to a beautiful and boundless horizon. A garden of four acres had been laid out by the taste of Mr. Deyverdun: from the garden a rich scenery of meadows and vineyards descends to the Leman Lake, and the prospect far beyond the Lake is crowned by the stupendous mountains of Savoy. My books and my acquaintance had been first united in London; but this happy position of my library in town and country was finally reserved for Lausanne. Possessed of every comfort in this triple alliance, I could not be tempted to change my habitation with the changes of the seasons.

My friends had been kindly apprehensive that I should not be able to exist in a Swiss town at the foot of the Alps, after having so long conversed with the first men of the first cities of the world. Such lofty connexions may attract the curious, and gratify the vain; but I am too modest, or too proud, to rate my own value by that of my associates; and whatsoever may be the fame of learning or genius, experience has shown me that the cheaper qualifications of politeness and good sense are of more useful currency in the commerce of life. By many, conversation is esteemed as a theatre or a school: but after the morning has been occupied by the labours of the library, I wish to unbend rather than to exercise my mind; and in the interval between tea and supper I am far from disdaining the innocent amusement of a game at cards.

Lausanne is peopled by a numerous gentry, whose companionable idleness is seldom disturbed by the pursuits of avarice or ambition: the women, though confined to a domestic education, are endowed for the most part with more taste and knowledge than their husbands and brothers: but the decent freedom of both sexes is equally remote from the extremes of simplicity and refinement. I shall add as a misfortune rather than a merit, that the situation and beauty of the Pays de Vaud, the long habits of the English, the medical reputation of Dr. Tissot, and the fashion of viewing the mountains and *Glaciers,* have opened us on all sides to the incursions of foreigners. The visits of Mr. and Madame Necker, of Prince Henry of Prussia, and of Mr. Fox, may form some pleasing exceptions; but, in general, Lausanne has appeared most agreeable in my eyes, when we have been abandoned to our own society. I had frequently seen Mr. Necker, in the summer of 1784, at a country house near Lausanne, where he composed his Treatise on the Administration of the Finances. I have since, in October, 1790, visited him in his present residence, the castle and barony of Copet, near Geneva. Of the merits and measures of that statesman various opinions may be entertained; but all impartial men must agree in their esteem of his integrity and patriotism.

In the month of August, 1784, Prince Henry of Prussia, in his way to Paris, passed three days at Lausanne. His military conduct has been praised by professional men; his character has been vilified by the wit and malice of a demon; but I was flattered by his affability, and entertained by his conversation.

In his tour to Switzerland (September, 1788) Mr. Fox gave me two days of free and private society. He seemed to feel, and even to envy, the happiness of my situation; while I admired the powers of a superior man, as they are blended in his attractive character with the softness and simplicity of a child. Perhaps no human being was ever more perfectly exempt from the taint of malevolence, vanity, or falsehood.

My transmigration from London to Lausanne could not be effected without interrupting the course of my historical labours. The hurry of my departure, the joy of my arrival, the delay of my tools, suspended their progress; and a full twelvemonth was lost before I could resume the thread of regular and daily industry. A number of books most requisite and least common had been previously selected; the academical library of Lausanne, which I could use as my own, contained at least the fathers and councils; and I have derived some occasional succour from the public collections of Berne and Geneva. The fourth volume was soon terminated, by an abstract of the controversies of the Incarnation, which the learned Dr. Prideaux was apprehensive of exposing to profane eyes. It had been the original design of the learned Dean Prideaux to write the history of the ruin of the Eastern Church. In this work it would have been necessary, not only to unravel all those controversies which the Christians made about the hypostatical union, but also to unfold all the niceties and subtle notions which each sect entertained concerning it. The pious historian was apprehensive of exposing that incomprehensible mystery to the cavils and objections of unbelievers; and he durst not, "seeing the nature of this book, venture it abroad in so wanton and lewd an age."

In the fifth and sixth volumes the revolutions of the empire and the world are most rapid, various, and instructive; and the Greek or Roman historians are checked by the hostile narratives of the barbarians of the East and the West.

It was not till after many designs, and many trials, that I preferred, as I still prefer, the method of grouping my picture by nations; and the seeming neglect of chronological order is surely compensated by the superior merits of interest and perspicuity. The style of the first volume is, in my opinion, somewhat crude and elaborate; in the second and third it is ripened into ease, correctness, and numbers; but in the three last I may have been seduced by the facility of my pen, and the constant habit of speaking one language and writing another may have infused some mixture of Gallic idioms. Happily for my eyes, I have always closed my studies with the day, and commonly with the morning; and a long, but temperate, labour has been accomplished, without fatiguing either the mind or body; but when I computed the remainder of my time and my task, it was apparent that, according to the season of publication, the delay of a month would be productive of that of a year. I was now straining for the goal, and in the last winter many evenings were borrowed from the social pleasures of Lausanne. I could now wish that a pause, an interval, had been allowed for a serious revisal.

I have presumed to mark the moment of conception: I shall now commemorate the hour of my final deliverance. It was on the day, or rather night, of the 27th of June, 1787, between the hours of eleven and twelve, that I wrote the last lines of the last page, in a summer-house in my garden. After laying down my pen, I took several turns in a *berceau*, or covered walk of acacias, which commands a prospect of the country, the lake, and the mountains. The air was temperate, the sky was serene, the silver orb of the moon was reflected from the waters, and all nature was silent. I will not dissemble the first emotions of joy on recovery of my freedom, and, perhaps, the establishment of my fame. But my pride was soon humbled, and a sober melancholy was spread over my mind, by the idea that I had taken an everlasting leave of an old and agreeable companion, and that whatsoever might be the future date of my *History,* the life of the historian must be short and precarious. I will add two facts, which have seldom occurred in the composition of six, or at least of five quartos. (1) My first rough manuscript, without any intermediate copy, has been sent to the press. (2) Not a sheet has been seen by any human eyes, excepting those of the author and the printer: the faults and the merits are exclusively my own.

PART II

The Decline and Fall
of the Roman Empire

1. The Empire of the Antonines

[Gibbon begins with a general account of the Roman Empire at the height from which he measured its decline: i.e., "the Age of the Antonines," the last phase of the century of peace and prosperity which ran from the death of Domitian (96 A.D.) to that of the second "Antonine," the Stoic Emperor Marcus Aurelius (180 A.D.). In his first chapter he describes the extent and military establishment of the Empire which, at that time, "comprehended the fairest part of the earth and the most civilised portion of mankind"—from the Atlantic to the frontiers of Persia and from the Atlas mountains to the Grampians, the Rhine and the Danube. In Chapter II he deals with its internal prosperity.]

It is not alone by the rapidity, or extent of conquest, that we should estimate the greatness of Rome. The sovereign of the Russian deserts commands a larger portion of the globe. In the seventh summer after his passage of the Hellespont, Alexander erected the Macedonian trophies on the banks of the Hyphasis. Within less than a century, the irresistible Zingis, and the Mogul princes of his race, spread their cruel devastations and transient empire from the sea of China to the confines of Egypt and Germany. But the firm edifice of Roman power was raised and preserved by the wisdom of ages. The obedient provinces of Trajan and the Antonines were united by laws and adorned by arts. They might occasionally suffer from the partial abuse of delegated authority; but the general principle of government was wise, simple, and beneficent.

They enjoyed the religion of their ancestors, whilst in civil honours and advantages they were exalted, by just degrees, to an equality with their conquerors.

I. The policy of the emperors and the senate, as far as it concerned religion, was happily seconded by the reflections of the enlightened, and by the habits of the superstitious, part of their subjects. The various modes of worship, which prevailed in the Roman world, were all considered by the people, as equally true; by the philosopher, as equally false; and by the magistrate, as equally useful. And thus toleration produced not only mutual indulgence, but even religious concord.

The superstition of the people was not embittered by any mixture of theological rancour; nor was it confined by the chains of any speculative system. The devout polytheist, though fondly attached to his national rites, admitted with implicit faith the different religions of the earth.[1] Fear, gratitude, and curiosity, a dream or an omen, a singular disorder, or a distant journey, perpetually disposed him to multiply the articles of his belief, and to enlarge the list of his protectors. The thin texture of the Pagan mythology was interwoven with various but not discordant materials. As soon as it was allowed that sages and heroes, who had lived, or who had died for the benefit of their country, were exalted to a state of power and immortality, it was universally confessed that they deserved, if not the adoration, at least the reverence of all mankind. The deities of a thousand groves and a thousand streams possessed, in peace, their local and respective influence; nor could the Roman who deprecated the wrath of the Tiber, deride the Egyptian who presented his offering to the beneficent genius of the Nile. The visible powers of Nature, the planets, and the elements, were the same throughout the universe. The

[1] There is not any writer who describes in so lively a manner as Herodotus, the true genius of Polytheism. The best commentary may be found in Mr. Hume's Natural History of Religion; and the best contrast in Bossuet's Universal History. Some obscure traces of an intolerant spirit appear in the conduct of the Egyptians; and the Christians as well as Jews, who lived under the Roman empire, formed a very important exception: so important, indeed, that the discussion will require a distinct chapter of this work.

invisible governors of the moral world were inevitably cast in a similar mould of fiction and allegory. Every virtue, and even vice, acquired its divine representative; every art and profession its patron, whose attributes, in the most distant ages and countries, were uniformly derived from the character of their peculiar votaries. A republic of gods of such opposite tempers and interest required, in every system, the moderating hand of a supreme magistrate, who, by the progress of knowledge and flattery, was gradually invested with the sublime perfections of an Eternal Parent, and an Omnipotent Monarch. Such was the mild spirit of antiquity, that the nations were less attentive to the difference than to the resemblance of their religious worship. The Greek, the Roman, and the Barbarian, as they met before their respective altars, easily persuaded themselves, that under various names, and with various ceremonies, they adored the same deities. The elegant mythology of Homer gave a beautiful, and almost a regular form, to the polytheism of the ancient world.

The philosophers of Greece deduced their morals from the nature of man, rather than from that of God. They meditated, however, on the Divine Nature, as a very curious and important speculation; and in the profound inquiry, they displayed the strength and weakness of the human understanding. Of the four most celebrated schools, the Stoics and the Platonists endeavoured to reconcile the jarring interests of reason and piety. They have left us the most sublime proofs of the existence and perfections of the first cause; but, as it was impossible for them to conceive the creation of matter, the workman in the Stoic philosophy was not sufficiently distinguished from the work; whilst, on the contrary, the spiritual God of Plato and his disciples resembled an idea rather than a substance. The opinions of the Academics and Epicureans were of a less religious cast; but whilst the modest science of the former induced them to doubt, the positive ignorance of the latter urged them to deny, the providence of a Supreme Ruler. The spirit of inquiry, prompted by emulation, and supported by freedom, had divided the public teachers of philosophy into a variety of contending sects; but the ingenuous youth who, from every part, resorted to Athens, and the other seats of learning in the Roman empire, were alike instructed in every school to reject and to despise the religion of the multitude. How, indeed, was it possible, that a philosopher should accept, as divine truths, the idle tales of the poets, and the incoherent traditions of antiquity; or, that he should adore, as gods, those imperfect beings whom he must have despised, as men! Against such unworthy adversaries, Cicero condescended to employ the arms of reason and eloquence; but the satire of Lucian was a much more adequate, as well as more efficacious weapon. We may be well assured, that a writer conversant with the world would never have ventured to expose the gods of his country to public ridicule, had they not already been the objects of secret contempt among the polished and enlightened orders of society.[2]

Notwithstanding the fashionable irreligion which prevailed in the age of the Antonines, both the interests of the priests and the credulity of the people were sufficiently respected. In their writings and conversation, the philosophers of antiquity asserted the independent dignity of reason; but they resigned their actions to the commands of law and of custom. Viewing, with a smile of pity and indulgence, the various errors of the vulgar, they diligently practised the ceremonies of their fathers, devoutly frequented the temples of the gods; and sometimes condescending to act a part on the theatre of superstition, they concealed the sentiments of an Atheist under the sacerdotal robes. Reasoners of such a temper were scarcely inclined to wrangle about their respective modes of faith, or of worship. It was indifferent to them what shape the folly of the multitude might choose to assume; and they approached, with the same inward contempt, and the same external reverence, the altars of the Libyan, the Olympian, or the Capitoline Jupiter.[3]

It is not easy to conceive from what motives a spirit of

---

[2] I do not pretend to assert, that, in this irreligious age, the natural terrors of superstition, dreams, omens, apparitions, etc., had lost their efficacy.

[3] Socrates, Epicurus, Cicero, and Plutarch, always inculcated

persecution could introduce itself into the Roman councils. The magistrates could not be actuated by a blind, though honest bigotry, since the magistrates were themselves philosophers; and the schools of Athens had given laws to the senate. They could not be impelled by ambition or avarice, as the temporal and ecclesiastical powers were united in the same hands. The pontiffs were chosen among the most illustrious of the senators; and the office of Supreme Pontiff was constantly exercised by the emperors themselves. They knew and valued the advantages of religion, as it is connected with civil government. They encouraged the public festivals which humanise the manners of the people. They managed the arts of divination, as a convenient instrument of policy; and they respected as the firmest bond of society, the useful persuasion that, either in this or in a future life, the crime of perjury is most assuredly punished by the avenging gods. But whilst they acknowledged the general advantages of religion, they were convinced that the various modes of worship contributed alike to the same salutary purposes; and that, in every country, the form of superstition, which had received the sanction of time and experience, was the best adapted to the climate and to its inhabitants. Avarice and taste very frequently despoiled the vanquished nations of the elegant statues of their gods, and the rich ornaments of their temples; but, in the exercise of the religion which they derived from their ancestors, they uniformly experienced the indulgence, and even protection, of the Roman conquerors. The province of Gaul seems, and indeed only seems, an exception to this universal toleration. Under the specious pretext of abolishing human sacrifices, the emperors Tiberius and Claudius suppressed the dangerous power of the Druids, but the priests themselves, their gods and their altars, subsisted in peaceful obscurity till the final destruction of Paganism.

Rome, the capital of a great monarchy, was incessantly filled with subjects and strangers from every part of the world, who all introduced and enjoyed the favourite su-

---

decent reverence for the religion of their own country, and of mankind. The devotion of Epicurus was assiduous and exemplary.

perstitions of their native country. Every city in the empire was justified in maintaining the purity of its ancient ceremonies; and the Roman senate, using the common privilege, sometimes interposed, to check this inundation of foreign rites. The Egyptian superstition, of all the most contemptible and abject, was frequently prohibited; the temples of Serapis and Isis demolished and their worshippers banished from Rome and Italy. But the zeal of fanaticism prevailed over the cold and feeble efforts of policy. The exiles returned, the proselytes multiplied, the temples were restored with increasing splendour, and Isis and Serapis at length assumed their place among the Roman deities. Nor was this indulgence a departure from the old maxims of government. In the purest ages of the commonwealth, Cybele and Æsculapius had been invited by solemn embassies; and it was customary to tempt the protectors of besieged cities, by the promise of more distinguished honours than they possessed in their native country. Rome gradually became the common temple of her subjects; and the freedom of the city was bestowed on all the gods of mankind.

II.   The narrow policy of preserving, without any foreign mixture, the pure blood of the ancient citizens, had checked the fortune, and hastened the ruin, of Athens and Sparta. The aspiring genius of Rome sacrificed vanity to ambition, and deemed it more prudent, as well as honourable, to adopt virtue and merit for her own wheresoever they were found, among slaves or strangers, enemies or barbarians. During the most flourishing era of the Athenian commonwealth, the number of citizens gradually decreased from about thirty to twenty-one thousand. If, on the contrary, we study the growth of the Roman republic, we may discover, that, notwithstanding the incessant demands of wars and colonies, the citizens, who, in the first census of Servius Tullius, amounted to no more than eighty-three thousand, were multiplied, before the commencement of the social war, to the number of four hundred and sixty-three thousand men, able to bear arms in the service of their country. When the allies of Rome claimed an equal share of honours and privileges, the senate indeed preferred the chance of arms to an ignominious concession. The Samnites and the Lucanians paid the severe penalty of their rashness; but the rest of the Italian states, as they successively returned to their duty, were admitted into the bosom of the republic, and soon contributed to the ruin of public freedom. Under a democratical government, the citizens exercise the powers of sovereignty; and those powers will be first abused, and afterwards lost, if they are committed to an unwieldy multitude. But when the popular assemblies had been suppressed by the administration of the emperors, the conquerors were distinguished from the vanquished nations, only as the first and most honourable order of subjects; and their increase, however rapid, was no longer exposed to the same dangers. Yet the wisest princes, who adopted the maxims of Augustus, guarded with the strictest care the dignity of the Roman name, and diffused the freedom of the city with a prudent liberality.

Till the privileges of Romans had been progressively extended to all the inhabitants of the empire, an important distinction was preserved between Italy and the provinces. The former was esteemed the centre of public unity, and the firm basis of the constitution. Italy claimed the birth, or at least the residence, of the emperors and the senate. The estates of the Italians were exempt from taxes, their persons from the arbitrary jurisdiction of governors. Their municipal corporations, formed after the perfect model of the capital, were intrusted, under the immediate eye of the supreme power, with the execution of the laws. From the foot of the Alps to the extremity of Calabria, all the natives of Italy were born citizens of Rome. Their partial distinctions were obliterated, and they insensibly coalesced into one great nation, united by language, manners, and civil institutions, and equal to the weight of a powerful empire. The republic gloried in her generous policy, and was frequently rewarded by the merit and services of her adopted sons. Had she always confined the distinction of Romans to the ancient families within the walls of the city, that immortal name would have been deprived of some of its noblest ornaments. Virgil was a native of Mantua; Hor-

ace was inclined to doubt whether he should call himself
an Apulian or a Lucanian: it was in Padua that an historian was found worthy to record the majestic series of
Roman victories. The patriot family of the Catos emerged
from Tusculum; and the little town of Arpinum claimed
the double honour of producing Marius and Cicero, the
former of whom deserved, after Romulus and Camillus,
to be styled the Third Founder of Rome; and the latter,
after saving his country from the designs of Catiline,
enabled her to contend with Athens for the palm of
eloquence.

The provinces of the empire (as they have been described in the preceding chapter) were destitute of any
public force, or constitutional freedom. In Etruria, in
Greece, and in Gaul, it was the first care of the senate
to dissolve those dangerous confederacies, which taught
mankind, that as the Roman arts prevailed by division,
they might be resisted by union. Those princes, whom the
ostentation of gratitude or generosity permitted for a
while to hold a precarious sceptre, were dismissed from
their thrones as soon as they had performed their appointed task of fashioning to the yoke the vanquished
nations. The free states and cities which had embraced
the cause of Rome, were rewarded with a nominal alliance, and insensibly sunk into real servitude. The public authority was everywhere exercised by the ministers
of the senate and of the emperors, and that authority was
absolute, and without control. But the same salutary
maxims of government, which had secured the peace
and obedience of Italy, were extended to the most distant conquests. A nation of Romans was gradually formed
in the provinces, by the double expedient of introducing
colonies, and of admitting the most faithful and deserving of the provincials to the freedom of Rome.

"Wheresoever the Roman conquers, he inhabits," is a
very just observation of Seneca, confirmed by history and
experience. The natives of Italy, allured by pleasure or
by interest, hastened to enjoy the advantages of victory;
and we may remark, that about forty years after the reduction of Asia, eighty thousand Romans were massacred
in one day, by the cruel orders of Mithridates. These

voluntary exiles were engaged, for the most part, in the occupations of commerce, agriculture, and the farm of the revenue. But after the legions were rendered permanent by the emperors, the provinces were peopled by a race of soldiers; and the veterans, whether they received the reward of their service in land or in money, usually settled with their families in the country where they had honourably spent their youth. Throughout the empire, but more particularly in the western parts, the most fertile districts, and the most convenient situations, were reserved for the establishment of colonies; some of which were of a civil, and others of a military nature. In their manners and internal policy, the colonies formed a perfect representation of their great parent; and as they were soon endeared to the natives by the ties of friendship and alliance, they effectually diffused a reverence for the Roman name, and a desire, which was seldom disappointed, of sharing, in due time, its honours and advantages. The municipal cities insensibly equalled the rank and splendour of the colonies; and in the reign of Hadrian, it was disputed which was the preferable condition, of those societies which had issued from, or those which had been received into the bosom of Rome. The right of Latium, as it was called, conferred on the cities to which it had been granted a more partial favour. The magistrates only, at the expiration of their office, assumed the quality of Roman citizens; but as those offices were annual, in a few years they circulated round the principal families. Those of the provincials who were permitted to bear arms in the legions; those who exercised any civil employment; all, in a word, who performed any public service, or displayed any personal talents, were rewarded with a present, whose value was continually diminished by the increasing liberality of the emperors. Yet even, in the age of the Antonines, when the freedom of the city had been bestowed on the greater number of their subjects, it was still accompanied with very solid advantages. The bulk of the people acquired, with that title, the benefit of the Roman laws, particularly in the interesting articles of marriage, testaments, and inheritances; and the road of fortune was open to those whose pretensions were seconded by favour or merit. The grandsons of the Gauls, who had besieged Julius Cæsar in Alesia, commanded legions, governed provinces, and were admitted into the senate of Rome. Their ambition, instead of disturbing the tranquillity of the state, was intimately connected with its safety and greatness.

So sensible were the Romans of the influence of language over national manners, that it was their most serious care to extend, with the progress of their arms, the use of the Latin tongue. The ancient dialects of Italy, the Sabine, the Etruscan, and the Venetian, sunk into oblivion; but in the provinces, the east was less docile than the west, to the voice of its victorious preceptors. This obvious difference marked the two portions of the empire with a distinction of colours, which, though it was in some degree concealed during the meridian splendour of prosperity, became gradually more visible as the shades of night descended upon the Roman world. The western countries were civilised by the same hands which subdued them. As soon as the barbarians were reconciled to obedience, their minds were opened to any new impressions of knowledge and politeness. The language of Virgil and Cicero, though with some inevitable mixture of corruption, was so universally adopted in Africa, Spain, Gaul, Britain, and Pannonia, that the faint traces of the Punic or Celtic idioms were preserved only in the mountains, or among the peasants. Education and study insensibly inspired the natives of those countries with the sentiments of Romans; and Italy gave fashions as well as laws to her Latin provincials. They solicited with more ardour, and obtained with more facility, the freedom and honours of the state; supported the national dignity in letters and in arms; and, at length, in the person of Trajan, produced an emperor whom the Scipios would not have disowned for their countryman. . . .

It was by such institutions that the nations of the empire insensibly melted away into the Roman name and people. But there still remained, in the centre of every province and of every family, an unhappy condition of men who endured the weight, without sharing the benefits, of society. In the free states of antiquity the domestic slaves were exposed to the wanton rigour of despotism. The perfect settlement of the Roman empire was preceded by ages of violence and rapine. The slaves consisted, for the most part, of barbarian captives, taken in thousands by the chance of war, purchased at a vile price, accustomed to a life of independence, and impatient to break and to revenge their fetters. Against such internal enemies, whose desperate insurrections had more than once reduced the republic to the brink of destruction, the most severe regulations, and the most cruel treatment, seemed almost justified by the great law of self-preservation. But when the principal nations of Europe, Asia, and Africa, were united under the laws of one sovereign, the source of foreign supplies flowed with much less abundance, and the Romans were reduced to the milder but more tedious method of propagation. In their numerous families, and particularly in their country estates, they encouraged the marriage of their slaves. The sentiments of nature, the habits of education, and the possession of a dependent species of property, contributed to alleviate the hardships of servitude. The existence of a slave became an object of greater value, and though his happiness still depended on the temper and circumstances of the master, the humanity of the latter, instead of being restrained by fear, was encouraged by the sense of his own interest. The progress of manners was accelerated by the virtue or policy of the emperors; and by the edicts of Hadrian and the Antonines, the protection of the laws were extended to the most abject part of mankind. The jurisdiction of life and death over the slaves, a power long exercised and often abused, was taken out of private hands, and reserved to the magistrates alone. The subterraneous prisons were abolished; and, upon a just complaint of intolerable treatment, the injured slave obtained either his deliverance, or a less cruel master.

Hope, the best comfort of our imperfect condition, was not denied to the Roman slave; and if he had any opportunity of rendering himself either useful or agreeable, he might very naturally expect that the diligence and fidelity of a few years would be rewarded with the inestimable gift of freedom. The benevolence of the master was so frequently prompted by the meaner suggestions of vanity and avarice, that the laws found it more necessary to restrain than to encourage a profuse and undistinguishing liberality, which might degenerate into a very dangerous abuse. It was a maxim of ancient jurisprudence, that a slave had not any country of his own; he acquired with his liberty an admission into the political society of which his patron was a member. The consequences of this maxim would have prostituted the privileges of the Roman city to a mean and promiscuous multitude. Some seasonable exceptions were therefore provided; and the honourable distinction was confined to such slaves only, as for just causes, and with the approbation of the magistrate, should receive a solemn and legal manumission. Even these chosen freed-men obtained no more than the private rights of citizens, and were rigorously excluded from civil or military honours. Whatever might be the merit or fortune of their sons, *they* likewise were esteemed unworthy of a seat in the senate; nor were the traces of a servile origin allowed to be completely obliterated till the third or fourth generation. Without destroying the distinction of ranks, a distant prospect of freedom and honours was presented, even to those whom pride and prejudice almost disdained to number among the human species. . . .

The number of subjects who acknowledged the laws of Rome, of citizens, of provincials, and of slaves, cannot now be fixed with such a degree of accuracy, as the importance of the object would deserve. We are informed that when the emperor Claudius exercised the office of censor, he took an account of six millions nine hundred and forty-five thousand Roman citizens, who, with the proportion of women and children, must have amounted to about twenty millions of souls. The multitude of subjects of an inferior rank was uncertain and fluctuating. But, after weighing with attention every circumstance which could influence the balance, it seems probable that there existed, in the time of Claudius, about twice as many provincials as there were citizens, of either sex, and of every age; and that the slaves were at least equal in number to the free inhabitants of the Roman world. The total amount of this imperfect calculation would rise to about one hundred and twenty millions of persons; a degree of population which possibly exceeds that of modern Europe, and forms the most numerous society that has ever been united under the same system of government.

Domestic peace and union were the natural consequences of the moderate and comprehensive policy embraced by the Romans. If we turn our eyes towards the monarchies of Asia, we shall behold despotism in the centre, and weakness in the extremities; the collection of the revenue, or the administration of justice, enforced by the presence of an army; hostile barbarians established in the heart of the country, hereditary satraps usurping the dominion of the provinces, and subjects inclined to rebellion, though incapable of freedom. But the obedience of the Roman world was uniform, voluntary, and permanent. The vanquished nations, blended into one great people, resigned the hope, nay even the wish, of resuming their independence, and scarcely considered their own existence as distinct from the existence of Rome. The established authority of the emperors pervaded without an effort the wide extent of their dominions, and was exercised with the same facility on the banks of the Thames, or of the Nile, as on those of the Tiber. The legions were destined to serve against the public enemy, and the civil magistrate seldom required the aid of a military force. In this state of general security, the leisure as well as opulence both of the prince and people were devoted to improve and to adorn the Roman empire.

Among the innumerable monuments of architecture constructed by the Romans, how many have escaped the notice of history, how few have resisted the ravages of time and barbarism! And yet even the majestic ruins that are still scattered over Italy and the provinces, would be sufficient to prove that those countries were once the seat of a polite and powerful empire. Their greatness alone, or their beauty, might deserve our attention; but they are rendered more interesting by two important circumstances, which connect the agreeable history of the arts with the more useful history of human manners. Many of those works were erected at private expense, and almost all were intended for public benefit.

It is natural to suppose that the greatest number, as well as the most considerable of the Roman edifices, were raised by the emperors, who possessed so unbounded a command both of men and money. Augustus was accustomed to boast that he had found his capital of brick, and that he had left it of marble. The strict economy of Vespasian was the source of his magnificence. The works of Trajan bear the stamp of his genius. The public monuments with which Hadrian adorned every province of the empire, were executed not only by his orders, but under his immediate inspection. He was himself an artist; and he loved the arts, as they conduced to the glory of the monarch. They were encouraged by the Antonines, as they contributed to the happiness of the people. But if the emperors were the first, they were not the only architects of their dominions. Their example was universally imitated by their principal subjects, who were not afraid of declaring to the world that they had spirit to conceive, and wealth to accomplish, the noblest undertakings. Scarcely had the proud structure of the Coliseum been dedicated at Rome, before the edifices of a smaller scale indeed, but of the same design and materials, were erected for the use, and at the expense, of the cities of Capua and Verona. The inscription of the stupendous bridge of Alcantara attests that it was thrown over the Tagus by the contribution of a few Lusitanian communities. When Pliny was intrusted with the government of Bithynia and Pontus, provinces by no means the richest or most considerable of the empire, he found the cities within his jurisdiction striving with each other in every useful and ornamental work, that might deserve the curiosity of strangers, or the gratitude of their citizens. It was the duty of the Proconsul to supply their deficiencies, to direct their taste, and sometimes to moderate their emulation. The opulent senators of Rome and the provinces esteemed it an honour, and almost an obligation, to adorn the splendour of their age and country; and the influence of fashion very frequently supplied the want of taste or generosity. Among a crowd of these private benefactors, we may select Herodes Atticus, an Athenian citizen, who lived in the age of the Antonines. Whatever might be the motive of his conduct, his magnificence would have been worthy of the greatest kings.

The family of Herod, at least after it had been favoured by fortune, was lineally descended from Cimon and Miltiades, Theseus and Cecrops, Æacus and Jupiter. But the posterity of so many gods and heroes was fallen into the most abject state. His grandfather had suffered by the hands of justice, and Julius Atticus, his father, must have ended his life in poverty and contempt, had he not discovered an immense treasure buried under an old house, the last remains of his patrimony. According to the rigour of law, the emperor might have asserted his claim, and the prudent Atticus prevented, by a frank confession, the officiousness of informers. But the equitable Nerva, who then filled the throne, refused to accept any part of it, and commanded him to use, without scruple, the present of fortune. The cautious Athenian still insisted that the treasure was too considerable for a subject, and that he knew not how to *use it. Abuse it, then,* replied the monarch, with a good-natured peevishness; for it is your own. Many will be of opinion that Atticus literally obeyed the emperor's last instructions; since he expended the greatest part of his fortune, which was much increased by an advantageous marriage, in the service of the Public. He had obtained for his son Herod the prefecture of the free cities of Asia; and the young magistrate, observing that the town of Troas was indifferently supplied with water, obtained from the munificence of Hadrian three hundred myriads of drachms (about a hundred thousand pounds) for the construction of a new aqueduct. But in the execution of the work the charge amounted to more than double the estimate, and the officers of the revenue began to murmur, till the generous Atticus silenced their complaints, by requesting that he might be permitted to take upon himself the whole additional expense.

The ablest preceptors of Greece and Asia had been invited by liberal rewards to direct the education of young Herod. Their pupil soon became a celebrated orator according to the useless rhetoric of that age, which, confining itself to the schools, disdained to visit either the Forum or the Senate. He was honoured with the consulship at Rome; but the greatest part of his life was spent in a philosophic retirement at Athens, and his adjacent villas; perpetually surrounded by sophists, who acknowledged, without reluctance, the superiority of a rich and generous rival. The monuments of his genius have perished; some considerable ruins still preserve the fame of his taste and munificence: modern travellers have measured the remains of the stadium which he constructed at Athens. It was six hundred feet in length, built entirely of white marble, capable of admitting the whole body of the people, and finished in four years, whilst Herod was president of the Athenian games. To the memory of his wife Regilla he dedicated a theatre, scarcely to be paralleled in the empire; no wood except cedar, very curiously carved, was employed in any part of the building. The Odeum, designed by Pericles for musical performances, and the rehearsal of new tragedies, had been a trophy of the victory of the arts over Barbaric greatness; as the timbers employed in the construction consisted chiefly of the masts of the Persian vessels. Notwithstanding the repairs bestowed on that ancient edifice by a king of Cappadocia, it was again fallen to decay. Herod restored its ancient beauty and magnificence. Nor was the liberality of that illustrious citizen confined to the walls of Athens. The most splendid ornaments bestowed on the temple of Neptune in the Isthmus, a theatre at Corinth, a stadium at Delphi, a bath at Thermopylæ, and an aqueduct at Canusium in Italy, were insufficient to exhaust his treasures. The people of Epirus, Thessaly, Eubœa, Bœotia, and Peloponnesus, experienced his favours; and many inscriptions of the cities of Greece and Asia gratefully style Herodes Atticus their patron and benefactor.

In the commonwealths of Athens and Rome, the modest simplicity of private houses announced the equal condition of freedom; whilst the sovereignty of the people was represented in the majestic edifices destined to the public use; nor was this republican spirit totally extinguished by the introduction of wealth and monarchy. It was in works of national honour and benefit, that the most virtuous of the emperors affected to display their magnificence. The golden palace of Nero excited a just indignation, but the vast extent of ground which had been usurped by his selfish luxury, was more nobly filled under the succeeding reigns by the Coliseum, the baths of Titus, the Claudian portico, and the temples dedicated to the goddess of Peace, and to the genius of Rome. These monuments of architecture, the property of the Roman people, were adorned with the most beautiful productions of Grecian painting and sculpture; and in the temple of Peace a very curious library was open to the curiosity of the learned. At a small distance from thence was situated the Forum of Trajan. It was surrounded with a lofty portico, in the form of a quadrangle, into which four triumphal arches opened a noble and spacious entrance: in the centre arose a column of marble, whose height, of one hundred and ten feet, denoted the elevation of the hill that had been cut away. This column, which still subsists in its ancient beauty, exhibited an exact representation of the Dacian victories of its founder. The veteran soldier contemplated the story of his own campaigns, and by an easy illusion of national vanity, the peaceful citizen associated himself to the honours of the triumph. All the other quarters of the capital, and all the provinces of the empire, were embellished by the same liberal spirit of public magnificence, and were filled with amphitheatres, theatres, temples, porticos, triumphal arches, baths, and aqueducts, all variously conducive to the health, the devotion, and the pleasures of the meanest citizen. The last mentioned of those edifices deserve our peculiar attention. The boldness of the enterprise, the solidity of the execution, and the uses to which they were subservient, rank the aqueducts among the noblest monuments of Roman genius and power. The aqueducts of the capital claim a just preeminence; but the curious traveller, who, without the light of history, should examine those of Spoleto, of Metz, or of Segovia, would very naturally conclude that those provincial towns had formerly been the residence of some potent monarch. The solitudes of Asia and Africa were once covered with flourishing cities, whose populousness, and even whose existence, was derived from such artificial supplies of a perennial stream of fresh water.

We have computed the inhabitants and contemplated the public works of the Roman empire. The observation of the number and greatness of its cities will serve to confirm the former, and to multiply the latter. It may not be unpleasing to collect a few scattered instances relative to that subject, without forgetting, however, that from the vanity of nations and the poverty of language, the vague appellation of city has been indifferently bestowed on Rome and upon Laurentum. I. *Ancient* Italy is said to have contained eleven hundred and ninety-seven cities; and for whatsoever era of antiquity the expression might be intended, there is not any reason to believe the country less populous in the age of the Antonines than in that of Romulus. The petty states of Latium were contained within the metropolis of the empire, by whose superior influence they had been attracted. Those parts of Italy which have so long languished under the lazy tyranny of priests, and viceroys, had been afflicted only by the more tolerable calamities of war; and the first symptoms of decay which *they* experienced were amply compensated by the rapid improvements of the Cisalpine Gaul. The splendour of Verona may be traced in its remains: yet Verona was less celebrated than Aquileia or Padua, Milan or Ravenna. II. The spirit of improvement had passed the Alps, and been felt even in the woods of Britain, which were gradually cleared away to open a free space for convenient and elegant habitations. York was the seat of government; London was already enriched by commerce; and Bath was celebrated for the salutary effects of its medicinal waters. Gaul could boast of her twelve hundred cities, and though, in the northern parts, many of them, without excepting Paris itself, were little more than the rude and imperfect townships of a rising people, the southern provinces imitated the wealth and elegance of Italy. Many were the cities of Gaul, Marseilles, Arles, Nîmes, Narbonne, Toulouse, Bordeaux, Autun, Vienna, Lyons, Langres, and Treves, whose ancient condition might sustain an equal, and perhaps advantageous comparison with their present state. With regard to Spain, that country flourished as a province, and has declined as a kingdom. Exhausted by the abuse of her strength, by America, and by superstition, her pride might possibly be confounded, if we required such a list of three hundred and sixty cities, as Pliny has exhibited under the reign of Vespasian. III. Three hundred African cities had once acknowledged the authority of Carthage, nor is it likely that their numbers diminished under the administration of the emperors: Carthage itself rose with new splendour from its ashes; and that capital, as well as Capua and Corinth, soon recovered all the advantages which can be separated from independent sovereignty. IV. The provinces of the east present the contrast of Roman magnificence with Turkish barbarism. The ruins of antiquity scattered over uncultivated fields, and ascribed, by ignorance, to the power of magic, scarcely afford a shelter to the oppressed peasant or wandering Arab. Under the reign of the Cæsars, the proper Asia alone contained five hundred populous cities, enriched with all the gifts of nature, and adorned with all the refinements of art. Eleven cities of Asia had once disputed the honour of dedicating a temple to Tiberius, and their respective merits were examined by the senate.[4] Four of them were immediately rejected as unequal to the burden; and among these was Laodicea, whose splendour is still displayed in its ruins. Laodicea collected a very considerable revenue from its flocks of

[4] I have taken some pains in consulting and comparing modern travellers, with regard to the fate of those eleven cities of Asia: seven or eight are totally destroyed, Hypæpe, Tralles, Laodicea, Ilium, Halicarnassus, Miletus, Ephesus, and we may add Sardis. Of the remaining three, Pergamus is a straggling village of two or three thousand inhabitants; Magnesia, under the name of Guzel-hissar, a town of some consequence, and Smyrna, a great city, peopled by an hundred thousand souls. But even at Smyrna, while the Franks have maintained commerce, the Turks have ruined the arts.

sheep, celebrated for the fineness of their wool, and had received, a little before the contest, a legacy of above four hundred thousand pounds by the testament of a generous citizen. If such was the poverty of Laodicea, what must have been the wealth of those cities, whose claim appeared preferable, and particularly of Pergamus, of Smyrna, and of Ephesus, who so long disputed with each other the titular primacy of Asia. The capitals of Syria and Egypt held a still superior rank in the empire: Antioch and Alexandria looked down with disdain on a crowd of dependent cities, and yielded, with reluctance, to the majesty of Rome itself.

All these cities were connected with each other, and with the capital, by the public highways, which, issuing from the Forum of Rome, traversed Italy, pervaded the provinces, and were terminated only by the frontiers of the empire. If we carefully trace the distance from the wall of Antoninus to Rome, and from thence to Jerusalem, it will be found that the great chain of communication, from the north-west to the south-east point of the empire, was drawn out to the length of four thousand and eighty Roman miles. The public roads were accurately divided by mile-stones, and ran in a direct line from one city to another, with very little respect for the obstacles either of nature or private property. Mountains were perforated, and bold arches thrown over the broadest and most rapid streams. The middle part of the road was raised into a terrace which commanded the adjacent country, consisted of several strata of sand, gravel, and cement, and was paved with large stones, or in some places, near the capital, with granite. Such was the solid construction of the Roman highways, whose firmness has not entirely yielded to the effort of fifteen centuries. They united the subjects of the most distant provinces by an easy and familiar intercourse; but their primary object had been to facilitate the marches of the legions; nor was any country considered as completely subdued, till it had been rendered, in all its parts, pervious to the arms and authority of the conqueror. The advantage of receiving the earliest intelligence, and of conveying their orders with celerity, induced the emperors to establish throughout their extensive dominions, the regular institution of posts. Houses were everywhere erected at the distance only of five or six miles; each of them was constantly provided with forty horses, and by the help of these relays it was easy to travel an hundred miles in a day along the Roman roads. The use of the posts was allowed to those who claimed it by an Imperial mandate; but though originally intended for the public service, it was sometimes indulged to the business or conveniency of private citizens. Nor was the communication of the Roman empire less free and open by sea than it was by land. The provinces surrounded and inclosed the Mediterranean; and Italy, in the shape of an immense promontory, advanced into the midst of that great lake. The coasts of Italy are, in general, destitute of safe harbours; but human industry had corrected the deficiencies of nature; and the artificial port of Ostia, in particular, situated at the mouth of the Tiber, and formed by the emperor Claudius, was a useful monument of Roman greatness. From this port, which was only sixteen miles from the capital, a favourable breeze frequently carried vessels in seven days to the columns of Hercules, and in nine or ten, to Alexandria in Egypt.

Whatever evils either reason or declamation have imputed to extensive empire, the power of Rome was attended with some beneficial consequences to mankind; and the same freedom of intercourse which extended the vices, diffused likewise the improvements of social life. In the more remote ages of antiquity, the world was unequally divided. The east was in the immemorial possession of arts and luxury; whilst the west was inhabited by rude and warlike barbarians, who either disdained agriculture, or to whom it was totally unknown. Under the protection of an established government, the productions of happier climates, and the industry of more civilised nations, were gradually introduced into the western countries of Europe; and the natives were encouraged, by an open and profitable commerce, to multiply the former, as well as to improve the latter. It would be almost impossible to enumerate all the articles, either of the animal or the vegetable reign, which were succes-

sively imported into Europe, from Asia and Egypt; but
it will not be unworthy of the dignity, and much less of
the utility, of an historical work, slightly to touch on a few
of the principal heads. 1. Almost all the flowers, the herbs,
and the fruits, that grow in our European gardens, are
of foreign extraction, which, in many cases, is betrayed
even by their names: the apple was a native of Italy,
and when the Romans had tasted the richer flavour of
the apricot, the peach, the pomegranate, the citron, and
the orange, they contented themselves with applying to
all these new fruits the common denomination of apple,
discriminating them from each other by the additional
epithet of their country. 2. In the time of Homer, the
vine grew wild in the island of Sicily, and most probably
in the adjacent continent; but it was not improved by
the skill, nor did it afford a liquor grateful to the taste,
of the savage inhabitants. A thousand years afterwards,
Italy could boast, that of the fourscore most generous
and celebrated wines, more than two-thirds were produced from her soil. The blessing was soon communicated
to the Narbonnese province of Gaul; but so intense was
the cold to the north of the Cevennes, that, in the time
of Strabo, it was thought impossible to ripen the grapes
in those parts of Gaul. This difficulty, however, was
gradually vanquished; and there is some reason to believe, that the vineyards of Burgundy are as old as the
age of the Antonines. The olive, in the western world,
followed the progress of peace, of which it was considered as the symbol. Two centuries after the foundation of Rome, both Italy and Africa were strangers to
that useful plant; it was naturalised in those countries;
and at length carried into the heart of Spain and Gaul.
The timid errors of the ancients, that it required a certain degree of heat, and could only flourish in the neighbourhood of the sea, were insensibly exploded by industry and experience. The cultivation of flax was transported from Egypt to Gaul, and enriched the whole country, however it might impoverish the particular lands on
which it was sown. 5. The use of artificial grasses became familiar to the farmers both of Italy and the provinces, particularly the Lucerne, which derived its name

and origin from Media. The assured supply of whole-some and plentiful food for the cattle during winter, multiplied the number of the flocks and herds, which in their turn contributed to the fertility of the soil. To all these improvements may be added an assiduous atten-tion to mines and fisheries, which, by employing a multi-tude of laborious hands, serve to increase the pleasures of the rich, and the subsistence of the poor. The elegant treatise of Columella describes the advanced state of the Spanish husbandry, under the reign of Tiberius; and it may be observed, that those famines which so frequently afflicted the infant republic, were seldom or never ex-perienced by the extensive empire of Rome. The acci-dental scarcity, in any single province, was immediately relieved by the plenty of its more fortunate neighbours.

Agriculture is the foundation of manufactures; since the productions of nature are the materials of art. Under the Roman empire, the labour of an industrious and in-genious people was variously, but incessantly employed, in the service of the rich. In their dress, their table, their houses and their furniture, the favourites of fortune united every refinement of conveniency, of elegance, and of splendour, whatever could soothe their pride or gratify their sensuality. Such refinements, under the odious name of luxury, have been severely arraigned by the moralists of every age; and it might perhaps be more conducive to the virtue, as well as happiness, of man-kind, if all possessed the necessaries, and none the super-fluities, of life. But in the present imperfect condition of society, luxury, though it may proceed from vice or folly, seems to be the only means that can correct the unequal distribution of property. The diligent mechanic, and the skilful artist, who have obtained no share in the division of the earth, receive a voluntary tax from the possessors of land; and the latter are prompted, by a sense of interest, to improve those estates, with whose produce they may purchase additional pleasures. This operation, the particular effects of which are felt in every society, acted with much more diffusive energy in the Roman world. The provinces would soon have been exhausted of their wealth, if the manufactures and commerce of luxury had not insensibly restored to the industrious subjects the sums which were exacted from them by the arms and authority of Rome. As long as the circulation was confined within the bounds of the empire, it impressed the political machine with a new degree of activity, and its consequences, sometimes beneficial, could never become pernicious.

But it is no easy task to confine luxury within the limits of an empire. The most remote countries of the ancient world were ransacked to supply the pomp and delicacy of Rome. The forests of Scythia afforded some valuable furs. Amber was brought over land from the shores of the Baltic to the Danube; and the barbarians were astonished at the price which they received in exchange for so useless a commodity. There was a considerable demand for Babylonian carpets and other manufactures of the East; but the most important and unpopular branch of foreign trade was carried on with Arabia and India. Every year, about the time of the summer solstice, a fleet of an hundred and twenty vessels sailed from Myos-hormos, a port of Egypt, on the Red Sea. By the periodical assistance of the Monsoons, they traversed the ocean in about forty days. The coast of Malabar, or the island of Ceylon, was the usual term of their navigation, and it was in those markets that the merchants from the more remote countries of Asia expected their arrival. The return of the fleet of Egypt was fixed to the months of December or January; and as soon as their rich cargo had been transported on the backs of camels, from the Red Sea to the Nile, and had descended that river as far as Alexandria, it was poured, without delay, into the capital of the empire. The objects of oriental traffic were splendid and trifling: silk, a pound of which was esteemed not inferior in value to a pound of gold; precious stones, among which the pearl claimed the first rank after the diamond; and a variety of aromatics, that were consumed in religious worship and the pomp of funerals. The labour and risk of the voyage was rewarded with almost incredible profit; but the profit was made upon Roman subjects, and a few individuals were enriched at the expense of the Public. As the natives of Arabia and India were contented with the productions and manufactures of their own country, silver, on the side of the Romans, was the principal, if not the only instrument of commerce. It was a complaint worthy of the gravity of the senate, that in the purchase of female ornaments, the wealth of the state was irrecoverably given away to foreign and hostile nations. The annual loss is computed, by a writer of an inquisitive but censorious temper, at upwards of eight hundred thousand pounds sterling. Such was the style of discontent, brooding over the dark prospect of approaching poverty. And yet, if we compare the proportion between gold and silver, as it stood in the time of Pliny, and as it was fixed in the reign of Constantine, we shall discover within that period a very considerable increase. There is not the least reason to suppose that gold was become more scarce; it is therefore evident that silver was grown more common; that whatever might be the amount of the Indian and Arabian exports, they were far from exhausting the wealth of the Roman world; and that the produce of the mines abundantly supplied the demands of commerce.

Notwithstanding the propensity of mankind to exalt the past, and to depreciate the present, the tranquil and prosperous state of the empire was warmly felt, and honestly confessed, by the provincials as well as Romans. "They acknowledged that the true principles of social life, laws, agriculture, and science, which had been first invented by the wisdom of Athens, were now firmly established by the power of Rome, under whose auspicious influence the fiercest barbarians were united by an equal government and common language. They affirm, that with the improvement of arts, the human species was visibly multiplied. They celebrate the increasing splendour of the cities, the beautiful face of the country, cultivated and adorned like an immense garden; and the long festival of peace, which was enjoyed by so many nations, forgetful of their ancient animosities, and delivered from the apprehension of future danger." Whatever suspicions may be suggested by the air of rhetoric and declamation, which seems to prevail in these passages, the substance of them is perfectly agreeable to historic truth.

It was scarcely possible that the eyes of contemporaries should discover in the public felicity the latent causes of decay and corruption. This long peace, and the uniform government of the Romans, introduced a slow and secret poison into the vitals of the empire. The minds of men were gradually reduced to the same level, the fire of genius was extinguished, and even the military spirit evaporated. The natives of Europe were brave and robust, Spain, Gaul, Britain, and Illyricum supplied the legions with excellent soldiers, and constituted the real strength of the monarchy. Their personal valour remained, but they no longer possessed that public courage which is nourished by the love of independence, the sense of national honour, the presence of danger, and the habit of command. They received laws and governors from the will of their sovereign, and trusted for their defence to a mercenary army. The posterity of their boldest leaders was contented with the rank of citizens and subjects. The most aspiring spirits resorted to the court or standard of the emperors; and the deserted provinces, deprived of political strength or union, insensibly sunk into the languid indifference of private life.

The love of letters, almost inseparable from peace and refinement, was fashionable among the subjects of Hadrian and the Antonines, who were themselves men of learning and curiosity. It was diffused over the whole extent of their empire; the most northern tribes of Britons had acquired a taste for rhetoric; Homer as well as Virgil were transcribed and studied on the banks of the Rhine and Danube; and the most liberal rewards sought out the faintest glimmerings of literary merit. The sciences of physic and astronomy were successfully cultivated by the Greeks; the observations of Ptolemy and the writings of Galen are studied by those who have improved their discoveries and corrected their errors; but if we except the inimitable Lucian, this age of indolence passed away without having produced a single writer of original genius, or who excelled in the arts of elegant composition. The authority of Plato and Aristotle, of Zeno and Epicurus, still reigned in the schools; and their systems, transmitted with blind deference from one generation of disciples to another, precluded every generous attempt to exercise the powers, or enlarge the limits, of the human mind. The beauties of the poets and orators, instead of kindling a fire like their own, inspired only cold and servile imitations: or if any ventured to deviate from those models, they deviated at the same time from good sense and propriety. On the revival of letters, the youthful vigour of the imagination, after a long repose, national emulation, a new religion, new languages, and a new world, called forth the genius of Europe. But the provincials of Rome, trained by a uniform artificial foreign education, were engaged in a very unequal competition with those bold ancients, who, by expressing their genuine feelings in their native tongue, had already occupied every place of honour. The name of Poet was almost forgotten; that of Orator was usurped by the sophists. A cloud of critics, of compilers, of commentators, darkened the face of learning, and the decline of genius was soon followed by the corruption of taste.

The sublime Longinus, who in somewhat a later period, and in the court of a Syrian queen, preserved the spirit of ancient Athens, observes and laments this degeneracy of his contemporaries, which debased their sentiments, enervated their courage, and depressed their talents. "In the same manner," says he, "as some children always remain pygmies, whose infant limbs have been too closely confined; thus our tender minds, fettered by the prejudices and habits of a just servitude, are unable to expand themselves, or to attain that well-proportioned greatness which we admire in the ancients; who living under a popular government, wrote with the same freedom as they acted."[5] This diminutive stature of mankind, if we pursue the metaphor, was daily sinking below the old standard, and the Roman world was indeed peopled by a race of pygmies; when the fierce giants of the north

---

5 [The *Treatise on the Sublime*, traditionally ascribed to Longinus, the minister of Zenobia, queen of Palmyra, is now thought to be by an earlier writer. Gibbon himself, in his Journal, foreshadowed this modern verdict. *Ed.*]

broke in, and mended the puny breed. They restored a manly spirit of freedom; and after the revolution of ten centuries, freedom became the happy parent of taste and science.

[*In chapter III Gibbon describes the political constitution of the Empire as established by Augustus and practised by his successors. These emperors no longer feared the senate, which they had deprived of power, but apprehended the power of the army, on which their own authority ultimately rested. They therefore sought to prevent a disputed succession by naming and training their successors. At the end of the chapter, Gibbon describes the planned succession of the golden age of the empire.*]

2. The Rise of Christianity

[The chapters on the rise of Christianity, and more particularly Chapters XV and XVI, with which Gibbon ended his first volume, proved the most controversial part of his work, provoking numerous attacks (see above pp. 45-48), and eliciting his own Vindication (below p. 440). In chapter XV, which is here printed almost entire, he describes the rise and progress of Christianity within the Roman Empire before its acceptance as the religion of state.]

A candid but rational inquiry into the progress and establishment of Christianity may be considered as a very essential part of the history of the Roman empire. While that great body was invaded by open violence, or undermined by slow decay, a pure and humble religion gently insinuated itself into the minds of men, grew up in silence and obscurity, derived new vigour from opposition, and finally erected the triumphant banner of the Cross on the ruins of the Capitol. Nor was the influence of Christianity confined to the period or to the limits of the Roman empire. After a revolution of thirteen or fourteen centuries, that religion is still professed by the nations of Europe, the most distinguished portion of human kind in arts and learning as well as in arms. By the industry and zeal of the Europeans it has been widely diffused to the most distant shores of Asia and Africa; and by the means of their colonies has been firmly established from Canada to Chile, in a world unknown to the ancients.

But this inquiry, however useful or entertaining, is attended with two peculiar difficulties. The scanty and suspicious materials of ecclesiastical history seldom enable us to dispel the dark cloud that hangs over the first age of the church. The great law of impartiality too often obliges us to reveal the imperfections of the uninspired teachers and believers of the Gospel; and, to a careless observer, *their* faults may seem to cast a shade on the faith which they professed. But the scandal of the pious Christian, and the fallacious triumph of the Infidel, should cease as soon as they recollect not only *by whom,* but likewise *to whom,* the Divine Revelation was given. The theologian may indulge the pleasing task of describing Religion as she descended from Heaven, arrayed in her native purity. A more melancholy duty is imposed on the historian. He must discover the inevitable mixture of error and corruption which she contracted in a long residence upon earth, among a weak and degenerate race of beings.

Our curiosity is naturally prompted to inquire by what means the Christian faith obtained so remarkable a victory over the established religions of the earth. To this inquiry an obvious but satisfactory answer may be returned; that it was owing to the convincing evidence of the doctrine itself, and to the ruling providence of its great Author. But as truth and reason seldom find so favourable a reception in the world, and as the wisdom of Providence frequently condescends to use the passions of the human heart, and the general circumstances of mankind, as instruments to execute its purpose, we may still be permitted, though with becoming submission, to ask, not indeed what were the first, but what were the secondary causes of the rapid growth of the Christian church? It will, perhaps, appear that it was most effectually favoured and assisted by the five following causes:—
I. The inflexible, and, if we may use the expression, the intolerant zeal of the Christians, derived, it is true, from the Jewish religion, but purified from the narrow and unsocial spirit which, instead of inviting, had deterred the Gentiles from embracing the law of Moses. II. The doctrine of a future life, improved by every additional circumstance which could give weight and effi-

cacy to that important truth III. The miraculous powers ascribed to the primitive church. IV. The pure and austere morals of the Christians. V. The union and discipline of the Christian republic, which gradually formed an independent and increasing state in the heart of the Roman empire.

I. We have already described the religious harmony of the ancient world, and the facility with which the most different and even hostile nations embraced, or at least respected, each other's superstitions. A single people refused to join in the common intercourse of mankind. The Jews, who, under the Assyrian and Persian monarchies, had languished for many ages the most despised portion of their slaves, emerged from obscurity under the successors of Alexander; and as they multiplied to a surprising degree in the East, and afterwards in the West, they soon excited the curiosity and wonder of other nations. The sullen obstinacy with which they maintained their peculiar rites and unsocial manners seemed to mark them out a distinct species of men, who boldly professed, or who faintly disguised, their implacable hatred to the rest of human kind. Neither the violence of Antiochus, nor the arts of Herod, nor the example of the circumjacent nations, could ever persuade the Jews to associate with the institutions of Moses the elegant mythology of the Greeks. According to the maxims of universal toleration, the Romans protected a superstition which they despised. The polite Augustus condescended to give orders that sacrifices should be offered for his prosperity in the temple of Jerusalem; while the meanest of the posterity of Abraham, who should have paid the same homage to the Jupiter of the Capitol, would have been an object of abhorrence to himself and to his brethren. But the moderation of the conquerors was insufficient to appease the jealous prejudices of their subjects, who were alarmed and scandalised at the ensigns of paganism, which necessarily introduced themselves into a Roman province. The mad attempt of Caligula to place his own statue in the temple of Jerusalem was defeated by the unanimous resolution of a people who dreaded death much less than such an idolatrous profanation. Their attachment to the law of Moses was equal to their detestation of foreign religions. The current of zeal and devotion, as it was contracted into a narrow channel, ran with the strength, and sometimes with the fury, of a torrent.

This inflexible perseverance, which appeared so odious or so ridiculous to the ancient world, assumes a more awful character, since Providence has deigned to reveal to us the mysterious history of the chosen people. But the devout and even scrupulous attachment to the Mosaic religion, so conspicuous among the Jews who lived under the second temple, becomes still more surprising if it is compared with the stubborn incredulity of their forefathers. When the law was given in thunder from Mount Sinai; when the tides of the ocean and the course of the planets were suspended for the convenience of the Isrælites; and when temporal rewards and punishments were the immediate consequences of their piety or disobedience, they perpetually relapsed into rebellion against the visible majesty of their Divine King, placed the idols of the nations in the sanctuary of Jehovah, and imitated every fantastic ceremony that was practised in the tents of the Arabs, or in the cities of Phœnicia. As the protection of Heaven was deservedly withdrawn from the ungrateful race, their faith acquired a proportionable degree of vigour and purity. The contemporaries of Moses and Joshua had beheld with careless indifference the most amazing miracles. Under the pressure of every calamity, the belief of those miracles has preserved the Jews of a later period from the universal contagion of idolatry; and in contradiction to every known principle of the human mind, that singular people seems to have yielded a stronger and more ready assent to the traditions of their remote ancestors than to the evidence of their own senses.

The Jewish religion was admirably fitted for defence, but it was never designed for conquest; and it seems probable that the number of proselytes was never much superior to that of apostates. The divine promises were originally made, and the distinguishing rite of circumcision was enjoined, to a single family. When the posterity of Abraham had multiplied like the sands of the sea, the Deity, from whose mouth they received a system of laws and ceremonies, declared himself the proper and as it were the national God of Israel; and with the most jealous care separated his favourite people from the rest of mankind. The conquest of the land of Canaan was accompanied with so many wonderful and with so many bloody circumstances, that the victorious Jews were left in a state of irreconcilable hostility with all their neighbours. They had been commanded to extirpate some of the most idolatrous tribes, and the execution of the Divine will had seldom been retarded by the weakness of humanity. With the other nations they were forbidden to contract any marriages or alliances; and the prohibition of receiving them into the congregation, which in some cases was perpetual, almost always extended to the third, to the seventh, or even to the tenth generation. The obligation of preaching to the Gentiles the faith of Moses had never been inculcated as a precept of the law, nor were the Jews inclined to impose it on themselves as a voluntary duty.

In the admission of new citizens that unsocial people was actuated by the selfish vanity of the Greeks rather than by the generous policy of Rome. The descendants of Abraham were flattered by the opinion that they alone were the heirs of the covenant, and they were apprehensive of diminishing the value of their inheritance by sharing it too easily with the strangers of the earth. A larger acquaintance with mankind extended their knowledge without correcting their prejudices; and whenever the God of Israel acquired any new votaries, he was much more indebted to the inconstant humour of polytheism than to the active zeal of his own missionaries. The religion of Moses seems to be instituted for a particular country as well as for a single nation; and if a strict obedience had been paid to the order that every male, three times in the year, should present himself before the Lord Jehovah, it would have been impossible that the Jews could ever have spread themselves beyond the narrow limits of the promised land. That obstacle was indeed removed by the destruction of the temple of Jerusalem; but the most considerable part of the Jewish religion was involved in its destruction; and the Pagans, who had long wondered at the strange report of an empty sanctuary, were at a loss to discover what could be the object, or what could be the instruments, of a worship which was destitute of temples and of altars, of priests and of sacrifices. Yet even in their fallen state, the Jews, still asserting their lofty and exclusive privileges, shunned, instead of courting, the society of strangers. They still insisted with inflexible rigour on those parts of the law which it was in their power to practise. Their peculiar distinctions of days, of meats, and a variety of trivial though burdensome observances, were so many objects of disgust and aversion for the other nations, to whose habits and prejudices they were diametrically opposite. The painful and even dangerous rite of circumcision was alone capable of repelling a willing proselyte from the door of the synagogue.

Under these circumstances, Christianity offered itself to the world, armed with the strength of the Mosaic law, and delivered from the weight of its fetters. An exclusive zeal for the truth of religion and the unity of God was as carefully inculcated in the new as in the ancient system: and whatever was now revealed to mankind concerning the nature and designs of the Supreme Being was fitted to increase their reverence for that mysterious doctrine. The divine authority of Moses and the prophets was admitted, and even established, as the firmest basis of Christianity. From the beginning of the world an uninterrupted series of predictions had announced and prepared the long-expected coming of the Messiah, who, in compliance with the gross apprehensions of the Jews, had been more frequently represented under the character of a King and Conqueror, than under that of a Prophet, a Martyr, and the Son of God. By his expiatory sacrifice the imperfect sacrifices of the temple were at once consummated and abolished. The ceremonial law, which consisted only of types and figures, was succeeded by a pure and spiritual worship, equally adapted to all climates, as well as to every condition of mankind; and to the initiation of blood, was substituted a more harm-

87

less initiation of water. The promise of divine favour, instead of being partially confined to the posterity of Abraham, was universally proposed to the freeman and the slave, to the Greek and to the barbarian, to the Jew and to the Gentile. Every privilege that could raise the proselyte from earth to heaven, that could exalt his devotion, secure his happiness, or even gratify that secret pride which, under the semblance of devotion, insinuates itself into the human heart, was still reserved for the members of the Christian church; but at the same time all mankind was permitted, and even solicited, to accept the glorious distinction, which was not only proffered as a favour, but imposed as an obligation. It became the most sacred duty of a new convert to diffuse among his friends and relations the inestimable blessing which he had received, and to warn them against a refusal that would be severely punished as a criminal disobedience to the will of a benevolent but all-powerful Deity.

The enfranchisement of the church from the bonds of the synagogue was a work, however, of some time and of some difficulty. The Jewish converts, who acknowledged Jesus in the character of the Messiah foretold by their ancient oracles, respected him as a prophetic teacher of virtue and religion; but they obstinately adhered to the ceremonies of their ancestors, and were desirous of imposing them on the Gentiles, who continually augmented the number of believers. These Judaising Christians seem to have argued with some degree of plausibility from the Divine origin of the Mosaic law, and from the immutable perfections of its great Author. They affirmed, *that,* if the Being who is the same through all eternity had designed to abolish those sacred rites which had served to distinguish his chosen people, the repeal of them would have been no less clear and solemn than their first promulgation: *that,* instead of those frequent declarations which either suppose or assert the perpetuity of the Mosaic religion, it would have been represented as a provisionary scheme intended to last only till the coming of the Messiah, who should instruct mankind in a more perfect mode of faith and of worship: *that* the Messiah himself, and his disciples who conversed with him on earth, instead of authorising by their example the most minute observances of the Mosaic law, would have published to the world the abolition of those useless and obsolete ceremonies, without suffering Christianity to remain during so many years obscurely confounded among the sects of the Jewish church. Arguments like these appear to have been used in the defence of the expiring cause of the Mosaic law; but the industry of our learned divines has abundantly explained the ambiguous language of the Old Testament, and the ambiguous conduct of the apostolic teachers. It was proper gradually to unfold the system of the Gospel, and to pronounce with the utmost caution and tenderness a sentence of condemnation so repugnant to the inclination and prejudices of the believing Jews. . . .

[*After describing, as evidence of "the necessity of these precautions," the conflict within the Church of Jerusalem between the Nazarenes, (and their extremists, the Ebionites) who clung to the Mosaic law, and their rivals, who rejected it, and incidentally thereby enjoyed Roman protection, Gibbon proceeds.*]

While the orthodox church preserved a just medium between excessive veneration and improper contempt for the law of Moses, the various heretics deviated into equal but opposite extremes of error and extravagance. From the acknowledged truth of the Jewish religion, the Ebionites had concluded that it could never be abolished. From its supposed imperfections, the Gnostics as hastily inferred that it never was instituted by the wisdom of the Deity. There are some objections against the authority of Moses and the prophets which too readily present themselves to the sceptical mind; though they can only be derived from our ignorance of remote antiquity, and from our incapacity to form an adequate judgment of the Divine economy. These objections were eagerly embraced and as petulantly urged by the vain science of the Gnostics. As those heretics were, for the most part, averse to the pleasures of sense, they morosely arraigned the polygamy of the patriarchs, the gallantries of David, and

the seraglio of Solomon. The conquest of the land of
Canaan, and the extirpation of the unsuspecting natives,
they were at a loss how to reconcile with the common notions of humanity and justice. But when they recollected
the sanguinary list of murders, of executions, and of
massacres, which stain almost every page of the Jewish
annals, they acknowledged that the barbarians of Palestine had exercised as much compassion towards their idolatrous enemies as they had ever shown to their friends or
countrymen. Passing from the sectaries of the law to the
law itself, they asserted that it was impossible that a
religion which consisted only of bloody sacrifices and
trifling ceremonies, and whose rewards as well as punishments were all of a carnal and temporal nature, could
inspire the love of virtue, or restrain the impetuosity of
passion. The Mosaic account of the creation and fall of
man was treated with profane derision by the Gnostics,
who would not listen with patience to the repose of the
Deity after six days' labour, to the rib of Adam, the
garden of Eden, the trees of life and of knowledge, the
speaking serpent, the forbidden fruit, and the condemnation pronounced against human kind for the venial
offence of their first progenitors. The God of Israel was
impiously represented by the Gnostics as a being liable
to passion and to error, capricious in his favour, implacable in his resentment, meanly jealous of his superstitious worship, and confining his partial providence to
a single people, and to this transitory life. In such a
character they could discover none of the features of the
wise and omnipotent Father of the universe. They allowed that the religion of the Jews was somewhat less
criminal than the idolatry of the Gentiles: but it was
their fundamental doctrine that the Christ whom they
adored as the first and brightest emanation of the Deity
appeared upon earth to rescue mankind from their various errors, and to reveal a *new* system of truth and perfection. The most learned of the fathers, by a very singular condescension, have imprudently admitted the sophistry of the Gnostics. Acknowledging that the literal
sense is repugnant to every principle of faith as well
as reason, they deem themselves secure and invulnerable

behind the ample veil of allegory, which they carefully spread over every tender part of the Mosaic dispensation.

It has been remarked with more ingenuity than truth that the virgin purity of the church was never violated by schism or heresy before the reign of Trajan or Hadrian, about one hundred years after the death of Christ. We may observe with much more propriety that, during that period, the disciples of the Messiah were indulged in a freer latitude both of faith and practice than has ever been allowed in succeeding ages. As the terms of communion were insensibly narrowed, and the spiritual authority of the prevailing party was exercised with increasing severity, many of its most respectable adherents, who were called upon to renounce, were provoked to assert their private opinions, to pursue the consequences of their mistaken principles, and openly to erect the standard of rebellion against the unity of the church. The Gnostics were distinguished as the most polite, the most learned, and the most wealthy of the Christian name; and that general appellation, which expressed a superiority of knowledge, was either assumed by their own pride, or ironically bestowed by the envy of their adversaries. They were almost without exception of the race of the Gentiles, and their principal founders seem to have been natives of Syria or Egypt, where the warmth of the climate disposes both the mind and the body to indolent and contemplative devotion. The Gnostics blended with the faith of Christ many sublime but obscure tenets, which they derived from oriental philosophy, and even from the religion of Zoroaster, concerning the eternity of matter, the existence of two principles, and the mysterious hierarchy of the invisible world. As soon as they launched out into that vast abyss, they delivered themselves to the guidance of a disordered imagination; and as the paths of error are various and infinite, the Gnostics were imperceptibly divided into more than fifty particular sects, of whom the most celebrated appear to have been the Basilidians, the Valentinians, the Marcionites, and, in a still later period, the Manichæans. Each of these sects could boast of its bishops and congregations, of its doctors and martyrs; and, instead of the Four

91

Gospels adopted by the church, the heretics produced a multitude of histories, in which the actions and discourses of Christ and of his apostles were adapted to their respective tenets. The success of the Gnostics was rapid and extensive. They covered Asia and Egypt, established themselves in Rome, and sometimes penetrated into the provinces of the West. For the most part they arose in the second century, flourished during the third, and were suppressed in the fourth or fifth, by the prevalence of more fashionable controversies, and by the superior ascendant of the reigning power. Though they constantly disturbed the peace, and frequently disgraced the name of religion, they contributed to assist rather than to retard the progress of Christianity. The Gentile converts, whose strongest objections and prejudices were directed against the law of Moses, could find admission into many Christian societies, which required not from their untutored mind any belief of an antecedent revelation. Their faith was insensibly fortified and enlarged, and the church was ultimately benefited by the conquests of its most inveterate enemies.

But whatever difference of opinion might subsist between the Orthodox, the Ebionites, and the Gnostics, concerning the divinity or the obligation of the Mosaic law, they were all equally animated by the same exclusive zeal, and by the same abhorrence for idolatry, which had distinguished the Jews from the other nations of the ancient world. The philosopher, who considered the system of polytheism as a composition of human fraud and error, could disguise a smile of contempt under the mask of devotion, without apprehending that either the mockery or the compliance would expose him to the resentment of any invisible, or, as he conceived them, imaginary powers. But the established religions of Paganism were seen by the primitive Christians in a much more odious and formidable light. It was the universal sentiment both of the church and of heretics, that the dæmons were the authors, the patrons, and the objects of idolatry. Those rebellious spirits who had been degraded from the rank of angels, and cast down into the infernal pit, were still permitted to roam upon earth, to torment the bodies and to seduce the minds of sinful men. The dæmons soon discovered and abused the natural propensity of the human heart towards devotion, and, artfully withdrawing the adoration of mankind from their Creator, they usurped the place and honours of the Supreme Deity. By the success of their malicious contrivances, they at once gratified their own vanity and revenge, and obtained the only comfort of which they were yet susceptible, the hope of involving the human species in the participation of their guilt and misery. It was confessed, or at least it was imagined, that they had distributed among themselves the most important characters of polytheism, one dæmon assuming the name and attributes of Jupiter, another of Æsculapius, a third of Venus, and a fourth perhaps of Apollo, and that, by the advantage of their long experience and aërial nature, they were enabled to execute, with sufficient skill and dignity, the parts which they had undertaken. They lurked in the temples, instituted festivals and sacrifices, invented fables, pronounced oracles, and were frequently allowed to perform miracles. The Christians, who, by the interposition of evil spirits, could so readily explain every præternatural appearance, were disposed and even desirous to admit the most extravagant fictions of the Pagan mythology. But the belief of the Christian was accompanied with horror. The most trifling mark of respect to the national worship he considered as a direct homage yielded to the dæmon, and as an act of rebellion against the majesty of God.

In consequence of this opinion, it was the first but arduous duty of a Christian to preserve himself pure and undefiled by the practice of idolatry. The religion of the nations was not merely a speculative doctrine professed in the schools or preached in the temples. The innumerable deities and rites of polytheism were closely interwoven with every circumstance of business or pleasure, of public or of private life; and it seemed impossible to escape the observance of them, without, at the same time, renouncing the commerce of mankind, and all the offices and amusements of society. The important transactions of peace and war were prepared or concluded by solemn sacrifices, in which the magistrate, the senator, and the

soldier were obliged to preside or to participate. The public spectacles were an essential part of the cheerful devotion of the Pagans, and the gods were supposed to accept, as the most grateful offering, the games that the
prince and people celebrated in honour of their peculiar
festivals.[1] The Christian, who with pious horror avoided
the abomination of the circus or the theatre, found himself encompassed with infernal snares in every convivial
entertainment, as often as his friends, invoking the hospitable deities, poured out libations to each other's happiness. When the bride, struggling with well-affected reluctance, was forced in hymenæal pomp over the threshold of her new habitation, or when the sad procession
of the dead slowly moved towards the funeral pile, the
Christian, on these interesting occasions, was compelled
to desert the persons who were the dearest to him, rather
than contract the guilt inherent to those impious ceremonies. Every art and every trade that was in the least
concerned in the framing or adorning of idols was polluted by the stain of idolatry; a severe sentence, since it
devoted to eternal misery the far greater part of the
community which is employed in the exercise of liberal
or mechanic professions. If we cast our eyes over the
numerous remains of antiquity, we shall perceive that,
besides the immediate representations of the gods and
the holy instruments of their worship, the elegant forms
and agreeable fictions consecrated by the imagination of
the Greeks were introduced as the richest ornaments of
the houses, the dress, and the furniture of the Pagans.
Even the arts of music and painting, of eloquence and
poetry, flowed from the same impure origin. In the style
of the fathers, Apollo and the Muses were the organs of
the infernal spirit; Homer and Virgil were the most
eminent of his servants; and the beautiful mythology
which pervades and animates the compositions of their
genius is destined to celebrate the glory of the dæmons.
Even the common language of Greece and Rome

---

[1] See Tertullian, *De Spectaculis*. This severe reformer shows
no more indulgence to a tragedy of Euripides than to a combat
of gladiators. The dress of the actors particularly offends him.
By the use of the lofty buskin they impiously strive to add a
cubit to their stature: c. 23.

abounded with familiar but impious expressions, which the imprudent Christian might too carelessly utter, or too patiently hear.

The dangerous temptations which on every side lurked in ambush to surprise the unguarded believer assailed him with redoubled violence on the days of solemn festivals. So artfully were they framed and disposed throughout the year, that superstition always wore the appearance of pleasure, and often of virtue. Some of the most sacred festivals in the Roman ritual were destined to salute the new calends of January with vows of public and private felicity; to indulge the pious remembrance of the dead and living; to ascertain the inviolable bounds of property; to hail, on the return of spring, the genial powers of fecundity; to perpetuate the two memorable eras of Rome, the foundation of the city, and that of the republic; and to restore, during the humane licence of the Saturnalia, the primitive equality of mankind. Some idea may be conceived of the abhorrence of the Christians for such impious ceremonies, by the scrupulous delicacy which they displayed on a much less alarming occasion. On days of general festivity it was the custom of the ancients to adorn their doors with lamps and with branches of laurel, and to crown their heads with a garland of flowers. This innocent and elegant practice might perhaps have been tolerated as a mere civil institution. But it most unluckily happened that the doors were under the protection of the household gods, that the laurel was sacred to the lover of Daphne, and that garlands of flowers, though frequently worn as a symbol either of joy or mourning, had been dedicated in their first origin to the service of superstition. The trembling Christians, who were persuaded in this instance to comply with the fashion of their country and the commands of the magistrate, laboured under the most gloomy apprehensions, from the reproaches of their own conscience, the censures of the church, and the denunciations of divine vengeance.

Such was the anxious diligence which was required to guard the chastity of the Gospel from the infectious breath of idolatry. The superstitious observances of pub-

lic or private rites were carelessly practised, from education and habit, by the followers of the established religion. But as often as they occurred, they afforded the
Christians an opportunity of declaring and confirming
their zealous opposition. By these frequent protestations
their attachment to the faith was continually fortified;
and in proportion to the increase of zeal, they combated
with the more ardour and success in the holy war which
they had undertaken against the empire of the dæmons.

II. The writings of Cicero represent in the most lively
colours the ignorance, the errors, and the uncertainty
of the ancient philosophers with regard to the immortality of the soul. When they are desirous of arming their
disciples against the fear of death, they inculcate, as
an obvious though melancholy position, that the fatal
stroke of our dissolution releases us from the calamities
of life; and that those can no longer suffer who no
longer exist. Yet there were a few sages of Greece and
Rome who had conceived a more exalted, and, in some
respects, a juster idea of human nature, though it must
be confessed that, in the sublime inquiry, their reason
had been often guided by their imagination, and that
their imagination had been prompted by their vanity.
When they viewed with complacency the extent of their
own mental powers, when they exercised the various
faculties of memory, of fancy, and of judgement, in the
most profound speculations or the most important labours, and when they reflected on the desire of fame,
which transported them into future ages, far beyond
the bounds of death and of the grave, they were unwilling to confound themselves with the beasts of the field,
or to suppose that a being, for whose dignity they entertained the most sincere admiration, could be limited
to a spot of earth, and to a few years of duration. With
this favourable prepossession they summoned to their
aid the science, or rather the language, of Metaphysics.
They soon discovered that, as none of the properties of
matter will apply to the operations of the mind, the human soul must consequently be a substance distinct from
the body, pure, simple, and spiritual, incapable of dissolution, and susceptible of a much higher degree of

virtue and happiness after the release from its corporeal prison. From these specious and noble principles the philosophers who trod in the footsteps of Plato deduced a very unjustifiable conclusion, since they asserted, not only the future immortality, but the past eternity of the human soul, which they were too apt to consider as a portion of the infinite and self-existing spirit which pervades and sustains the universe. A doctrine thus removed beyond the senses and the experience of mankind might serve to amuse the leisure of a philosophic mind; or, in the silence of solitude, it might sometimes impart a ray of comfort to desponding virtue; but the faint impression which had been received in the schools was soon obliterated by the commerce and business of active life. We are sufficiently acquainted with the eminent persons who flourished in the age of Cicero and of the first Cæsars, with their actions, their characters, and their motives, to be assured that their conduct in this life was never regulated by any serious conviction of the rewards or punishments of a future state. At the bar and in the senate of Rome the ablest orators were not apprehensive of giving offence to their hearers by exposing that doctrine as an idle and extravagant opinion, which was rejected with contempt by every man of a liberal education and understanding.

Since therefore the most sublime efforts of philosophy can extend no farther than feebly to point out the desire, the hope, or, at most, the probability of a future state, there is nothing, except a divine revelation that can ascertain the existence and describe the condition of the invisible country which is destined to receive the souls of men after their separation from the body. But we may perceive several defects inherent to the popular religions of Greece and Rome which rendered them very unequal to so arduous a task. 1. The general system of their mythology was unsupported by any solid proofs; and the wisest among the Pagans had already disclaimed its usurped authority. 2. The description of the infernal regions had been abandoned to the fancy of painters and of poets, who peopled them with so many phantoms and monsters who dispensed their rewards and punishments with so little equity, that a solemn truth, the most congenial to the human heart, was oppressed and disgraced by the absurd mixture of the wildest fictions. 3. The doctrine of a future state was scarcely considered among the devout polytheists of Greece and Rome as a fundamental article of faith. The providence of the gods, as it related to public communities rather than to private individuals, was principally displayed on the visible theatre of the present world. The petitions which were offered on the altars of Jupiter or Apollo expressed the anxiety of their worshippers for temporal happiness, and their ignorance or indifference concerning a future life. The important truth of the immortality of the soul was inculcated with more diligence as well as success in India, in Assyria, in Egypt, and in Gaul; and since we cannot attribute such a difference to the superior knowledge of the barbarians, we must ascribe it to the influence of an established priesthood, which employed the motives of virtue as the instrument of ambition.

We might naturally expect that a principle so essential to religion would have been revealed in the clearest terms to the chosen people of Palestine, and that it might safely have been intrusted to the hereditary priesthood of Aaron. It is incumbent on us to adore the mysterious dispensations of Providence, when we discover that the doctrine of the immortality of the soul is omitted in the law of Moses; it is darkly insinuated by the prophets; and during the long period which elapsed between the Egyptian and the Babylonian servitudes, the hopes as well as fears of the Jews appear to have been confined within the narrow compass of the present life. After Cyrus had permitted the exiled nation to return into the promised land, and after Ezra had restored the ancient records of their religion, two celebrated sects, the Sadducees and the Pharisees, insensibly arose at Jerusalem. The former, selected from the more opulent and distinguished ranks of society, were strictly attached to the literal sense of the Mosaic law, and they piously rejected the immortality of the soul as an opinion that received no countenance from the divine book, which they revered as the only rule of their faith. To the authority of Scripture the Pharisees added that of tradition, and they accepted, under the name of traditions, several speculative tenets from the philosophy or religion of the eastern nations. The doctrines of fate or predestination, of angels and spirits, and of a future state of rewards and punishments, were in the number of these new articles of belief; and as the Pharisees, by the austerity of their manners, had drawn into their party the body of the Jewish people, the immortality of the soul became the prevailing sentiment of the synagogue under the reign of the Asmonæan princes and pontiffs. The temper of the Jews was incapable of contenting itself with such a cold and languid assent as might satisfy the mind of a Polytheist; and as soon as they admitted the idea of a future state, they embraced it with the zeal which has always formed the characteristic of the nation. Their zeal, however, added nothing to its evidence, or even probability; and it was still necessary that the doctrine of life and immortality, which had been dictated by nature, approved by reason, and received by superstition, should obtain the sanction of divine truth from the authority and example of Christ.

When the promise of eternal happiness was proposed to mankind on condition of adopting the faith, and of observing the precepts, of the Gospel, it is no wonder that so advantageous an offer should have been accepted by great numbers of every religion, of every rank, and of every province in the Roman empire. The ancient Christians were animated by a contempt for their present existence, and by a just confidence of immortality, of which the doubtful and imperfect faith of modern ages cannot give us any adequate notion. In the primitive church the influence of truth was very powerfully strengthened by an opinion which, however it may deserve respect for its usefulness and antiquity, has not been found agreeable to experience. It was universally believed that the end of the world, and the kingdom of heaven, were at hand. The near approach of this wonderful event had been predicted by the apostles; the tradition of it was preserved by their earliest disciples, and those who understood in their literal sense the discourses of Christ himself were obliged to expect the second and glorious coming of the Son of Man in the clouds, before that generation was totally extinguished which had beheld his humble condition upon earth, and which might still be witness of the calamities of the Jews under Vespasian or Hadrian. The revolution of seventeen centuries has instructed us not to press too closely the mysterious language of prophecy and revelation; but as long as, for wise purposes, this error was permitted to subsist in the church, it was productive of the most salutary effects on the faith and practice of Christians, who lived in the awful expectation of that moment when the globe itself, and all the various race of mankind, should tremble at the appearance of their divine Judge.[2]

The ancient and popular doctrine of the Millennium was intimately connected with the second coming of Christ. As the works of the creation had been finished in six days, their duration in their present state, according to a tradition which was attributed to the prophet Elijah, was fixed to six thousand years. By the same analogy it was inferred that this long period of labour and contention, which was now almost elapsed, would be succeeded by a joyful Sabbath of a thousand years; and that Christ, with the triumphant band of the saints and the elect who had escaped death, or who had been miraculously revived, would reign upon earth till the time appointed for the last and general resurrection. So pleasing was this hope to the mind of believers, that the *New Jerusalem*, the seat of this blissful kingdom, was quickly adorned with all the gayest colours of the imagination. A felicity consisting only of pure and spiritual pleasure would have appeared too refined for its inhabitants, who were still supposed to possess their human nature and senses. A garden of Eden, with the amusements of the pastoral life, was no longer suited to the advanced state of society which prevailed under the Roman empire. A city was therefore erected of gold and precious stones,

---

[2] This expectation was countenanced by the twenty-fourth chapter of St. Matthew, and by the first epistle of St. Paul to the Thessalonians. Erasmus removes the difficulty by the help of allegory and metaphor; and the learned Grotius ventures to insinuate, that, for wise purposes, the pious deception was permitted to take place.

and a supernatural plenty of corn and wine was bestowed on the adjacent territory; in the free enjoyment of whose spontaneous productions the happy and benevolent people was never to be restrained by any jealous laws of exclusive property. The assurance of such a Millennium was carefully inculcated by a succession of fathers from Justin Martyr and Irenæus, who conversed with the immediate disciples of the apostles, down to Lactantius, who was preceptor to the son of Constantine. Though it might not be universally received, it appears to have been the reigning sentiment of the orthodox believers; and it seems so well adapted to the desires and apprehensions of mankind, that it must have contributed in a very considerable degree to the progress of the Christian faith. But when the edifice of the church was almost completed, the temporary support was laid aside. The doctrine of Christ's reign upon earth was at first treated as a profound allegory, was considered by degrees as a doubtful and useless opinion, and was at length rejected as the absurd invention of heresy and fanaticism. A mysterious prophecy, which still forms a part of the sacred canon, but which was thought to favour the exploded sentiment, has very narrowly escaped the proscription of the church.[3]

Whilst the happiness and glory of a temporal reign were promised to the disciples of Christ, the most dread-

---

[3] In the council of Laodicea (about the year 360) the Apocalypse was tacitly excluded from the sacred canon by the same churches of Asia to which it is addressed; and we may learn from the complaint of Sulpicius Severus that their sentence had been ratified by the greater number of Christians of his time. From what causes then is the Apocalypse at present so generally received by the Greek, the Roman, and the Protestant churches? The following ones may be assigned:—1. The Greeks were subdued by the authority of an impostor, who, in the sixth century, assumed the character of Dionysius the Areopagite. 2. A just apprehension that the grammarians might become more important than the theologians engaged the council of Trent to fix the seal of their infallibility on all the books of Scripture contained in the Latin Vulgate, in the number of which the Apocalypse was fortunately included. 3. The advantage of turning those mysterious prophecies against the See of Rome inspired the Protestants with uncommon veneration for so useful an ally. See the ingenious and elegant discourses of the present bishop of Lichfield on that unpromising subject.

ful calamities were denounced against an unbelieving world. The edification of the new Jerusalem was to advance by equal steps with the destruction of the mystic Babylon; and as long as the emperors who reigned before Constantine persisted in the profession of idolatry, the epithet of Babylon was applied to the city and to the empire of Rome. A regular series was prepared of all the moral and physical evils which can afflict a flourishing nation; intestine discord, and the invasion of the fiercest barbarians from the unknown regions of the North; pestilence and famine, comets and eclipses, earthquakes and inundations. All these were only so many preparatory and alarming signs of the great catastrophe of Rome, when the country of the Scipios and Cæsars should be consumed by a flame from Heaven, and the city of the seven hills, with her palaces, her temples, and her triumphal arches, should be buried in a vast lake of fire and brimstone. It might, however, afford some consolation to Roman vanity, that the period of their empire would be that of the world itself; which, as it had once perished by the element of water, was destined to experience a second and a speedy destruction from the element of fire. In the opinion of a general conflagration the faith of the Christian very happily coincided with the tradition of the East, the philosophy of the Stoics, and the analogy of Nature; and even the country which, from religious motives, had been chosen for the origin and principal scene of the conflagration, was the best adapted for that purpose by natural and physical causes—by its deep caverns, beds of sulphur, and numerous volcanoes, of which those of Ætna, of Vesuvius, and of Lipari exhibit a very imperfect representation. The calmest and most intrepid sceptic could not refuse to acknowledge that the destruction of the present system of the world by fire was in itself extremely probable. The Christian, who founded his belief much less on the fallacious arguments of reason than on the authority of tradition and the interpretation of Scripture, expected it with terror and confidence as a certain and approaching event; and as his mind was perpetually filled with the solemn idea, he considered every disaster that happened to the empire as an infallible symptom of an expiring world.

The condemnation of the wisest and most virtuous of the Pagans, on account of their ignorance or disbelief of the divine truth, seems to offend the reason and the humanity of the present age. But the primitive church, whose faith was of a much firmer consistence, delivered over, without hesitation, to eternal torture the far greater part of the human species. A charitable hope might perhaps be indulged in favour of Socrates, or some other sages of antiquity, who had consulted the light of reason before that of the Gospel had arisen. But it was unanimously affirmed that those who, since the birth or the death of Christ, had obstinately persisted in the worship of the dæmons, neither deserved nor could expect a pardon from the irritated justice of the Deity. These rigid sentiments, which had been unknown to the ancient world, appear to have infused a spirit of bitterness into a system of love and harmony. The ties of blood and friendship were frequently torn asunder by the difference of religious faith; and the Christians, who, in this world, found themselves oppressed by the power of the Pagans, were sometimes seduced by resentment and spiritual pride to delight in the prospect of their future triumph. "You are fond of spectacles," exclaims the stern Tertullian, "expect the greatest of all spectacles, the last and eternal judgment of the universe. How shall I admire, how laugh, how rejoice, how exult, when I behold so many proud monarchs, and fancied gods, groaning in the lowest abyss of darkness; so many magistrates, who persecuted the name of the Lord, liquefying in fiercer fires than they ever kindled against the Christians; so many sage philosophers blushing in red-hot flames with their deluded scholars; so many celebrated poets trembling before the tribunal, not of Minos, but of Christ; so many tragedians, more tuneful in the expression of their own sufferings; so many dancers—" But the humanity of the reader will permit me to draw a veil over the rest of this infernal description, which the zealous African pursues in a long variety of affected and unfeeling witticisms.

Doubtless there were many among the primitive Christians of a temper more suitable to the meekness and charity of their profession. There were many who felt a sincere compassion for the danger of their friends and countrymen, and who exerted the most benevolent zeal to save them from the impending destruction. The careless Polytheist, assailed by new and unexpected terrors, against which neither his priests nor his philosophers could afford him any certain protection, was very frequently terrified and subdued by the menace of eternal tortures. His fears might assist the progress of his faith and reason; and if he could once persuade himself to suspect that the Christian religion might possibly be true, it became an easy task to convince him that it was the safest and most prudent party that he could possibly embrace.

III. The supernatural gifts, which even in this life were ascribed to the Christians above the rest of mankind, must have conduced to their own comfort, and very frequently to the conviction of infidels. Besides the occasional prodigies, which might sometimes be effected by the immediate interposition of the Deity when he suspended the laws of Nature for the service of religion, the Christian church, from the time of the apostles and their first disciples, has claimed an uninterrupted succession of miraculous powers, the gift of tongues, of vision, and of prophecy, the power of expelling dæmons, of healing the sick, and of raising the dead. The knowledge of foreign languages was frequently communicated to the contemporaries of Irenæus, though Irenæus himself was left to struggle with the difficulties of a barbarous dialect whilst he preached the Gospel to the natives of Gaul. The divine inspiration, whether it was conveyed in the form of a waking or of a sleeping vision, is described as a favour very liberally bestowed on all ranks of the faithful, on women as on elders, on boys as well as upon bishops. When their devout minds were sufficiently prepared by a course of prayer, of fasting, and of vigils, to receive the extraordinary impulse, they were transported out of their senses, and delivered in ecstasy what was inspired, being mere organs of the Holy Spirit, just as a pipe or flute is of him who blows into it. We may add that the design of these visions was, for the most part, either to disclose the future history, or to guide the present administration, of the church. The expulsion of the dæmons from the bodies of those unhappy persons whom they had been permitted to torment was considered as a signal though ordinary triumph of religion, and is repeatedly alleged by the ancient apologists as the most convincing evidence of the truth of Christianity. The awful ceremony was usually performed in a public manner, and in the presence of a great number of spectators; the patient was relieved by the power or skill of the exorcist, and the vanquished dæmon was heard to confess that he was one of the fabled gods of antiquity, who had impiously usurped the adoration of mankind. But the miraculous cure of diseases of the most inveterate or even præternatural kind can no longer occasion any surprise, when we recollect that in the days of Irenæus, about the end of the second century, the resurrection of the dead was very far from being esteemed an uncommon event; that the miracle was frequently performed on necessary occasions, by great fasting and the joint supplication of the church of the place, and that the persons thus restored to their prayers had lived afterwards among them many years. At such a period, when faith could boast of so many wonderful victories over death, it seems difficult to account for the scepticism of those philosophers who still rejected and derided the doctrine of the resurrection. A noble Grecian had rested on this important ground the whole controversy, and promised Theophilus, bishop of Antioch, that, if he could be gratified with the sight of a single person who had been actually raised from the dead, he would immediately embrace the Christian religion. It is somewhat remarkable that the prelate of the first eastern church, however anxious for the conversion of his friend, thought proper to decline this fair and reasonable challenge.

The miracles of the primitive church, after obtaining the sanction of ages, have been lately attacked in a very free and ingenious inquiry;[4] which, though it has met with the most favourable reception from the public, appears to have excited a general scandal among the divines of our own as well as of the other Protestant churches of Europe.[5] Our different sentiments on this subject will be much less influenced by any particular arguments than by our habits of study and reflection, and, above all, by the degree of the evidence which we have accustomed ourselves to require for the proof of a miraculous event. The duty of an historian does not call upon him to interpose his private judgment in this nice and important controversy; but he ought not to dissemble the difficulty of adopting such a theory as may reconcile the interest of religion with that of reason, of making a proper application of that theory, and of defining with precision the limits of that happy period, exempt from error and from deceit, to which we might be disposed to extend the gift of supernatural powers. From the first of the fathers to the last of the popes, a succession of bishops, of saints, of martyrs, and of miracles, is continued without interruption; and the progress of superstition was so gradual and almost imperceptible, that we know not in what particular link we should break the chain of tradition. Every age bears testimony to the wonderful events by which it was distinguished, and its testimony appears no less weighty and respectable than that of the preceding generation, till we are insensibly led on to accuse our own inconsistency if, in the eighth or in the twelfth century, we deny to the venerable Bede, or to the holy Bernard, the same degree of confidence which, in the second century, we had so liberally granted to Justin or to Irenæus.[6] If the truth of any of those mir-

---

4 Dr. Middleton sent out his Introduction in the year 1747, published his Free Inquiry in 1749, and before his death, which happened in 1750, he had prepared a vindication of it against his numerous adversaries.

5 The university of Oxford conferred degrees on his opponents. From the indignation of Mosheim we may discover the sentiments of the Lutheran divines.

6 It may seem somewhat remarkable that Bernard of Clairvaux, who records so many miracles of his friend St. Malachi, never takes any notice of his own, which, in their turn, however, are

acles is appreciated by their apparent use and propriety, every age had unbelievers to convince, heretics to confute, and idolatrous nations to convert; and sufficient motives might always be produced to justify the interposition of Heaven. And yet, since every friend to revelation is persuaded of the reality, and every reasonable man is convinced of the cessation, of miraculous powers, it is evident that there must have been *some period* in which they were either suddenly or gradually withdrawn from the Christian church. Whatever era is chosen for that purpose, the death of the apostles, the conversion of the Roman empire, or the extinction of the Arian heresy, the insensibility of the Christians who lived at that time will equally afford a just matter of surprise. They still supported their pretensions after they had lost their power. Credulity performed the office of faith; fanaticism was permitted to assume the language of inspiration, and the effects of accident or contrivance were ascribed to supernatural causes. The recent experience of genuine miracles should have instructed the Christian world in the ways of Providence, and habituated their eye (if we may use a very inadequate expression) to the style of the Divine artist. Should the most skilful painter of modern Italy presume to decorate his feeble imitations with the name of Raphael or of Correggio, the insolent fraud would be soon discovered and indignantly rejected.

Whatever opinion may be entertained of the miracles of the primitive church since the time of the apostles, this unresisting softness of temper, so conspicuous among the believers of the second and third centuries, proved of some accidental benefit to the cause of truth and religion. In modern times, a latent and even involuntary scepticism adheres to the most pious dispositions. Their admission of supernatural truths is much less an active consent than a cold and passive acquiescence. Accustomed long since to observe and to respect the invariable order of Nature, our reason, or at least our imagination, is not sufficiently prepared to sustain the

carefully related by his companions and disciples. In the long series of ecclesiastical history, does there exist a single instance of a saint asserting that he himself possessed the gift of miracles?

visible action of the Deity. But in the first ages of Christianity the situation of mankind was extremely different. The most curious, or the most credulous, among the Pagans were often persuaded to enter into a society which asserted an actual claim of miraculous powers. The primitive Christians perpetually trod on mystic ground, and their minds were exercised by the habits of believing the most extraordinary events. They felt, or they fancied, that on every side they were incessantly assaulted by dæmons, comforted by visions, instructed by prophecy, and surprisingly delivered from danger, sickness, and from death itself, by the supplications of the church. The real or imaginary prodigies, of which they so frequently conceived themselves to be the objects, the instruments, or the spectators, very happily disposed them to adopt with the same ease, but with far greater justice, the authentic wonders of the evangelic history; and thus miracles that exceeded not the measure of their own experience inspired them with the most lively assurance of mysteries which were acknowledged to surpass the limits of their understanding. It is this deep impression of supernatural truths which has been so much celebrated under the name of faith; a state of mind described as the surest pledge of the Divine favour and of future felicity, and recommended as the first or perhaps the only merit of a Christian. According to the more rigid doctors, the moral virtues, which may be equally practised by infidels, are destitute of any value or efficacy in the work of our justification.

IV. But the primitive Christian demonstrated his faith by his virtues; and it was very justly supposed that the Divine persuasion, which enlightened or subdued the understanding, must at the same time purify the heart and direct the actions of the believer. The first apologists of Christianity who justify the innocence of their brethren, and the writers of a later period who celebrate the sanctity of their ancestors, display, in the most lively colours, the reformation of manners which was introduced into the world by the preaching of the Gospel. As it is my intention to remark only such human causes as were permitted to second the influence of revelation, I shall slightly mention two motives which might naturally render the lives of the primitive Christians much purer and more austere than those of their Pagan contemporaries or their degenerate successors—repentance for their past sins, and the laudable desire of supporting the reputation of the society in which they were engaged.

It is a very ancient reproach, suggested by the ignorance or the malice of infidelity, that the Christians allured into their party the most atrocious criminals, who, as soon as they were touched by a sense of remorse, were easily persuaded to wash away, in the water of baptism, the guilt of their past conduct, for which the temples of the gods refused to grant them any expiation. But this reproach, when it is cleared from misrepresentation, contributes as much to the honour as it did to the increase of the church. The friends of Christianity may acknowledge without a blush that many of the most eminent saints had been before their baptism the most abandoned sinners. Those persons who in the world had followed, though in an imperfect manner, the dictates of benevolence and propriety, derived such a calm satisfaction from the opinion of their own rectitude as rendered them much less susceptible of the sudden emotions of shame, of grief, and of terror, which have given birth to so many wonderful conversions. After the example of their Divine Master, the missionaries of the Gospel disdained not the society of men, and especially of women, oppressed by the consciousness, and very often by the effects, of their vices. As they emerged from sin and superstition to the glorious hope of immortality, they resolved to devote themselves to a life, not only of virtue, but of penitence. The desire of perfection became the ruling passion of their soul; and it is well known that, while reason embraces a cold mediocrity, our passions hurry us with rapid violence over the space which lies between the most opposite extremes.

When the new converts had been enrolled in the number of the faithful, and were admitted to the sacraments of the church, they found themselves restrained from relapsing into their past disorders by another consideration of a less spiritual but of a very innocent and respectable nature. Any particular society that has departed from the great body of the nation, or the religion to which it belonged, immediately becomes the object of universal as well as invidious observation. In proportion to the smallness of its numbers, the character of the society may be affected by the virtue and vices of the persons who compose it; and every member is engaged to watch with the most vigilant attention over his own behaviour, and over that of his brethren, since, as he must expect to incur a part of the common disgrace, he may hope to enjoy a share of the common reputation. When the Christians of Bithynia were brought before the tribunal of the younger Pliny, they assured the proconsul that, far from being engaged in any unlawful conspiracy, they were bound by a solemn obligation to abstain from the commission of those crimes which disturb the private or public peace of society, from theft, robbery, adultery, perjury, and fraud. Near a century afterwards, Tertullian with an honest pride could boast that very few Christians had suffered by the hand of the executioner, except on account of their religion. Their serious and sequestered life, averse to the gay luxury of the age, inured them to chastity, temperance, economy, and all the sober and domestic virtues. As the greater number were of some trade or profession, it was incumbent on them, by the strictest integrity and the fairest dealing, to remove the suspicions which the profane are too apt to conceive against the appearances of sanctity. The contempt of the world exercised them in the habits of humility, meekness, and patience. The more they were persecuted, the more closely they adhered to each other. Their mutual charity and unsuspecting confidence has been remarked by infidels, and was too often abused by perfidious friends.

It is a very honourable circumstance for the morals of the primitive Christians, that even their faults, or rather errors, were derived from an excess of virtue. The bishops and doctors of the church, whose evidence attests, and whose authority might influence, the professions, the principles, and even the practice of their contemporaries, had studied the Scriptures with less skill than devotion; and they often received in the most literal sense those rigid precepts of Christ and the apostles to which the prudence of succeeding commentators has applied a looser and more figurative mode of interpretation. Ambitious to exalt the perfection of the Gospel above the wisdom of philosophy, the zealous fathers have carried the duties of self-mortification, of purity, and of patience, to a height which it is scarcely possible to attain, and much less to preserve, in our present state of weakness and corruption. A doctrine so extraordinary and so sublime must inevitably command the veneration of the people; but it was ill calculated to obtain the suffrage of those worldly philosophers who, in the conduct of this transitory life, consult only the feelings of nature and the interest of society.

There are two very natural propensities which we may distinguish in the most virtuous and liberal dispositions, the love of pleasure and the love of action. If the former is refined by art and learning, improved by the charms of social intercourse, and corrected by a just regard to economy, to health, and to reputation, it is productive of the greatest part of the happiness of private life. The love of action is a principle of a much stronger and more doubtful nature. It often leads to anger, to ambition, and to revenge; but when it is guided by the sense of propriety and benevolence, it becomes the parent of every virtue, and, if those virtues are accompanied with equal abilities, a family, a state, or an empire may be indebted for their safety and prosperity to the undaunted courage of a single man. To the love of pleasure we may therefore ascribe most of the agreeable, to the love of action we may attribute most of the useful and respectable, qualifications. The character in which both the one and the other should be united and harmonised would seem to constitute the most perfect idea of human nature. The insensible and inactive disposition, which should be supposed alike destitute of both, would be rejected, by the common consent of mankind, as utterly incapable of procuring any happiness to the individual, or any public benefit to the world. But it was not in *this* world that the primitive Christians were desirous of making themselves either agreeable or useful.

111

The acquisition of knowledge, the exercise of our reason or fancy, and the cheerful flow of unguarded conversation, may employ the leisure of a liberal mind. Such amusements, however, were rejected with abhorrence, or admitted with the utmost caution, by the severity of the fathers, who despised all knowledge that was not useful to salvation, and who considered all levity of discourse as a criminal abuse of the gift of speech. In our present state of existence the body is so inseparably connected with the soul, that it seems to be our interest to taste, with innocence and moderation, the enjoyments of which that faithful companion is susceptible. Very different was the reasoning of our devout predecessors; vainly aspiring to imitate the perfection of angels, they disdained, or they affected to disdain, every earthly and corporeal delight. Some of our senses indeed are necessary for our preservation, others for our subsistence, and others again for our information; and thus far it was impossible to reject the use of them. The first sensation of pleasure was marked as the first moment of their abuse. The unfeeling candidate for heaven was instructed, not only to resist the grosser allurements of the taste or smell, but even to shut his ears against the profane harmony of sounds, and to view with indifference the most finished productions of human art. Gay apparel, magnificent houses, and elegant furniture were supposed to unite the double guilt of pride and of sensuality: a simple and mortified appearance was more suitable to the Christian who was certain of his sins and doubtful of his salvation. In their censures of luxury the fathers are extremely minute and circumstantial; and among the various articles which excite their pious indignation, we may enumerate false hair, garments of any colour except white, instruments of music, vases of gold or silver, downy pillows (as Jacob reposed his head on a stone), white bread, foreign wines, public salutations, the use of warm baths, and the practice of shaving the beard, which, according to the expression of Tertullian, is a lie against our own faces, and an impious attempt to improve the works of the Creator. When Christianity was introduced among the rich and the polite, the observation of these singular laws was left, as it would be at present, to the few who were ambitious of superior sanctity. But it is always easy, as well as agreeable, for the inferior ranks of mankind to claim a merit from the contempt of that pomp and pleasure which fortune has placed beyond their reach. The virtue of the primitive Christians, like that of the first Romans, was very frequently guarded by poverty and ignorance.

The chaste severity of the fathers in whatever related to the commerce of the two sexes flowed from the same principle—their abhorrence of every enjoyment which might gratify the sensual and degrade the spiritual nature of man. It was their favourite opinion, that if Adam had preserved his obedience to the Creator, he would have lived for ever in a state of virgin purity, and that some harmless mode of vegetation might have peopled paradise with a race of innocent and immortal beings. The use of marriage was permitted only to his fallen posterity, as a necessary expedient to continue the human species, and as a restraint, however imperfect, on the natural licentiousness of desire. The hesitation of the orthodox casuists on this interesting subject betrays the perplexity of men unwilling to approve an institution which they were compelled to tolerate. The enumeration of the very whimsical laws which they most circumstantially imposed on the marriage-bed would force a smile from the young and a blush from the fair. It was their unanimous sentiment that a first marriage was adequate to all the purposes of nature and of society. The sensual connection was refined into a resemblance of the mystic union of Christ with his church, and was pronounced to be indissoluble either by divorce or by death. The practice of second nuptials was branded with the name of a legal adultery; and the persons who were guilty of so scandalous an offence against Christian purity were soon excluded from the honours, and even from the arms, of the church. Since desire was imputed as a crime, and marriage was tolerated as a defect, it was consistent with the same principles to consider a state of celibacy as the nearest approach to the Divine perfection. It was with the utmost difficulty that ancient Rome could support the institution of six vestals; but the primitive church was filled with a great number of persons of either sex who had devoted themselves to the profession of perpetual chastity. A few of these, among whom we may reckon the learned Origen, judged it the most prudent to disarm the tempter.[7] Some were insensible and some were invincible against the assaults of the flesh. Disdaining an ignominious flight, the virgins of the warm climate of Africa encountered the enemy in the closest engagement; they permitted priests and deacons to share their bed, and gloried amidst the flames in their unsullied purity. But insulted Nature sometimes vindicated her rights, and this new species of martyrdom served only to introduce a new scandal into the church.[8] Among the Christian ascetics, however (a name which they soon acquired from their painful exercise), many, as they were less presumptuous, were probably more successful. The loss of sensual pleasure was supplied and compensated by spiritual pride. Even the multitude of Pagans were inclined to estimate the merit of the sacrifice by its apparent difficulty; and it was in the praise of these chaste spouses of Christ that the fathers have poured forth the troubled stream of their eloquence. Such are the early traces of monastic principles and institutions, which, in a subsequent age, have counterbalanced all the temporal advantages of Christianity.

The Christians were not less averse to the business than to the pleasures of this world. The defence of our persons and property they knew not how to reconcile with the patient doctrine which enjoined an unlimited forgiveness of past injuries, and commanded them to invite the repetition of fresh insults. Their simplicity was offended by the use of oaths, by the pomp of magistracy,

---

[7] Before the fame of Origen had excited envy and persecution, this extraordinary action was rather admired than censured. As it was his general practice to allegorise Scripture, it seems unfortunate that, in this instance only, he should have adopted the literal sense. [Origen castrated himself, taking too literally the Pauline text, "Some have made themselves eunuchs for the sake of Christ." Ed.]

[8] Something like this rash attempt was long afterwards imputed to the founder of the order of Fontevrault. Bayle has amused himself and his readers on that very delicate subject.

and by the active contention of public life; nor could their humane ignorance be convinced that it was lawful on any occasion to shed the blood of our fellow-creatures, either by the sword of justice or by that of war, even though their criminal or hostile attempts should threaten the peace and safety of the whole community. It was acknowledged that, under a less perfect law, the powers of the Jewish constitution had been exercised, with the approbation of Heaven, by inspired prophets and by anointed kings. The Christians felt and confessed that such institutions might be necessary for the present system of the world, and they cheerfully submitted to the authority of their Pagan governors. But while they inculcated the maxims of passive obedience, they refused to take any active part in the civil administration or the military defence of the empire. Some indulgence might perhaps be allowed to those persons who, before their conversion, were already engaged in such violent and sanguinary occupations; but it was impossible that the Christians, without renouncing a more sacred duty, could assume the character of soldiers, of magistrates, or of princes. This indolent, or even criminal disregard to the public welfare, exposed them to the contempt and reproaches of the Pagans, who very frequently asked, what must be the fate of the empire, attacked on every side by the barbarians, if all mankind should adopt the pusillanimous sentiments of the new sect? To this insulting question the Christian apologists returned obscure and ambiguous answers, as they were unwilling to reveal the secret cause of their security: the expectation that, before the conversion of mankind was accomplished, war, government, the Roman empire, and the world itself, would be no more. It may be observed that, in this instance likewise, the situation of the first Christians coincided very happily with their religious scruples, and that their aversion to an active life contributed rather to excuse them from the service than to exclude them from the honours of the state and army.

V. But the human character, however it may be exalted or depressed by a temporary enthusiasm, will return by degrees to its proper and natural level, and will resume those passions that seem the most adapted to its present condition. The primitive Christians were dead to the business and pleasures of the world; but their love of action, which could never be entirely extinguished, soon revived, and found a new occupation in the government of the church. A separate society, which attacked the established religion of the empire, was obliged to adopt some form of internal policy, and to appoint a sufficient number of ministers, intrusted not only with the spiritual functions, but even with the temporal direction of the Christian commonwealth. The safety of the society, its honour, its aggrandisement, were productive, even in the most pious minds, of a spirit of patriotism, such as the first of the Romans had felt for the republic, and sometimes of a similar indifference in the use of whatever means might probably conduce to so desirable an end. The ambition of raising themselves or their friends to the honours and offices of the church was disguised by the laudable intention of devoting to the public benefit the power and consideration which, for that purpose only, it became their duty to solicit. In the exercise of their functions they were frequently called upon to detect the errors of heresy or the arts of faction, to oppose the designs of perfidious brethren, to stigmatise their characters with deserved infamy, and to expel them from the bosom of a society whose peace and happiness they had attempted to disturb. The ecclesiastical governors of the Christians were taught to unite the wisdom of the serpent with the innocence of the dove; but as the former was refined, so the latter was insensibly corrupted, by the habits of government. In the church as well as in the world, the persons who were placed in any public station rendered themselves considerable by their eloquence and firmness, by their knowledge of mankind, and by their dexterity in business; and while they concealed from others, and perhaps from themselves, the secret motives of their conduct, they too frequently relapsed into all the turbulent passions of active life, which were tinctured with an additional degree of bitterness and obstinacy from the infusion of spiritual zeal.

The government of the church has often been the subject, as well as the prize, of religious contention. The hostile disputants of Rome, of Paris, of Oxford, and of Geneva, have alike struggled to reduce the primitive and apostolic model to the respective standards of their own policy. The few who have pursued this inquiry with more candour and impartiality are of opinion that the apostles declined the office of legislation, and rather chose to endure some partial scandals and divisions, than to exclude the Christians of a future age from the liberty of varying their forms of ecclesiastical government according to the changes of times and circumstances. The scheme of policy which, under their approbation, was adopted for the use of the first century, may be discovered from the practice of Jerusalem, of Ephesus, or of Corinth. The societies which were instituted in the cities of the Roman empire were united only by the ties of faith and charity. Independence and equality formed the basis of their internal constitution. The want of discipline and human learning was supplied by the occasional assistance of the *prophets*, who were called to that function without distinction of age, of sex, or of natural abilities, and who, as often as they felt the divine impulse, poured forth the effusions of the Spirit in the assembly of the faithful. But these extraordinary gifts were frequently abused or misapplied by the prophetic teachers. They displayed them at an improper season, presumptuously disturbed the service of the assembly, and by their pride or mistaken zeal they introduced, particularly into the apostolic church of Corinth, a long and melancholy train of disorders. As the institution of prophets became useless, and even pernicious, their powers were withdrawn, and their office abolished.

The public functions of religion were solely intrusted to the established ministers of the church, the *bishops* and the *presbyters;* two appellations which, in their first origin, appear to have distinguished the same office and the same order of persons. The name of Presbyter was expressive of their age, or rather of their gravity and wisdom. The title of Bishop denoted their inspection over the faith and manners of the Christians who were committed to their pastoral care. In proportion to the respective numbers of the faithful, a larger or smaller number of these *episcopal presbyters* guided each infant congregation with equal authority and with united counsels.

But the most perfect equality of freedom requires the directing hand of a superior magistrate: and the order of public deliberations soon introduces the office of a president, invested at least with the authority of collecting the sentiments, and of executing the resolutions, of the assembly. A regard for the public tranquillity, which would so frequently have been interrupted by annual or by occasional elections, induced the primitive Christians to constitute an honorable and perpetual magistracy, and to choose one of the wisest and most holy among their presbyters to execute, during his life, the duties of their ecclesiastical governor. It was under these circumstances that the lofty title of Bishop began to raise itself above the humble appellation of Presbyter; and while the latter remained the most natural distinction for the members of every Christian senate, the former was appropriated to the dignity of its new president. The advantages of this episcopal form of government, which appears to have been introduced before the end of the first century, were so obvious, and so important for the future greatness, as well as the present peace, of Christianity, that it was adopted without delay by all the societies which were already scattered over the empire, had acquired in a very early period the sanction of antiquity, and is still revered by the most powerful churches, both of the East and of the West, as a primitive and even as a divine establishment. It is needless to observe that the pious and humble presbyters who were first dignified with the episcopal title could not possess, and would probably have rejected, the power and pomp which now encircles the tiara of the Roman pontiff, or the mitre of a German prelate. But we may define in a few words the narrow limits of their original jurisdiction, which was chiefly of a spiritual, though in some instances of a temporal nature. It consisted in the administration of the sacraments and discipline of the church, the superintendency of religious ceremonies, which imperceptibly increased in number and variety, the consecration of ecclesiastical ministers, to whom the bishop assigned their respective functions, the management of the public fund, and the determination of all such differences as the faithful were unwilling to expose before the tribunal of an idolatrous judge. These powers, during a short period, were exercised according to the advice of the presbyteral college, and with the consent and approbation of the assembly of Christians. The primitive bishops were considered only as the first of their equals, and the honourable servants of a free people. Whenever the episcopal chair became vacant by death, a new president was chosen among the presbyters by the suffrage of the whole congregation, every member of which supposed himself invested with a sacred and sacerdotal character.

Such was the mild and equal constitution by which the Christians were governed more than an hundred years after the death of the apostles. Every society formed within itself a separate and independent republic; and although the most distant of these little states maintained a mutual as well as friendly intercourse of letters and deputations, the Christian world was not yet connected by any supreme authority or legislative assembly. As the numbers of the faithful were gradually multiplied, they discovered the advantages that might result from a closer union of their interest and designs. Towards the end of the second century, the churches of Greece and Asia adopted the useful institutions of provincial synods, and they may justly be supposed to have borrowed the model of a representative council from the celebrated examples of their own country, the Amphictyons, the Achæan league, or the assemblies of the Ionian cities. It was soon established as a custom and as a law, that the bishops of the independent churches should meet in the capital of the province at the stated periods of spring and autumn. Their deliberations were assisted by the advice of a few distinguished presbyters, and moderated by the presence of a listening multitude. Their decrees, which were styled Canons, regulated every important

119

controversy of faith and discipline; and it was natural to believe that a liberal effusion of the Holy Spirit would be poured on the united assembly of the delegates of the Christian people. The institution of synods was so well suited to private ambition and to public interest, that in the space of a few years it was received throughout the whole empire. A regular correspondence was established between the provincial councils, which mutually communicated and approved their respective proceedings; and the catholic church soon assumed the form, and acquired the strength, of a great federative republic.

As the legislative authority of the particular churches was insensibly superseded by the use of councils, the bishops obtained by their alliance a much larger share of executive and arbitrary power; and as soon as they were connected by a sense of their common interest, they were enabled to attack, with united vigour, the original rights of their clergy and people. The prelates of the third century imperceptibly changed the language of exhortation into that of command, scattered the seeds of future usurpations, and supplied, by Scripture allegories and declamatory rhetoric, their deficiency of force and of reason. They exalted the unity and power of the church, as it was represented in the EPISCOPAL OFFICE, of which every bishop enjoyed an equal and undivided portion. Princes and magistrates, it was often repeated, might boast an earthly claim to a transitory dominion: it was the episcopal authority alone which was derived from the Deity, and extended itself over this and over another world. The bishops were the vice-regents of Christ, the successors of the apostles, and the mystic substitutes of the high priest of the Mosaic law. Their exclusive privilege of conferring the sacerdotal character invaded the freedom both of clerical and of popular elections: and if, in the administration of the church, they still consulted the judgment of the presbyters or the inclination of the people, they most carefully inculcated the merit of such a voluntary condescension. The bishops acknowledged the supreme authority which resided in the assembly of their brethren; but in the government of his peculiar diocese each of them exacted from his *flock* the same implicit obedience as if that favourite metaphor had been literally just, and as if the shepherd had been of a more exalted nature than that of his sheep. This obedience, however, was not imposed without some efforts on one side, and some resistance on the other. The democratical part of the constitution was, in many places, very warmly supported by the zealous or interested opposition of the inferior clergy. But their patriotism received the ignominious epithets of faction and schism, and the episcopal cause was indebted for its rapid progress to the labours of many active prelates, who, like Cyprian of Carthage, could reconcile the arts of the most ambitious statesman with the Christian virtues which seem adapted to the character of a saint and martyr.

The same causes which at first had destroyed the equality of the presbyters introduced among the bishops a pre-eminence of rank, and from thence a superiority of jurisdiction. As often as in the spring and autumn they met in provincial synod, the difference of personal merit and reputation was very sensibly felt among the members of the assembly, and the multitude was governed by the wisdom and eloquence of the few. But the order of public proceedings required a more regular and less invidious distinction; the office of perpetual presidents in the councils of each province was conferred on the bishops of the principal city; and these aspiring prelates, who soon acquired the lofty titles of Metropolitans and Primates, secretly prepared themselves to usurp over their episcopal brethren the same authority which the bishops had so lately assumed above the college of presbyters. Nor was it long before an emulation of pre-eminence and power prevailed among the Metropolitans themselves, each of them affecting to display, in the most pompous terms, the temporal honours and advantages of the city over which he presided; the numbers and opulence of the Christians who were subject to their pastoral care; the saints and martyrs who had arisen among them; and the purity with which they preserved the tradition of the faith as it had been transmitted through a series of orthodox bishops from the apostle or the apostolic disciple to whom the foundation of their church was ascribed. From every cause, either of a civil or of an ecclesiastical nature, it was easy to foresee that Rome must enjoy the respect, and would soon claim the obedience, of the provinces. The society of the faithful bore a just proportion to the capital of the empire; and the Roman church was the greatest, the most numerous, and, in regard to the West, the most ancient of all the Christian establishments, many of which had received their religion from the pious labours of her missionaries. Instead of *one* apostolic founder, the utmost boast of Antioch, of Ephesus, or of Corinth, the banks of the Tiber were supposed to have been honoured with the preaching and martyrdom of the *two* most eminent among the apostles; and the bishops of Rome very prudently claimed the inheritance of whatsoever prerogatives were attributed either to the person or to the office of St. Peter. The bishops of Italy and of the provinces were disposed to allow them a primacy of order and association (such was their very accurate expression) in the Christian aristocracy. But the power of a monarch was rejected with abhorrence, and the aspiring genius of Rome experienced from the nations of Asia and Africa a more vigorous resistance to her spiritual than she had formerly done to her temporal dominion. The patriotic Cyprian, who ruled with the most absolute sway the church of Carthage and the provincial synods, opposed with resolution and success the ambition of the Roman pontiff, artfully connected his own cause with that of the eastern bishops, and, like Hannibal, sought out new allies in the heart of Asia. If this Punic war was carried on without any effusion of blood, it was owing much less to the moderation than to the weakness of the contending prelates. Invectives and excommunications were *their* only weapons; and these, during the progress of the whole controversy, they hurled against each other with equal fury and devotion. The hard necessity of censuring either a pope or a saint and martyr distresses the modern Catholics whenever they are obliged to relate the particulars of a dispute in which the champions of religion indulged such passions as seem much more adapted to the senate or to the camp.

The progress of the ecclesiastical authority gave birth to the memorable distinction of the laity and of the clergy, which had been unknown to the Greeks and Romans. The former of these appellations comprehended the body of the Christian people; the latter, according to the signification of the word, was appropriated to the chosen portion that had been set apart for the service of religion; a celebrated order of men which has furnished the most important, though not always the most edifying, subjects for modern history. Their mutual hostilities sometimes disturbed the peace of the infant church, but their zeal and activity were united in the common cause, and the love of power, which (under the most artful disguises) could insinuate itself into the breasts of bishops and martyrs, animated them to increase the number of their subjects, and to enlarge the limits of the Christian empire. They were destitute of any temporal force, and they were for a long time discouraged and oppressed, rather than assisted, by the civil magistrate; but they had acquired, and they employed within their own society, the two most efficacious instruments of government, rewards and punishments; the former derived from the pious liberality, the latter from the devout apprehensions, of the faithful. . . .

[*After describing the gradual acquisition of wealth by the church, at the disposal of its bishops, and the development of ecclesiastical penalties, especially excommunication, Gibbon goes on.*]

The well-tempered mixture of liberality and rigour, the judicious dispensation of rewards and punishments, according to the maxims of policy as well as justice, constituted the *human* strength of the church. The bishops, whose paternal care extended itself to the government of both worlds, were sensible of the importance of these prerogatives; and, covering their ambition with the fair pretence of the love of order, they were jealous of any rival in the exercise of a discipline so necessary to prevent the desertion of those troops which had enlisted themselves under the banner of the Cross, and whose numbers every day became more considerable. From the imperious declamations of Cyprian we should naturally conclude that the doctrines of excommunication and penance formed the most essential part of religion; and that it was much less dangerous for the disciples of Christ to neglect the observance of the moral duties than to despise the censures and authority of their bishops. Sometimes we might imagine that we were listening to the voice of Moses, when he commanded the earth to open, and to swallow up, in consuming flames, the rebellious race which refused obedience to the priesthood of Aaron; and we should sometimes suppose that we heard a Roman consul asserting the majesty of the republic, and declaring his inflexible resolution to enforce the rigour of the laws. "If such irregularities are suffered with impunity" (it is thus that the bishop of Carthage chides the lenity of his colleague), "if such irregularities are suffered, there is an end of EPISCOPAL VIGOUR; an end of the sublime and divine power of governing the Church; an end of Christianity itself." Cyprian had renounced those temporal honours which it is probable he would never have obtained; but the acquisition of such absolute command over the consciences and understanding of a congregation, however obscure or despised by the world, is more truly grateful to the pride of the human heart than the possession of the most despotic power imposed by arms and conquest on a reluctant people.

In the course of this important, though perhaps tedious, inquiry, I have attempted to display the secondary causes which so efficaciously assisted the truth of the Christian religion. If among these causes we have discovered any artificial ornaments, any accidental circumstances, or any mixture of error and passion, it cannot appear surprising that mankind should be the most sensibly affected by such motives as were suited to their imperfect nature. It was by the aid of these causes—exclusive zeal, the immediate expectation of another world, the claim of miracles, the practice of rigid virtue, and the constitution of the primitive church—that Christianity spread itself with so much success in the Roman empire. To the first of these the Christians were indebted for their invincible valour, which disdained to capitulate with the enemy whom they were resolved to vanquish. The three succeeding causes supplied their valour with the most formidable arms. The last of these causes united their courage, directed their arms, and gave their efforts that irresistible weight which even a small band of well-trained and intrepid volunteers has so often possessed over an undisciplined multitude, ignorant of the subject and careless of the event of the war. In the various religions of Polytheism, some wandering fanatics of Egypt and Syria, who addressed themselves to the credulous superstition of the populace, were perhaps the only order of priests that derived their whole support and credit from their sacerdotal profession, and were very deeply affected by a personal concern for the safety or prosperity of their tutelar deities. The ministers of Polytheism, both in Rome and in the provinces, were, for the most part, men of a noble birth and of an affluent fortune, who received, as an honourable distinction, the care of a celebrated temple or of a public sacrifice, exhibited, very frequently at their own expense, the sacred games, and with cold indifference performed the ancient rites, according to the laws and fashion of their country. As they were engaged in the ordinary occupations of life, their zeal and devotion were seldom animated by a sense of interest, or by the habits of an ecclesiastical character. Confined to their respective temples and cities, they remained without any connection of discipline or government; and whilst they acknowledged the supreme jurisdiction of the senate, of the college of pontiffs, and of the emperor, those civil magistrates contented themselves with the easy task of maintaining in peace and dignity the general worship of mankind. We have already seen how various, how loose, and how uncertain were the religious sentiments of Polytheists. They were abandoned, almost without control, to the natural workings of a superstitious fancy. The accidental circumstances of their life and situation determined the object as well as the degree of their devotion; and as long as their adoration was successively prostituted to a thousand deities, it was scarcely possible that their hearts could be susceptible of a very sincere or lively passion for any of them.

When Christianity appeared in the world, even these faint and imperfect impressions had lost much of their original power. Human reason, which by its unassisted strength is incapable of perceiving the mysteries of faith, had already obtained an easy triumph over the folly of Paganism; and when Tertullian or Lactantius employ their labours in exposing its falsehood and extravagance, they are obliged to transcribe the eloquence of Cicero or the wit of Lucian. The contagion of these sceptical writings had been diffused far beyond the number of their readers. The fashion of incredulity was communicated from the philosopher to the man of pleasure or business, from the noble to the plebeian, and from the master to the menial slave who waited at his table, and who eagerly listened to the freedom of his conversation. On public occasions the philosophic part of mankind affected to treat with respect and decency the religious institutions of their country, but their secret contempt penetrated through the thin and awkward disguise; and even the people, when they discovered that their deities were rejected and derided by those whose rank or understanding they were accustomed to reverence, were filled with doubts and apprehensions concerning the truth of those doctrines to which they had yielded the most implicit belief. The decline of ancient prejudice exposed a very numerous portion of human kind to the danger of a painful and comfortless situation. A state of scepticism and suspense may amuse a few inquisitive minds. But the practice of superstition is so congenial to the multitude that, if they are forcibly awakened, they still regret the loss of their pleasing vision. Their love of the marvellous and supernatural, their curiosity with regard to future events, and their strong propensity to extend their hopes and fears beyond the limits of the visible world, were the principal causes which favoured the establishment of Polytheism. So urgent on the vulgar is the necessity of believing, that the fall of any system of mythology will most probably be succeeded by the introduction of some other mode of superstition. Some deities of a more recent and fashionable cast might soon have occupied the deserted temples of Jupiter and Apollo, if, in the decisive moment, the wisdom of Providence had not interposed a genuine revelation fitted to inspire the most rational esteem and conviction, whilst, at the same time, it was adorned with all that could attract the curiosity, the wonder, and the veneration of the people. In their actual disposition, as many were almost disengaged from their artificial prejudices, but equally susceptible and desirous of a devout attachment, an object much less deserving would have been sufficient to fill the vacant place in their hearts, and to gratify the uncertain eagerness of their passions. Those who are inclined to pursue this reflection, instead of viewing with astonishment the rapid progress of Christianity, will perhaps be surprised that its success was not still more rapid and still more universal.

It has been observed, with truth as well as propriety, that the conquests of Rome prepared and facilitated those of Christianity. In the second chapter of this work we have attempted to explain in what manner the most civilised provinces of Europe, Asia, and Africa were united under the dominion of one sovereign, and gradually connected by the most intimate ties of laws, of manners, and of language. The Jews of Palestine, who had fondly expected a temporal deliverer, gave so cold a reception to the miracles of the divine prophet, that it was found unnecessary to publish, or at least to preserve, any Hebrew gospel.[9] The authentic histories of the actions of Christ were composed in the Greek language, at a considerable distance from Jerusalem, and after the Gentile converts were grown extremely numerous. As soon as those histories were translated into the Latin tongue they were perfectly intelligible to all the subjects

---

[9] The modern critics are not disposed to believe what the fathers almost unanimously assert, that St. Matthew composed a Hebrew gospel, of which only the Greek translation is extant. It seems, however, dangerous to reject their testimony.

of Rome, excepting only to the peasants of Syria and Egypt, for whose benefit particular versions were afterwards made. The public highways, which had been constructed for the use of the legions, opened an easy passage for the Christian missionaries from Damascus to Corinth, and from Italy to the extremity of Spain or Britain; nor did those spiritual conquerors encounter any of the obstacles which usually retard or prevent the introduction of a foreign religion into a distant country. There is the strongest reason to believe that before the reigns of Diocletian and Constantine the faith of Christ had been preached in every province, and in all the great cities of the empire; but the foundation of the several congregations, the numbers of the faithful who composed them, and their proportion to the unbelieving multitude, are now buried in obscurity or disguised by fiction and declamation. Such imperfect circumstances, however, as have reached our knowledge concerning the increase of the Christian name in Asia and Greece, in Egypt, in Italy, and in the West, we shall now proceed to relate, without neglecting the real or imaginary acquisitions which lay beyond the frontiers of the Roman empire.

The rich provinces that extend from the Euphrates to the Ionian sea were the principal theatre on which the apostle of the Gentiles displayed his zeal and piety. The seeds of the Gospel, which he had scattered in a fertile soil, were diligently cultivated by his disciples; and it should seem that, during the two first centuries, the most considerable body of Christians was contained within those limits. Among the societies which were instituted in Syria, none were more ancient or more illustrious than those of Damascus, of Berœa or Aleppo, and of Antioch. The prophetic introduction of the Apocalypse has described and immortalised the seven churches of Asia—Ephesus, Smyrna, Pergamus, Thyatira, Sardes, Laodicea, and Philadelphia; and their colonies were soon diffused over that populous country. In a very early period, the islands of Cyprus and Crete, the provinces of Thrace and Macedonia, gave a favourable reception to the new religion; and Christian republics were soon founded in the cities of Corinth, of Sparta, and of Athens. The antiquity of the Greek and Asiatic churches allowed a sufficient space of time for their increase and multiplication; and even the swarms of Gnostics and other heretics serve to display the flourishing condition of the orthodox church, since the appellation of heretics has always been applied to the less numerous party. To these domestic testimonies we may add the confession, the complaints, and the apprehensions of the Gentiles themselves. From the writings of Lucian, a philosopher who had studied mankind, and who describes their manners in the most lively colours, we may learn that, under the reign of Commodus, his native country of Pontus was filled with Epicureans and *Christians*. Within fourscore years after the death of Christ, the humane Pliny laments the magnitude of the evil which he vainly attempted to eradicate. In his very curious epistle to the emperor Trajan he affirms that the temples were almost deserted, that the sacred victims scarcely found any purchasers, and that the superstition had not only infected the cities, but had even spread itself into the villages and the open country of Pontus and Bithynia.

Without descending into a minute scrutiny of the expressions or of the motives of those writers who either celebrate or lament the progress of Christianity in the East, it may in general be observed that none of them have left us any grounds from whence a just estimate might be formed of the real numbers of the faithful in those provinces. One circumstance, however, has been fortunately preserved, which seems to cast a more distinct light on this obscure but interesting subject. Under the reign of Theodosius, after Christianity had enjoyed, during more than sixty years, the sunshine of Imperial favour, the ancient and illustrious church of Antioch consisted of one hundred thousand persons, three thousand of whom were supported out of the public oblations. The splendour and dignity of the queen of the East, the acknowledged populousness of Cæsarea, Seleucia, and Alexandria, and the destruction of two hundred and fifty thousand souls in the earthquake which afflicted Antioch under the elder Justin, are so many convincing proofs that the whole number of its inhabitants was not less than half a million, and that the Christians, however multiplied by zeal and power, did not exceed a fifth part of that great city. How different a proportion must we adopt when we compare the persecuted with the triumphant church, the West with the East, remote villages with populous towns, and countries recently converted to the faith with the place where the believers first received the appellation of Christians! It must not, however, be dissembled that, in another passage, Chrysostom, to whom we are indebted for this useful information, computes the multitude of the faithful as even superior to that of the Jews and Pagans. But the solution of this apparent difficulty is easy and obvious. The eloquent preacher draws a parallel between the civil and the ecclesiastical constitution of Antioch; between the list of Christians who had acquired heaven by baptism, and the list of citizens who had a right to share the public liberality. Slaves, strangers, and infants were comprised in the former; they were excluded from the latter.

The extensive commerce of Alexandria, and its proximity to Palestine, gave an easy entrance to the new religion. It was at first embraced by great numbers of the Therapeutæ, or Essenians, of the lake Mareotis, a Jewish sect which had abated much of its reverence for the Mosaic ceremonies. The austere life of the Essenians, their fasts and excommunications, the community of goods, the love of celibacy, their zeal for martyrdom, and the warmth though not the purity of their faith, already offered a very lively image of the primitive discipline. It was in the school of Alexandria that the Christian theology appears to have assumed a regular and scientifical form; and when Hadrian visited Egypt, he found a church composed of Jews and of Greeks, sufficiently important to attract the notice of that inquisitive prince. But the progress of Christianity was for a long time confined within the limits of a single city, which was itself a foreign colony, and till the close of the second century the predecessors of Demetrius were the only prelates of the Egyptian church. Three bishops were consecrated by the hands of Demetrius, and the number was increased to twenty by his successor Heraclas. The body of the natives, a people distinguished by a sullen inflexibility of temper, entertained the new doctrine with coldness and reluctance; and even in the time of Origen it was rare to meet with an Egyptian who had surmounted his early prejudices in favour of the sacred animals of his country. As soon, indeed, as Christianity ascended the throne, the zeal of those barbarians obeyed the prevailing impulsion; the cities of Egypt were filled with bishops, and the deserts of Thebais swarmed with hermits.

A perpetual stream of strangers and provincials flowed into the capacious bosom of Rome. Whatever was strange or odious, whoever was guilty or suspected, might hope, in the obscurity of that immense capital, to elude the vigilance of the law. In such a various conflux of nations, every teacher, either of truth or of falsehood, every founder, whether of a virtuous or a criminal association, might easily multiply his disciples or accomplices. The Christians of Rome, at the time of the accidental persecution of Nero, are represented by Tacitus as already amounting to a very great multitude, and the language of that great historian is almost similar to the style employed by Livy, when he relates the introduction and the suppression of the rites of Bacchus. After the Bacchanals had awakened the severity of the senate, it was likewise apprehended that a very great multitude, as it were *another people,* had been initiated into those abhorred mysteries. A more careful inquiry soon demonstrated that the offenders did not exceed seven thousand; a number indeed sufficiently alarming when considered as the object of public justice. It is with the same candid allowance that we should interpret the vague expressions of Tacitus, and in a former instance of Pliny, when they exaggerate the crowds of deluded fanatics who had forsaken the established worship of the gods. The church of Rome was undoubtedly the first and most populous of the empire; and we are possessed of an authentic record which attests the state of religion in that city about the middle of the

131

third century, and after a peace of thirty-eight years. The clergy, at that time, consisted of a bishop, forty-six presbyters, seven deacons, as many sub-deacons, forty-two acolytes, and fifty readers, exorcists, and porters. The number of widows, of the infirm, and of the poor, who were maintained by the oblations of the faithful, amounted to fifteen hundred. From reason, as well as from the analogy of Antioch, we may venture to estimate the Christians of Rome at about fifty thousand. The populousness of that great capital cannot perhaps be exactly ascertained; but the most modest calculation will not surely reduce it lower than a million of inhabitants, of whom the Christians might constitute at the most a twentieth part.

The western provincials appeared to have derived the knowledge of Christianity from the same source which had diffused among them the language, the sentiments, and the manners of Rome. In this more important circumstance, Africa, as well as Gaul, was gradually fashioned to the imitation of the capital. Yet notwithstanding the many favourable occasions which might invite the Roman missionaries to visit their Latin provinces, it was late before they passed either the sea or the Alps; nor can we discover in those great countries any assured traces either of faith or of persecution that ascend higher than the reign of the Antonines. The slow progress of the Gospel in the cold climate of Gaul was extremely different from the eagerness with which it seems to have been received on the burning sands of Africa. The African Christians soon formed one of the principal members of the primitive church. The practice introduced into that province of appointing bishops to the most inconsiderable towns, and very frequently to the most obscure villages, contributed to multiply the splendour and importance of their religious societies, which during the course of the third century were animated by the zeal of Tertullian, directed by the abilities of Cyprian, and adorned by the eloquence of Lactantius. But if, on the contrary, we turn our eyes towards Gaul, we must content ourselves with discovering, in the time of Marcus Antoninus, the feeble and united congregations of Lyons and Vienne; and even as late as the reign of Decius we are assured that in a few cities only—Arles, Narbonne, Toulouse, Limoges, Clermont, Tours, and Paris—some scattered churches were supported by the devotion of a small number of Christians. Silence is indeed very consistent with devotion; but as it is seldom compatible with zeal we may perceive and lament the languid state of Christianity in those provinces which had exchanged the Celtic for the Latin tongue, since they did not, during the three first centuries, give birth to a single ecclesiastical writer. From Gaul, which claimed a just pre-eminence of learning and authority over all the countries on this side of the Alps, the light of the Gospel was more faintly reflected on the remote provinces of Spain and Britain; and if we may credit the vehement assertions of Tertullian, they had already received the first rays of the faith when he addressed his Apology to the magistrates of the emperor Severus. But the obscure and imperfect origin of the western churches of Europe has been so negligently recorded, that, if we would relate the time and manner of their foundation, we must supply the silence of antiquity by those legends which avarice or superstition long afterwards dictated to the monks in the lazy gloom of their convents.[10] Of these holy romances, that of the apostle St. James can alone, by its singular extravagance, deserve to be mentioned. From a peaceful fisherman of the lake of Gennesareth, he was transformed into a valorous knight, who charged at the head of the Spanish chivalry in their battles against the Moors. The gravest historians have celebrated his exploits; the miraculous shrine of Compostella displayed his power; and the sword of a military order, assisted by the terrors of the Inquisition, was sufficient to remove every objection of profane criticism.

The progress of Christianity was not confined to the Roman empire; and, according to the primitive fathers, who interpret facts by prophecy, the new religion, within

---

10 In the fifteenth century there were few who had either inclination or courage to question whether Joseph of Arimathea founded the monastery of Glastonbury, and whether Dionysius the Areopagite preferred the residence of Paris to that of Athens.

a century after the death of its Divine Author, had already visited every part of the globe. "There exists not," says Justin Martyr, "a people, whether Greek or barbarian, or any other race of men, by whatsoever appellation or manners they may be distinguished, however ignorant of arts or agriculture, whether they dwell under tents, or wander about in covered waggons, among whom prayers are not offered up in the name of a crucified Jesus to the Father and Creator of all things." But this splendid exaggeration, which even at present it would be extremely difficult to reconcile with the real state of mankind, can be considered only as the rash sally of a devout but careless writer, the measure of whose belief was regulated by that of his wishes. But neither the belief nor the wishes of the fathers can alter the truth of history. It will still remain an undoubted fact that the barbarians of Scythia and Germany, who afterwards subverted the Roman monarchy, were involved in the darkness of paganism; and that even the conversion of Iberia, of Armenia, or of Æthiopia, was not attempted with any degree of success till the sceptre was in the hands of an orthodox emperor. Before that time the various accidents of war and commerce might indeed diffuse an imperfect knowledge of the Gospel among the tribes of Caledonia, and among the borders of the Rhine, the Danube, and the Euphrates. Beyond the last-mentioned river, Edessa was distinguished by a firm and early adherence to the faith. From Edessa the principles of Christianity were easily introduced into the Greek and Syrian cities which obeyed the successors of Artaxerxes; but they do not appear to have made any deep impression on the minds of the Persians, whose religious system, by the labours of a well-disciplined order of priests, had been constructed with much more art and solidity than the uncertain mythology of Greece and Rome.

From this impartial though imperfect survey of the progress of Christianity, it may perhaps seem probable that the number of its proselytes has been excessively magnified by fear on the one side, and by devotion on the other. According to the irreproachable testimony of

Origen, the proportion of the faithful was very inconsiderable, when compared with the multitude of an unbelieving world; but, as we are left without any distinct information, it is impossible to determine, and it is difficult even to conjecture, the real numbers of the primitive Christians. The most favourable calculation, however, that can be deduced from the examples of Antioch and of Rome will not permit us to imagine that more than a twentieth part of the subjects of the empire had enlisted themselves under the banner of the Cross before the important conversion of Constantine. But their habits of faith, of zeal, and of union, seemed to multiply their numbers; and the same causes which contributed to their future increase served to render their actual strength more apparent and more formidable.

Such is the constitution of civil society, that, whilst a few persons are distinguished by riches, by honours, and by knowledge, the body of the people is condemned to obscurity, ignorance, and poverty. The Christian religion, which addressed itself to the whole human race, must consequently collect a far greater number of proselytes from the lower than from the superior ranks of life. This innocent and natural circumstance has been improved into a very odious imputation, which seems to be less strenuously denied by the apologists than it is urged by the adversaries of the faith; that the new sect of Christians was almost entirely composed of the dregs of the populace, of peasants and mechanics, of boys and women, of beggars and slaves, the last of whom might sometimes introduce the missionaries into the rich and noble families to which they belonged. These obscure teachers (such was the charge of malice and infidelity) are as mute in public as they are loquacious and dogmatical in private. Whilst they cautiously avoid the dangerous encounter of philosophers, they mingle with the rude and illiterate crowd, and insinuate themselves into those minds whom their age, their sex, or their education has the best disposed to receive the impression of superstitious terrors.

This unfavourable picture, though not devoid of a faint resemblance, betrays, by its dark colouring and distorted features, the pencil of an enemy. As the humble faith of Christ diffused itself through the world, it was embraced by several persons who derived some consequence from the advantages of nature or fortune. Aristides, who presented an eloquent apology to the emperor Hadrian, was an Athenian philosopher. Justin Martyr had sought divine knowledge in the schools of Zeno, of Aristotle, of Pythagoras, and of Plato, before he fortunately was accosted by the old man, or rather the angel, who turned his attention to the study of the Jewish prophets. Clemens of Alexandria had acquired much various reading in the Greek, and Tertullian in the Latin, language. Julius Africanus and Origen possessed a very considerable share of the learning of their times; and although the style of Cyprian is very different from that of Lactantius, we might almost discover that both those writers had been public teachers of rhetoric. Even the study of philosophy was at length introduced among the Christians, but it was not always productive of the most salutary effects; knowledge was as often the parent of heresy as of devotion, and the description which was designed for the followers of Artemon may, with equal propriety, be applied to the various sects that resisted the successors of the apostles. "They presume to alter the holy Scriptures, to abandon the ancient rule of faith, and to form their opinions according to the subtile precepts of logic. The science of the church is neglected for the study of geometry, and they lose sight of heaven while they are employed in measuring the earth. Euclid is perpetually in their hands. Aristotle and Theophrastus are the objects of their admiration; and they express an uncommon reverence for the works of Galen. Their errors are derived from the abuse of the arts and sciences of the infidels, and they corrupt the simplicity of the Gospel by the refinements of human reason." Nor can it be affirmed with truth that the advantages of birth and fortune were always separated from the profession of Christianity. Several Roman citizens were brought before the tribunal of Pliny, and he soon discovered that a great number of persons of *every order* of men in Bithynia had deserted the religion of their ancestors. His unsuspected testimony may, in this instance, obtain more credit than the bold challenge of Tertullian, when he addresses himself to the fears as well as to the humanity of the proconsul of Africa, by assuring him that if he persists in his cruel intentions he must decimate Carthage, and that he will find among the guilty many persons of his own rank, senators and matrons of noblest extraction, and the friends or relations of his most intimate friends. It appears, however, that about forty years afterwards the emperor Valerian was persuaded of the truth of this assertion, since in one of his rescripts he evidently supposes that senators, Roman knights, and ladies of quality, were engaged in the Christian sect. The church still continued to increase its outward splendour as it lost its internal purity; and, in the reign of Diocletian, the palace, the courts of justice, and even the army, concealed a multitude of Christians, who endeavoured to reconcile the interests of the present with those of a future life.

And yet these exceptions are either too few in number, or too recent in time, entirely to remove the imputation of ignorance and obscurity which has been so arrogantly cast on the first proselytes of Christianity. Instead of employing in our defence the fictions of later ages, it will be more prudent to convert the occasion of scandal into a subject of edification. Our serious thoughts will suggest to us that the apostles themselves were chosen by Providence among the fishermen of Galilee, and that, the lower we depress the temporal condition of the first Christians, the more reason we shall find to admire their merit and success. It is incumbent on us diligently to remember that the kingdom of heaven was promised to the poor in spirit, and that minds afflicted by calamity and the contempt of mankind cheerfully listen to the divine promise of future happiness; while, on the contrary, the fortunate are satisfied with the possession of this world; and the wise abuse in doubt and dispute their vain superiority of reason and knowledge.

We stand in need of such reflections to comfort us for the loss of some illustrious characters, which in our eyes might have seemed the most worthy of the heavenly present. The names of Seneca, of the elder and the younger Pliny, of Tacitus, of Plutarch, of Galen, of the slave Epictetus, and of the emperor Marcus Antoninus, adorn the age in which they flourished, and exalt the dignity of human nature. They filled with glory their respective stations, either in active or contemplative life; their excellent understandings were improved by study; philosophy had purified their minds from the prejudices of the popular superstition; and their days were spent in the pursuit of truth and the practice of virtue. Yet all these sages (it is no less an object of surprise than of concern) overlooked or rejected the perfection of the Christian system. Their language or their silence equally discover their contempt for the growing sect which in their time had diffused itself over the Roman empire. Those among them who condescend to mention the Christians consider them only as obstinate and perverse enthusiasts, who exacted an implicit submission to their mysterious doctrines, without being able to produce a single argument that could engage the attention of men of sense and learning.

It is at least doubtful whether any of these philosophers perused the apologies which the primitive Christians repeatedly published in behalf of themselves and of their religion; but it is much to be lamented that such a cause was not defended by abler advocates. They expose with superfluous wit and eloquence the extravagance of Polytheism. They interest our compassion by displaying the innocence and sufferings of their injured brethren. But when they would demonstrate the divine origin of Christianity, they insist much more strongly on the predictions which announced, than on the miracles which accompanied, the appearance of the Messiah. Their favourite argument might serve to edify a Christian or to convert a Jew, since both the one and the other acknowledge the authority of those prophecies, and both are obliged, with devout reverence, to search for their sense and their accomplishment. But this mode of persuasion loses much of its weight and influence when it is addressed to those who neither understand nor respect the Mosaic dispensation and the prophetic style.

In the unskilful hands of Justin and of the succeeding apologists, the sublime meaning of the Hebrew oracles evaporates in distant types, affected conceits, and cold allegories; and even their authenticity was rendered suspicious to an unenlightened Gentile, by the mixture of pious forgeries which, under the names of Orpheus, Hermes, and the Sibyls, were obtruded on him as of equal value with the genuine inspirations of Heaven. The adoption of fraud and sophistry in the defence of revelation too often reminds us of the injudicious conduct of those poets who load their *invulnerable* heroes with a useless weight of cumbersome and brittle armour.

But how shall we excuse the supine inattention of the Pagan and philosophic world to those evidences which were presented by the hand of Omnipotence, not to their reason, but to their senses? During the age of Christ, of his apostles, and of their first disciples, the doctrine which they preached was confirmed by innumerable prodigies. The lame walked, the blind saw, the sick were healed, the dead were raised, dæmons were expelled, and the laws of Nature were frequently suspended for the benefit of the church. But the sages of Greece and Rome turned aside from the awful spectacle, and, pursuing the ordinary occupations of life and study, appeared unconscious of any alterations in the moral or physical government of the world. Under the reign of Tiberius, the whole earth, or at least a celebrated province of the Roman empire, was involved in a preternatural darkness of three hours. Even this miraculous event, which ought to have excited the wonder, the curiosity, and the devotion of mankind, passed without notice in an age of science and history. It happened during the lifetime of Seneca and the elder Pliny, who must have experienced the immediate effects, or received the earliest intelligence, of the prodigy. Each of these philosophers, in a laborious work, has recorded all the great phenomena of Nature, earthquakes, meteors, comets, and eclipses, which his indefatigable curiosity could collect. Both the one and the other have omitted to mention the greatest phenomenon to which the mortal eye has been witness since the creation of the globe. A distinct chapter of Pliny is designed for eclipses of an extraordinary nature and unusual duration; but he contents himself with describing the singular defect of light which followed the murder of Cæsar, when, during the greatest part of a year, the orb of the sun appeared pale and without splendour. This season of obscurity, which cannot surely be compared with the preternatural darkness of the Passion, had been already celebrated by most of the poets and historians of that memorable age.

3. Church and State in the Roman Empire: The Persecution of Diocletian

[*For the first two centuries after Christ, the Roman State had generally tolerated the Christian Church as one religion among many. But in the convulsions of the third century, the claims of the Church seemed to threaten society, and under Diocletian (284-305), the great Illyrian emperor who reorganised the imperial system, a direct collision occurred. Diocletian finally ranged himself against the Church; it was the continuator of his political work, Constantine the Great (306-337) who reversed his religious policy and adopted Christianity as the religion of the Empire. In the last part of Chapter XVI Gibbon describes the situation under Diocletian.*]

Amidst the frequent revolutions of the empire the Christians still flourished in peace and prosperity; and notwithstanding a celebrated era of martyrs has been deduced from the accession of Diocletian, the new system of policy, introduced and maintained by the wisdom of that prince, continued, during more than eighteen years, to breathe the mildest and most liberal spirit of religious toleration. The mind of Diocletian himself was less adapted indeed to speculative inquiries than to the active labours of war and government. His prudence rendered him averse to any great innovation, and, though his temper was not very susceptible of zeal or enthusiasm, he always maintained an habitual regard for the ancient deities of the empire. But the leisure of the two empresses, of his wife Prisca, and of Valeria his daughter, permitted them to listen with more at-

141

tention and respect to the truths of Christianity, which
in every age has acknowledged its important obligations
to female devotion. The principal eunuchs, Lucian and
Dorotheus, Gorgonius and Andrew, who attended the
person, possessed the favour, and governed the household of Diocletian, protected by their powerful influence
the faith which they had embraced. Their example was
imitated by many of the most considerable officers of the
palace, who, in their respective stations, had the care of
the Imperial ornaments, of the robes, of the furniture,
of the jewels, and even of the private treasury; and,
though it might sometimes be incumbent on them to
accompany the emperor when he sacrificed in the temple,
they enjoyed, with their wives, their children, and their
slaves, the free exercise of the Christian religion. Diocletian and his colleagues frequently conferred the most
important offices on those persons who avowed their abhorrence for the worship of the gods, but who had displayed abilities proper for the service of the state. The
bishops held an honourable rank in their respective
provinces, and were treated with distinction and respect,
not only by the people, but by the magistrates themselves. Almost in every city the ancient churches were
found insufficient to contain the increasing multitude of
proselytes; and in their place more stately and capacious
edifices were erected for the public worship of the faithful. The corruption of manners and principles, so forcibly
lamented by Eusebius, may be considered, not only as a
consequence, but as a proof, of the liberty which the
Christians enjoyed and abused under the reign of
Diocletian. Prosperity had relaxed the nerves of discipline.
Fraud, envy, and malice prevailed in every congregation.
The presbyters aspired to the episcopal office, which
every day became an object more worthy of their ambition. The bishops, who contended with each other for ecclesiastical pre-eminence, appeared by their conduct to
claim a secular and tyrannical power in the church; and
the lively faith which still distinguished the Christians
from the Gentiles was shown much less in their lives
than in their controversial writings.

Notwithstanding this seeming security, an attentive

observer might discern some symptoms that threatened the church with a more violent persecution than any which she had yet endured. The zeal and rapid progress of the Christians awakened the Polytheists from their supine indifference in the cause of those deities whom custom and education had taught them to revere. The mutual provocations of a religious war, which had already continued above two hundred years, exasperated the animosity of the contending parties. The Pagans were incensed at the rashness of a recent and obscure sect, which presumed to accuse their countrymen of error, and to devote their ancestors to eternal misery. The habits of justifying the popular mythology against the invectives of an implacable enemy, produced in their minds some sentiments of faith and reverence for a system which they had been accustomed to consider with the most careless levity. The supernatural powers assumed by the church inspired at the same time terror and emulation. The followers of the established religion intrenched themselves behind a similar fortification of prodigies; invented new modes of sacrifice, of expiation, and of initiation;[1] attempted to revive the credit of their expiring oracles; and listened with eager credulity to every impostor who flattered their prejudices by a tale of wonders. Both parties seemed to acknowledge the truth of those miracles which were claimed by their adversaries; and while they were contented with ascribing them to the arts of magic, and to the power of dæmons, they mutually concurred in restoring and establishing the reign of superstition. Philosophy, her most dangerous enemy, was now converted into her most useful ally. The groves of the Academy, the gardens of Epicurus, and even the portico of the Stoics, were almost deserted, as so many different schools of scepticism or impiety; and many among the Romans were desirous that the writings of Cicero should be condemned and suppressed by the authority of the senate. The prevailing sect of the new Platonicians judged

---

[1] We might quote, among a great number of instances, the mysterious worship of Mithras and the Taurobolia; the latter of which became fashionable in the time of the Antonines. The romance of Apuleius is as full of devotion as of satire.

it prudent to connect themselves with the priest, whom perhaps they despised, against the Christians, whom they had reason to fear. These fashionable philosophers prosecuted the design of extracting allegorical wisdom from the fictions of the Greek poets; instituted mysterious rites of devotion for the use of their chosen disciples; recommended the worship of the ancient gods as the emblems or ministers of the Supreme Deity, and composed against the faith of the Gospel many elaborate treatises, which have since been committed to the flames by the prudence of orthodox emperors.

Although the policy of Diocletian and the humanity of Constantius inclined them to preserve inviolate the maxims of toleration, it was soon discovered that their two associates, Maximian and Galerius, entertained the most implacable aversion for the name and religion of the Christians. The minds of those princes had never been enlightened by science; education had never softened their temper. They owed their greatness to their swords, and in their most elevated fortune they still retained their superstitious prejudices of soldiers and peasants. In the general administration of the provinces they obeyed the laws which their benefactor had established; but they frequently found occasions of exercising within their camp and palaces a secret persecution,[2] for which the imprudent zeal of the Christians sometimes offered the most specious pretences. A sentence of death was executed upon Maximilianus, an African youth, who had been produced by his own father before the magistrate as a sufficient and legal recruit, but who obstinately

---

[2] Eusebius, limits the number of military martyrs, by a remarkable expression (σπανίως τούτων εἶς που καὶ δεύτερος), of which neither his Latin nor French translator have rendered the energy. Notwithstanding the authority of Eusebius, and the silence of Lactantius, Ambrose, Sulpicius, Orosius, etc., it has been long believed that the Thebæan legion, consisting of 6000 Christians, suffered martyrdom by the order of Maximian, in the valley of the Pennine Alps. The story was first published about the middle of the fifth century, by Eucherius bishop of Lyons, who received it from certain persons, who received it from Isaac bishop of Geneva, who is said to have received it from Theodore bishop of Octodurum. The abbey of St. Maurice still subsists, a rich monument of the credulity of Sigismund, king of Burgundy.

persisted in declaring that his conscience would not permit him to embrace the profession of a soldier. It could scarcely be expected that any government should suffer the action of Marcellus the centurion to pass with impunity. On the day of a public festival, that officer threw away his belt, his arms, and the ensigns of his office, and exclaimed with a loud voice that he would obey none but Jesus Christ the eternal King, and that he renounced for ever the use of carnal weapons, and the service of an idolatrous master. The soldiers, as soon as they recovered from their astonishment, secured the person of Marcellus. He was examined in the city of Tingi by the president of that part of Mauritania; and as he was convicted by his own confession, he was condemned and beheaded for the crime of desertion. Examples of such a nature savour much less of religious persecution than of martial or even civil law: but they served to alienate the mind of the emperors; to justify the severity of Galerius, who dismissed a great number of Christian officers from their employments; and to authorise the opinion that a sect of enthusiasts, which avowed principles so repugnant to the public safety, must either remain useless, or would soon become dangerous subjects of the empire.

After the success of the Persian war had raised the hopes and the reputation of Galerius, he passed a winter with Diocletian in the palace of Nicomedia; and the fate of Christianity became the object of their secret consultations. The experienced emperor was still inclined to pursue measures of lenity; and though he readily consented to exclude the Christians from holding any employments in the household or the army, he urged in the strongest terms the danger as well as cruelty of shedding the blood of those deluded fanatics. Galerius at length extorted from him the permission of summoning a council, composed of a few persons the most distinguished in the civil and military departments of the state. The important question was agitated in their presence, and those ambitious courtiers easily discerned that it was incumbent on them to second, by their eloquence, the importunate violence of the Cæsar.

It may be presumed that they insisted on every topic which might interest the pride, the piety, or the fears, of their sovereign in the destruction of Christianity. Perhaps they represented that the glorious work of the deliverance of the empire was left imperfect, as long as an independent people was permitted to subsist and multiply in the heart of the provinces. The Christians (it might speciously be alleged), renouncing the gods and the institutions of Rome, had constituted a distinct republic, which might yet be suppressed before it had acquired any military force; but which was already governed by its own laws and magistrates, was possessed of a public treasure, and was intimately connected in all its parts by the frequent assemblies of the bishops, to whose decrees their numerous and opulent congregations yielded an implicit obedience. Arguments like these may seem to have determined the reluctant mind of Diocletian to embrace a new system of persecution: but though we may suspect, it is not in our power to relate, the secret intrigues of the palace, the private views and resentments, the jealousy of women or eunuchs, and all those trifling but decisive causes which so often influence the fate of empires and the councils of the wisest monarchs.

The pleasure of the emperors was at length signified to the Christians, who, during the course of this melancholy winter, had expected, with anxiety, the result of so many secret consultations. The twenty-third of February, which coincided with the Roman festival of the Terminalia, was appointed (whether from accident or design) to set bounds to the progress of Christianity. At the earliest dawn of day the Prætorian præfect, accompanied by several generals, tribunes, and officers of the revenue, repaired to the principal church of Nicomedia, which was situated on an eminence in the most populous and beautiful part of the city. The doors were instantly broke open; they rushed into the sanctuary; and as they searched in vain for some visible object of worship, they were obliged to content themselves with committing to the flames the volumes of Holy Scripture. The ministers of Diocletian were followed by a numerous body of guards and pioneers, who marched in order of battle, and were provided with all the instruments used in the destruction of fortified cities. By their incessant labour, a sacred edifice, which towered above the Imperial palace, and had long excited the indignation and envy of the Gentiles, was in a few hours levelled with the ground.

The next day the general edict of persecution was published; and though Diocletian, still averse to the effusion of blood, had moderated the fury of Galerius, who proposed that every one refusing to offer sacrifice should immediately be burnt alive, the penalties inflicted on the obstinacy of the Christians might be deemed sufficiently rigorous and effectual. It was enacted that their churches, in all the provinces of the empire, should be demolished to their foundations; and the punishment of death was denounced against all who should presume to hold any secret assemblies for the purpose of religious worship. The philosophers, who now assumed the unworthy office of directing the blind zeal of persecution, had diligently studied the nature and genius of the Christian religion; and as they were not ignorant that the speculative doctrines of the faith were supposed to be contained in the writings of the prophets, of the evangelists, and of the apostles, they most probably suggested the order that the bishops and presbyters should deliver all their sacred books into the hands of the magistrates; who were commanded, under the severest penalties, to burn them in a public and solemn manner. By the same edict, the property of the church was at once confiscated; and the several parts of which it might consist were either sold to the highest bidder, united to the Imperial domain, bestowed on the cities and corporations, or granted to the solicitations of rapacious courtiers. After taking such effectual measures to abolish the worship and to dissolve the government of the Christians, it was thought necessary to subject to the most intolerable hardships the condition of those perverse individuals who should still reject the religion of nature, of Rome, and of their ancestors. Persons of a liberal birth were declared incapable of holding any honours or employments; slaves were for ever deprived of the hopes of freedom; and the whole body of the people were put out of the protection of the law. The judges were authorised to hear and to determine every action that was brought against a Christian. But the Christians were not permitted to complain of any injury which they themselves had suffered; and thus those unfortunate sectaries were exposed to the severity, while they were excluded from the benefits, of public justice. This new species of martyrdom, so painful and lingering, so obscure and ignominious, was, perhaps, the most proper to weary the constancy of the faithful: nor can it be doubted that the passions and interest of mankind were disposed on this occasion to second the designs of the emperors. But the policy of a well-ordered government must sometimes have interposed in behalf of the oppressed Christians; nor was it possible for the Roman princes entirely to remove the apprehension of punishment, or to connive at every act of fraud and violence, without exposing their own authority and the rest of their subjects to the most alarming dangers.

This edict was scarcely exhibited to the public view, in the most conspicuous place of Nicomedia, before it was torn down by the hands of a Christian, who expressed at the same time, by the bitterest invectives, his contempt as well as abhorrence for such impious and tyrannical governors. His offence, according to the mildest laws, amounted to treason, and deserved death. And if it be true that he was a person of rank and education, those circumstances could serve only to aggravate his guilt. He was burnt, or rather roasted, by a slow fire; and his executioners, zealous to revenge the personal insult which had been offered to the emperors, exhausted every refinement of cruelty, without being able to subdue his patience, or to alter the steady and insulting smile which, in his dying agonies, he still preserved in his countenance. The Christians, though they confessed that his conduct had not been strictly conformable to the laws of prudence, admired the divine fervour of his zeal; and the excessive commendations which they lavished on the memory of their hero and martyr contributed to fix a deep impression of terror and hatred in the mind of Diocletian.

His fears were soon alarmed by the view of a danger from which he very narrowly escaped. Within fifteen days the palace of Nicomedia, and even the bedchamber of Diocletian, were twice in flames; and though both times they were extinguished without any material damage, the singular repetition of the fire was justly considered as an evident proof that it had not been the effect of chance or negligence. The suspicion naturally fell on the Christians; and it was suggested, with some degree of probability, that those desperate fanatics, provoked by their present sufferings, and apprehensive of impending calamities, had entered into a conspiracy with their faithful brethren, the eunuchs of the palace, against the lives of two emperors whom they detested as the irreconcilable enemies of the church of God. Jealousy and resentment prevailed in every breast, but especially in that of Diocletian. A great number of persons, distinguished either by the offices which they had filled or by the favour which they had enjoyed, were thrown into prison. Every mode of torture was put in practice, and the court, as well as city, was polluted with many bloody executions. But as it was found impossible to extort any discovery of this mysterious transaction, it seems incumbent on us either to presume the innocence, or to admire the resolution, of the sufferers. A few days afterwards Galerius hastily withdrew himself from Nicomedia, declaring that, if he delayed his departure from that devoted palace, he should fall a sacrifice to the rage of the Christians. The ecclesiastical historians, from whom alone we derive a partial and imperfect knowledge of this persecution, are at a loss how to account for the fears and danger of the emperors. Two of these writers, a prince and a rhetorician, were eye-witnesses of the fire of Nicomedia. The one ascribes it to lightning and the divine wrath, the other affirms that it was kindled by the malice of Galerius himself.

As the edict against the Christians was designed for a general law of the whole empire, and as Diocletian and Galerius, though they might not wait for the consent, were assured of the concurrence, of the Western princes, it would appear more consonant to our ideas of policy that the governors of all the provinces should have received secret instructions to publish, on one and the same day, this declaration of war within their respective departments. It was at least to be expected that the convenience of the public highways and established posts would have enabled the emperors to transmit their orders with the utmost despatch from the palace of Nicomedia to the extremities of the Roman world; and that they would not have suffered fifty days to elapse before the edict was published in Syria, and near four months before it was signified to the cities of Africa. This delay may perhaps be imputed to the cautious temper of Diocletian, who had yielded a reluctant consent to the measures of persecution, and who was desirous of trying the experiment under his more immediate eye before he gave way to the disorders and discontent which it must inevitably occasion in the distant provinces. At first, indeed, the magistrates were restrained from the effusion of blood; but the use of every other severity was permitted, and even recommended to their zeal; nor could the Christians, though they cheerfully resigned the ornaments of their churches, resolve to interrupt their religious assemblies, or to deliver their sacred books to the flames. The pious obstinacy of Felix, an African bishop, appears to have embarrassed the subordinate ministers of the government. The curator of his city sent him in chains to the proconsul. The proconsul transmitted him to the Prætorian præfect of Italy; and Felix, who disdained even to give an evasive answer, was at length beheaded at Venusia, in Lucania, a place on which the birth of Horace has conferred fame. This precedent, and perhaps some Imperial rescript, which was issued in consequence of it, appeared to authorise the governors of provinces in punishing with death the refusal of the Christians to deliver up their sacred books. There were undoubtedly many persons who embraced this opportunity of obtaining the crown of martyrdom; but there were likewise too many who purchased an ignominious life by discovering and betraying the Holy Scripture into the hands of infidels. A great number even of bishops and presbyters acquired, by this criminal compliance, the opprobrious epithet of *Traditors;* and their offence was productive of much present scandal and of much future discord in the African church.

The copies as well as the versions of Scripture were already so multiplied in the empire, that the most severe inquisition could no longer be attended with any fatal consequences; and even the sacrifice of those volumes which, in every congregation, were preserved for public use, required the consent of some treacherous and unworthy Christians. But the ruin of the churches was easily effected by the authority of the government and by the labour of the Pagans. In some provinces, however, the magistrates contented themselves with shutting up the places of religious worship. In others they more literally complied with the terms of the edict; and, after taking away the doors, the benches, and the pulpit, which they burnt as it were in a funeral pile, they completely demolished the remainder of the edifice. It is perhaps to this melancholy occasion that we should apply a very remarkable story, which is related with so many circumstances of variety and improbability that it serves rather to excite than to satisfy our curiosity. In a small town in Phrygia, of whose name as well as situation we are left ignorant, it should seem that the magistrates and the body of the people had embraced the Christian faith; and as some resistance might be apprehended to the execution of the edict, the governor of the province was supported by a numerous detachment of legionaries. On their approach the citizens threw themselves into the church, with the resolution either of defending by arms that sacred edifice or of perishing in its ruins. They indignantly rejected the notice and permission which was given them to retire, till the soldiers, provoked by their obstinate refusal, set fire to the building on all sides, and consumed, by this extraordinary kind of martyrdom, a great number of Phrygians, with their wives and children.

Some slight disturbances, though they were suppressed almost as soon as excited, in Syria and the frontiers of Armenia, afforded the enemies of the church a very plausible occasion to insinuate that those troubles had been secretly fomented by the intrigues of the bishops, who had already forgotten their ostentatious professions of passive and unlimited obedience. The resentment, or the fears, of Diocletian at length transported him beyond the bounds of moderation which he had hitherto preserved, and he declared, in a series of cruel edicts, his intention of abolishing the Christian name. By the first of these edicts the governors of the provinces were directed to apprehend all persons of the ecclesiastical order; and the prisons destined for the vilest criminals were soon filled with a multitude of bishops, presbyters, deacons, readers, and exorcists. By a second edict the magistrates were commanded to employ every method of severity which might reclaim them from their odious superstition, and oblige them to return to the established worship of the gods. This rigorous order was extended, by a subsequent edict, to the whole body of Christians, who were exposed to a violent and general persecution. Instead of those salutary restraints which had required the direct and solemn testimony of an accuser, it became the duty as well as the interest of the Imperial officers to discover, to pursue, and to torment the most obnoxious among the faithful. Heavy penalties were denounced against all who should presume to save a proscribed sectary from the just indignation of the gods and of the emperors. Yet, notwithstanding the severity of this law, the virtuous courage of many of the Pagans, in concealing their friends or relations, affords an honourable proof that the rage of superstition had not extinguished in their minds the sentiments of nature and humanity.

Diocletian had no sooner published his edicts against the Christians than, as if he had been desirous of committing to other hands the work of persecution, he divested himself of the Imperial purple. The character and situation of his colleagues and successors sometimes urged them to enforce, and sometimes inclined them to suspend, the execution of these rigorous laws; nor can we acquire a just and distinct idea of this important period of ecclesiastical history unless we separately consider the state of Christianity, in the different parts of the empire, during the space of ten years which elapsed between the first edicts of Diocletian and the final peace of the church.

The mild and humane temper of Constantius was averse to the oppression of any part of his subjects. The principal offices of his palace were exercised by Christians. He loved their persons, esteemed their fidelity, and entertained not any dislike to their religious principles. But as long as Constantius remained in the subordinate station of Cæsar, it was not in his power openly to reject the edicts of Diocletian, or to disobey the commands of Maximian. His authority contributed, however, to alleviate the sufferings which he pitied and abhorred. He consented with reluctance to the ruin of the churches, but he ventured to protect the Christians themselves from the fury of the populace and from the rigour of the laws. The provinces of Gaul (under which we may probably include those of Britain) were indebted for the singular tranquillity which they enjoyed to the gentle interposition of their sovereign. But Datianus, the president or governor of Spain, actuated either by zeal or policy, chose rather to execute the public edicts of the emperors than to understand the secret intentions of Constantius; and it can scarcely be doubted that his provincial administration was stained with the blood of a few martyrs. The elevation of Constantius to the supreme and independent dignity of Augustus gave a free scope to the exercise of his virtues, and the shortness of his reign did not prevent him from establishing a system of toleration of which he left the precept and the example to his son Constantine. His fortunate son, from the first moment of his accession declaring himself the protector of the church, at length deserved the appellation of the first emperor who publicly professed and established the Christian religion. The motives of his conversion, as they may variously be deduced from benevolence, from policy, from conviction, or from remorse, and the progress of the revolution, which, under his powerful influence and that of his sons, rendered Christianity the reigning religion of the Roman empire, will form a very interesting and important chapter in the second volume of this history. At present it may be sufficient to observe that every victory of Constantine was productive of some relief or benefit to the church.

The provinces of Italy and Africa experienced a short but violent persecution. The rigorous edicts of Diocletian were strictly and cheerfully executed by his associate Maximian, who had long hated the Christians, and who delighted in acts of blood and violence. In the autumn of the first year of the persecution the two emperors met at Rome to celebrate their triumph; several oppressive laws appear to have issued from their secret consultations, and the diligence of the magistrates was animated by the presence of their sovereigns. After Diocletian had divested himself of the purple, Italy and Africa were administered under the name of Severus, and were exposed, without defence, to the implacable resentment of his master Galerius. Among the martyrs of Rome, Adauctus deserves the notice of posterity. He was of a noble family in Italy, and had raised himself, through the successive honours of the palace, to the important office of treasurer of the private demesnes. Adauctus is the more remarkable for being the only person of rank and distinction who appears to have suffered death during the whole course of this general persecution.

The revolt of Maxentius immediately restored peace to the churches of Italy and Africa, and the same tyrant who oppressed every other class of his subjects showed himself just, humane, and even partial, towards the afflicted Christians. He depended on their gratitude and affection, and very naturally presumed that the injuries which they had suffered, and the dangers which they still apprehended, from his most inveterate enemy, would secure the fidelity of a party already considerable by their numbers and opulence. Even the conduct of Maxentius towards the bishops of Rome and Carthage may be considered as the proof of his toleration, since it is probable that the most orthodox princes would adopt the same measures with regard to their established clergy. Marcellus, the former of those prelates, had thrown the capital into confusion by the severe penance which he imposed on a great number of Christians who, during the late persecution, had renounced or dissembled their religion. The rage of faction broke out in frequent and violent seditions; the blood of the faithful was shed by each other's hands; and the exile of Marcellus, whose prudence seems to have been less eminent than his zeal, was found to be the only measure capable of restoring peace to the distracted church of Rome. The behaviour of Mensurius, bishop of Carthage, appears to have been still more reprehensible. A deacon of that city had published a libel against the emperor. The offender took refuge in the episcopal palace, and, though it was somewhat early to advance any claims of ecclesiastical immunities, the bishop refused to deliver him up to the officers of justice. For this treasonable resistance Mensurius was summoned to court, and, instead of receiving a legal sentence of death or banishment, he was permitted, after a short examination, to return to his diocese. Such was the happy condition of the Christian subjects of Maxentius, that, whenever they were desirous of procuring for their own use any bodies of martyrs, they were obliged to purchase them from the most distant provinces of the East. A story is related of Algæ, a Roman lady, descended from a consular family, and possessed of so ample an estate that it required the management of seventy-three stewards. Among these Boniface was the favourite of his mistress, and, as Algæ mixed love with devotion, it is reported that he was admitted to share her bed. Her fortune enabled her to gratify the pious desire of obtaining some sacred relics from the East. She intrusted Boniface with a considerable sum of gold and a large quantity of aromatics, and her lover, attended by twelve horsemen and three covered chariots, undertook a remote pilgrimage as far as Tarsus in Cilicia.

The sanguinary temper of Galerius, the first and principal author of the persecution, was formidable to those Christians whom their misfortunes had placed within the limits of his dominions; and it may fairly be presumed that many persons of a middle rank, who were not confined by the chains either of wealth or of poverty, very frequently deserted their native country, and sought a refuge in the milder climate of the West. As long as he commanded only the armies and provinces of Illyricum, he could with difficulty either find or make a considerable number of martyrs in a warlike country which had entertained the missionaries of the Gospel with more coldness and reluctance than any other part of the empire. But when Galerius had obtained the supreme power and the government of the East, he indulged in their fullest extent his zeal and cruelty, not only in the provinces of Thrace and Asia, which acknowledged his immediate jurisdiction, but in those of Syria, Palestine, and Egypt, where Maximian gratified his own inclination by yielding a rigorous obedience to the stern commands of his benefactor.

The frequent disappointments of his ambitious views, the experience of six years of persecution, and the salutary reflections which a lingering and painful distemper suggested to the mind of Galerius, at length convinced him that the most violent efforts of despotism are insufficient to extirpate a whole people, or to subdue their religious prejudices. Desirous of repairing the mischief that he had occasioned, he published in his own name, and in those of Licinius and Constantine, a general edict, which, after a pompous recital of the Imperial titles, proceeded in the following manner:

"Among the important cares which have occupied our mind for the utility and preservation of the empire, it was our intention to correct and re-establish all things according to the ancient laws and public discipline of the Romans. We were particularly desirous of reclaiming into the way of reason and nature the deluded Christians who had renounced the religion and ceremonies instituted by their fathers, and, presumptuously despising the practice of antiquity, had invented extravagant laws and opinions according to the dictates of their fancy, and had collected a various society from the different provinces of our empire. The edicts which we have published to enforce the worship of the gods having exposed many of the Christians to danger and distress, many having suffered death, and many more, who still persist in their impious folly, being left destitute of *any* public exercise of religion, we are disposed to extend to those unhappy men the effects of our wonted clemency. We permit them, therefore, freely to profess their private opinions, and to assemble in their conventicles without fear or molestation, provided always that they preserve a due respect to the established laws and government. By another rescript we shall signify our intentions to the judges and magistrates, and we hope that our indulgence will engage the Christians to offer up their prayers to the Deity whom they adore for our safety and prosperity, for their own, and for that of the republic." It is not usually in the language of edicts and manifestos that we should search for the real character of the secret motives of princes; but as these were the words of a dying emperor, his situation, perhaps, may be admitted as a pledge of his sincerity.

When Galerius subscribed this edict of toleration, he was well assured that Licinius would readily comply with the inclinations of his friend and benefactor, and that any measures in favour of the Christians would obtain the approbation of Constantine. But the emperor would not venture to insert in the preamble the name of Maximian, whose consent was of the greatest importance, and who succeeded a few days afterwards to the provinces of Asia. In the first six months, however, of his new reign, Maximian affected to adopt the prudent counsels of his predecessor; and though he never condescended to secure the tranquillity of the church by a public edict, Sabinus, his Prætorian præfect, addressed a circular letter to all the governors and magistrates of the provinces, expatiating on the Imperial clemency, acknowledging the invincible obstinacy of the Christians, and directing the officers of justice to cease their ineffectual prosecutions, and to connive at the secret assemblies of those enthusiasts. In consequence of these orders, great numbers of Christians were released from prison, or delivered from the mines. The confessors, singing hymns of triumph, returned into their own countries, and those who had yielded to the violence of the tempest, solicited with tears of repentance their re-admission into the bosom of the church.

But this treacherous calm was of short duration; nor

could the Christians of the East place any confidence in the character of their sovereign. Cruelty and superstition were the ruling passions of the soul of Maximian. The former suggested the means, the latter pointed out the objects, of persecution. The emperor was devoted to the worship of the gods, to the study of magic, and to the belief of oracles. The prophets or philosophers, whom he revered as the favourites of Heaven, were frequently raised to the government of provinces, and admitted into his most secret councils. They easily convinced him that the Christians had been indebted for their victories to their regular discipline, and that the weakness of polytheism had principally flowed from a want of union and subordination among the ministers of religion. A system of government was therefore instituted, which was evidently copied from the policy of the church. In all the great cities of the empire, the temples were repaired and beautified by the order of Maximian, and the officiating priests of the various deities were subjected to the authority of a superior pontiff destined to oppose the bishop, and to promote the cause of paganism. These pontiffs acknowledged, in their turn, the supreme jurisdiction of the metropolitans or high priests of the province, who acted as the immediate viceregents of the emperor himself. A white robe was the ensign of their dignity; and these new prelates were carefully selected from the most noble and opulent families. By the influence of the magistrates, and of the sacerdotal order, a great number of dutiful addresses were obtained, particularly from the cities of Nicomedia, Antioch, and Tyre, which artfully represented the well-known intentions of the court as the general sense of the people; solicited the emperor to consult the laws of justice rather than the dictates of his clemency; expressed their abhorrence of the Christians, and humbly prayed that those impious sectaries might at least be excluded from the limits of their respective territories. The answer of Maximian to the address which he obtained from the citizens of Tyre is still extant. He praises their zeal and devotion in terms of the highest satisfaction, descants on the obstinate impiety of the Christians, and betrays, by the readiness with which he consents to their banishment, that he considered himself as receiving, rather than as conferring, an obligation. The priests as well as the magistrates were empowered to enforce the execution of his edicts, which were engraved on tables of brass; and though it was recommended to them to avoid the effusion of blood, the most cruel and ignominious punishments were inflicted on the refractory Christians.

The Asiatic Christians had everything to dread from the severity of a bigoted monarch who prepared his measures of violence with such deliberate policy. But a few months had scarcely elapsed before the edicts published by the two Western emperors obliged Maximian to suspend the prosecution of his designs: the civil war which he so rashly undertook against Licinius employed all his attention; and the defeat and death of Maximian soon delivered the church from the last and most implacable of her enemies.

In this general view of the persecution which was first authorised by the edicts of Diocletian, I have purposely refrained from describing the particular sufferings and deaths of the Christian martyrs. It would have been an easy task, from the history of Eusebius, from the declamations of Lactantius, and from the most ancient acts, to collect a long series of horrid and disgusting pictures, and to fill many pages with racks and scourges, with iron hooks and red-hot beds, and with all the variety of tortures which fire and steel, savage beasts, and more savage executioners, could inflict on the human body. These melancholy scenes might be enlivened by a crowd of visions and miracles destined either to delay the death, to celebrate the triumph, or to discover the relics of those canonised saints who suffered for the name of Christ. But I cannot determine what I ought to transcribe, till I am satisfied how much I ought to believe. The gravest of the ecclesiastical historians, Eusebius himself, indirectly confesses that he has related whatever might redound to the glory, and that he has suppressed all that could tend to the disgrace, of religion. Such an acknowledgment will naturally excite a suspicion that a writer who has so openly violated one of the fundamental laws of history has not paid a very strict regard to the observance of the other; and the suspicion will derive additional credit from the character of Eusebius, which was less tinctured with credulity, and more practised in the arts of courts, than that of almost any of his contemporaries. On some particular occasions, when the magistrates were exasperated by some personal motives of interest or resentment, when the zeal of the martyrs urged them to forget the rules of prudence, and perhaps of decency, to overturn the altars, to pour out imprecations against the emperors, or to strike the judge as he sat on his tribunal, it may be presumed that every mode of torture which cruelty could invent, or constancy could endure, was exhausted on those devoted victims. Two circumstances, however, have been unwarily mentioned, which insinuate that the general treatment of the Christians who had been apprehended by the officers of justice was less intolerable than it is usually imagined to have been. 1. The confessors who were condemned to work in the mines were permitted by the humanity or the negligence of their keepers to build chapels, and freely to profess their religion in the midst of those dreary habitations. 2. The bishops were obliged to check and to censure the forward zeal of the Christians, who voluntarily threw themselves into the hands of the magistrates. Some of these were persons oppressed by poverty and debts, who blindly sought to terminate a miserable existence by a glorious death. Others were allured by the hope that a short confinement would expiate the sins of a whole life; and others again were actuated by the less honourable motive of deriving a plentiful subsistence, and perhaps a considerable profit, from the alms which the charity of the faithful bestowed on the prisoners. After the church had triumphed over all her enemies, the interest as well as vanity of the captives prompted them to magnify the merit of their respective suffering. A convenient distance of time or place gave an ample scope to the progress of fiction; and the frequent instances which might be alleged of holy martyrs whose wounds had been instantly healed, whose strength had been renewed, and whose lost members had miraculously been restored, were extremely convenient for the purpose of removing every difficulty, and of silencing every objection. The most extravagant legends, as they conduced to the honour of the church, were applauded by the credulous multitude, countenanced by the power of the clergy, and attested by the suspicious evidence of ecclesiastical history.

The vague descriptions of exile and imprisonment, of pain and torture, are so easily exaggerated or softened by the pencil of an artful orator, that we are naturally induced to inquire into a fact of a more distinct and stubborn kind; the number of persons who suffered death in consequence of the edicts published by Diocletian, his associates, and his successors. The recent legendaries record whole armies and cities which were at once swept away by the undistinguishing rage of persecution. The more ancient writers content themselves with pouring out a liberal effusion of loose and tragical invectives, without condescending to ascertain the precise number of those persons who were permitted to seal with their blood their belief of the Gospel. From the history of Eusebius it may however be collected that only nine bishops were punished with death; and we are assured, by his particular enumeration of the martyrs of Palestine, that no more than ninety-two Christians were entitled to that honourable appellation. As we are unacquainted with the degree of episcopal zeal and courage which prevailed at that time, it is not in our power to draw any useful inferences from the former of these facts: but the latter may serve to justify a very important and probable conclusion. According to the distribution of Roman provinces, Palestine may be considered as the sixteenth part of the Eastern empire: and since there were some governors who, from a real or affected clemency, had preserved their hands unstained with the blood of the faithful, it is reasonable to believe that the country which had given birth to Christianity produced at least the sixteenth part of the martyrs who suffered death within the dominions of Galerius and Maximian; the whole might consequently amount to about fifteen hundred, a number which, if it is equally divided between the ten years of the persecution, will allow an annual consumption of one hundred and fifty martyrs. Allotting the same proportion to the provinces of Italy, Africa, and perhaps Spain, where, at the end of two or three years, the rigour of the penal laws was either suspended or abolished, the multitude of Christians in the Roman empire, on whom a capital punishment was inflicted by a judicial sentence, will be reduced to somewhat less than two thousand persons. Since it cannot be doubted that the Christians were more numerous, and their enemies more exasperated, in the time of Diocletian than they had ever been in any former persecution, this probable and moderate computation may teach us to estimate the number of primitive saints and martyrs who sacrificed their lives for the important purpose of introducing Christianity into the world.

We shall conclude this chapter by a melancholy truth which obtrudes itself on the reluctant mind; that, even admitting, without hesitation or inquiry, all that history has recorded, or devotion has feigned, on the subject of martyrdoms, it must still be acknowledged that the Christians, in the course of their intestine dissensions, have inflicted far greater severities on each other than they had experienced from the zeal of infidels. During the ages of ignorance which followed the subversion of the Roman empire in the West, the bishops of the Imperial city extended their dominion over the laity as well as clergy of the Latin church. The fabric of superstition which they had erected, and which might long have defied the feeble efforts of reason, was at length assaulted by a crowd of daring fanatics, who, from the twelfth to the sixteenth century, assumed the popular character of reformers. The church of Rome defended by violence the empire which she had acquired by fraud; a system of peace and benevolence was soon disgraced by the proscriptions, wars, massacres, and the institution of the holy office. And as the reformers were animated by the love of civil as well as of religious freedom, the Catholic princes connected their own interest with that of the clergy, and enforced by fire and the sword the terrors of spiritual censures. In the Netherlands alone more than one hundred thousand of the subjects of Charles V are said to have suffered by the hand of the executioner; and this extraordinary number is attested by Grotius, a man of genius and learning, who preserved his moderation amidst the fury of contending sects, and who composed the annals of his own age and country at a time when the invention of printing had facilitated the means of intelligence and increased the danger of detection. If we are obliged to submit our belief to the authority of Grotius, it must be allowed that the number of Protestants who were executed in a single province and a single reign far exceeded that of the primitive martyrs in the space of three centuries and of the Roman empire. But if the improbability of the fact itself should prevail over the weight of evidence; if Grotius should be convicted of exaggerating the merit and sufferings of the reformers; we shall be naturally led to inquire what confidence can be placed in the doubtful and imperfect monuments of ancient credulity; what degree of credit can be assigned to a courtly bishop and a passionate declaimer, who, under the protection of Constantine, enjoyed the exclusive privilege of recording the persecutions inflicted on the Christians by the vanquished rivals or disregarded predecessors of their gracious sovereign.

4. The Rise of Monasticism

[*In chapter XXXVI Gibbon describes "the origins, progress, and effects of the monastic life." He admits that it is there "delayed"; for convenience of arrangement I have here brought it forward.*]

Prosperity and peace introduced the distinction of the *vulgar* and the *Ascetic Christians*. The loose and imperfect practice of religion satisfied the conscience of the multitude. The prince or magistrate, the soldier or merchant, reconciled their fervent zeal and implicit faith with the exercise of their profession, the pursuit of their interest, and the indulgence of their passions: but the Ascetics, who obeyed and abused the rigid precepts of the Gospel, were inspired by the savage enthusiasm which represents man as a criminal, and God as a tyrant. They seriously renounced the business and the pleasures of the age; abjured the use of wine, of flesh, and of marriage; chastised their body, mortified their affections, and embraced a life of misery, as the price of eternal happiness. In the reign of Constantine the Ascetics fled from a profane and degenerate world to perpetual solitude or religious society. Like the first Christians of Jerusalem, they resigned the use or the property of their temporal possessions; established regular communities of the same sex and a similar disposition; and assumed the names of *Hermits, Monks*, and *Anachorets*, expressive of their lonely retreat in a natural or artificial desert. They soon acquired the respect of the world, which they despised; and the loudest applause was bestowed on this DIVINE PHILOSOPHY, which surpassed, without the aid of science or reason, the laborious virtues of the Grecian schools. The monks might indeed con-

tend with the Stoics in the contempt of fortune, of pain,
and of death: the Pythagorean silence and submission
were revived in their servile discipline; and they disdained as firmly as the Cynics themselves all the forms
and decencies of civil society. But the votaries of this
Divine Philosophy aspired to imitate a purer and more
perfect model. They trod in the footsteps of the prophets,
who had retired to the desert; and they restored the devout and contemplative life, which had been instituted
by the Essenians in Palestine and Egypt. The philosophic eye of Pliny had surveyed with astonishment a
solitary people, who dwelt among the palm-trees near
the Dead Sea; who subsisted without money; who were
propagated without women; and who derived from the
disgust and repentance of mankind a perpetual supply
of voluntary associates.

Egypt, the fruitful parent of superstition, afforded the
first example of the monastic life. Antony, an illiterate
youth of the lower parts of Thebais, distributed his patrimony, deserted his family and native home, and executed
his *monastic* penance with original and intrepid fanaticism. After a long and painful novitiate among the
tombs and in a ruined tower, he boldly advanced into
the desert three days' journey to the eastward of the
Nile; discovered a lonely spot, which possessed the advantages of shade and water; and fixed his last residence
on Mount Colzim, near the Red Sea, where an ancient
monastery still preserves the name and memory of the
saint. The curious devotion of the Christians pursued him
to the desert; and when he was obliged to appear at
Alexandria, in the face of mankind, he supported his
fame with discretion and dignity. He enjoyed the friendship of Athanasius, whose doctrine he approved; and
the Egyptian peasant respectfully declined a respectful
invitation from the emperor Constantine. The venerable
patriarch (for Antony attained the age of one hundred
and five years) beheld the numerous progeny which had
been formed by his example and his lessons. The pro-
lific colonies of monks multiplied with rapid increase
on the sands of Libya, upon the rocks of Thebais, and
in the cities of the Nile. To the south of Alexandria, the

mountain, and adjacent desert, of Nitria was peopled by five thousand anachorets; and the traveller may still investigate the ruins of fifty monasteries, which were planted in that barren soil by the disciples of Antony. In the Upper Thebais, the vacant island of Tabenne was occupied by Pachomius and fourteen hundred of his brethren. That holy abbot successively founded nine monasteries of men, and one of women; and the festival of Easter sometimes collected fifty thousand religious persons, who followed his *angelic* rule of discipline. The stately and populous city of Oxyrinchus, the seat of Christian orthodoxy, had devoted the temples, the public edifices, and even the ramparts, to pious and charitable uses; and the bishop, who might preach in twelve churches, computed ten thousand females, and twenty thousand males, of the monastic profession. The Egyptians, who gloried in this marvellous revolution, were disposed to hope, and to believe, that the number of the monks was equal to the remainder of the people; and posterity might repeat the saying which had formerly been applied to the sacred animals of the same country, that in Egypt it was less difficult to find a god than a man.

Athanasius introduced into Rome the knowledge and practice of the monastic life; and a school of this new philosophy was opened by the disciples of Antony, who accompanied their primate to the holy threshold of the Vatican. The strange and savage appearance of these Egyptians excited, at first, horror and contempt, and, at length, applause and zealous imitation. The senators, and more especially the matrons, transformed their palaces and villas into religious houses; and the narrow institution of *six* Vestals was eclipsed by the frequent monasteries, which were seated on the ruins of ancient temples and in the midst of the Roman forum. Inflamed by the example of Antony, a Syrian youth, whose name was Hilarion,[1] fixed his dreary abode on a sandy beach

---

[1] See the Life of Hilarion, by St. Jerom. The stories of Paul, Hilarion, and Malchus, by the same author, are admirably told; and the only defect of these pleasing compositions is the want of truth and common sense.

between the sea and a morass, about seven miles from Gaza. The austere penance, in which he persisted forty-eight years, diffused a similar enthusiasm; and the holy man was followed by a train of two or three thousand anachorets, whenever he visited the innumerable monasteries of Palestine. The fame of Basil is immortal in the monastic history of the East. With a mind that had tasted the learning and eloquence of Athens; with an ambition scarcely to be satisfied by the archbishopric of Cæsarea, Basil retired to a savage solitude in Pontus; and deigned, for a while, to give laws to the spiritual colonies which he profusely scattered along the coast of the Black Sea. In the West, Martin of Tours, a soldier, a hermit, a bishop, and a saint, established the monasteries of Gaul; two thousand of his disciples followed him to the grave; and his eloquent historian challenges the deserts of Thebais to produce, in a more favourable climate, a champion of equal virtue. The progress of the monks was not less rapid or universal than that of Christianity itself. Every province, and, at last, every city, of the empire was filled with their increasing multitudes; and the bleak and barren isles, from Lerins to Lipari, that arise out of the Tuscan Sea, were chosen by the anachorets for the place of their voluntary exile. An easy and perpetual intercourse by sea and land connected the provinces of the Roman world; and the life of Hilarion displays the facility with which an indigent hermit of Palestine might traverse Egypt, embark for Sicily, escape to Epirus, and finally settle in the island of Cyprus. The Latin Christians embraced the religious institutions of Rome. The pilgrims who visited Jerusalem eagerly copied, in the most distant climates of the earth, the faithful model of the monastic life. The disciples of Antony spread themselves beyond the tropic, over the Christian empire of Æthiopia. The monastery of Banchor, in Flintshire, which contained above two thousand brethren, dispersed a numerous colony among the barbarians of Ireland; and Iona, one of the Hebrides, which was planted by the Irish monks, diffused over the northern regions a doubtful ray of science and superstition.[2]

---

[2] This small though not barren spot, Iona, Hy, or Columbkill,

These unhappy exiles from social life were impelled by the dark and implacable genius of superstition. Their mutual resolution was supported by the example of millions, of either sex, of every age, and of every rank; and each proselyte who entered the gates of a monastery was persuaded that he trod the steep and thorny path of eternal happiness. But the operation of these religious motives was variously determined by the temper and situation of mankind. Reason might subdue, or passion might suspend, their influence; but they acted most forcibly on the infirm minds of children and females; they were strengthened by secret remorse or accidental misfortune; and they might derive some aid from the temporal considerations of vanity or interest. It was naturally supposed that the pious and humble monks, who had renounced the world to accomplish the work of their salvation, were the best qualified for the spiritual government of the Christians. The reluctant hermit was torn from his cell, and seated, amidst the acclamations of the people, on the episcopal throne: the monasteries of Egypt, of Gaul, and of the East, supplied a regular succession of saints and bishops; and ambition soon discovered the secret road which led to the possession of wealth and honours. The popular monks, whose reputation was connected with the fame and success of the order, assiduously laboured to multiply the number of their fellow-captives. They insinuated themselves into noble and opulent families; and the specious arts of flattery and seduction were employed to secure those proselytes who might bestow wealth or dignity on the monastic profession. The indignant father bewailed the loss, perhaps, of an only son; the credulous maid was betrayed by vanity to violate the laws of nature; and the matron aspired to imaginary perfection by renouncing the virtues of domestic life. Paula yielded to the persuasive eloquence of Jerom; and the profane title of mother-in-law of God tempted that

only two miles in length and one mile in breadth, has been distinguished—1. By the monastery of St. Columba, founded A.D. 566, whose abbot exercised an extraordinary jurisdiction over the bishops of Caledonia; 2. By a *classic* library, which afforded some hopes of an entire Livy; and, 3. By the tombs of sixty kings, Scots, Irish, and Norwegians, who reposed in holy ground.

illustrious widow to consecrate the virginity of her daughter Eustochium. By the advice, and in the company, of her spiritual guide, Paula abandoned Rome and her infant son; retired to the holy village of Bethlem; founded an hospital and four monasteries; and acquired, by her alms and penance, an eminent and conspicuous station in the catholic church. Such rare and illustrious penitents were celebrated as the glory and example of their age; but the monasteries were filled by a crowd of obscure and abject plebeians, who gained in the cloister much more than they had sacrificed in the world. Peasants, slaves, and mechanics might escape from poverty and contempt to a safe and honourable profession, whose apparent hardships were mitigated by custom, by popular applause, and by the secret relaxation of discipline. The subjects of Rome, whose persons and fortunes were made responsible for unequal and exorbitant tributes, retired from the oppression of the Imperial government; and the pusillanimous youth preferred the penance of a monastic, to the dangers of a military, life. The affrighted provincials of every rank, who fled before the barbarians, found shelter and subsistence; whole legions were buried in these religious sanctuaries; and the same cause which relieved the distress of individuals impaired the strength and fortitude of the empire.

The monastic profession of the ancients was an act of voluntary devotion. The inconstant fanatic was threatened with eternal vengeance of the God whom he deserted; but the doors of the monastery were still open for repentance. Those monks whose conscience was fortified by reason or passion were at liberty to resume the character of men and citizens; and even the spouses of Christ might accept the legal embraces of an earthly lover. The examples of scandal, and the progress of superstition, suggested the propriety of more forcible restraints. After a sufficient trial, the fidelity of the novice was secured by a solemn and perpetual vow; and his irrevocable engagement was ratified by the laws of the church and state. A guilty fugitive was pursued, arrested, and restored to his perpetual prison; and the interposition of the magistrate oppressed the freedom and merit which had alleviated, in some degree, the abject slavery of the monastic discipline. The actions of a monk, his words, and even his thoughts, were determined by an inflexible rule or a capricious superior: the slightest offences were corrected by disgrace or confinement, extraordinary fasts, or bloody flagellation; and disobedience, murmur, or delay were ranked in the catalogue of the most heinous sins.[3] A blind submission to the commands of the abbot, however absurd, or even criminal, they might seem, was the ruling principle, the first virtue of the Egyptian monks; and their patience was frequently exercised by the most extravagant trials. They were directed to remove an enormous rock; assiduously to water a barren staff that was planted in the ground, till, at the end of three years, it should vegetate and blossom like a tree; to walk into a fiery furnace; or to cast their infant into a deep pond: and several saints, or madmen, have been immortalised in monastic story by their thoughtless and fearless obedience. The freedom of the mind, the source of every generous and rational sentiment, was destroyed by the habits of credulity and submission; and the monk, contracting the vices of a slave, devoutly followed the faith and passions of his ecclesiastical tyrant. The peace of the Eastern church was invaded by a swarm of fanatics, incapable of fear, or reason, or humanity; and the Imperial troops acknowledged, without shame, that they were much less apprehensive of an encounter with the fiercest barbarians.

Superstition has often framed and consecrated the fantastic garments of the monks: but their apparent singularity sometimes proceeds from their uniform attachment to a simple and primitive model, which the revolutions of fashion have made ridiculous in the eyes

---

[3] The rule of Columbanus, so prevalent in the West, inflicts one hundred lashes for very slight offences. Before the time of Charlemagne the abbots indulged themselves in mutilating their monks, or putting out th ir eyes—a punishment much less cruel than the tremendous *vade in pace* (the subterraneous dungeon, or sepulchre), which was af. r invented. See an admirable discourse of the learned Mabillon, who, on this occasion, seems to be inspired by the g niu of ait . For such an effort, I can forgive his defence of the holy tear of Vendome.

of mankind. The father of the Benedictines expressly disclaims all idea of choice or merit; and soberly exhorts his disciples to adopt the coarse and convenient dress of the countries which they may inhabit. The monastic habits of the ancients varied with the climate and their mode of life; and they assumed, with the same indifference, the sheepskin of the Egyptian peasants or the cloak of the Grecian philosophers. They allowed themselves the use of linen in Egypt, where it was a cheap and domestic manufacture; but in the West they rejected such an expensive article of foreign luxury. It was the practice of the monks either to cut or shave their hair; they wrapped their heads in a cowl, to escape the sight of profane objects; their legs and feet were naked, except in the extreme cold of winter; and their slow and feeble steps were supported by a long staff. The aspect of a genuine anachoret was horrid and disgusting: every sensation that is offensive to man was thought acceptable to God; and the angelic rule of Tabenne condemned the salutary custom of bathing the limbs in water and of anointing them with oil. The austere monks slept on the ground, on a hard mat or a rough blanket; and the same bundle of palm-leaves served them as a seat in the day and a pillow in the night. Their original cells were low narrow huts, built of the slightest materials; which formed, by the regular distribution of the streets, a large and populous village, enclosing, within the common wall, a church, a hospital, perhaps a library, some necessary offices, a garden, and a fountain or reservoir of fresh water. Thirty or forty brethren composed a family of separate discipline and diet; and the great monasteries of Egypt consisted of thirty or forty families.

Pleasure and guilt are synonymous terms in the language of the monks, and they had discovered, by experience, that rigid fasts and abstemious diet are the most effectual preservatives against the impure desires of the flesh. The rules of abstinence which they imposed, or practised, were not uniform or perpetual: the cheerful festival of the Pentecost was balanced by the extraordinary mortification of Lent; the fervour of new monasteries was insensibly relaxed; and the voracious appetite of the Gauls could not imitate the patient and temperate virtue of the Egyptians. The disciples of Antony and Pachomius were satisfied with their daily pittance[4] of twelve ounces of bread, or rather biscuit, which they divided into two frugal repasts, of the afternoon and of the evening. It was esteemed a merit, and almost a duty, to abstain from the boiled vegetables which were provided for the refectory; but the extraordinary bounty of the abbot sometimes indulged them with the luxury of cheese, fruit, salad, and the small dried fish of the Nile. A more ample latitude of sea and river fish was gradually allowed or assumed; but the use of flesh was long confined to the sick or travellers: and when it gradually prevailed in the less rigid monasteries of Europe, a singular distinction was introduced; as if birds, whether wild or domestic, had been less profane than the grosser animals of the field. Water was the pure and innocent beverage of the primitive monks; and the founder of the Benedictines regrets the daily portion of half a pint of wine which had been extorted from him by the intemperance of the age. Such an allowance might be easily supplied by the vineyards of Italy; and his victorious disciples, who passed the Alps, the Rhine, and the Baltic, required, in the place of wine, an adequate compensation of strong beer or cider.

The candidate who aspired to the virtue of evangelical poverty, abjured, at his first entrance into a regular community, the idea, and even the name, of all separate or exclusive possession. The brethren were supported by their manual labour; and the duty of labour was strenuously recommended as a penance, as an exercise, and as the most laudable means of securing their daily subsistence. The garden and fields, which the industry of the monks had often rescued from the forest or the morass, were diligently cultivated by their hands. They performed, without reluctance, the menial offices of slaves and domestics; and the several trades that were necessary to provide their habits, their utensils, and their

---

[4] "Those who drink only water, and have no nutritious liquor, ought at least to have a pound and a half (*twenty-four ounces*) of bread every day." State of Prisons, p. 40, by Mr. Howard.

lodging, were exercised within the precincts of the great monasteries. The monastic studies have tended, for the most part, to darken, rather than to dispel, the cloud of superstition. Yet the curiosity or zeal of some learned solitaries has cultivated the ecclesiastical and even the profane sciences: and posterity must gratefully acknowledge that the monuments of Greek and Roman literature have been preserved and multiplied by their indefatigable pens. But the more humble industry of the monks, especially in Egypt, was contented with the silent, sedentary occupation of making wooden sandals, or of twisting the leaves of the palm-tree into mats and baskets. The superfluous stock, which was not consumed in domestic use, supplied, by trade, the wants of the community: the boats of Tabenne, and the other monasteries of Thebais, descended the Nile as far as Alexandria; and, in a Christian market, the sanctity of the workmen might enhance the intrinsic value of the work.

But the necessity of manual labour was insensibly superseded. The novice was tempted to bestow his fortune on the saints in whose society he was resolved to spend the remainder of his life; and the pernicious indulgence of the laws permitted him to receive, for their use, any future accessions of legacy or inheritance. Melania contributed her plate, three hundred pounds' weight of silver, and Paula contracted an immense debt for the relief of their favourite monks, who kindly imparted the merits of their prayers and penance to a rich and liberal sinner. Time continually increased, and accidents could seldom diminish, the estates of the popular monasteries, which spread over the adjacent country and cities: and, in the first century of their institution, the infidel Zosimus has maliciously observed, that, for the benefit of the poor, the Christian monks had reduced a great part of mankind to a state of beggary. As long as they maintained their original fervour, they approved themselves, however, the faithful and benevolent stewards of the charity which was intrusted to their care. But their discipline was corrupted by prosperity: they gradually assumed the pride of wealth, and at last indulged the luxury of expense. Their public luxury might be excused by the magnificence of religious worship, and the decent motive of erecting durable habitations for an immortal society. But every age of the church has accused the licentiousness of the degenerate monks; who no longer remembered the object of their institution, embraced the vain and sensual pleasures of the world which they had renounced, and scandalously abused the riches which had been acquired by the austere virtues of their founders.[5] Their natural descent, from such painful and dangerous virtue, to the common vices of humanity, will not, perhaps, excite much grief or indignation in the mind of a philosopher.

The lives of the primitive monks were consumed in penance and solitude, undisturbed by the various occupations which fill the time, and exercise the faculties, of reasonable, active, and social beings. Whenever they were permitted to step beyond the precincts of the monastery, two jealous companions were the mutual guards and spies of each other's actions; and, after their return, they were condemned to forget, or, at least, to suppress, whatever they had seen or heard in the world. Strangers, who professed the orthodox faith, were hospitably entertained in a separate apartment; but their dangerous conversation was restricted to some chosen elders of approved discretion and fidelity. Except in their presence, the monastic slave might not receive the visits of his friends or kindred; and it was deemed highly meritorious, if he afflicted a tender sister, or an aged parent, by the obstinate refusal of a word or look.[6] The monks themselves passed their lives, without personal attachments, among a crowd which had been formed by accident, and was detained, in the same prison, by force or prejudice. Recluse fanatics have few ideas or sentiments to communicate: a special licence of the abbot regulated the

---

[5] I have somewhere heard or read the frank confession of a Benedictine abbot: "My vow of poverty has given me an hundred thousand crowns a year; my vow of obedience has raised me to the rank of a sovereign prince." I forget the consequences of his vow of chastity.

[6] Pior, an Egyptian monk, allowed his sister to see him; but he shut his eyes during the whole visit. Many such examples might be added.

time and duration of their familiar visits; and, at their silent meals, they were enveloped in their cowls, inaccessible, and almost invisible, to each other. Study is the resource of solitude; but education had not prepared and qualified for any liberal studies the mechanics and peasants who filled the monastic communities. They might work; but the vanity of spiritual perfection was tempted to disdain the exercise of manual labour; and the industry must be faint and languid which is not excited by the sense of personal interest.

According to their faith and zeal, they might employ the day, which they passed in their cells, either in vocal or mental prayer: they assembled in the evening, and they were awakened in the night, for the public worship of the monastery. The precise moment was determined by the stars, which are seldom clouded in the serene sky of Egypt; and a rustic horn, or trumpet, the signal of devotion, twice interrupted the vast silence of the desert. Even sleep, the last refuge of the unhappy, was rigorously measured: the vacant hours of the monk heavily rolled along, without business or pleasure; and, before the close of each day, he had repeatedly accused the tedious progress of the sun. In this comfortless state, superstition still pursued and tormented her wretched votaries. The repose which they had sought in the cloister was disturbed by tardy repentance, profane doubts, and guilty desires; and, while they considered each natural impulse as an unpardonable sin, they perpetually trembled on the edge of a flaming and bottomless abyss. From the painful struggles of disease and despair, these unhappy victims were sometimes relieved by madness or death; and, in the sixth century, a hospital was founded at Jerusalem for a small portion of the austere penitents who were deprived of their senses. Their visions, before they attained this extreme and acknowledged term of frenzy, have afforded ample materials of supernatural history. It was their firm persuasion that the air which they breathed was peopled with invisible enemies; with innumerable dæmons, who watched every occasion, and assumed every form, to terrify, and above all to tempt, their unguarded virtue. The imagination, and even the senses, were deceived by the illusions of distempered fanaticism; and the hermit, whose midnight prayer was oppressed by involuntary slumber, might easily confound the phantoms of horror or delight which had occupied his sleeping and his waking dreams.

The monks were divided into two classes: the *Cœnobites*, who lived under a common and regular discipline; and the *Anachorets*, who indulged their unsocial, independent fanaticism. The most devout, or the most ambitious, of the spiritual brethren renounced the convent, as they had renounced the world. The fervent monasteries of Egypt, Palestine, and Syria were surrounded by a *Laura*, a distant circle of solitary cells; and the extravagant penance of the Hermits was stimulated by applause and emulation. They sunk under the painful weight of crosses and chains; and their emaciated limbs were confined by collars, bracelets, gauntlets, and greaves of massy and rigid iron. All superfluous incumbrance of dress they contemptuously cast away; and some savage saints of both sexes have been admired, whose naked bodies were only covered by their long hair. They aspired to reduce themselves to the rude and miserable state in which the human brute is scarcely distinguished above his kindred animals; and the numerous sect of Anachorets derived their name from their humble practice of grazing in the fields of Mesopotamia with the common herd. They often usurped the den of some wild beast whom they affected to resemble; they buried themselves in some gloomy cavern, which art or nature had scooped out of the rock; and the marble quarries of Thebais are still inscribed with the monuments of their penance. The most perfect Hermits are supposed to have passed many days without food, many nights without sleep, and many years without speaking; and glorious was the *man* (I abuse that name) who contrived any cell, or seat, of a peculiar construction, which might expose him, in the most inconvenient posture, to the inclemency of the seasons.

Among these heroes of the monastic life, the name and genius of Simeon Stylites have been immortalised by the singular invention of an aërial penance. At the age of thirteen the young Syrian deserted the profession of a shepherd, and threw himself into an austere monastery. After a long and painful novitiate, in which Simeon was repeatedly saved from pious suicide, he established his residence on a mountain, about thirty or forty miles to the east of Antioch. Within the space of a *mandra*, or circle of stones, to which he had attached himself by a ponderous chain, he ascended a column, which was successively raised from the height of nine, to that of sixty, feet from the ground. In this last and lofty station, the Syrian Anachoret resisted the heat of thirty summers, and the cold of as many winters. Habit and exercise instructed him to maintain his dangerous situation without fear or giddiness, and successively to assume the different postures of devotion. He sometimes prayed in an erect attitude, with his outstretched arms in the figure of a cross; but his most familiar practice was that of bending his meagre skeleton from the forehead to the feet; and a curious spectator, after numbering twelve hundred and forty-four repetitions, at length desisted from the endless account. The progress of an ulcer in his thigh[7] might shorten, but it could not disturb, this *celestial* life; and the patient Hermit expired without descending from his column. A prince, who should capriciously inflict such tortures, would be deemed a tyrant; but it would surpass the power of a tyrant to impose a long and miserable existence on the reluctant victims of his cruelty. This voluntary martyrdom must have gradually destroyed the sensibility both of the mind and body; nor can it be presumed that the fanatics who torment themselves are susceptible of any lively affection for the rest of mankind. A cruel, unfeeling temper has distinguished the monks of every age and country: their stern indifference, which is seldom mollified by personal friendship, is inflamed by religious hatred; and their

---

[7] I must not conceal a piece of ancient scandal concerning the origin of this ulcer. It has been reported that the Devil, assuming an angelic form, invited him to ascend, like Elijah, into a fiery chariot. The saint too hastily raised his foot, and Satan seized the moment of inflicting this chastisement on his vanity.

merciless zeal has strenuously administered the holy office of the Inquisition.

The monastic saints, who excite only the contempt and pity of a philosopher, were respected and almost adored by the prince and people. Successive crowds of pilgrims from Gaul and India saluted the divine pillar of Simeon; the tribes of Saracens disputed in arms the honour of his benediction; the queens of Arabia and Persia gratefully confessed his supernatural virtue; and the angelic Hermit was consulted by the younger Theodosius in the most important concerns of the church and state. His remains were transported from the mountain of Telenissa, by a solemn procession of the patriarch, the master-general of the East, six bishops, twenty-one counts or tribunes, and six thousand soldiers; and Antioch revered his bones as her glorious ornament and impregnable defence. The fame of the apostles and martyrs was gradually eclipsed by these recent and popular Anachorets; the Christian world fell prostrate before their shrines; and the miracles ascribed to their relics exceeded, at least in number and duration, the spiritual exploits of their lives. But the golden legend of their lives was embellished by the artful credulity of their interested brethren; and a believing age was easily persuaded that the slightest caprice of an Egyptian or a Syrian monk had been sufficient to interrupt the eternal laws of the universe. The favourites of Heaven were accustomed to cure inveterate diseases with a touch, a word, or a distant message; and to expel the most obstinate dæmons from the souls or bodies which they possessed. They familiarly accosted, or imperiously commanded, the lions and serpents of the desert; infused vegetation into a sapless trunk; suspended iron on the surface of the water; passed the Nile on the back of a crocodile; and refreshed themselves in a fiery furnace. These extravagant tales, which display the fiction, without the genius, of poetry, have seriously affected the reason, the faith, and the morals of the Christians. Their credulity debased and vitiated the faculties of the mind: they corrupted the evidence of history; and superstition gradually extinguished the hostile light of philosophy and science. Every mode of religious worship which had been practised by the saints, every mysterious doctrine which they believed, was fortified by the sanction of divine revelation, and all the manly virtues were oppressed by the servile and pusillanimous reign of the monks. If it be possible to measure the interval between the philosophic writings of Cicero and the sacred legend of Theodoret, between the character of Cato and that of Simeon, we may appreciate the memorable revolution which was accomplished in the Roman empire within a period of five hundred years.

Nerva had scarcely accepted the purple from the assassins of Domitian before he discovered that his feeble age was unable to stem the torrent of public disorders, which had multiplied under the long tyranny of his predecessor. His mild disposition was respected by the good; but the degenerate Romans required a more vigorous character, whose justice should strike terror into the guilty. Though he had several relations, he fixed his choice on a stranger. He adopted Trajan, then about forty years of age, and who commanded a powerful army in the Lower Germany; and immediately, by a decree of the senate, declared him his colleague and successor in the empire. It is sincerely to be lamented, that whilst we are fatigued with the disgustful relation of Nero's crimes and follies, we are reduced to collect the actions of Trajan from the glimmerings of an abridgment, or the doubtful light of a panegyric. There remains, however, one panegyric far removed beyond the suspicion of flattery. Above two hundred and fifty years after the death of Trajan, the senate, in pouring out the customary acclamations on the accession of a new emperor, wished that he might surpass the felicity of Augustus, and the virtue of Trajan.

We may readily believe, that the father of his country hesitated whether he ought to intrust the various and doubtful character of his kinsman Hadrian with sovereign power. In his last moments, the arts of the empress Plotina either fixed the irresolution of Trajan, or boldly supposed a fictitious adoption; the truth of which could not be safely disputed, and Hadrian was peaceably acknowledged as his lawful successor. Under his reign, as has been already mentioned, the empire flourished in peace and prosperity. He encouraged the arts, reformed the laws, asserted military discipline, and visited all his provinces in person. His vast and active genius was equally suited to the most enlarged views, and the minute details of civil policy. But the ruling passions of his soul were curiosity and vanity. As they prevailed, and as they were attracted by different objects, Hadrian was, by turns, an excellent prince, a ridiculous sophist, and a jealous tyrant. The general tenor of his conduct deserved praise for its equity and moderation. Yet in the first days of his reign, he put to death four consular senators, his personal enemies, and men who had been judged worthy of empire; and the tediousness of a painful illness rendered him, at last, peevish and cruel. The senate doubted whether they should pronounce him a god or a tyrant; and the honours decreed to his memory were granted to the prayers of the pious Antoninus.

The caprice of Hadrian influenced his choice of a successor. After revolving in his mind several men of distinguished merit, whom he esteemed and hated, he adopted Ælius Verus, a gay and voluptuous nobleman, recommended by uncommon beauty to the lover of Antinous.[8] But while Hadrian was delighting himself with his own applause, and the acclamations of the soldiers, whose consent had been secured by an immense donative, the new Cæsar was ravished from his embraces by an untimely death. He left only one son. Hadrian commended the boy to the gratitude of the Antonines. He was adopted by Pius; and, on the accession of Marcus, was invested with an equal share of sovereign power. Among the many vices of this younger Verus he possessed one virtue; a dutiful reverence for his wiser colleague, to whom he willingly abandoned the ruder cares of empire. The philosophic emperor dissembled his follies, lamented his early death, and cast a decent veil over his memory.

---

[8] The deification of Antinous, his medals, statues, temples, city, oracles, and constellation, are well known, and still dishonour the memory of Hadrian. Yet we may remark, that of the first fifteen emperors, Claudius was the only one whose taste in love was entirely correct.

As soon as Hadrian's passion was either gratified or disappointed, he resolved to deserve the thanks of posterity, by placing the most exalted merit on the Roman throne. His discerning eye easily discovered a senator about fifty years of age, blameless in all the offices of life, and a youth of about seventeen, whose riper years opened the fair prospect of every virtue: the elder of these was declared the son and successor of Hadrian, on condition, however, that he himself should immediately adopt the younger. The two Antonines (for it is of them that we are now speaking) governed the Roman world forty-two years, with the same invariable spirit of wisdom and virtue. Although Pius had two sons,[9] he preferred the welfare of Rome to the interest of his family, gave his daughter Faustina in marriage to young Marcus, obtained from the senate the tribunitian and proconsular powers, and with a noble disdain, or rather ignorance of jealousy, associated him to all the labours of government. Marcus, on the other hand, revered the character of his benefactor, loved him as a parent, obeyed him as his sovereign, and, after he was no more, regulated his own administration by the example and maxims of his predecessor. Their united reigns are possibly the only period of history in which the happiness of a great people was the sole object of government.

Titus Antoninus Pius has been justly denominated a second Numa. The same love of religion, justice, and peace, was the distinguishing characteristic of both princes. But the situation of the latter opened a much larger field for the exercise of those virtues. Numa could only prevent a few neighbouring villages from plundering each other's harvests. Antoninus diffused order and tranquillity over the greatest part of the earth. His reign is marked by the rare advantage of furnishing very few materials for history; which is, indeed, little more than the register of the crimes, follies, and misfortunes of mankind. In private life, he was an amiable as well as a good man. The native simplicity of his virtue was a stranger to vanity or affectation. He enjoyed with modera-

---

[9] Without the help of medals and inscriptions we should be ignorant of this fact, so honourable to the memory of Pius.

tion the conveniencies of his fortune, and the innocent pleasures of society: and the benevolence of his soul displayed itself in a cheerful serenity of temper.

The virtue of Marcus Aurelius Antoninus was of a severer and more laborious kind. It was the well-earned harvest of many a learned conference, of many a patient lecture, and many a midnight lucubration. At the age of twelve years he embraced the rigid system of the Stoics, which taught him to submit his body to his mind, his passions to his reason; to consider virtue as the only good, vice as the only evil, all things external as things indifferent. His meditations, composed in the tumult of a camp, are still extant; and he even condescended to give lessons of philosophy in a more public manner than was perhaps consistent with the modesty of a sage, or the dignity of an emperor. But his life was the noblest commentary on the precepts of Zeno. He was severe to himself, indulgent to the imperfections of others, just and beneficent to all mankind. He regretted that Avidius Cassius, who excited a rebellion in Syria, had disappointed him, by a voluntary death, of the pleasure of converting an enemy into a friend; and he justified the sincerity of that sentiment, by moderating the zeal of the senate against the adherents of the traitor. War he detested, as the disgrace and calamity of human nature; but when the necessity of a just defence called upon him to take up arms, he readily exposed his person to eight winter campaigns on the frozen banks of the Danube, the severity of which was at last fatal to the weakness of his constitution. His memory was revered by a grateful posterity, and above a century after his death, many persons preserved the image of Marcus Antoninus, among those of their household gods.

If a man were called to fix the period in the history of the world, during which the condition of the human race was most happy and prosperous, he would, without hesitation, name that which elapsed from the death of Domitian to the accession of Commodus. The vast extent of the Roman empire was governed by absolute power, under the guidance of virtue and wisdom. The armies were restrained by the firm but gentle hand of four succesive emperors, whose characters and authority commanded involuntary respect. The forms of the civil administration were carefully preserved by Nerva, Trajan, Hadrian, and the Antonines, who delighted in the image of liberty, and were pleased with considering themselves as the accountable ministers of the laws. Such princes deserved the honour of restoring the republic had the Romans of their days been capable of enjoying a rational freedom.

The labours of these monarchs were overpaid by the immense reward that inseparably waited on their success; by the honest pride of virtue, and by the exquisite delight of beholding the general happiness of which they were the authors. A just, but melancholy reflection embittered, however, the noblest of human enjoyments. They must often have recollected the instability of a happiness which depended on the character of a single man. The fatal moment was perhaps approaching, when some licentious youth, or some jealous tyrant, would abuse, to the destruction, that absolute power which they had exerted for the benefit of their people. The ideal restraints of the senate and the laws might serve to display the virtues, but could never correct the vices, of the emperor. The military force was a blind and irresistible instrument of oppression; and the corruption of Roman manners would always supply flatterers eager to applaud, and ministers prepared to serve the fear or the avarice, the lust or the cruelty, of their masters.

5. The Foundation of Constantinople

[Diocletian had reorganised the Empire; Con-
stantine, who ultimately succeeded to his power
and policy, drew two important conclusions from
the work of his predecessor. He came to terms with
Christianity, which Diocletian had persecuted;
and he completed Diocletian's administrative re-
distribution by founding a new capital, Con-
stantinople. In chapter XVII Gibbon describes
the foundation of this "new Rome" which was to
continue the name of the Roman Empire, and
part of its substance, for a thousand years after
the collapse of the old Rome, itself now a thousand
years old.]

After the defeat and abdication of Licinius his victorious rival proceeded to lay the foundations of a city
destined to reign in future times the mistress of the
East, and to survive the empire and religion of Constantine. The motives, whether of pride or of policy, which
first induced Diocletian to withdraw himself from the
ancient seat of government, had acquired additional
weight by the example of his successors and the habits
of forty years. Rome was insensibly confounded with the
dependent kingdoms which had once acknowledged her
supremacy; and the country of the Cæsars was viewed
with cold indifference by a martial prince, born in the
neighbourhood of the Danube, educated in the courts
and armies of Asia, and invested with the purple by the
legions of Britain. The Italians, who had received Constantine as their deliverer, submissively obeyed the edicts
which he sometimes condescended to address to the

senate and people of Rome; but they were seldom honoured with the presence of their new sovereign. During the vigour of his age Constantine, according to the various exigencies of peace and war, moved with slow dignity or with active diligence along the frontiers of his extensive dominions; and was always prepared to take the field either against a foreign or a domestic enemy. But as he gradually reached the summit of prosperity and the decline of life, he began to meditate the design of fixing in a more permanent station the strength as well as majesty of the throne. In the choice of an advantageous situation he preferred the confines of Europe and Asia; to curb with a powerful arm the barbarians who dwelt between the Danube and the Tanais; to watch with an eye of jealousy the conduct of the Persian monarch, who indignantly supported the yoke of an ignominious treaty. With these views Diocletian had selected and embellished the residence of Nicomedia: but the memory of Diocletian was justly abhorred by the protector of the church; and Constantine was not insensible to ambition of founding a city which might perpetuate the glory of his own name. During the late operations of the war against Licinius he had sufficient opportunity to contemplate, both as a soldier and as a statesman, the incomparable position of Byzantium; and to observe how strongly it was guarded by nature against an hostile attack, whilst it was accessible on every side to the benefits of commercial intercourse. Many ages before Constantine, one of the most judicious historians of antiquity had described the advantages of a situation from whence a feeble colony of Greeks derived the command of the sea, and the honours of a flourishing and independent republic.

If we survey Byzantium in the extent which it acquired with the august name of Constantinople, the figure of the Imperial city may be represented under that of an unequal triangle. The obtuse point, which advances towards the east and the shores of Asia, meets and repels the waves of the Thracian Bosphorus. The northern side of the city is bounded by the harbour, and the southern is washed by the Propontis or Sea of Marmora. The basis

185

of the triangle is opposed to the west, and terminates the continent of Europe. But the admirable form and division of the circumjacent land and water cannot, without a more ample explanation, be clearly or sufficiently understood.

The winding channel through which the waters of the Euxine flow with a rapid and incessant course towards the Mediterranean received the appellation of Bosphorus, a name not less celebrated in the history than in the fables of antiquity. A crowd of temples and of votive altars, profusely scattered along its steep and woody banks, attested the unskilfulness, the terrors, and the devotion of the Grecian navigators who, after the example of the Argonauts, explored the dangers of the inhospitable Euxine. On these banks tradition long preserved the memory of the palace of Phineus, infested by the obscene harpies;[1] and of the sylvan reign of Amycus, who defied the son of Leda to the combat of the Cestus.[2] The straits of the Bosphorus are terminated by the Cyanean rocks, which, according to the description of the poets, had once floated on the face of the waters, and were destined by the gods to protect the entrance of the Euxine against the eye of profane curiosity. From the Cyanean rocks to the point and harbour of Byzantium the winding length of the Bosphorus extends about sixteen miles, and its most ordinary breadth may be computed at about one mile and a half. The *new* castles of Europe and Asia are constructed, on either continent, upon the foundations of two celebrated temples, of Serapis and of Jupiter Urius. The *old* castles, a work of the Greek emperors, command the narrowest part of the channel, in a place where the opposite banks advance within five hundred paces of each other. These fortresses were restored and strengthened by Mahomet the Second when he meditated the siege of Constantinople: but the Turkish conqueror was most

---

[1] There are very few conjectures so happy as that of Le Clerc who supposes that the harpies were only locusts. The Syriac or Phœnician name of those insects, their noisy flight, the stench and devastation which they occasion, and the north wind which drives them into the sea, all contribute to form the striking resemblance.

[2] [*Cestus*—the ancient boxing glove. *Ed.*]

probably ignorant that, near two thousand years before his reign, Darius had chosen the same situation to connect the two continents by a bridge of boats. At a small distance from the old castles we discover the little town of Chrysopolis, or Scutari, which may almost be considered as the Asiatic suburb of Constantinople. The Bosphorus, as it begins to open into the Propontis, passes between Byzantium and Chalcedon. The latter of those cities was built by the Greeks a few years before the former; and the blindness of its founders, who overlooked the superior advantages of the opposite coast, has been stigmatised by a proverbial expression of contempt.

The harbour of Constantinople, which may be considered as an arm of the Bosphorus, obtained, in a very remote period, the denomination of the *Golden Horn*. The curve which it describes might be compared to the horn of a stag, or as it should seem, with more propriety, to that of an ox. The epithet of *golden* was expressive of the riches which every wind wafted from the most distant countries into the secure and capacious port of Constantinople. The river Lycus, formed by the conflux of two little streams, pours into the harbour a perpetual supply of fresh water, which serves to cleanse the bottom and to invite the periodical shoals of fish to seek their retreat in that convenient recess. As the vicissitudes of tides are scarcely felt in those seas, the constant depth of the harbour allows goods to be landed on the quays without the assistance of boats; and it has been observed that, in many places, the largest vessels may rest their prows against the houses while their sterns are floating in the water. From the mouth of the Lycus to that of the harbour this arm of the Bosphorus is more than seven miles in length. The entrance is about five hundred yards broad, and a strong chain could be occasionally drawn across it to guard the port and city from the attack of an hostile navy.

Between the Bosphorus and the Hellespont, the shores of Europe and Asia receding on either side inclose the Sea of Marmora, which was known to the ancients by the denomination of Propontis. The navigation from the issue of the Bosphorus to the entrance of the Hellespont

187

is about one hundred and twenty miles. Those who steer their westward course through the middle of the Propontis may at once descry the high lands of Thrace and Bithynia, and never lose sight of the lofty summit of Mount Olympus, covered with eternal snows. They leave on the left a deep gulf, at the bottom of which Nicomedia was seated, the imperial residence of Diocletian; and they pass the small islands of Cyzicus and Proconnesus before they cast anchor at Gallipoli, where the sea, which separates Asia from Europe, is again contracted into a narrow channel.

The geographers who, with the most skilful accuracy, have surveyed the form and extent of the Hellespont, assign about sixty miles for the winding course, and about three miles for the ordinary breadth, of those celebrated straits. But the narrowest part of the channel is found to the northward of the old Turkish castles, between the cities of Sestus and Abydus. It was here that the adventurous Leander braved the passage of the flood for the possession of his mistress. It was here likewise, in a place where the distance between the opposite banks cannot exceed five hundred paces, that Xerxes imposed a stupendous bridge of boats, for the purpose of transporting into Europe a hundred and seventy myriads of barbarians. A sea contracted within such narrow limits may seem but ill to deserve the singular epithet of *broad*, which Homer, as well as Orpheus, has frequently bestowed on the Hellespont. But our ideas of greatness are of a relative nature: the traveller, and especially the poet, who sailed along the Hellespont, who pursued the windings of the stream, and contemplated the rural scenery, which appeared on every side to terminate the prospect, insensibly lost the remembrance of the sea; and his fancy painted those celebrated straits with all the attributes of a mighty river, flowing with a swift current, in the midst of a woody and inland country, and at length, through a wide mouth, discharging itself into the Ægean or Archipelago. Ancient Troy, seated on an eminence at the foot of Mount Ida, overlooked the mouth of the Hellespont, which scarcely received an accession of waters from the tribute of those immortal rivulets the Simois and Scamander. The Grecian camp had stretched twelve miles along the shore, from the Sigean to the Rhœtean promontory; and the flanks of the army were guarded by the bravest chiefs who fought under the banners of Agamemnon. The first of those promontories was occupied by Achilles with his invincible myrmidons, and the dauntless Ajax pitched his tents on the other. After Ajax had fallen a sacrifice to his disappointed pride and to the ingratitude of the Greeks, his sepulchre was erected on the ground where he had defended the navy against the rage of Jove and of Hector; and the citizens of the rising town of Rhœteum celebrated his memory with divine honours. Before Constantine gave a just preference to the situation of Byzantium, he had conceived the design of erecting the seat of empire on this celebrated spot, from whence the Romans derived their fabulous origin. The extensive plain which lies below ancient Troy, towards the Rhœtean promontory and the tomb of Ajax, was first chosen for his new capital; and, though the undertaking was soon relinquished, the stately remains of unfinished walls and towers attracted the notice of all who sailed through the straits of the Hellespont.

We are at present qualified to view the advantageous position of Constantinople, which appears to have been formed by nature for the centre and capital of a great monarchy. Situated in the forty-first degree of latitude, the Imperial city commanded, from her seven hills, the opposite shores of Europe and Asia; the climate was healthy and temperate, the soil fertile, the harbour secure and capacious, and the approach on the side of the continent was of small extent and easy defence. The Bosphorus and the Hellespont may be considered as the two gates of Constantinople, and the prince who possessed those important passages could always shut them against a naval enemy and open them to the fleets of commerce. The preservation of the eastern provinces may, in some degree, be ascribed to the policy of Constantine, as the barbarians of the Euxine, who in the preceding age had poured their armaments into the heart of the Mediterranean, soon desisted from the exercise of piracy, and despaired of forcing this insurmountable barrier. When the gates of the Hellespont and Bosphorus were shut, the capital still enjoyed within their spacious enclosure every production which could supply the wants or gratify the luxury of its numerous inhabitants. The sea-coasts of Thrace and Bithynia, which languish under the weight of Turkish oppression, still exhibit a rich prospect of vineyards, of gardens, and of plentiful harvests; and the Propontis has ever been renowned for an inexhaustible store of the most exquisite fish, that are taken in their stated seasons, without skill, and almost without labour. But when the passages of the straits were thrown open for trade, they alternately admitted the natural and artificial riches of the north and south, of the Euxine and of the Mediterranean. Whatever rude commodities were collected in the forests of Germany and Scythia, as far as the sources of the Tanais and the Borysthenes; whatsoever was manufactured by the skill of Europe or Asia; the corn of Egypt, and the gems and spices of the farthest India, were brought by the varying winds into the port of Constantinople, which, for many ages, attracted the commerce of the ancient world.

The prospect of beauty, of safety, and of wealth, united in a single spot, was sufficient to justify the choice of Constantine. But as some decent mixture of prodigy and fable has, in every age, been supposed to reflect a becoming majesty on the origin of great cities, the emperor was desirous of ascribing his resolution not so much to the uncertain counsels of human policy as to the infallible and eternal decrees of divine wisdom. In one of his laws he has been careful to instruct posterity that, in obedience to the commands of God, he laid the everlasting foundations of Constantinople; and though he has not condescended to relate in what manner the celestial inspiration was communicated to his mind, the defect of his modest silence has been liberally supplied by the ingenuity of succeeding writers, who describe the nocturnal vision which appeared to the fancy of Constantine as he slept within the walls of Byzantium. The tutelar genius of the city, a venerable matron sinking under the weight of years and infirmities, was suddenly transformed into a blooming maid, whom his own hands adorned with all the symbols of Imperial greatness. The monarch awoke, interpreted the auspicious omen, and obeyed, without hesitation, the will of Heaven. The day which gave birth to a city or colony was celebrated by the Romans with such ceremonies as had been ordained by a generous superstition; and though Constantine might omit some rites which savoured too strongly of their Pagan origin, yet he was anxious to leave a deep impression of hope and respect on the minds of the spectators. On foot, with a lance in his hand, the emperor himself led the solemn procession, and directed the line which was traced as the boundary of the destined capital, till the growing circumference was observed with astonishment by the assistants, who, at length, ventured to observe that he had already exceeded the most ample measure of the great city. "I shall still advance," replied Constantine, "till HE, the invisible guide who marches before me, thinks proper to stop." Without presuming to investigate the nature or motives of this extraordinary conductor, we shall content ourselves with the more humble task of describing the extent and limits of Constantinople.

In the actual state of the city, the palace and gardens of the Seraglio occupy the eastern promontory, the first of the seven hills, and cover about one hundred and fifty acres of our own measure. The seat of Turkish jealousy and despotism is erected on the foundations of a Grecian republic; but it may be supposed that the Byzantines were tempted by the conveniency of the harbour to extend their habitations on that side beyond the modern limits of the Seraglio. The new walls of Constantine stretched from the port to the Propontis across the enlarged breadth of the triangle, at the distance of fifteen stadia from the ancient fortification, and with the city of Byzantium they enclosed five of the seven hills which, to the eyes of those who approach Constantinople, appear to rise above each other in beautiful order. About a century after the death of the founder, the new buildings, extending on one side up the harbour, and on the other along the Propontis, already covered the narrow ridge of the sixth and the broad summit of the seventh hill. The necessity of protecting those suburbs from the incessant inroads of the barbarians engaged the younger Theodosius to surround his capital with an adequate and permanent enclosure of walls. From the eastern promontory to the golden gate, the extreme length of Constantinople was about three Roman miles, the circumference measured between ten and eleven, and the surface might be computed as equal to about two thousand English acres. It is impossible to justify the vain and credulous exaggerations of modern travellers, who have sometimes stretched the limits of Constantinople over the adjacent villages of the European and even of the Asiatic coast. But the suburbs of Pera and Galata, though situated beyond the harbour, may deserve to be considered as a part of the city; and this addition may perhaps authorise the measure of a Byzantine historian, who assigns sixteen Greek (about fourteen Roman) miles for the circumference of his native city. Such an extent may seem not unworthy of an Imperial residence. Yet Constantinople must yield to Babylon and Thebes, to ancient Rome, to London, and even to Paris.

The master of the Roman world, who aspired to erect an eternal monument of the glories of his reign, could employ in the prosecution of that great work the wealth, the labour, and all that yet remained of the genius, of obedient millions. Some estimate may be formed of the expense bestowed with Imperial liberality on the foundation of Constantinople by the allowance of about two millions five hundred thousand pounds for the construction of the walls, the porticoes, and the aqueducts. The forests that overshadowed the shores of the Euxine, and the celebrated quarries of white marble in the little island of Proconnesus, supplied an inexhaustible stock of materials, ready to be conveyed, by the convenience of a short water-carriage, to the harbour of Byzantium. A multitude of labourers and artificers urged the conclusion of the work with incessant toil; but the impatience of Constantine soon discovered that, in the decline of the arts, the skill as well as numbers of his architects bore a very unequal proportion to the greatness of his designs.

The magistrates of the most distant provinces were there-fore directed to institute schools, to appoint professors, and, by the hopes of rewards and privileges, to engage in the study and practice of architecture a sufficient num-ber of ingenious youths who had received a liberal educa-tion. The buildings of the new city were executed by such artificers as the reign of Constantine could afford; but they were decorated by the hands of the most cele-brated masters of the age of Pericles and Alexander. To revive the genius of Phidias and Lysippus surpassed in-deed the power of a Roman emperor; but the immortal productions which they had bequeathed to posterity were exposed without defence to the rapacious vanity of a despot. By his commands the cities of Greece and Asia were despoiled of their most valuable ornaments. The trophies of memorable wars, the objects of religious veneration, the most finished statues of the gods and heroes, of the sages and poets of ancient times, contrib-uted to the splendid triumph of Constantinople; and gave occasion to the remark of the historian Cedrenus, who observes, with some enthusiasm, that nothing seemed wanting except the souls of the illustrious men whom these admirable monuments were intended to represent. But it is not in the city of Constantine, nor in the declining period of an empire, when the human mind was depressed by civil and religious slavery, that we should seek for the souls of Homer and of Demos-thenes.

During the siege of Byzantium the conqueror had pitched his tent on the commanding eminence of the second hill. To perpetuate the memory of his success, he chose the same advantageous position for the principal Forum, which appears to have been of a circular or rather elliptical form. The two opposite entrances formed triumphal arches; the porticoes, which enclosed it on every side, were filled with statues, and the centre of the Forum was occupied by a lofty column, of which a mutilated fragment is now degraded by the appellation of the *burnt pillar*. This column was erected on a pedes-tal of white marble twenty feet high, and was composed of ten pieces of porphyry, each of which measured about ten feet in height, and about thirty-three in circumference. On the summit of the pillar, above one hundred and twenty feet from the ground, stood the colossal statue of Apollo. It was of bronze, had been transported either from Athens or from a town of Phrygia, and was supposed to be the work of Phidias. The artist had represented the god of day, or, as it was afterwards interpreted, the emperor Constantine himself, with a sceptre in his right hand, the globe of the world in his left, and a crown of rays glittering on his head. The Circus, or Hippodrome, was a stately building about four hundred paces in length, and one hundred in breadth. The space between the two *metæ* or goals was filled with statues and obelisks; and we may still remark a very singular fragment of antiquity, the bodies of three serpents twisted into one pillar of brass. Their triple heads had once supported the golden tripod which, after the defeat of Xerxes, was consecrated in the temple of Delphi by the victorious Greeks. The beauty of the Hippodrome has been long since defaced by the rude hands of the Turkish conquerors, but, under the similar appellation of Atmeidan, it still serves as a place of exercise for their horses. From the throne, whence the emperor viewed the Circensian games, a winding staircase descended to the palace; a magnificent edifice, which scarcely yielded to the residence of Rome itself, and which, together with the dependent courts, gardens, and porticoes, covered a considerable extent of ground upon the banks of the Propontis, between the Hippodrome and the church of St. Sophia. We might likewise celebrate the baths, which still retained the name of Zeuxippus, after they had been enriched by the munificence of Constantine, with lofty columns, various marbles, and above threescore statues of bronze. But we should deviate from the design of this history if we attempted minutely to describe the different buildings or quarters of the city. It may be sufficient to observe that whatever could adorn the dignity of a great capital, or contribute to the benefit or pleasure of its numerous inhabitants, was contained within the walls of Constantinople. A particular description, composed about a century after its foundation, enumerates a capitol or school of learning, a circus, two theatres, eight public and one hundred and fifty-three private baths, fifty-two porticoes, five granaries, eight aqueducts or reservoirs of water, four spacious halls for the meetings of the senate or courts of justice, fourteen churches, fourteen palaces, and four thousand three hundred and eighty-eight houses which, for their size or beauty, deserved to be distinguished from the multitude of plebeian habitations.

The populousness of his favoured city was the next and most serious object of the attention of its founder. In the dark ages which succeeded the translation of the empire, the remote and the immediate consequences of that memorable event were strangely confounded by the vanity of the Greeks and the credulity of the Latins. It was asserted and believed that all the noble families of Rome, the senate, and the equestrian order, with their innumerable attendants, had followed their emperor to the banks of the Propontis; that a spurious race of strangers and plebeians was left to possess the solitude of the ancient capital; and that the lands of Italy, long since converted into gardens, were at once deprived of cultivation and inhabitants. In the course of this history such exaggerations will be reduced to their just value; yet, since the growth of Constantinople cannot be ascribed to the general increase of mankind and of industry, it must be admitted that this artificial colony was raised at the expense of the ancient cities of the empire. Many opulent senators of Rome and of the eastern provinces were probably invited by Constantine to adopt for their country the fortunate spot which he had chosen for his own residence. The invitations of a master are scarcely to be distinguished from commands, and the liberality of the emperor obtained a ready and cheerful obedience. He bestowed on his favourites the palaces which he had built in the several quarters of the city, assigned them lands and pensions for the support of their dignity, and alienated the demesnes of Pontus and Asia to grant hereditary estates by the easy tenure of maintaining a house in the capital. But these encouragements and obligations soon became superfluous, and were gradually abolished. Wherever the seat of government is fixed, a considerable part of the public revenue will be expended by the prince himself, by his ministers, by the officers of justice, and by the domestics of the palace. The most wealthy of the provincials will be attracted by the powerful motives of interest and duty, of amusement and curiosity. A third and more numerous class of inhabitants will insensibly be formed, of servants, of artificers, and of merchants, who derive their subsistence from their own labour, and from the wants or luxury of the superior ranks. In less than a century Constantinople disputed with Rome itself the pre-eminence of riches and numbers. New piles of buildings, crowded together with too little regard to health or convenience, scarcely allowed the intervals of narrow streets for the perpetual throng of men, of horses, and of carriages. The allotted space of ground was insufficient to contain the increasing people, and the additional foundations, which on either side were advanced into the sea, might alone have composed a very considerable city.

The frequent and regular distributions of wine and oil, of corn or bread, of money or provisions, had almost exempted the poorer citizens of Rome from the necessity of labour. The magnificence of the first Cæsars was in some measure imitated by the founder of Constantinople: but his liberality, however it might excite the applause of the people, has incurred the censure of posterity. A nation of legislators and conquerors might assert their claim to the harvests of Africa, which had been purchased with their blood; and it was artfully contrived by Augustus, that, in the enjoyment of plenty, the Romans should lose the memory of freedom. But the prodigality of Constantine could not be excused by any consideration either of public or private interest; and the annual tribute of corn imposed upon Egypt for the benefit of his new capital was applied to feed a lazy and insolent populace, at the expense of the husbandmen of an industrious province. Some other regulations of this emperor are less liable to blame, but they are less deserving of notice. He divided Constantinople into fourteen regions or quarters, dignified the public council with the appellation of senate, communicated to the citizens the privileges of Italy, and bestowed on the rising city the title of Colony, the first and most favoured daughter of ancient Rome. The venerable parent still maintained the legal and acknowledged supremacy, which was due to her age, to her dignity, and to the remembrance of her former greatness.

As Constantine urged the progress of the work with the impatience of a lover, the walls, the porticoes, and the principal edifices were completed in a few years, or, according to another account, in a few months: but this extraordinary diligence should excite the less admiration, since many of the buildings were finished in so hasty and imperfect a manner, that, under the succeeding reign, they were preserved with difficulty from impending ruin. But while they displayed the vigour and freshness of youth, the founder prepared to celebrate the dedication of his city. The games and largesses which crowned the pomp of this memorable festival may easily be supposed; but there is one circumstance of a more singular and permanent nature, which ought not entirely to be overlooked. As often as the birthday of the city returned, the statue of Constantine, framed by his order, of gilt wood, and bearing in its right hand a small image of the genius of the place, was erected on a triumphal car. The guards, carrying white tapers, and clothed in their richest apparel, accompanied the solemn procession as it moved through the Hippodrome. When it was opposite to the throne of the reigning emperor, he rose from his seat, and with grateful reverence adored the memory of his predecessor. At the festival of the dedication, an edict, engraved on a column of marble, bestowed the title of SECOND or NEW ROME on the city of Constantine. But the name of Constantinople has prevailed over that honourable epithet, and after the revolution of fourteen centuries still perpetuates the fame of its author.

The foundation of a new capital is naturally connected with the establishment of a new form of civil and military administration. The distinct view of the complicated system of policy introduced by Diocletian, improved by Constantine, and completed by his immediate successors, may not only amuse the fancy by the singular picture of a great empire, but will tend to illustrate the secret and internal causes of its rapid decay. In the pursuit of any remarkable institution, we may be frequently led into the more early or the more recent times of the Roman history; but the proper limits of this inquiry will be included within a period of about one hundred and thirty years, from the accession of Constantine to the publication of the Theodosian code; from which, as well as from the *Notitia* of the East and West, we derive the most copious and authentic information of the state of the empire. This variety of objects will suspend, for some time, the course of the narrative; but the interruption will be censured only by those readers who are insensible to the importance of laws and manners, while they peruse, with eager curiosity, the transient intrigues of a court, or the accidental event of a battle.

The manly pride of the Romans, content with substantial power, had left to the vanity of the East the forms and ceremonies of ostentatious greatness. But when they lost even the semblance of those virtues which were derived from their ancient freedom, the simplicity of Roman manners was insensibly corrupted by the stately affectation of the courts of Asia. The distinctions of personal merit and influence, so conspicuous in a republic, so feeble and obscure under a monarchy, were abolished by the despotism of the emperors; who substituted in their room a severe subordination of rank and office, from the titled slaves who were seated on the steps of the throne, to the meanest instruments of arbitrary power. This multitude of abject dependents was interested in the support of the actual government, from the dread of a revolution which might at once confound their hopes and intercept the reward of their services. In this divine hierarchy (for such it is frequently styled) every rank was marked with the most scrupulous exactness, and its dignity was displayed in a variety of trifling and solemn ceremonies, which it was a study to learn, and a sacrilege to neglect. The purity of the Latin language was debased, by adopting, in the intercourse of pride and flattery, a profusion of epithets which Tully would scarcely have understood, and which Augustus would have rejected with indignation. The principal officers of the empire were saluted, even by the sovereign himself, with the deceitful titles of your *Sincerity*, your *Gravity*, your *Excellency*, your *Eminence*, your *sublime and wonderful Magnitude*, your *illustrious and magnificent Highness*. The codicils or patents of their office were curiously emblazoned with such emblems as were best adapted to explain its nature and high dignity—the image or portrait of the reigning emperors; a triumphal car; the book of mandates placed on a table, covered with a rich carpet, and illuminated by four tapers; the allegorical figures of the provinces which they governed; or the appellations and standards of the troops whom they commanded. Some of these official ensigns were really exhibited in their hall of audience; others preceded their pompous march whenever they appeared in public; and every circumstance of their demeanour, their dress, their ornaments, and their train, was calculated to inspire a deep reverence for the representatives of supreme majesty. By a philosophic observer the system of the Roman government might have been mistaken for a splendid theatre, filled with players of every character and degree, who repeated the language, and imitated the passions, of their original model.

6. Julian the Apostle and the Pagan Reaction

[*For three-quarters of a century, the heirs and successors of Constantine struggled to maintain the reorganised, Christianised empire against the onslaughts of barbarians, Persians, heretics, and usurpers. Only one of them, Constantine's nephew Julian, educated in the old philosophy, sought to reject both the new religion and the new despotism and to return to the paganism and stoic virtue of the Antonines. In chapters XXXII and XXXIII Gibbon describes, first, the political reforms of Julian, then his attempt to restore paganism in the Empire.*]

Julian was not insensible of the advantages of freedom. From his studies he had imbibed the spirit of ancient sages and heroes; his life and fortunes had depended on the caprice of a tyrant; and, when he ascended the throne, his pride was sometimes mortified by the reflection that the slaves who would not dare to censure his defects were not worthy to applaud his virtues. He sincerely abhorred the system of oriental despotism which Diocletian, Constantine, and the patient habits of fourscore years, had established in the empire. A motive of superstition prevented the execution of the design which Julian had frequently meditated, of relieving his head from the weight of a costly diadem; but he absolutely refused the title of *Dominus* or *Lord,* a word which was grown so familiar to the ears of the Romans, that they no longer remembered its servile and humiliating origin. The office, or rather the name, of consul was cherished by a prince who contemplated with reverence the ruins of the republic; and the same behaviour which had been assumed by the prudence of Augustus was adopted by Julian from choice and inclination. On the calends of January, at break of day, the new consuls, Mamertinus and Nevitta, hastened to the palace to salute the emperor. As soon as he was informed of their approach, he leaped from his throne, eagerly advanced to meet them, and compelled the blushing magistrates to receive the demonstrations of his affected humility. From the palace they proceeded to the senate. The emperor, on foot, marched before their litters, and the gazing multitude admired the image of ancient times, or secretly blamed a conduct which, in their eyes, degraded the majesty of the purple. But the behaviour of Julian was uniformly supported. During the games of the Circus, he had, imprudently or designedly, performed the manumission of a slave in the presence of the consul. The moment he was reminded that he had trespassed on the jurisdiction of *another* magistrate, he condemned himself to pay a fine of ten pounds of gold, and embraced this public occasion of declaring to the world that he was subject, like the rest of his fellow-citizens, to the laws, and even to the forms, of the republic. The spirit of his administration, and his regard for the place of his nativity, induced Julian to confer on the senate of Constantinople the same honours, privileges, and authority which were still enjoyed by the senate of ancient Rome. A legal fiction was introduced and gradually established, that one half of the national council had migrated into the East, and the despotic successors of Julian, accepting the title of Senators, acknowledged themselves the members of a respectable body which was permitted to represent the majesty of the Roman name. From Constantinople the attention of the monarch was extended to the municipal senates of the provinces. He abolished, by repeated edicts, the unjust and pernicious exemptions which had withdrawn so many idle citizens from the service of their country; and by imposing an equal distribution of public duties, he restored the strength, the splendour, or, according to the glowing expression of Libanius, the soul of the expiring cities of his empire. The venerable age of Greece excited the most tender compassion in the mind of Julian, which kindled into rapture when he recollected the gods, the heroes, and the men superior to heroes and to gods, who had bequeathed to the latest posterity the monuments of their genius or the example of their virtues. He relieved the distress and restored the beauty of the cities of Epirus and Peloponnesus. Athens acknowledged him for her benefactor, Argos for her deliverer. The pride of Corinth, again rising from her ruins with the honours of a Roman colony, exacted a tribute from the adjacent republics for the purpose of defraying the games of the Isthmus, which were celebrated in the amphitheatre with the hunting of bears and panthers. From this tribute the cities of Elis, of Delphi, and of Argos, which had inherited from their remote ancestors the sacred office of perpetuating the Olympic, the Pythian, and the Nemean games, claimed a just exemption. The immunity of Elis and Delphi was respected by the Corinthians, but the poverty of Argos tempted the insolence of oppression, and the feeble complaints of its deputies were silenced by the decree of a provincial magistrate, who seems to have consulted only the interest of the capital in which he resided. Seven years after the sentence Julian allowed the cause to be referred to a superior tribunal, and his eloquence was interposed, most probably with success, in the defence of a city which had been the royal seat of Agamemnon, and had given to Macedonia a race of kings and conquerors.

The laborious administration of military and civil affairs, which were multiplied in proportion to the extent of the empire, exercised the abilities of Julian; but he frequently assumed the two characters of Orator and of Judge, which are almost unknown to the modern sovereigns of Europe. The arts of persuasion, so diligently cultivated by the first Cæsars, were neglected by the military ignorance and Asiatic pride of their successors, and, if they condescended to harangue the soldiers, whom they feared, they treated with silent disdain the senators, whom they despised. The assemblies of the senate, which Constantius had avoided, were considered by Julian as the place where he could exhibit with the most propriety the maxims of a republican and the talents of a rhetorician. He alternately practised, as in a school of declamation, the several modes of praise, of censure, of exhortation; and his friend Libanius has remarked that the study of Homer taught him to imitate the simple, concise style of Menelaus, the copiousness of Nestor, whose words descended like the flakes of a winter's snow, or the pathetic and forcible eloquence of Ulysses. The functions of a judge, which are sometimes incompatible with those of a prince, were exercised by Julian not only as a duty, but as an amusement; and although he might have trusted the integrity and discernment of his Prætorian præfects, he often placed himself by their side on the seat of judgment. The acute penetration of his mind was agreeably occupied in detecting and defeating the chicanery of the advocates, who laboured to disguise the truth of facts and to pervert the sense of the laws. He sometimes forgot the gravity of his station, asked indiscreet or unseasonable questions, and betrayed, by the loudness of his voice and the agitation of his body, the earnest vehemence with which he maintained his opinion against the judges, the advocates, and their clients. But his knowledge of his own temper prompted him to encourage, and even to solicit, the reproof of his friends and ministers: and whenever they ventured to oppose the irregular sallies of his passions, the spectators could observe the shame as well as the gratitude of their monarch. The decrees of Julian were almost always founded on the principles of justice, and he had the firmness to resist the two most dangerous temptations which assault the tribunal of a sovereign under the specious forms of compassion and equity. He decided the merits of the cause without weighing the circumstances of the parties; and the poor, whom he wished to relieve, were condemned to satisfy the just demands of a noble and wealthy adversary. He carefully distinguished the judge from the legislator; and though he meditated a necessary reformation of the Roman jurisprudence, he pronounced sentence according to the strict and literal interpretation of those laws which the magistrates were bound to execute and the subjects to obey.

The generality of princes, if they were stripped of their purple and cast naked into the world, would immediately sink to the lowest rank of society, without a hope of emerging from their obscurity. But the personal merit of Julian was, in some measure, independent of his fortune. Whatever had been his choice of life, by the force of intrepid courage, lively wit, and intense application, he would have obtained, or at least he would have deserved, the highest honours of his profession, and Julian might have raised himself to the rank of minister or general of the state in which he was born a private citizen. If the jealous caprice of power had disappointed his expectations; if he had prudently declined the paths of greatness, the employment of the same talents in studious solitude would have placed beyond the reach of kings his present happiness and his immortal fame. When we inspect with minute, or perhaps malevolent, attention the portrait of Julian, something seems wanting to the grace and perfection of the whole figure. His genius was less powerful and sublime than that of Cæsar, nor did he possess the consummate prudence of Augustus. The virtues of Trajan appear more steady and natural, and the philosophy of Marcus is more simple and consistent. Yet Julian sustained adversity with firmness, and prosperity with moderation. After an interval of one hundred and twenty years from the death of Alexander Severus, the Romans beheld an emperor who made no distinction between his duties and his pleasures, who laboured to relieve the distress and to revive the spirit of his subjects, and who endeavoured always to connect authority with merit, and happiness with virtue. Even faction, and religious faction, was constrained to acknowledge the superiority of his genius in peace as well as in war, and to confess, with a sigh, that the apostate Julian was a lover of his country, and that he deserved the empire of the world.

The character of Apostate has injured the reputation of Julian; and the enthusiasm which clouded his virtues has exaggerated the real and apparent magnitude of his faults. Our partial ignorance may represent him as a philosophic monarch, who studied to protect, with an equal hand, the religious factions of the empire, and to allay the theological fever which had inflamed the minds of the people from the edicts of Diocletian to the exile of Athanasius. A more accurate view of the character and conduct of Julian will remove this favourable prepossession for a prince who did not escape the general contagion of the times. We enjoy the singular advantage of comparing the pictures which have been delineated by his fondest admirers and his implacable enemies. The actions of Julian are faithfully related by a judicious and candid historian, the impartial spectator of his life and death. The unanimous evidence of his contemporaries is confirmed by the public and private declarations of the emperor himself; and his various writings express the uniform tenor of his religious sentiments, which policy would have prompted him to dissemble rather than to affect. A devout and sincere attachment for the gods of Athens and Rome constituted the ruling passion of Julian; the powers of an enlightened understanding were betrayed and corrupted by the influence of superstitious prejudice; and the phantoms which existed only in the mind of the emperor had a real and pernicious effect on the government of the empire. The vehement zeal of the Christians, who despised the worship, and overturned the altars, of those fabulous deities, engaged their votary in a state of irreconcilable hostility with a very numerous party of his subjects; and he was sometimes tempted, by the desire of victory or the shame of a repulse, to violate the laws of prudence, and even of justice. The triumph of the party which he deserted and opposed has fixed a stain of infamy on the name of Julian; and the unsuccessful apostate has been overwhelmed with a torrent of pious invectives, of which the signal was given by the sonorous trumpet of Gregory Nazianzen. The interesting nature of the events which were crowded into the short reign of this active emperor deserves a just and circumstantial narrative. His motive, his counsels, and his actions, as far as they are connected with the history of religion, will be the subject of the present chapter.

The cause of his strange and fatal apostasy may be derived from the early period of his life when he was left an orphan in the hands of the murderers of his family.[1] The names of Christ and of Constantius, the ideas of slavery and of religion, were soon associated in a youthful imagination, which was susceptible of the most lively impressions. The care of his infancy was intrusted to Eusebius, bishop of Nicomedia, who was related to him on the side of his mother; and till Julian reached the twentieth year of his age, he received from his Christian preceptors the education not of a hero but of a saint. The emperor, less jealous of a heavenly than of an earthly crown, contented himself with the imperfect character of a catechumen, while he bestowed the advantages of baptism on the nephews of Constantine. They were even admitted to the inferior offices of the ecclesiastical order; and Julian publicly read the Holy Scriptures in the church of Nicomedia. The study of religion, which they assiduously cultivated, appeared to produce the fairest fruits of faith and devotion.[2] They prayed, they fasted, they distributed alms to the poor, gifts to the clergy, and oblations to the tombs of the martyrs; and the splendid monument of St. Mamas, at Cæsarea, was erected, or at least was undertaken, by the joint labour of Gallus and Julian. They respectfully conversed with the bishops who were eminent for superior sanctity, and solicited the benediction of the monks and hermits who had introduced into Cappadocia the voluntary hardships of the ascetic life. As the two princes advanced towards the years of manhood, they discovered, in their religious sentiments, the difference of their characters. The dull and obstinate understanding of Gallus embraced, with implicit zeal, the doctrines of Chris-

---

[1] [On the death of Constantine, his son Constantius II secured his power by a general massacre of his collateral kinsmen, of whom only Julian and his brother Gallus survived. Ed.]

[2] See his Christian, and even ecclesiastical education, in Gregory, Socrates, and Sozomen. He escaped very narrowly from being a bishop, and perhaps a saint.

tianity, which never influenced his conduct, or moderated his passions. The mild disposition of the younger brother was less repugnant to the precepts of the Gospel; and his active curiosity might have been gratified by a theological system which explains the mysterious essence of the Deity, and opens the boundless prospect of invisible and future worlds. But the independent spirit of Julian refused to yield the passive and unresisting obedience which was required, in the name of religion, by the haughty ministers of the church. Their speculative opinions were imposed as positive laws, and guarded by the terrors of eternal punishments; but while they prescribed the rigid formulary of the thoughts, the words, and the actions of the young prince, whilst they silenced his objections, and severely checked the freedom of his inquiries, secretly provoked his impatient genius to disclaim the authority of his ecclesiastical guides. He was educated in the Lesser Asia, amidst the scandals of the Arian controversy. The fierce contests of the Eastern bishops, the incessant alterations of their creeds, and the profane motives which appeared to actuate their conduct, insensibly strengthened the prejudice of Julian that they neither understood nor believed the religion for which they so fiercely contended. Instead of listening to the proofs of Christianity with that favourable attention which adds weight to the most respectable evidence, he heard with suspicion, and disputed with obstinacy and acuteness, the doctrines for which he already entertained an invincible aversion. Whenever the young princes were directed to compose declamations on the subject of the prevailing controversies, Julian always declared himself the advocate of Paganism, under the specious excuse that, in the defence of the weaker cause, his learning and ingenuity might be more advantageously exercised and displayed. . . .

[*From scepticism Julian proceeded to anti-Christian faith. At the age of twenty he was initiated into the Eleusinian mysteries in a cave at Ephesus. But he prudently concealed his views during the reign of his cousin Constantius.*]

The dissimulation of Julian lasted above ten years, from his secret initiation of Ephesus at the beginning of the civil war; when he declared himself at once the implacable enemy of Christ and of Constantius. This state of constraint might contribute to strengthen his devotion; and as soon as he had satisfied the obligation of assisting, on solemn festivals, at the assemblies of the Christians, Julian returned, with the impatience of a lover, to burn his free and voluntary incense in the domestic chapels of Jupiter and Mercury. But as every act of dissimulation must be painful to an ingenuous spirit, the profession of Christianity increased the aversion of Julian for a religion which oppressed the freedom of his mind, and compelled him to hold a conduct repugnant to the noblest attributes of human nature—sincerity and courage.

The inclination of Julian might prefer the gods of Homer and of the Scipios to the new faith which his uncle had established in the Roman empire, and in which he himself had been sanctified by the sacrament of baptism. But, as a philosopher, it was incumbent on him to justify his dissent from Christianity, which was supported by the number of its converts, by the chain of prophecy, the splendour of miracles, and the weight of evidence. The elaborate work which he composed amidst the preparations of the Persian war contained the substance of those arguments which he had long revolved in his mind. Some fragments have been transcribed and preserved by his adversary, the vehement Cyril of Alexandria; and they exhibit a very singular mixture of wit and learning, of sophistry and fanaticism. The elegance of the style and the rank of the author recommended his writings to the public attention; and in the impious list of the enemies of Christianity the celebrated name of Porphyry was effaced by the superior merit or reputation of Julian. The minds of the faithful were either seduced, or scandalised, or alarmed; and the Pagans, who sometimes presumed to engage in the unequal dispute, derived, from the popular work of their Imperial missionary, an inexhaustible supply of fallacious objections. But in the assiduous prosecution of these theological studies the emperor of the Romans imbibed the illiberal prejudices and passions of a polemic divine. He contracted an irrevocable obligation to maintain and propagate his religious opinions; and whilst he secretly applauded the strength and dexterity with which he wielded the weapons of controversy, he was tempted to distrust the sincerity, or to despise the understandings, of his antagonists, who could obstinately resist the force of reason and eloquence.

The Christians, who beheld with horror and indignation the apostasy of Julian, had much more to fear from his power than from his arguments. The Pagans, who were conscious of his fervent zeal, expected, perhaps with impatience, that the flames of persecution should be immediately kindled against the enemies of the gods; and that the ingenious malice of Julian would invent some cruel refinements of death and torture which had been unknown to the rude and inexperienced fury of his predecessors. But the hopes, as well as the fears, of the religious factions were apparently disappointed by the prudent humanity of a prince who was careful of his own fame, of the public peace, and of the rights of mankind. Instructed by history and reflection, Julian was persuaded that, if the diseases of the body may sometimes be cured by salutary violence, neither steel nor fire can eradicate the erroneous opinions of the mind. The reluctant victim may be dragged to the foot of the altar; but the heart still abhors and disclaims the sacrilegious act of the hand. Religious obstinacy is hardened and exasperated by oppression; and, as soon as the persecution subsides, those who have yielded are restored as penitents, and those who have resisted are honoured as saints and martyrs. If Julian adopted the unsuccessful cruelty of Diocletian and his colleagues, he was sensible that he should stain his memory with the name of tyrant, and add new glories to the catholic church, which had derived strength and increase from the severity of the Pagan magistrates. Actuated by these motives, and apprehensive of disturbing the repose of an unsettled reign, Julian surprised the world by an edict which was not unworthy of a statesman or a philosopher. He extended to all the inhabitants of the Roman world the benefits of a free and equal toleration; and the only hardship which he inflicted on the Christians was to deprive them of the power of tormenting their fellow-subjects, whom they stigmatised with the odious titles of idolaters and heretics. The Pagans received a gracious permission, or rather an express order, to open ALL their temples; and they were at once delivered from the oppressive laws and arbitrary vexations which they had sustained under the reign of Constantine and of his sons. At the same time, the bishops and clergy who had been banished by the Arian monarch were recalled from exile, and restored to their respective churches; the Donatists, the Novatians, the Macedonians, the Eunomians, and those who, with a more prosperous fortune, adhered to the doctrine of the council of Nice. Julian, who understood and derided their theological disputes, invited to the palace the leaders of the hostile sects, that he might enjoy the agreeable spectacle of their furious encounters. The clamour of controversy sometimes provoked the emperor to exclaim, "Hear me! the Franks have heard me, and the Alemanni;" but he soon discovered that he was now engaged with more obstinate and implacable enemies; and though he exerted the powers of oratory to persuade them to live in concord, or at least in peace, he was perfectly satisfied, before he dismissed them from his presence, that he had nothing to dread from the union of the Christians. The impartial Ammianus has ascribed this affected clemency to the desire of fomenting the intestine divisions of the church; and the insidious design of undermining the foundations of Christianity was inseparably connected with the zeal which Julian professed to restore the ancient religion of the empire.

As soon as he ascended the throne, he assumed, according to the custom of his predecessors, the character of supreme pontiff; not only as the most honourable title of Imperial greatness, but as a sacred and important office, the duties of which he was resolved to execute with pious diligence. As the business of the state prevented the emperor from joining every day in the public devotion of his subjects, he dedicated a domestic chapel to his tutelar deity the Sun; his gardens were filled with statues and altars of the gods; and each apartment of the palace displayed the appearance of a magnificent temple. Every morning he saluted the parent of light with a sacrifice; the blood of another victim was shed at the moment when the Sun sunk below the horizon; and the Moon, the Stars, and the Genii of the night received their respective and seasonable honours from the indefatigable devotion of Julian. On solemn festivals he regularly visited the temple of the god or goddess to whom the day was peculiarly consecrated, and endeavoured to excite the religion of the magistrates and people by the example of his own zeal. Instead of maintaining the lofty state of a monarch, distinguished by the splendour of his purple, and encompassed by the golden shields of his guards, Julian solicited, with respectful eagerness, the meanest offices which contributed to the worship of the gods. Amidst the sacred but licentious crowd of priests, of inferior ministers, and of female dancers, who were dedicated to the service of the temple, it was the business of the emperor to bring the wood, to blow the fire, to handle the knife, to slaughter the victim, and, thrusting his bloody hands into the bowels of the expiring animal, to draw forth the heart or liver, and to read, with the consummate skill of an haruspex, the imaginary signs of future events. The wisest of the Pagans censured this extravagant superstition, which affected to despise the restraints of prudence and decency. Under the reign of a prince who practised the rigid maxims of economy, the expense of religious worship consumed a very large portion of the revenue; a constant supply of the scarcest and most beautiful birds was transported from distant climates, to bleed on the altars of the gods; an hundred oxen were frequently sacrificed by Julian on one and the same day; and it soon became a popular jest, that, if he should return with conquest from the Persian war, the breed of horned cattle must infallibly be extinguished. Yet this expense may appear inconsiderable, when it is compared with the splendid presents which were offered, either by the hand or by order of the emperor, to all the celebrated places of de-

votion in the Roman world; and with the sums allotted
to repair and decorate the ancient temples, which had
suffered the silent decay of time, or the recent injuries of
Christian rapine. Encouraged by the example, the ex-
hortations, the liberality of their pious sovereign, the
cities and families resumed the practice of their neglected ceremonies, "Every part of the world," exclaims
Libanius, with devout transport, "displayed the triumph
of religion, and the grateful prospect of flaming altars,
bleeding victims, the smoke of incense, and a solemn
train of priests and prophets, without fear and without
danger. The sound of prayer and of music was heard on
the tops of the highest mountains; and the same ox
afforded a sacrifice for the gods, and a supper for their
joyous votaries."

But the genius and power of Julian were unequal to
the enterprise of restoring a religion which was destitute
of theological principles, of moral precepts, and of ecclesiastical discipline; which rapidly hastened to decay
and dissolution, and was not susceptible of any solid or
consistent reformation. The jurisdiction of the supreme
pontiff, more especially after that office had been united
with the Imperial dignity, comprehended the whole extent of the Roman empire. Julian named for his vicars,
in the several provinces, the priests and philosophers,
whom he esteemed the best qualified to co-operate in the
execution of his great design; and his pastoral letters, if
we may use that name, still represent a very curious
sketch of his wishes and intentions. He directs that in
every city the sacerdotal order should be composed, without any distinction of birth or fortune, of those persons
who were the most conspicuous for their love of the gods
and of men. "If they are guilty," continues he, "'of any
scandalous offence, they should be censured or degraded
by the superior pontiff; but as long as they retain their
rank, they are entitled to the respect of the magistrates
and people. Their humility may be shown in the plain-
ness of their domestic garb; their dignity, in the pomp
of holy vestments. When they are summoned in their
turn to officiate before the altar, they ought not, during
the appointed number of days, to depart from the pre-

cincts of the temple; nor should a single day be suffered to elapse without the prayers and the sacrifice which they are obliged to offer for the prosperity of the state and of individuals. The exercise of their sacred functions requires an immaculate purity both of mind and body; and even when they are dismissed from the temple to the occupations of common life, it is incumbent on them to excel in decency and virtue the rest of their fellow-citizens. The priest of the gods should never be seen in theatres or taverns. His conversation should be chaste, his diet temperate, his friends of honourable reputation; and if he sometimes visits the Forum or the Palace, he should appear only as the advocate of those who have vainly solicited either justice or mercy. His studies should be suited to the sanctity of his profession. Licentious tales, or comedies, or satires, must be banished from his library, which ought solely to consist of historical and philosophical writings; of history, which is founded in truth, and of philosophy, which is connected with religion. The impious opinions of the Epicureans and sceptics deserve his abhorrence and contempt;[3] but he should diligently study the systems of Pythagoras, of Plato, and of the Stoics, which unanimously teach that there *are* gods; that the world is governed by their providence; that their goodness is the source of every temporal blessing; and that they have prepared for the human soul a future state of reward or punishment." The Imperial pontiff inculcates, in the most persuasive language, the duties of benevolence and hospitality; exhorts his inferior clergy to recommend the universal practice of those virtues; promises to assist their indigence from the public treasury; and declares his resolution of establishing hospitals in every city, where the poor should be received without any invidious distinction of country or of religion. Julian beheld with envy the wise and humane regulations of the church; and he very frankly confesses

---

[3] The exultation of Julian that these impious sects, and even their writings, are extinguished, may be consistent enough with the sacerdotal character; but it is unworthy of a philosopher to wish that any opinions and arguments the most repugant to his own should be concealed from the knowledge of mankind.

his intention to deprive the Christians of the applause, as well as advantage, which they had acquired by the exclusive practice of charity and beneficence. The same spirit of imitation might dispose the emperor to adopt several ecclesiastical institutions, the use and importance of which were approved by the success of his enemies. But if these imaginary plans of reformation had been realised, the forced and imperfect copy would have been less beneficial to Paganism than honourable to Christianity. The Gentiles, who peaceably followed the customs of their ancestors, were rather surprised than pleased with the introduction of foreign manners; and, in the short period of his reign, Julian had frequent occasions to complain of the want of fervour of his own party. . . .

[*Gibbon gives various instances of the violence caused by Julian's acts of restitution, which included an attempt to restore the Temple of Jerusalem, and concludes with the spectacular episode of George of Cappadocia, archbishop of Alexandria, who is presumed (though, as Gibbon admits, not with certainty) to be the original St. George.*]

George, from his parents or his education, surnamed the Cappadocian, was born at Epiphania in Cilicia, in a fuller's shop. From this obscure and servile origin he raised himself by the talents of a parasite; and the patrons whom he assiduously flattered procured for their worthless dependent a lucrative commission, or contract, to supply the army with bacon. His employment was mean; he rendered it infamous. He accumulated wealth by the basest arts of fraud and corruption; but his malversations were so notorious, that George was compelled to escape from the pursuits of justice. After this disgrace, in which he appears to have saved his fortune at the expense of his honour, he embraced, with real or affected zeal, the profession of Arianism. From the love, or the ostentation, of learning, he collected a valuable library of history, rhetoric, philosophy, and theology; and the choice of the prevailing faction promoted George of Cappadocia to the throne of Athanasius. The entrance of the new archbishop was that of a barbarian conqueror; and each moment of his reign was polluted by cruelty and avarice. The catholics of Alexandria and Egypt were abandoned to a tyrant, qualified by nature and education to exercise the office of persecution; but he oppressed with an impartial hand the various inhabitants of his extensive diocese. The primate of Egypt assumed the pomp and insolence of his lofty station; but he still betrayed the vices of his base and servile extraction. The merchants of Alexandria were impoverished by the unjust and almost universal monopoly, which he acquired, of nitre, salt, paper, funerals, etc.: and the spiritual father of a great people condescended to practise the vile and pernicious arts of an informer. The Alexandrians could never forget, nor forgive, the tax which he suggested on all the houses of the city, under an obsolete claim that the royal founder had conveyed to his successors, the Ptolemies and the Cæsars, the perpetual property of the soil. The Pagans, who had been flattered with the hopes of freedom and toleration, excited his devout avarice; and the rich temples of Alexandria were either pillaged or insulted by the haughty prelate, who exclaimed in a loud and threatening tone, "How long will these sepulchres be permitted to stand?" Under the reign of Constantius he was expelled by the fury, or rather by the justice, of the people; and it was not without a violent struggle that the civil and military powers of the state could restore his authority, and gratify his revenge. The messenger who proclaimed at Alexandria the accession of Julian announced the downfall of the archbishop. George, with two of his obsequious ministers, Count Diodorus, and Dracontius, master of the mint, were ignominiously dragged in chains to the public prison. At the end of twenty-four days the prison was forced open by the rage of a superstitious multitude, impatient of the tedious forms of judicial proceedings. The enemies of gods and men expired under their cruel insults; the lifeless bodies of the archbishop and his associates were carried in triumph through the streets on the back of a camel; and the inactivity of the Athanasian party was esteemed a shining example of evangelical patience. The remains of these guilty wretches were thrown into the sea; and the popular leaders of the tumult declared their resolution to disappoint the devotion of the Christians, and to intercept the future honours of these *martyrs,* who had been punished, like their predecessors, by the enemies of their religion. The fears of the Pagans were just, and their precautions ineffectual. The meritorious death of the archbishop obliterated the memory of his life. The rival of Athanasius was dear and sacred to the Arians, and the seeming conversion of those sectaries introduced his worship into the bosom of the catholic church. The odious stranger, disguising every circumstance of time and place, assumed the mask of a martyr, a saint, and a Christian hero; and the infamous George of Cappadocia has been transformed into the renowned St. George of England, the patron of arms, of chivalry, and of the garter.

[*The murder of the Arian archbishop George opened the way for the return to Alexandria of his rival Athanasius, who quickly established himself as "ecclesiastical dictator"; but Julian interposed and issued an edict exiling Athanasius from Egypt.*]

The execution of the sentence was still delayed by the caution or negligence of Ecdicius, præfect of Egypt, who was at length awakened from his lethargy by a severe reprimand. "Though you neglect," says Julian, "to write to me on any other subject, at least it is your duty to inform me of your conduct towards Athanasius, the enemy of the gods. My intentions have been long since communicated to you. I swear by the great Serapis, that unless, on the calends of December, Athanasius has departed from Alexandria, nay, from Egypt, the officers of your government shall pay a fine of one hundred pounds of gold. You know my temper: I am slow to condemn, but I am still slower to forgive." This epistle was enforced by a short postscript written with the emperor's own hand. "The contempt that is shown for all the gods fills me with grief and indignation. There is nothing that

I should see, nothing that I should hear, with more pleasure, than the expulsion of Athanasius from all Egypt. The abominable wretch! Under my reign, the baptism of several Grecian ladies of the highest rank has been the effect of his persecutions." The death of Athanasius was not *expressly* commanded; but the præfect of Egypt understood that it was safer for him to exceed than to neglect the orders of an irritated master. The archbishop prudently retired to the monasteries of the Desert; eluded, with his usual dexterity, the snares of the enemy; and lived to triumph over the ashes of a prince who, in words of formidable import, had declared his wish that the whole venom of the Galilæan school were contained in the single person of Athanasius.

I have endeavoured faithfully to represent the artful system by which Julian proposed to obtain the effects, without incurring the guilt or reproach, of persecution. But if the deadly spirit of fanaticism perverted the heart and understanding of a virtuous prince, it must, at the same time, be confessed, that the *real* sufferings of the Christians were inflamed and magnified by human passions and religious enthusiasm. The meekness and resignation which had distinguished the primitive disciples of the Gospel was the object of the applause, rather than of the imitation, of their successors. The Christians, who had now possessed above forty years the civil and ecclesiastical government of the empire, had contracted the insolent vices of prosperity, and the habit of believing that the saints alone were entitled to reign over the earth. As soon as the enmity of Julian deprived the clergy of the privileges which had been conferred by the favour of Constantine, they complained of the most cruel oppression; and the free toleration of idolaters and heretics was a subject of grief and scandal to the orthodox party. The acts of violence, which were no longer countenanced by the magistrates, were still committed by the zeal of the people. At Pessinus the altar of Cybele was overturned almost in the presence of the emperor; and in the city of Cæsarea, in Cappadocia, the temple of Fortune, the sole place of worship which had been left to the Pagans, was destroyed by the rage of a popular tumult.

On these occasions, a prince who felt for the honour of the gods was not disposed to interrupt the course of justice; and his mind was still more deeply exasperated when he found that the fanatics, who had deserved and suffered the punishment of incendiaries, were rewarded with the honours of martyrdom. The Christian subjects of Julian were assured of the hostile designs of their sovereign; and, to their jealous apprehension, every circumstance of his government might afford some grounds of discontent and suspicion. In the ordinary administration of the laws, the Christians, who formed so large a part of the people, must frequently be condemned; but their indulgent brethren, without examining the merits of the cause, presumed their innocence, allowed their claims, and imputed the severity of their judge to the partial malice of religious persecution. These present hardships, intolerable as they might appear, were represented as a slight prelude of the impending calamities. The Christians considered Julian as a cruel and crafty tyrant, who suspended the execution of his revenge till he should return victorious from the Persian war. They expected that, as soon as he had triumphed over the foreign enemies of Rome, he would lay aside the irksome mask of dissimulation; that the amphitheatres would stream with the blood of hermits and bishops; and that the Christians who still persevered in the profession of the faith would be deprived of the common benefits of nature and society. Every calumny that could wound the reputation of the Apostate was credulously embraced by the fears and hatred of his adversaries; and their indiscreet clamours provoked the temper of a sovereign whom it was their duty to respect, and their interest to flatter. They still protested that prayers and tears were their only weapons against the impious tyrant, whose head they devoted to the justice of offended Heaven. But they insinuated, with sullen resolution, that their submission was no longer the effect of weakness; and that, in the imperfect state of human virtue, the patience which is founded on principle may be exhausted by persecution. It is impossible to determine how far the zeal of Julian would have prevailed over his good sense and humanity; but, if we seriously reflect on the strength and spirit of the church, we shall be convinced that, before the emperor could have extinguished the religion of Christ, he must have involved his country in the horrors of a civil war.

7. Theodosius the Great and the Final Destruction of Paganism

[The hope of a successful return to paganism was dashed by the death of Julian in the Persian War (363 A.D.) after a reign of only two years. Thereafter, the emperors were Christian; but Arians (who exalted God above Christ) and Athanasians (whose doctrine of an equal Trinity had been promulgated at the Council of Nice or Nicæa in 325) still contended for supremacy, and Arianism was particularly strong in the East. The decisive change came in 378, when the Arian emperor Valens, who administered the Eastern provinces, was defeated and killed by the Goths at Adrianople, and his Western colleague Gratian adopted, in his place, the Spanish-born General Theodosius, "the first of the Emperors baptised in the true faith of the Trinity." The reign of Theodosius, who became sole emperor after his defeat of the usurper Maximus in 388, is as important as that of Constantine himself. By his own military genius he secured, for a time, the safety of the whole empire; and thanks to the support, not to say domination, of St. Ambrose, bishop of Milan, he achieved the final triumph of Athanasian Christianity over both Arianism and paganism. In Chapter XXVII Gibbon describes Theodosius' intervention in the ecclesiastical politics of Constantinople and the ruin of the Arian party at the Council of Constantinople (381); in chapter XXVIII (from which the following passage is taken) he describes his final destruction of paganism and the introduction of the worship of saints and relics among Christians.]

220

The ruin of Paganism, in the age of Theodosius, is perhaps the only example of the total extirpation of any ancient and popular superstition, and may therefore deserve to be considered as a singular event in the history of the human mind. The Christians, more especially the clergy, had impatiently supported the prudent delays of Constantine and the equal toleration of the elder Valentinian; nor could they deem their conquest perfect or secure as long as their adversaries were permitted to exist. The influence which Ambrose and his brethren had acquired over the youth of Gratian and the piety of Theodosius was employed to infuse the maxims of persecution into the breasts of their Imperial proselytes. Two specious principles of religious jurisprudence were established, from whence they deduced a direct and rigorous conclusion against the subjects of the empire who still adhered to the ceremonies of their ancestors: *that* the magistrate is, in some measure, guilty of the crimes which he neglects to prohibit or to punish; and *that* the idolatrous worship of fabulous deities and real dæmons is the most abominable crime against the supreme majesty of the Creator. The laws of Moses and the examples of Jewish history were hastily, perhaps erroneously, applied by the clergy to the mild and universal reign of Christianity. The zeal of the emperors was excited to vindicate their own honour and that of the Deity; and the temples of the Roman world were subverted about sixty years after the conversion of Constantine.

From the age of Numa to the reign of Gratian, the Romans preserved the regular succession of the several colleges of the sacerdotal order. Fifteen PONTIFFS exercised their supreme jurisdiction over all things and persons that were consecrated to the service of the gods; and the various questions which perpetually arose in a loose and traditionary system were submitted to the judgment of their holy tribunal. Fifteen grave and learned AUGURS observed the face of the heavens, and prescribed the actions of heroes according to the flight of birds. Fifteen keepers of the Sibylline books (their name of QUINDECEMVIRS was derived from their number) occasionally consulted the history of future, and,

as it should seem, of contingent events. Six VESTALS devoted their virginity to the guard of the sacred fire and
of the unknown pledges of the duration of Rome, which
no mortal had been suffered to behold with impunity.
Seven EPULOS prepared the table of the gods, conducted
the solemn procession, and regulated the ceremonies of
the annual festival. The three FLAMENS of Jupiter, of
Mars, and of Quirinus, were considered as the peculiar
ministers of the three most powerful deities, who watched
over the fate of Rome and of the universe. The KING of
the SACRIFICES represented the person of Numa and of
his successors in the religious functions, which could be
performed only by royal hands. The confraternities of the
SALIANS, the LUPERCALS, etc., practised such rites as
might extort a smile of contempt from every reasonable
man, with a lively confidence of recommending themselves to the favour of the immortal gods. The authority
which the Roman priests had formerly obtained in the
counsels of the republic was gradually abolished by the
establishment of monarchy and the removal of the seat
of empire. But the dignity of their sacred character was
still protected by the laws and manners of their country;
and they still continued, more especially the college of
pontiffs, to exercise in the capital, and sometimes in the
provinces, the rights of their ecclesiastical and civil jurisdiction. Their robes of purple, chariots of state, and
sumptuous entertainments attracted the admiration of
the people; and they received, from the consecrated lands
and the public revenue, an ample stipend, which liberally
supported the splendour of the priesthood and all the expenses of the religious worship of the state. As the
service of the altar was not incompatible with the command of armies, the Romans, after their consulships and
triumphs, aspired to the place of pontiff or of augur;
the seats of Cicero[1] and Pompey were filled, in the fourth
century, by the most illustrious members of the senate;
and the dignity of their birth reflected additional splen-

---

[1] Cicero frankly or indirectly confesses that the *Augurate* is the
supr... obj:t of his wishes. Pliny is proud to tread in the footsteps of Cicero, and the chain of tradition might be continued
from history and marbles.

dour on their sacerdotal character. The fifteen priests who composed the college of pontiffs enjoyed a more distinguished rank as the companions of their sovereign; and the Christian emperors condescended to accept the robe and ensigns which were appropriated to the office of supreme pontiff. But when Gratian ascended the throne, more scrupulous or more enlightened, he sternly rejected those profane symbols; applied to the service of the state or of the church the revenues of the priests and vestals; abolished their honours and immunities; and dissolved the ancient fabric of Roman superstition, which was supported by the opinions and habits of eleven hundred years. Paganism was still the constitutional religion of the senate. The hall or temple in which they assembled was adorned by the statue and altar of Victory: a majestic female standing on a globe, with flowing garments, expanded wings, and a crown of laurel in her outstretched hand. The senators were sworn on the altar of the goddess to observe the laws of the emperor and of the empire; and a solemn offering of wine and incense was the ordinary prelude of their public deliberations. The removal of this ancient monument was the only injury which Constantius had offered to the superstition of the Romans. The altar of Victory was again restored by Julian, tolerated by Valentinian, and once more banished from the senate by the zeal of Gratian. But the emperor yet spared the statues of the gods which were exposed to the public veneration: four hundred and twenty-four temples, or chapels, still remained to satisfy the devotion of the people, and in every quarter of Rome the delicacy of the Christians was offended by the fumes of idolatrous sacrifice.

But the Christians formed the least numerous party in the senate of Rome; and it was only by their absence that they could express their dissent from the legal, though profane, acts of a Pagan majority. In that assembly the dying embers of freedom were, for a moment, revived and inflamed by the breath of fanaticism. Four respectable deputations were successively voted to the Imperial court, to represent the grievances of the priesthood and the senate, and to solicit the restoration of the altar of Victory. The conduct of this important business was intrusted to the eloquent Symmachus, a wealthy and noble senator, who united the sacred characters of pontiff and augur with the civil dignities of proconsul of Africa and præfect of the city. The breast of Symmachus was animated by the warmest zeal for the cause of expiring Paganism; and his religious antagonists lamented the abuse of his genius and the inefficacy of his moral virtues. The orator, whose petition is extant to the emperor Valentinian, was conscious of the difficulty and danger of the office which he had assumed. He cautiously avoids every topic which might appear to reflect on the religion of his sovereign; humbly declares that prayers and entreaties are his only arms; and artfully draws his arguments from the schools of rhetoric rather than from those of philosophy. Symmachus endeavours to seduce the imagination of a young prince, by displaying the attributes of the goddess of Victory; he insinuates that the confiscation of the revenues which were consecrated to the service of the gods was a measure unworthy of his liberal and disinterested character; and he maintains that the Roman sacrifices would be deprived of their force and energy, if they were no longer celebrated at the expense as well as in the name of the republic. Even scepticism is made to supply an apology for superstition. The great and incomprehensible *secret* of the universe eludes the inquiry of man. Where reason cannot instruct, custom may be permitted to guide; and every nation seems to consult the dictates of prudence, by a faithful attachment to those rites and opinions which have received the sanction of ages. If those ages have been crowned with glory and prosperity—if the devout people has frequently obtained the blessings which they have solicited at the altars of the gods—it must appear still more advisable to persist in the same salutary practice, and not to risk the unknown perils that may attend any rash innovations. The test of antiquity and success was applied with singular advantage to the religion of Numa; and ROME herself, the celestial genius that presided over the fates of the city, is introduced by the orator to plead her own cause before the tribunal of the emperors. "Most excellent princes," says the venerable matron, "fathers of your country! pity and respect my age, which has hitherto flowed in an uninterrupted course of piety. Since I do not repent, permit me to continue in the practice of my ancient rites. Since I am born free, allow me to enjoy my domestic institutions. This religion has reduced the world under my laws. These rites have repelled Hannibal from the city, and the Gauls from the Capitol. Were my grey hairs reserved for such intolerable disgrace? I am ignorant of the new system that I am required to adopt; but I am well assured that the correction of old age is always an ungrateful and ignominious office." The fears of the people supplied what the discretion of the orator had suppressed; and the calamities which afflicted or threatened the declining empire were unanimously imputed by the Pagans to the new religion of Christ and of Constantine.

But the hopes of Symmachus were repeatedly baffled by the firm and dextrous opposition of the archbishop of Milan, who fortified the emperors against the fallacious eloquence of the advocate of Rome. In this controversy Ambrose condescends to speak the language of a philosopher, and to ask, with some contempt, why it should be thought necessary to introduce an imaginary and invisible power as the cause of those victories, which were sufficiently explained by the valour and discipline of the legions. He justly derides the absurd reverence for antiquity, which could only tend to discourage the improvements of art and to replunge the human race into their original barbarism. From thence gradually rising to a more lofty and theological tone, he pronounces that Christianity alone is the doctrine of truth and salvation, and that every mode of Polytheism conducts its deluded votaries through the paths of error to the abyss of eternal perdition. Arguments like these, when they were suggested by a favourite bishop, had power to prevent the restoration of the altar of Victory; but the same arguments fell with much more energy and effect from the mouth of a conqueror, and the gods of antiquity were dragged in triumph at the chariot-wheels of Theodosius. In a full meeting of the senate the emperor proposed, according to the forms of the republic, the important question, whether the worship of Jupiter or that of Christ should be the religion of the Romans. The liberty of suffrages, which he affected to allow, was destroyed by the hopes and fears that his presence inspired; and the arbitrary exile of Symmachus was a recent admonition that it might be dangerous to oppose the wishes of the monarch. On a regular division of the senate, Jupiter was condemned and degraded by the sense of a very large majority; and it is rather surprising that any members should be found bold enough to declare, by their speeches and votes, that they were still attached to the interest of an abdicated deity. The hasty conversion of the senate must be attributed either to supernatural or to sordid motives; and many of these reluctant proselytes betrayed, on every favourable occasion, their secret disposition to throw aside the mask of odious dissimulation. But they were gradually fixed in the new religion, as the cause of the ancient became more hopeless; they yielded to the authority of the emperor, to the fashion of the times, and to the entreaties of their wives and children,[2] who were instigated and governed by the clergy of Rome and the monks of the East. The edifying example of the Anician family was soon imitated by the rest of the nobility: the Bassi, the Paullini, the Gracchi, embraced the Christian religion; and "the luminaries of the world, the venerable assembly of Catos (such are the high-flown expressions of Prudentius), were impatient to strip themselves of their pontifical garment—to cast the skin of the old serpent—to assume the snowy robes of baptismal innocence—and to humble the pride of the consular fasces before the tombs of the martyrs." The citizens, who subsisted by their own industry, and the populace, who were supported by the public liberality, filled the churches of the Lateran and Vatican with an incessant throng of devout proselytes. The decrees of the senate, which proscribed the worship of idols, were

---

2 Jerome specifies the pontiff Albinus, who was surrounded with such a believing family of children and grandchildren as would have been sufficient to convert even Jupiter himself—an extraordinary proselyte!

ratified by the general consent of the Romans; the splendour of the Capitol was defaced, and the solitary temples were abandoned to ruin and contempt. Rome submitted to the yoke of the Gospel; and the vanquished provinces had not yet lost their reverence for the name and authority of Rome.

The filial piety of the emperors themselves engaged them to proceed with some caution and tenderness in the reformation of the eternal city. Those absolute monarchs acted with less regard to the prejudices of the provincials. The pious labour, which had been suspended near twenty years since the death of Constantius, was vigorously resumed, and finally accomplished, by the zeal of Theodosius. Whilst that warlike prince yet struggled with the Goths, not for the glory, but for the safety of the republic, he ventured to offend a considerable party of his subjects, by some acts which might perhaps secure the protection of Heaven, but which must seem rash and unseasonable in the eye of human prudence. The success of his first experiments against the Pagans encouraged the pious emperor to reiterate and enforce his edicts of proscription: the same laws which had been originally published in the provinces of the East, were applied, after the defeat of Maximus, to the whole extent of the Western empire; and every victory of the orthodox Theodosius contributed to the triumph of the Christian and catholic faith. He attacked superstition in her most vital part, by prohibiting the use of sacrifices, which he declared to be criminal as well as infamous; and if the terms of his edicts more strictly condemned the impious curiosity which examined the entrails of the victims, every subsequent explanation tended to involve in the same guilt the general practice of *immolation,* which essentially constituted the religion of the Pagans. As the temples had been erected for the purpose of sacrifice, it was the duty of a benevolent prince to remove from his subjects the dangerous temptation of offending against the laws which he had enacted. A special commission was granted to Cynegius, the Prætorian præfect of the East, and afterwards to the Counts Jovius and Gaudentius, two officers of distinguished rank in the West, by

which they were directed to shut the temples, to seize
or destroy the instruments of idolatry, to abolish the
privileges of the priests, and to confiscate the consecrated property for the benefit of the emperor, of the
church, or of the army. Here the desolation might have
stopped: and the naked edifices, which were no longer
employed in the service of idolatry, might have been protected from the destructive rage of fanaticism. Many of
those temples were the most splendid and beautiful
monuments of Grecian architecture: and the emperor
himself was interested not to deface the splendour of
his own cities, or to diminish the value of his own possessions. Those stately edifices might be suffered to remain, as so many lasting trophies of the victory of
Christ. In the decline of the arts, they might be usefully
converted into magazines, manufactures, or places of
public assembly: and perhaps, when the walls of the
temple had been sufficiently purified by holy rites, the
worship of the true Deity might be allowed to expiate the
ancient guilt of idolatry. But as long as they subsisted,
the Pagans fondly cherished the secret hope that an auspicious revolution, a second Julian, might again restore
the altars of the gods: and the earnestness with which
they addressed their unavailing prayers to the throne
increased the zeal of the Christian reformers to extirpate,
without mercy, the root of superstition. The laws of the
emperors exhibit some symptoms of a milder disposition:
but their cold and languid efforts were insufficient to
stem the torrent of enthusiasm and rapine, which was
conducted, or rather impelled, by the spiritual rulers of
the church. In Gaul, the holy Martin, bishop of Tours,
marched at the head of his faithful monks to destroy the
idols, the temples, and the consecrated trees of his extensive diocese; and, in the execution of this arduous
task, the prudent reader will judge whether Martin was
supported by the aid of miraculous powers or of carnal
weapons. In Syria, the divine and excellent Marcellus, as
he is styled by Theodoret, a bishop animated with apostolic fervour, resolved to level with the ground the stately
temples within the diocese of Apamea. His attack was
resisted by the skill and solidity with which the temple

of Jupiter had been constructed. The building was seated on an eminence: on each of the four sides the lofty roof was supported by fifteen massy columns, sixteen feet in circumference; and the large stones of which they were composed were firmly cemented with lead and iron. The force of the strongest and sharpest tools had been tried without effect. It was found necessary to undermine the foundations of the columns, which fell down as soon as the temporary wooden props had been consumed with fire; and the difficulties of the enterprise are described under the allegory of a black dæmon, who retarded, though he could not defeat, the operations of the Christian engineers. Elated with victory, Marcellus took the field in person against the powers of darkness; a numerous troop of soldiers and gladiators marched under the episcopal banner, and he successively attacked the villages and country temples of the diocese of Apamea. Whenever any resistance or danger was apprehended, the champion of the faith, whose lameness would not allow him either to fight or fly, placed himself at a convenient distance, beyond the reach of darts. But this prudence was the occasion of his death; he was surprised and slain by a body of exasperated rustics; and the synod of the province pronounced, without hesitation, that the holy Marcellus had sacrificed his life in the cause of God. In the support of this cause, the monks, who rushed with tumultuous fury from the desert, distinguished themselves by their zeal and diligence. They deserved the enmity of the Pagans; and some of them might deserve the reproaches of avarice and intemperance—of avarice, which they gratified with holy plunder; and of intemperance, which they indulged at the expense of the people, who foolishly admired their tattered garments, loud psalmody, and artificial paleness. A small number of temples was protected by the fears, the venality, the taste, or the prudence of the civil and ecclesiastical governors. The temple of the Celestial Venus at Carthage, whose sacred precincts formed a circumference of two miles, was judiciously converted into a Christian church; and a similar consecration has preserved inviolate the majestic dome of the Pantheon at Rome. But in almost every province of the Roman world, an army of fanatics, without authority and without discipline, invaded the peaceful inhabitants; and the ruin of the fairest structures of antiquity still displays the ravages of *those* barbarians who alone had time and inclination to execute such laborious destruction.

In this wide and various prospect of devastation, the spectator may distinguish the ruins of the temple of Serapis, at Alexandria. Serapis does not appear to have been one of the native gods, or monsters, who sprung from the fruitful soil of superstitious Egypt. The first of the Ptolemies had been commanded, by a dream, to import the mysterious stranger from the coast of Pontus, where he had been long adored by the inhabitants of Sinope; but his attributes and his reign were so imperfectly understood, that it became a subject of dispute whether he represented the bright orb of day, or the gloomy monarch of the subterraneous regions. The Egyptians, who were obstinately devoted to the religion of their fathers, refused to admit this foreign deity within the walls of their cities. But the obsequious priests, who were seduced by the liberality of the Ptolemies, submitted, without resistance, to the power of the god of Pontus: an honourable and domestic genealogy was provided; and this fortunate usurper was introduced into the throne and bed of Osiris, the husband of Isis, and the celestial monarch of Egypt. Alexandria, which claimed his peculiar protection, gloried in the name of the city of Serapis. His temple, which rivalled the pride and magnificence of the Capitol, was erected on the spacious summit of an artificial mount, raised one hundred steps above the level of the adjacent parts of the city; and the interior cavity was strongly supported by arches, and distributed into vaults and subterraneous apartments. The consecrated buildings were surrounded by a quadrangular portico; the stately halls and exquisite statues displayed the triumph of the arts; and the treasures of ancient learning were preserved in the famous Alexandrian library, which had arisen with new splendour from its ashes. After the edicts of Theodosius had severely prohibited the sacrifices of the Pagans, they were still tolerated in the city and temple of Serapis; and this singular indulgence was imprudently ascribed to the superstitious terrors of the Christians themselves: as if they had feared to abolish those ancient rites which could alone secure the inundations of the Nile, the harvests of Egypt, and the subsistence of Constantinople.

At that time the archiepiscopal throne of Alexandria was filled by Theophilus, the perpetual enemy of peace and virtue; a bold, bad man, whose hands were alternately polluted with gold and with blood. His pious indignation was excited by the honours of Serapis; and the insults which he offered to an ancient chapel of Bacchus convinced the Pagans that he meditated a more important and dangerous enterprise. In the tumultuous capital of Egypt, the slightest provocation was sufficient to inflame a civil war. The votaries of Serapis, whose strength and numbers were much inferior to those of their antagonists, rose in arms at the instigation of the philosopher Olympius, who exhorted them to die in the defence of the altars of the gods. These Pagan fanatics fortified themselves in the temple, or rather fortress, of Serapis; repelled the besiegers by daring sallies and a resolute defence; and, by the inhuman cruelties which they exercised on their Christian prisoners, obtained the last consolation of despair. The efforts of the prudent magistrate were usefully exerted for the establishment of a truce till the answer of Theodosius should determine the fate of Serapis. The two parties assembled, without arms, in the principal square; and the Imperial rescript was publicly read. But when a sentence of destruction against the idols of Alexandria was pronounced, the Christians sent up a shout of joy and exultation, whilst the unfortunate Pagans, whose fury had given way to consternation, retired with hasty and silent steps, and eluded, by their flight or obscurity, the resentment of their enemies. Theophilus proceeded to demolish the temple of Serapis, without any other difficulties than those which he found in the weight and solidity of the materials; but these obstacles proved so insuperable that he was obliged to leave the foundations, and to content himself with reducing the edifice itself to a heap of rubbish,

231

a part of which was soon afterwards cleared away, to make room for a church erected in honour of the Christian martyrs. The valuable library of Alexandria was pillaged or destroyed; and near twenty years afterwards, the appearance of the empty shelves excited the regret and indignation of every spectator whose mind was not totally darkened by religious prejudice. The compositions of ancient genius, so many of which have irretrievably perished, might surely have been excepted from the wreck of idolatry, for the amusement and instruction of succeeding ages; and either the zeal or the avarice of the archbishop might have been satiated with the rich spoils which were the reward of his victory. While the images and vases of gold and silver were carefully melted, and those of a less valuable metal were contemptuously broken and cast into the streets, Theophilus laboured to expose the frauds and vices of the ministers of the idols: their dexterity in the management of the loadstone; their secret methods of introducing an human actor into a hollow statue; and their scandalous abuse of the confidence of devout husbands and unsuspecting females. Charges like these may seem to deserve some degree of credit, as they are not repugnant to the crafty and interested spirit of superstition. But the same spirit is equally prone to the base practice of insulting and calumniating a fallen enemy; and our belief is naturally checked by the reflection that it is much less difficult to invent a fictitious story than to support a practical fraud. The colossal statue of Serapis was involved in the ruin of his temple and religion. A great number of plates of different metals, artificially joined together, composed the majestic figure of the deity, who touched on either side the walls of the sanctuary. The aspect of Serapis, his sitting posture, and the sceptre which he bore in his left hand, were extremely similar to the ordinary representations of Jupiter. He was distinguished from Jupiter by the basket, or bushel, which was placed on his head; and by the emblematic monster which he held in his right hand; the head and body of a serpent branching into three tails, which were again terminated by the triple heads of a dog, a lion, and a wolf. It was confidently affirmed that, if any impious hand should dare to violate the majesty of the god, the heavens and the earth would instantly return to their original chaos. An intrepid soldier, animated by zeal, and armed with a weighty battle-axe, ascended the ladder; and even the Christian multitude expected with some anxiety the event of the combat. He aimed a vigorous stroke against the cheek of Serapis; the cheek fell to the ground; the thunder was still silent, and both the heavens and the earth continued to preserve their accustomed order and tranquillity. The victorious soldier repeated his blows: the huge idol was overthrown and broken in pieces; and the limbs of Serapis were ignominiously dragged through the streets of Alexandria. His mangled carcase was burnt in the amphitheatre, amidst the shouts of the populace; and many persons attributed their conversion to this discovery of the impotence of their tutelar deity. The popular modes of religion, that propose any visible and material objects of worship, have the advantage of adapting and familiarising themselves to the senses of mankind; but this advantage is counterbalanced by the various and inevitable accidents to which the faith of the idolater is exposed. It is scarcely possible that, in every disposition of mind, he should preserve his implicit reverence for the idols, or the relics, which the naked eye and the profane hand are unable to distinguish from the most common productions of art or nature; and if, in the hour of danger, their secret and miraculous virtue does not operate for their own preservation, he scorns the vain apologies of his priests, and justly derides the object and the folly of his superstitious attachment. After the fall of Serapis, some hopes were still entertained by the Pagans that the Nile would refuse his annual supply to the impious masters of Egypt; and the extraordinary delay of the inundation seemed to announce the displeasure of the river-god. But this delay was soon compensated by the rapid swell of the waters. They suddenly rose to such an unusual height as to comfort the discontented party with the pleasing expectation of a deluge; till the peaceful river again subsided to the well-known and fertilising level of sixteen cubits, or about thirty English feet.

The temples of the Roman empire were deserted or destroyed; but the ingenious superstition of the Pagans still attempted to elude the laws of Theodosius, by which all sacrifices had been severely prohibited. The inhabitants of the country, whose conduct was less exposed to the eye of malicious curiosity, disguised their *religious* under the appearance of *convivial* meetings. On the days of solemn festivals they assembled in great numbers under the spreading shade of some consecrated trees; sheep and oxen were slaughtered and roasted; and this rural entertainment was sanctified by the use of incense and by the hymns which were sung in honour of the gods. But it was alleged that, as no part of the animal was made a burnt-offering, as no altar was provided to receive the blood, and as the previous oblation of salt cakes and the concluding ceremony of libations were carefully omitted, these festal meetings did not involve the guests in the guilt or penalty of an illegal sacrifice. Whatever might be the truth of the facts or the merit of the distinction, these vain pretences were swept away by the last edict of Theodosius, which inflicted a deadly wound on the superstition of the Pagans. This prohibitory law is expressed in the most absolute and comprehensive terms. "It is our will and pleasure," says the emperor, "that none of our subjects, whether magistrates or private citizens, however exalted or however humble may be their rank and condition, shall presume in any city or in any place to worship an inanimate idol by the sacrifice of a guiltless victim." The act of sacrificing and the practice of divination by the entrails of the victim are declared (without any regard to the object of the inquiry) a crime of high treason against the state, which can be expiated only by the death of the guilty. The rites of Pagan superstition which might seem less bloody and atrocious are abolished as highly injurious to the truth and honour of religion; luminaries, garlands, frankincense, and libations of wine are specially enumerated and condemned; and the harmless claims of the domestic genius, of the household gods, are included in this rigorous proscription. The use of any of these profane and illegal ceremonies subjects the offender to the forfeiture of the house or estate where they have been performed; and if he has artfully chosen the property of another for the scene of his impiety, he is compelled to discharge, without delay, a heavy fine of twenty-five pounds of gold, or more than one thousand pounds sterling. A fine not less considerable is imposed on the connivance of the secret enemies of religion who shall neglect the duty of their respective stations, either to reveal or to punish the guilt of idolatry. Such was the persecuting spirit of the laws of Theodosius, which were repeatedly enforced by his sons and grandsons, with the loud and unanimous applause of the Christian world. . . .

The ruin of the Pagan religion is described by the sophists as a dreadful and amazing prodigy, which covered the earth with darkness and restored the ancient dominion of chaos and of night. They relate in solemn and pathetic strains that the temples were converted into sepulchres, and that the holy places, which had been adorned by the statues of the gods, were basely polluted by the relics of Christian martyrs. "The monks" (a race of filthy animals, to whom Eunapius is tempted to refuse the name of men) "are the authors of the new worship, which, in the place of those deities who are conceived by the understanding, has substituted the meanest and most contemptible slaves. The heads, salted and pickled, of those infamous malefactors, who for the multitude of their crimes have suffered a just and ignominious death; their bodies, still marked by the impression of the lash and the scars of those tortures which were inflicted by the sentence of the magistrate; such" (continues Eunapius) "are the gods which the earth produces in our days; such are the martyrs, the supreme arbitrators of our prayers and petitions to the Deity, whose tombs are now consecrated as the objects of the veneration of the people." Without approving the malice, it is natural enough to share the surprise of the sophist, the spectator of a revolution which raised those obscure victims of the laws of Rome to the rank of celestial and invisible protectors of the Roman empire. The grateful respect of the Christians for the martyrs of the faith was exalted, by time and victory, into religious adoration; and the most illustrious of the saints and prophets were deservedly associated to the honours of the martyrs. One hundred and fifty years after the glorious deaths of St. Peter and St. Paul, the Vatican and the Ostian road were distinguished by the tombs, or rather by the trophies, of those spiritual heroes. In the age which followed the conversion of Constantine, the emperors, the consuls, and the generals of armies devoutly visited the sepulchres of a tentmaker and a fisherman; and their venerable bones were deposited under the altars of Christ, on which the bishops of the royal city continually offered the unbloody sacrifice. The new capital of the Eastern world, unable to produce any ancient and domestic trophies, was enriched by the spoils of dependent provinces. The bodies of St. Andrew, St. Luke, and St. Timothy had reposed near three hundred years in the obscure graves from whence they were transported, in solemn pomp, to the church of the apostles, which the magnificence of Constantine had founded on the banks of the Thracian Bosphorus. About fifty years afterwards the same banks were honoured by the presence of Samuel, the judge and prophet of the people of Israel. His ashes, deposited in a golden vase, and covered with a silken veil, were delivered by the bishops into each other's hands. The relics of Samuel were received by the people with the same joy and reverence which they would have shown to the living prophet; the highways, from Palestine to the gates of Constantinople, were filled with an uninterrupted procession; and the emperor Arcadius himself, at the head of the most illustrious members of the clergy and senate, advanced to meet his extraordinary guest, who had always deserved and claimed the homage of kings. The example of Rome and Constantinople confirmed the faith and discipline of the catholic world. The honours of the saints and martyrs, after a feeble and ineffectual murmur of profane reason,[3] were universally established; and in the

---

[3] The presbyter Vigilantius, the protestant of his age, firmly, though ineffectually, withstood the superstition of monks, relics,

age of Ambrose and Jerom something was still deemed wanting to the sanctity of a Christian church, till it had been consecrated by some portion of holy relics, which fixed and inflamed the devotion of the faithful.

In the long period of twelve hundred years, which elapsed between the reign of Constantine and the reformation of Luther, the worship of saints and relics corrupted the pure and perfect simplicity of the Christian model; and some symptoms of degeneracy may be observed even in the first generations which adopted and cherished this pernicious innovation.

I. The satisfactory experience that the relics of saints were more valuable than gold or precious stones stimulated the clergy to multiply the treasures of the church. Without much regard for truth or probability, they invented names for skeletons, and actions for names. The fame of the apostles, and of the holy men who had imitated their virtues, was darkened by religious fiction. To the invincible band of genuine and primitive martyrs they added myriads of imaginary heroes, who had never existed, except in the fancy of crafty or credulous legendaries; and there is reason to suspect that Tours might not be the only diocese in which the bones of a malefactor were adored instead of those of a saint. A superstitious practice, which tended to increase the temptations of fraud and credulity, insensibly extinguished the light of history and of reason in the Christian world.

II. But the progress of superstition would have been much less rapid and victorious if the faith of the people had not been assisted by the seasonable aid of visions and miracles to ascertain the authenticity and virtue of the most suspicious relics. In the reign of the younger Theodosius, Lucian, a presbyter of Jerusalem, and the ecclesiastical minister of the village of Caphargamala, about twenty miles from the city, related a very singular dream, which, to remove his doubts, had been repeated

---

saints, fasts, etc., for which Jerom compares him to the Hydra, Cerberus, the Centaurs, etc., and considers him only as the organ of the Dæmon. Whoever will peruse the controversy of St. Jerom and Vigilantius, and St. Augustin's account of the miracles of St. Stephen, may speedily gain some idea of the spirit of the Fathers.

on three successive Saturdays. A venerable figure stood before him, in the silence of the night, with a long beard, a white robe, and a gold rod; announced himself by the name of Gamaliel; and revealed to the astonished presbyter, that his own corpse, with the bodies of his son Abibas, his friend Nicodemus, and the illustrious Stephen, the first martyr of the Christian faith, were secretly buried in the adjacent field. He added, with some impatience, that it was time to release himself and his companions from their obscure prison; that their appearance would be salutary to a distressed world; and that they had made choice of Lucian to inform the bishop of Jerusalem of their situation and their wishes. The doubts and difficulties which still retarded this important discovery were successively removed by new visions; and the ground was opened by the bishop, in the presence of an innumerable multitude. The coffins of Gamaliel, of his son, and of his friend, were found in regular order; but when the fourth coffin, which contained the remains of Stephen, was shown to the light, the earth trembled, and an odour such as that of Paradise was smelt, which instantly cured the various diseases of seventy-three of the assistants. The companions of Stephen were left in their peaceful residence of Caphargamala; but the relics of the first martyr were transported, in solemn procession, to a church constructed in their honour on Mount Sion; and the minute particles of those relics, a drop of blood, or the scrapings of a bone, were acknowledged, in almost every province of the Roman world, to possess a divine and miraculous virtue. The grave and learned Augustin, whose understanding scarcely admits the excuse of credulity, has attested the innumerable prodigies which were performed in Africa by the relics of St. Stephen; and this marvellous narrative is inserted in the elaborate work of the City of God, which the bishop of Hippo designed as a solid and immortal proof of the truth of Christianity. Augustin solemnly declares that he has selected those miracles only which were publicly certified by the persons who were either the objects, or the spectators, of the power of the martyr. Many prodigies were omitted or forgotten; and Hippo had been less favourably treated than the other cities of the province. And yet the bishop enumerates above seventy miracles, of which three were resurrections from the dead, in the space of two years, and within the limits of his own diocese. If we enlarge our view to all the dioceses, and all the saints, of the Christian world, it will not be easy to calculate the fables, and the errors, which issued from this inexhaustible source. But we may surely be allowed to observe that a miracle, in that age of superstition and credulity, lost its name and its merit, since it could scarcely be considered as a deviation from the ordinary and established laws of nature.

III. The innumerable miracles, of which the tombs of the martyrs were the perpetual theatre, revealed to the pious believer the actual state and constitution of the invisible world; and his religious speculations appeared to be founded on the firm basis of fact and experience. Whatever might be the condition of vulgar souls in the long interval between the dissolution and the resurrection of their bodies, it was evident that the superior spirits of the saints and martyrs did not consume that portion of their existence in silent and inglorious sleep. It was evident (without presuming to determine the place of their habitation, or the nature of their felicity) that they enjoyed the lively and active consciousness of their happiness, their virtue, and their powers; and that they had already secured the possession of their eternal reward. The enlargement of their intellectual faculties surpassed the measure of the human imagination; since it was proved by *experience* that they were capable of hearing and understanding the various petitions of their numerous votaries, who, in the same moment of time, but in the most distant parts of the world, invoked the name and assistance of Stephen or of Martin. The confidence of their petitioners was founded on the persuasion that the saints, who reigned with Christ, cast an eye of pity upon earth; that they were warmly interested in the prosperity of the catholic church; and that the individuals who imitated the example of their faith and piety were the peculiar and favourite objects of their most tender regard. Sometimes, indeed, their friendship might be influenced by considerations of a less exalted kind: they viewed with partial affection the places which had been consecrated by their birth, their residence, their death, their burial, or the possession of their relics. The meaner passions of pride, avarice, and revenge, may be deemed unworthy of a celestial breast; yet the saints themselves condescended to testify their grateful approbation of the liberality of their votaries; and the sharpest bolts of punishment were hurled against those impious wretches who violated their magnificent shrines, or disbelieved their supernatural power. Atrocious, indeed, must have been the guilt, and strange would have been the scepticism, of those men, if they had obstinately resisted the proofs of a divine agency, which the elements, the whole range of the animal creation, and even the subtle and invisible operations of the human mind, were compelled to obey.[4] The immediate, and almost instantaneous, effects, that were supposed to follow the prayer, or the offence, satisfied the Christians of the ample measure of favour and authority which the saints enjoyed in the presence of the Supreme God; and it seemed almost superfluous to inquire whether they were continually obliged to intercede before the throne of grace, or whether they might not be permitted to exercise, according to the dictates of their benevolence and justice, the delegated powers of their subordinate ministry. The imagination, which had been raised by a painful effort to the contemplation and worship of the Universal Cause, eagerly embraced such inferior objects of adoration as were more proportioned to its gross conceptions and imperfect faculties. The sublime and simple theology of the primitive Christians was gradually corrupted: and the MONARCHY of heaven, already clouded by metaphysical subtleties, was degraded by the introduction of a popular mythology which tended to restore the reign of polytheism.

IV. As the objects of religion were gradually reduced

---

[4] At Minorca, the relics of St. Stephen converted in eight days 540 Jews; with the help, indeed, of some wholesome severities, such as burning the synagogue, driving the obstinate infidels to starve among the rocks, etc.

to the standard of the imagination, the rites and ceremonies were introduced that seemed most powerfully
to affect the senses of the vulgar. If, in the beginning
of the fifth century, Tertullian, or Lactantius, had been
suddenly raised from the dead, to assist at the festival
of some popular saint or martyr, they would have gazed
with astonishment and indignation on the profane
spectacle which had succeeded to the pure and spiritual
worship of a Christian congregation. As soon as the
doors of the church were thrown open, they must have
been offended by the smoke of incense, the perfume of
flowers, and the glare of lamps and tapers, which diffused, at noon-day, a gaudy, superfluous, and, in their
opinion, a sacrilegious light. If they approached the
balustrade of the altar, they made their way through the
prostrate crowd, consisting, for the most part, of strangers and pilgrims, who resorted to the city on the vigil
of the feast; and who already felt the strong intoxication of fanaticism, and, perhaps, of wine. Their devout
kisses were imprinted on the walls and pavement of
the sacred edifice; and their fervent prayers were directed,
whatever might be the language of their church, to the
bones, the blood, or the ashes of the saint, which were
usually concealed, by a linen or silken veil, from the eyes
of the vulgar. The Christians frequented the tombs of
the martyrs, in the hope of obtaining, from their powerful intercession, every sort of spiritual, but more especially of temporal, blessings. They implored the preservation of their health, or the cure of their infirmities; the
fruitfulness of their barren wives, or the safety and
happiness of their children. Whenever they undertook
any distant or dangerous journey, they requested that
the holy martyrs would be their guides and protectors
on the road; and if they returned without having experienced any misfortune, they again hastened to the
tombs of the martyrs, to celebrate, with grateful thanks-
givings, their obligations to the memory and relics of
those heavenly patrons. The walls were hung round with
symbols of the favours which they had received; eyes,
and hands, and feet, of gold and silver: and edifying
pictures, which could not long escape the abuse of in-

discreet or idolatrous devotion, represented the image, the attributes, and the miracles of the tutelar saint. The same uniform original spirit of superstition might suggest, in the most distant ages and countries, the same methods of deceiving the credulity, and of affecting the senses of mankind: but it must ingenuously be confessed that the ministers of the Catholic Church thereby imitated the profane model which they were impatient to destroy. The most respectable bishops had persuaded themselves that the ignorant rustics would more cheerfully renounce the superstitions of Paganism, if they found some resemblance, some compensation, in the bosom of Christianity. The religion of Constantine achieved, in less than a century, the final conquest of the Roman empire: but the victors themselves were insensibly subdued by the arts of their vanquished rivals.

8. Theology and Faction in the Eastern Empire

["The genius of Rome," says Gibbon, "expired with Theodosius, the last of the successors of Augustus and Constantine who appeared in the field at the head of their armies and whose authority was recognised throughout the whole extent of the empire." After his death (395 A.D.), Rome and Constantinople became the separate capitals of his sons, Arcadius and Honorius, and were never effectively reunited. Their courses also diverged. While Rome, united in religious uniformity, crumbled beneath barbarian attacks, Constantinople survived the attacks but was convulsed by theological controversy. Whatever its intellectual significance, this controversy was sharpened by the rivalry between the patriarchs of the two greatest cities of the East, Alexandria and Constantinople. In chapter XXXII Gibbon describes the fate of St. John Chrysostom, archbishop of Constantinople, in the court of Arcadius, which was managed by "the mild and absolute dominion of his wife, the fair and artful Eudoxia" and by the "deformed and decrepit eunuch" Eutropius.]

After the death of the indolent Nectarius, the successor of Gregory Nazianzen, the church of Constantinople was distracted by the ambition of rival candidates, who were not ashamed to solicit, with gold or flattery, the suffrage of the people or of the favourite. On this occasion Eutropius seems to have deviated from his ordinary maxims; and his uncorrupted judgement was determined only by the superior merit of a stranger. In a late journey into the East he had admired the sermons of John, a native and presbyter of Antioch, whose name has been distinguished by the epithet of Chrysostom, or the Golden Mouth. A private order was despatched to the governor of Syria; and as the people might be unwilling to resign their favourite preacher, he was transported, with speed and secrecy, in a post-chariot, from Antioch to Constantinople. The unanimous and unsolicited consent of the court, the clergy, and the people ratified the choice of the minister; and, both as a saint and as an orator, the new archbishop surpassed the sanguine expectations of the public. Born of a noble and opulent family in the capital of Syria, Chrysostom had been educated, by the care of a tender mother, under the tuition of the most skilful masters. He studied the art of rhetoric in the school of Libanius; and that celebrated sophist, who soon discovered the talents of his disciple, ingenuously confessed that John would have deserved to succeed him had he not been stolen away by the Christians. His piety soon disposed him to receive the sacrament of baptism; to renounce the lucrative and honourable profession of the law; and to bury himself in the adjacent desert, where he subdued the lusts of the flesh by an austere penance of six years. His infirmities compelled him to return to the society of mankind; and the authority of Meletius devoted his talents to the service of the church: but in the midst of his family, and afterwards on the archiepiscopal throne, Chrysostom still persevered in the practice of the monastic virtues. The ample revenues, which his predecessors had consumed in pomp and luxury, he diligently applied to the establishment of hospitals; and the multitudes who were supported by his charity preferred the eloquent and edifying discourses of their archbishop to the amusements of the theatre or the circus. The monuments of that eloquence, which was admired near twenty years at Antioch and Constantinople, have been carefully preserved; and the possession of near one thousand sermons or homilies has authorised the critics of succeeding times to appreciate the genuine merit of Chrysostom. They unanimously attribute to the Christian orator the free command of an elegant and copious language; the judgment to conceal the advantages which he derived from the knowledge of rhetoric and philosophy; an inexhaustible fund of metaphors and similitudes, of ideas and images, to vary and illustrate the most familiar topics; the happy art of engaging the passions in the service of virtue, and of exposing the folly as well as the turpitude of vice almost with the truth and spirit of a dramatic representation.

The pastoral labours of the archbishop of Constantinople provoked and gradually united against him two sorts of enemies; the aspiring clergy, who envied his success, and the obstinate sinners, who were offended by his reproofs. When Chrysostom thundered from the pulpit of St. Sophia against the degeneracy of the Christians, his shafts were spent among the crowd, without wounding or even marking the character of any individual. When he declaimed against the peculiar vices of the rich, poverty might obtain a transient consolation from his invectives: but the guilty were still sheltered by their numbers; and the reproach itself was dignified by some ideas of superiority and enjoyment. But as the pyramid rose towards the summit, it insensibly diminished to a point; and the magistrates, the ministers, the favourite eunuchs, the ladies of the court, the empress Eudoxia herself, had a much larger share of guilt to divide among a smaller proportion of criminals. The personal applications of the audience were anticipated or confirmed by the testimony of their own conscience; and the intrepid preacher assumed the dangerous right of exposing both the offence and the offender to the public abhorrence. The secret resentment of the court encouraged the discontent of the clergy and monks of Constantinople, who were too hastily reformed by the fervent zeal of their archbishop. He had condemned from the pulpit the domestic females of the clergy of Constantinople, who, under the name of servants or sisters, afforded a perpetual occasion either of sin or of scandal. The silent and solitary ascetics, who had secluded themselves from the world, were entitled to the warmest approbation of Chrysostom; but he despised and stigmatised, as the disgrace of their holy profession, the crowd of degenerate monks, who, from some unworthy motives of pleasure or profit, so frequently infested the streets of the capital. To the voice of persuasion the archbishop was obliged to add the terrors of authority; and his ardour in the exercise of ecclesiastical jurisdiction was not always exempt from passion; nor was it always guided by prudence. Chrysostom was naturally of a choleric disposition. Although he struggled, according to the precepts of the Gospel, to love his private enemies, he indulged himself in the privilege of hating the enemies of God and of the church; and his sentiments were sometimes delivered with too much energy of countenance and expression. He still maintained, from some considerations of health or abstinence, his former habits of taking his repasts alone; and this inhospitable custom, which his enemies imputed to pride, contributed at least to nourish the infirmity of a morose and unsocial humour. Separated from that familiar intercourse which facilitates the knowledge and the despatch of business, he reposed an unsuspecting confidence in his deacon Serapion; and seldom applied his speculative knowledge of human nature to the particular characters either of his dependents or of his equals. Conscious of the purity of his intentions, and perhaps of the superiority of his genius, the archbishop of Constantinople extended the jurisdiction of the Imperial city, that he might enlarge the sphere of his pastoral labours; and the conduct which the profane imputed to an ambitious motive, appeared to Chrysostom himself in the light of a sacred and indispensable duty. In his visitation through the Asiatic provinces he deposed thirteen bishops of Lydia and Phrygia; and indiscreetly declared that a deep corruption of simony and licentiousness had infected the whole episcopal order. If those bishops were innocent, such a rash and unjust condemnation must excite a well-grounded discontent. If they were guilty, the numerous associates of their guilt would soon discover that their own safety depended on the ruin of the archbishop, whom they studied to represent as the tyrant of the Eastern church.

This ecclesiastical conspiracy was managed by Theophilus, archbishop of Alexandria, an active and ambitious prelate, who displayed the fruits of rapine in monuments of ostentation. His national dislike to the rising greatness of a city which degraded him from the second to the third rank in the Christian world was exasperated by some personal disputes with Chrysostom himself. By the private invitation of the empress, Theophilus landed at Constantinople, with a stout body of Egyptian mariners, to encounter the populace; and a train of dependent bishops, to secure by their voices the majority of a synod. The synod was convened in the suburb of Chalcedon, surnamed the *Oak*, where Rufinus had erected a stately church and monastery; and their proceedings were continued during fourteen days or sessions. A bishop and a deacon accused the archbishop of Constantinople; but the frivolous or improbable nature of the forty-seven articles which they presented against him may justly be considered as a fair and unexceptionable panegyric. Four successive summons were signified to Chrysostom; but he still refused to trust either his person or his reputation in the hands of his implacable enemies, who, prudently declining the examination of any particular charges, condemned his contumacious disobedience, and hastily pronounced a sentence of deposition. The synod of the *Oak* immediately addressed the emperor to ratify and execute their judgement, and charitably insinuated that the penalties of treason might be inflicted on the audacious preacher, who had reviled, under the name of Jezebel, the empress Eudoxia herself. The archbishop was rudely arrested, and conducted through the city, by one of the Imperial messengers, who landed him, after a short navigation, near the entrance of the Euxine; from whence, before the expiration of two days, he was gloriously recalled.

The first astonishment of his faithful people had been mute and passive: they suddenly rose with unanimous and irresistible fury. Theophilus escaped, but the promiscuous crowd of monks and Egyptian mariners was slaughtered without pity in the streets of Constantinople. A seasonable earthquake justified the interposition of Heaven; the torrent of sedition rolled forwards to the gates of the palace; and the empress, agitated by fear or remorse, threw herself at the feet of Arcadius, and confessed that the public safety could be purchased only by the restoration of Chrysostom. The Bosphorus was covered with innumerable vessels; the shores of Europe and Asia were profusely illuminated; and the acclamations of a victorious people accompanied, from the port to the cathedral, the triumph of the archbishop, who too easily consented to resume the exercise of his functions, before his sentence had been legally reversed by the authority of an ecclesiastical synod. Ignorant, or careless, of the impending danger, Chrysostom indulged his zeal, or perhaps his resentment; declaimed with peculiar asperity against *female* vices; and condemned the profane honours which were addressed, almost in the precincts of St. Sophia, to the statue of the empress. His imprudence tempted his enemies to inflame the haughty spirit of Eudoxia, by reporting, or perhaps inventing, the famous exordium of a sermon, "Herodias is again furious; Herodias again dances; she once more requires the head of John": an insolent allusion, which, as a woman and a sovereign, it was impossible for her to forgive. The short interval of a perfidious truce was employed to concert more effectual measures for the disgrace and ruin of the archbishop. A numerous council of the Eastern prelates, who were guided from a distance by the advice of Theophilus, confirmed the validity, without examining the justice, of the former sentence; and a detachment of barbarian troops was introduced into the city, to suppress the emotions of the people. On the vigil of Easter the solemn administration of baptism was rudely interrupted by the soldiers, who alarmed the modesty of the naked catechumens, and violated, by their presence, the awful mysteries of the Christian worship. Arsacius occupied the church of St. Sophia and the archiepiscopal throne. The catholics retreated to the baths of Constantine, and afterwards to the fields, where they were still pursued and insulted by the guards, the bishops, and the magistrates. The fatal day of the second and final exile of Chrysostom was marked by the conflagration of the cathedral, of the senate-house, and of the adjacent buildings; and this calamity was imputed, without proof, but not without probability, to the despair of a persecuted faction.

Cicero might claim some merit if his voluntary banishment preserved the peace of the republic; but the submission of Chrysostom was the indispensable duty of a Christian and a subject. Instead of listening to his humble prayer that he might be permitted to reside at Cyzicus or Nicomedia, the inflexible empress assigned for his exile the remote and desolate town of Cucusus, among the ridges of Mount Taurus, in the Lesser Armenia. A secret hope was entertained that the archbishop might perish in a difficult and dangerous march of seventy days in the heat of summer, through the provinces of Asia Minor, where he was continually threatened by the hostile attacks of the Isaurians, and the more implacable fury of the monks. Yet Chrysostom arrived in safety at the place of his confinement; and the three years which he spent at Cucusus, and the neighbouring town of Arabissus, were the last and most glorious of his life. His character was consecrated by absence and persecution; the faults of his administration were no longer remembered; but every tongue repeated the praises of his genius and virtue: and the respectful attention of the Christian world was fixed on a desert spot among the mountains of Taurus. From that solitude the archbishop, whose active mind was invigorated by misfortunes, maintained a strict and frequent correspondence with the most distant provinces; exhorted the separate congregation of his faithful adherents to persevere in their allegiance; urged the destruction of the temples of Phœnicia, and the extirpation of heresy in the isle of Cyprus; extended his pastoral care to the missions of Persia and Scythia; negotiated, by his ambassadors, with the Roman pontiff and the emperor Honorius; and boldly appealed, from a partial synod, to the supreme tribunal of a free and general council. The mind of the illustrious exile was still independent;

but his captive body was exposed to the revenge of the oppressors, who continued to abuse the name and authority of Arcadius.[1] An order was despatched for the instant removal of Chrysostom to the extreme desert of Pityus: and his guards so faithfully obeyed their cruel instructions, that, before he reached the sea-coast of the Euxine, he expired at Comana, in Pontus, in the sixtieth year of his age. The succeeding generation acknowledged his innocence and merit. The archbishops of the East, who might blush that their predecessors had been the enemies of Chrysostom, were gradually disposed, by the firmness of the Roman pontiff, to restore the honours of that venerable name. At the pious solicitation of the clergy and people of Constantinople, his relics, thirty years after his death, were transported from their obscure sepulchre to the royal city. The emperor Theodosius[2] advanced to receive them as far as Chalcedon; and, falling prostrate on the coffin, implored, in the name of his guilty parents, Arcadius and Eudoxia, the forgiveness of the injured saint.

[*The rivalry of Chrysostom and Theophilus was consecrated by rival theories about the incarnation of Christ. In chapter XLVII Gibbon goes more closely into these theories, which, in the succeeding reign of Theodosius II, provided the fuel for yet greater controversies, first between Cyril (the nephew and successor of Theophilus) in Alexandria and Nestorius in Constantinople, then between their successors in the same sees, Dioscorus and Flavian.*]

All those who believe the immateriality of the soul, a specious and noble tenet, must confess, from their

---

[1] After the exile of Chrysostom, Theophilus published an *enormous* and *horrible* volume against him, in which he perpetually repeats the polite expressions of *hosten humanitatis, sacrilegorum principem immundum dæmonem;* he affirms that John Chrysostom had delivered his soul to be adulterated by the devil; and wishes that some farther punishment, adequate (if possible) to the magnitude of his crimes, may be inflicted on him. St. Jerom, at the request of his friend Theophilus, translated this edifying performance from Greek into Latin.

[2] [i.e., Theodosius II, the son of Arcadius, who reigned 408-450. Ed.]

present experience, the incomprehensible union of mind and matter. A similar union is not inconsistent with a much higher, or even with the highest, degree of mental faculties; and the incarnation of an æon or archangel, the most perfect of created spirits, does not involve any positive contradiction or absurdity. In the age of religious freedom, which was determined by the council of Nice, the dignity of Christ was measured by private judgment according to the indefinite rule of Scripture, or reason, or tradition. But when his pure and proper divinity had been established on the ruins of Arianism, the faith of the Catholics trembled on the edge of a precipice where it was impossible to recede, dangerous to stand, dreadful to fall; and the manifold inconveniences of their creed were aggravated by the sublime character of their theology. They hesitated to pronounce—*that* God himself, the second person of an equal and consubstantial trinity, was manifested in the flesh; *that* a being who pervades the universe had been confined in the womb of Mary; *that* his eternal duration had been marked by the days, and months, and years of human existence; *that* the Almighty had been scourged and crucified; *that* his impassible essence had felt pain and anguish; *that* his omniscience was not exempt from ignorance; and *that* the source of life and immortality expired on Mount Calvary. These alarming consequences were affirmed with unblushing simplicity by Apollinaris, bishop of Laodicea, and one of the luminaries of the church. The son of a learned grammarian, he was skilled in all the sciences of Greece; eloquence, erudition, and philosophy, conspicuous in the volumes of Apollinaris, were humbly devoted to the service of religion. The worthy friend of Athanasius, the worthy antagonist of Julian, he bravely wrestled with the Arians and Polytheists, and, though he affected the rigour of geometrical demonstration, his commentaries revealed the literal and allegorical sense of the Scriptures. A mystery which had long floated in the looseness of popular belief was defined by his perverse diligence in a technical form; and he first proclaimed the memorable words, "One incarnate nature of Christ," which are still re-echoed with hostile clam-

251

ours in the churches of Asia, Egypt, and Æthiopia. He taught that the Godhead was united or mingled with the body of a man; and that the *Logos*, the eternal wisdom, supplied in the flesh the place and office of a human soul. Yet, as the profound doctor had been terrified at his own rashness, Apollinaris was heard to mutter some faint accents of excuse and explanation. He acquiesced in the old distinction of the Greek philosophers between the rational and sensitive soul of man; that he might reserve the *Logos* for intellectual functions, and employ the subordinate human principle in the meaner actions of animal life. With the moderate Docetes he revered Mary as the spiritual, rather than as the carnal, mother of Christ, whose body either came from heaven, impassible and incorruptible, or was absorbed, and as it were transformed, into the essence of the Deity. The system of Apollinaris was strenuously encountered by the Asiatic and Syrian divines, whose schools are honoured by the names of Basil, Gregory, and Chrysostom, and tainted by those of Diodorus, Theodore, and Nestorius. But the person of the aged bishop of Laodicea, his character and dignity, remained inviolate; and his rivals, since we may not suspect them of the weakness of toleration, were astonished, perhaps, by the novelty of the argument, and diffident of the final sentence of the Catholic church. Her judgment at length inclined in their favour; the heresy of Apollinaris was condemned, and the separate congregations of his disciples were proscribed by the Imperial laws. But his principles were secretly entertained in the monasteries of Egypt, and his enemies felt the hatred of Theophilus and Cyril, the successive patriarchs of Alexandria.

The grovelling Ebionite and the fantastic Docetes were rejected and forgotten: the recent zeal against the errors of Apollinaris reduced the Catholics to a seeming agreement with the double nature of Cerinthus.[3] But instead of a temporary and occasional alliance, *they* established, and *we* still embrace, the substantial, indissoluble, and everlasting union of a perfect God with a perfect man,

---

[3] Cerinthus of Asia was the original theorist of the complete separation of the divine and human nature of Christ. *Ed.*]

of the second person of the trinity with a reasonable soul and human flesh. In the beginning of the fifth century the *unity* of the *two natures* was the prevailing doctrine of the church. On all sides it was confessed that the mode of their co-existence could neither be represented by our ideas nor expressed by our language. Yet a secret and incurable discord was cherished between those who were most apprehensive of confounding, and those who were most fearful of separating, the divinity and the humanity of Christ. Impelled by religious frenzy, they fled with adverse haste from the error which they mutually deemed most destructive of truth and salvation. On either hand they were anxious to guard, they were jealous to defend, the union and the distinction of the two natures, and to invent such forms of speech, such symbols of doctrine, as were least susceptible of doubt or ambiguity. The poverty of ideas and language tempted them to ransack art and nature for every possible comparison, and each comparison misled their fancy in the explanation of an incomparable mystery. In the polemic microscope an atom is enlarged to a monster, and each party was skilful to exaggerate the absurd or impious conclusions that might be extorted from the principles of their adversaries. To escape from each other they wandered through many a dark and devious thicket, till they were astonished by the horrid phantoms of Cerinthus and Apollinaris, who guarded the opposite issues of the theological labyrinth. As soon as they beheld the twilight of sense and heresy, they started, measured back their steps, and were again involved in the gloom of impenetrable orthodoxy. To purge themselves from the guilt or reproach of damnable error, they disavowed their consequences, explained their principles, excused their indiscretions, and unanimously pronounced the sounds of concord and faith. Yet a latent and almost invisible spark still lurked among the embers of controversy: by the breath of prejudice and passion it was quickly kindled to a mighty flame, and the verbal disputes of the Oriental sects have shaken the pillars of the church and state.

The name of CYRIL of Alexandria is famous in controversial story, and the title of *saint* is a mark that his opinions and his party have finally prevailed. In the house of his uncle, the archbishop Theophilus, he imbibed the orthodox lessons of zeal and dominion, and five years of his youth were profitably spent in the adjacent monasteries of Nitria. Under the tuition of the abbot Serapion, he applied himself to ecclesiastical studies with such indefatigable ardour, that in the course of *one* sleepless night he has perused the four gospels, the catholic epistles, and the epistle to the Romans. Origen he detested; but the writings of Clemens and Dionysius, of Athanasius and Basil, were continually in his hands: by the theory and practice of dispute, his faith was confirmed and his wit was sharpened; he extended round his cell the cobwebs of scholastic theology, and meditated the works of allegory and metaphysics, whose remains, in seven verbose folios, now peaceably slumber by the side of their rivals. Cyril prayed and fasted in the desert, but his thoughts (it is the reproach of a friend) were still fixed on the world; and the call of Theophilus, who summoned him to the tumult of cities and synods, was too readily obeyed by the aspiring hermit. With the approbation of his uncle he assumed the office and acquired the fame of a popular preacher. His comely person adorned the pulpit; the harmony of his voice resounded in the cathedral; his friends were stationed to lead or second the applause of the congregation; and the hasty notes of the scribes preserved his discourses, which, in their effect, though not in their composition, might be compared with those of the Athenian orators. The death of Theophilus expanded and realised the hopes of his nephew. The clergy of Alexandria was divided; the soldiers and their general supported the claims of the archdeacon; but a resistless multitude, with voices and with hands, asserted the cause of their favourite; and after a period of thirty-nine years Cyril was seated on the throne of Athanasius.

The prize was not unworthy of his ambition. At a distance from the court, and at the head of an immense capital, the patriarch, as he was now styled, of Alexandria had gradually usurped the state and authority of a civil magistrate. The public and private charities of the city were managed by his discretion; his voice inflamed or appeased the passions of the multitude; his commands were blindly obeyed by his numerous and fanatic *parabolani*,[4] familiarised in their daily office with scenes of death; and the præfects of Egypt were awed or provoked by the temporal power of these Christian pontiffs. Ardent in the prosecution of heresy, Cyril auspiciously opened his reign by oppressing the Novatians, the most innocent and harmless of the sectaries. The interdiction of their religious worship appeared in his eyes a just and meritorious act; and he confiscated their holy vessels, without apprehending the guilt of sacrilege. The toleration, and even the privileges of the Jews, who had multiplied to the number of forty thousand, were secured by the laws of the Cæsars and Ptolemies, and a long prescription of seven hundred years since the foundation of Alexandria. Without any legal sentence, without any royal mandate, the patriarch, at the dawn of day, led a seditious multitude to the attack of the synagogues. Unarmed and unprepared, the Jews were incapable of resistance; their houses of prayer were levelled with the ground, and the episcopal warrior, after rewarding his troops with the plunder of their goods, expelled from the city the remnant of the unbelieving nation. Perhaps he might plead the insolence of their prosperity, and their deadly hatred of the Christians, whose blood they had recently shed in a malicious or accidental tumult. Such crimes would have deserved the animadversion of the magistrate; but in this promiscuous outrage the innocent were confounded with the guilty, and Alexandria was impoverished by the loss of a wealthy and industrious colony. The zeal of Cyril exposed him to the penalties of the Julian law; but in a feeble government and a superstitious age he was secure

---

4 The *Parabolani* of Alexandria were a charitable corporation, instituted during the plague of Gallienus, to visit the sick and to bury the dead. They gradually enlarged, abused, and sold the privileges of their order. Their outrageous conduct during the reign of Cyril provoked the emperor to deprive the patriarch of their nomination, and to restrain their number to five or six hundred. But these restraints were transient and ineffectual.

of impunity, and even of praise. Orestes complained; but his just complaints were too quickly forgotten by the ministers of Theodosius, and too deeply remembered by a priest who affected to pardon, and continued to hate, the præfect of Egypt. As he passed through the streets his chariot was assaulted by a band of five hundred of the Nitrian monks; his guards fled from the wild beasts of the desert; his protestations that he was a Christian and a Catholic were answered by a volley of stones, and the face of Orestes was covered with blood. The loyal citizens of Alexandria hastened to his rescue; he instantly satisfied his justice and revenge against the monk by whose hand he had been wounded, and Ammonius expired under the rod of the lictor. At the command of Cyril his body was raised from the ground, and transported in solemn procession to the cathedral; the name of Ammonius was changed to that of Thaumasius, the *wonderful;* his tomb was decorated with the trophies of martyrdom; and the patriarch ascended the pulpit to celebrate the magnanimity of an assassin and a rebel. Such honours might incite the faithful to combat and die under the banners of the saint; and he soon prompted, or accepted, the sacrifice of a virgin, who professed the religion of the Greeks, and cultivated the friendship of Orestes. Hypatia, the daughter of Theon the mathematician, was initiated in her father's studies; her learned comments have elucidated the geometry of Apollonius and Diophantus; and she publicly taught, both at Athens and Alexandria, the philosophy of Plato and Aristotle. In the bloom of beauty, and in the maturity of wisdom, the modest maid refused her lovers and instructed her disciples; the persons most illustrious for their rank or merit were impatient to visit the female philosopher; and Cyril beheld with a jealous eye the gorgeous train of horses and slaves who crowded the door of her academy. A rumour was spread among the Christians that the daughter of Theon was the only obstacle to the reconciliation of the præfect and the archbishop; and that obstacle was speedily removed. On a fatal day, in the holy season of Lent, Hypatia was torn from her chariot, stripped naked, dragged to the church, and inhumanly butchered by the hands of Peter the reader and a troop of savage and merciless fanatics: her flesh was scraped from her bones with sharp oystershells, and her quivering limbs were delivered to the flames. The just progress of inquiry and punishment was stopped by seasonable gifts; but the murder of Hypatia has imprinted an indelible stain on the character and religion of Cyril of Alexandria.[5]

Superstition, perhaps, would more gently expiate the blood of a virgin than the banishment of a saint; and Cyril had accompanied his uncle to the iniquitous synod of the Oak.[6] When the memory of Chrysostom was restored and consecrated, the nephew of Theophilus, at the head of a dying faction, still maintained the justice of his sentence; nor was it till after a tedious delay and an obstinate resistance that he yielded to the consent of the Catholic world. His enmity to the Byzantine pontiffs was a sense of interest, not a sally of passion: he envied their fortunate station in the sunshine of the Imperial court; and he dreaded their upstart ambition, which oppressed the metropolitans of Europe and Asia, invaded the provinces of Antioch and Alexandria, and measured their diocese by the limits of the empire. The long moderation of Atticus, the mild usurper of the throne of Chrysostom, suspended the animosities of the Eastern patriarchs; but Cyril was at length awakened by the exaltation of a rival more worthy of his esteem and hatred. After the short and troubled reign of Sisinnius, bishop of Constantinople, the factions of the clergy and people were appeased by the choice of the emperor, who, on this occasion, consulted the voice of fame, and invited the merit of a stranger. Nestorius, a native of

---

5 These exploits of St. Cyril are recorded by Socrates (1. vii. c. 13, 14, 15); and the most reluctant bigotry is compelled to copy an historian who coolly styles the murders of Hypatia ἄνδρες τὸ φρόνημα ἔνθερμοι [men of warm zeal. *Ed.*] At the mention of that injured name, I am pleased to observe a blush even on the cheek of Baronius.

6 He was deaf to the entreaties of Atticus of Constantinople, and of Isidore of Pelusium, and yielded only (if we may believe Nicephorus) to the personal intercession of the Virgin. Yet in his last years he still muttered that John Chrysostom had been justly condemned.

Germanicia and a monk of Antioch, was recommended by the austerity of his life and the eloquence of his sermons; but the first homily which he preached before the devout Theodosius betrayed the acrimony and impatience of his zeal. "Give me, O Cæsar!" he exclaimed, "give me the earth purged of heretics, and I will give you in exchange the kingdom of heaven. Exterminate with me the heretics, and with you I will exterminate the Persians." On the fifth day, as if the treaty had been already signed, the patriarch of Constantinople discovered, surprised, and attacked a secret conventicle of the Arians; they preferred death to submission; the flames that were kindled by their despair soon spread to the neighbouring houses, and the triumph of Nestorius was clouded by the name of *incendiary*. On either side of the Hellespont his episcopal vigour imposed a rigid formulary of faith and discipline—a chronological error concerning the festival of Easter was punished as an offence against the church and state. Lydia and Caria, Sardes and Miletus, were purified with the blood of the obstinate Quartodecimans; and the edict of the emperor, or rather of the patriarch, enumerates three-and-twenty degrees and denominations in the guilt and punishment of heresy. But the sword of persecution which Nestorius so furiously wielded was soon turned against his own breast. Religion was the pretence; but, in the judgement of a contemporary saint, ambition was the genuine motive of episcopal warfare.

In the Syrian school Nestorius had been taught to abhor the confusion of the two natures, and nicely to discriminate the humanity of his *master* Christ from the divinity of the *Lord* Jesus. The Blessed Virgin he revered as the mother of Christ, but his ears were offended with the rash and recent title of mother of God, which had been insensibly adopted since the origin of the Arian controversy. From the pulpit of Constantinople, a friend of the patriarch, and afterwards the patriarch himself, repeatedly preached against the use, or the abuse, of a word unknown to the apostles, unauthorised by the church, and which could only tend to alarm the timorous, to mislead the simple, to amuse the profane, and to justify, by a seeming resemblance, the old genealogy of Olympus. In his calmer moments Nestorius confessed that it might be tolerated or excused by the union of the two natures, and the communication of their *idioms:* but he was exasperated by contradiction to disclaim the worship of a new-born, an infant Deity, to draw his inadequate similes from the conjugal or civil partnerships of life, and to describe the manhood of Christ as the robe, the instrument, the tabernacle of his Godhead. At these blasphemous sounds the pillars of the sanctuary were shaken. The unsuccessful competitors of Nestorius indulged their pious or personal resentment, the Byzantine clergy was secretly displeased with the intrusion of a stranger: whatever is superstitious or absurd might claim the protection of the monks; and the people was interested in the glory of their virgin patroness. The sermons of the archbishop, and the service of the altar, were disturbed by seditious clamour; his authority and doctrine were renounced by separate congregations; every wind scattered round the empire the leaves of controversy; and the voice of the combatants on a sonorous theatre re-echoed in the cells of Palestine and Egypt. It was the duty of Cyril to enlighten the zeal and ignorance of his innumerable monks: in the school of Alexandria he had imbibed and professed the incarnation of one nature; and the successor of Athanasius consulted his pride and ambition when he rose in arms against another Arius, more formidable and more guilty, on the second throne of the hierarchy. After a short correspondence, in which the rival prelates disguised their hatred in the hollow language of respect and charity, the patriarch of Alexandria denounced to the prince and people, to the East and to the West, the damnable errors of the Byzantine pontiff. From the East, more especially from Antioch, he obtained the ambiguous counsels of toleration and silence, which were addressed to both parties while they favoured the cause of Nestorius. But the Vatican received with open arms the messengers of Egypt. The vanity of Celestine was flattered by the appeal; and the partial version of a monk decided the faith of the pope, who, with his

259

Latin clergy, was ignorant of the language, the arts, and the theology of the Greeks. At the head of an Italian synod, Celestine weighed the merits of the cause, approved the creed of Cyril, condemned the sentiments and person of Nestorius, degraded the heretic from his episcopal dignity, allowed a respite of ten days for recantation and penance, and delegated to his enemy the execution of this rash and illegal sentence. But the patriarch of Alexandria, whilst he darted the thunders of a god, exposed the errors and passions of a mortal; and his twelve anathemas still torture the orthodox slaves who adore the memory of a saint without forfeiting their allegiance to the synod of Chalcedon. These bold assertions are indelibly tinged with the colours of the Apollinarian heresy; but the serious, and perhaps the sincere, professions of Nestorius have satisfied the wiser and less partial theologians of the present times.

Yet neither the emperor nor the primate of the East were disposed to obey the mandate of an Italian priest; and a synod of the Catholic, or rather of the Greek, church was unanimously demanded as the sole remedy that could appease or decide this ecclesiastical quarrel. Ephesus, on all sides accessible by sea and land, was chosen for the place, the festival of Pentecost for the day, of the meeting; a writ of summons was despatched to each metropolitan, and a guard was stationed to protect and confine the fathers till they should settle the mysteries of heaven and the faith of the earth. Nestorius appeared not as a criminal, but as a judge; he depended on the weight rather than the number of his prelates, and his sturdy slaves from the baths of Zeuxippus were armed for every service of injury or defence. But his adversary Cyril was more powerful in the weapons both of the flesh and of the spirit. Disobedient to the letter, or at least to the meaning, of the royal summons, he was attended by fifty Egyptian bishops, who expected from their patriarch's nod the inspiration of the Holy Ghost. He had contracted an intimate alliance with Memnon bishop of Ephesus. The despotic primate of Asia disposed of the ready succours of thirty or forty episcopal votes: a crowd of peasants, the slaves of the church, was poured into the city to support with blows and clamours a metaphysical argument; and the people zealously asserted the honour of the Virgin, whose body reposed within the walls of Ephesus.[7] The fleet which had transported Cyril from Alexandria was laden with the riches of Egypt; and he disembarked a numerous body of mariners, slaves, and fanatics, enlisted with blind obedience under the banner of St. Mark and the mother of God. The fathers, and even the guards, of the council were awed by this martial array; the adversaries of Cyril and Mary were insulted in the streets or threatened in their houses; his eloquence and liberality made a daily increase in the number of his adherents; and the Egyptian soon computed that he might command the attendance and the voices of two hundred bishops. But the author of the twelve anathemas foresaw and dreaded the opposition of John of Antioch, who, with a small though respectable train of metropolitans and divines, was advancing by slow journeys from the distant capital of the East. Impatient of a delay which he stigmatised as voluntary and culpable, Cyril announced the opening of the synod sixteen days after the festival of Pentecost. Nestorius, who depended on the near approach of his Eastern friends, persisted, like his predecessor Chrysostom, to disclaim the jurisdiction, and to disobey the summons, of his enemies: they hastened his trial and his accuser presided in the seat of judgment. Sixty-eight bishops, twenty-two of metropolitan rank, defended his cause by a modest and temperate protest: they were excluded from the councils of their brethren. Candidian, in the emperor's name, requested a delay of four days; the profane magistrate was driven with outrage and insult from the assembly of the saints. The whole of this momentous transaction was crowded into the compass of a summer's day: the bishops delivered their separate opinions; but the uniformity of

---

[7] The Christians of the four first centuries were ignorant of the death and burial of Mary. The tradition of Ephesus is affirmed by the synod; yet it has been superseded by the claim of Jerusalem; and her *empty* sepulchre, as it was shown to the pilgrims, produced the fable of her resurrection and assumption, in which the Greek and Latin churches have piously acquiesced.

style reveals the influence or the hand of a master, who has been accused of corrupting the public evidence of their acts and subscriptions. Without a dissenting voice they recognised in the epistles of Cyril the Nicene creed and the doctrine of the fathers: but the partial extracts from the letters and homilies of Nestorius were interrupted by curses and anathemas; and the heretic was degraded from his episcopal and ecclesiastical dignity. The sentence, maliciously inscribed to the new Judas, was affixed and proclaimed in the streets of Ephesus: the weary prelates, as they issued from the church of the mother of God, were saluted as her champions; and her victory was celebrated by the illuminations, the songs, and the tumult of the night.

On the fifth day the triumph was clouded by the arrival and indignation of the Eastern bishops. In a chamber of the inn, before he had wiped the dust from his shoes, John of Antioch gave audience to Candidian the Imperial minister, who related his ineffectual efforts to prevent or to annul the hasty violence of the Egyptian. With equal haste and violence the Oriental synod of fifty bishops degraded Cyril and Memnon from their episcopal honours; condemned, in the twelve anathemas, the purest venom of the Apollinarian heresy; and described the Alexandrian primate as a monster, born and educated for the destruction of the church. His throne was distant and inaccessible; but they instantly resolved to bestow on the flock of Ephesus the blessing of a faithful shepherd. By the vigilance of Memnon the churches were shut against them, and a strong garrison was thrown into the cathedral. The troops, under the command of Candidian, advanced to the assault; the outguards were routed and put to the sword, but the place was impregnable: the besiegers retired; their retreat was pursued by a vigorous sally; they lost their horses, and many of the soldiers were dangerously wounded with clubs and stones. Ephesus, the city of the Virgin, was defiled with rage and clamour, with sedition and blood; the rival synods darted anathemas and excommunications from their spiritual engines; and the court of Theodosius was perplexed by the adverse and contradictory narratives of the Syrian and Egyptian factions. During a busy period of three months the emperor tried every method, except the most effectual means of indifference and contempt, to reconcile this theological quarrel. He attempted to remove or intimidate the leaders by a common sentence of acquittal or condemnation; he invested his representatives at Ephesus with ample power and military force; he summoned from either party eight chosen deputies to a free and candid conference in the neighbourhood of the capital, far from the contagion of popular frenzy. But the Orientals refused to yield, and the Catholics, proud of their numbers and of their Latin allies, rejected all terms of union or toleration. The patience of the meek Theodosius was provoked, and he dissolved in anger this episcopal tumult, which at the distance of thirteen centuries assumes the venerable aspect of the third œcumenical council. "God is my witness," said the pious prince, "that I am not the author of this confusion. His providence will discern and punish the guilty. Return to your provinces, and may your private virtues repair the mischief and scandal of your meeting." They returned to their provinces; but the same passions which had distracted the synod of Ephesus were diffused over the Eastern world. After three obstinate and equal campaigns, John of Antioch and Cyril of Alexandria condescended to explain and embrace: but their seeming re-union must be imputed rather to prudence than to reason, to the mutual lassitude rather than to the Christian charity of the patriarchs.

The Byzantine pontiff had instilled into the royal ear a baleful prejudice against the character and conduct of his Egyptian rival. An epistle of menace and invective, which accompanied the summons, accused him as a busy, insolent, and envious priest, who perplexed the simplicity of the faith, violated the peace of the church and state, and, by his artful and separate addresses to the wife and sister of Theodosius, presumed to suppose, or to scatter, the seeds of discord in the Imperial family. At the stern command of his sovereign, Cyril had repaired to Ephesus, where he was resisted, threatened, and confined, by the magistrates in the interest of Nestorius and the Orientals, who assembled the troops of Lydia and Ionia to suppress the fanatic and disorderly train of the patriarch. Without expecting the royal licence, he escaped from his guards, precipitately embarked, deserted the imperfect synod, and retired to his episcopal fortress of safety and independence. But his artful emissaries, both in the court and city, successfully laboured to appease the resentment, and to conciliate the favour, of the emperor. The feeble son of Arcadius was alternately swayed by his wife and sister, by the eunuchs and women of the palace: superstition and avarice were their ruling passions; and the orthodox chiefs were assiduous in their endeavours to alarm the former and to gratify the latter. Constantinople and the suburbs were sanctified with frequent monasteries, and the holy abbots, Dalmatius and Eutyches, had devoted their zeal and fidelity to the cause of Cyril, the worship of Mary, and the unity of Christ. From the first moment of their monastic life they had never mingled with the world, or trod the profane ground of the city. But in this awful moment of the danger of the church, their vow was superseded by a more sublime and indispensable duty. At the head of a long order of monks and hermits, who carried burning tapers in their hands, and chanted litanies to the mother of God, they proceeded from their monasteries to the palace. The people was edified and inflamed by this extraordinary spectacle, and the trembling monarch listened to the prayers and adjurations of the saints, who boldly pronounced that none could hope for salvation unless they embraced the person and the creed of the orthodox successor of Athanasius. At the same time every avenue of the throne was assaulted with gold. Under the decent names of *eulogies* and *benedictions,* the courtiers of both sexes were bribed according to the measure of their power and rapaciousness. But their incessant demands despoiled the sanctuaries of Constantinople and Alexandria; and the authority of the patriarch was unable to silence the just murmur of his clergy, that a debt of sixty thousand pounds had already been contracted to support the expense of this scandalous corruption. Pulcheria, who relieved her brother from the weight of an empire, was the firmest pillar of orthodoxy; and so intimate was the alliance between the thunders of the synod and the whispers of the court, that Cyril was assured of success if he could displace one eunuch, and substitute another in the favour of Theodosius. Yet the Egyptian could not boast of a glorious or decisive victory. The emperor, with unaccustomed firmness, adhered to his promise of protecting the innocence of the Oriental bishops; and Cyril softened his anathemas, and confessed, with ambiguity and reluctance, a twofold nature of Christ, before he was permitted to satiate his revenge against the unfortunate Nestorius.

The rash and obstinate Nestorius, before the end of the synod, was oppressed by Cyril, betrayed by the court, and faintly supported by his Eastern friends. A sentiment of fear or indignation prompted him, while it was yet time, to affect the glory of a voluntary abdication: his wish, or at least his request, was readily granted; he was conducted with honour from Ephesus to his old monastery of Antioch; and, after a short pause, his successors, Maximian and Proclus, were acknowledged as the lawful bishops of Constantinople. But in the silence of his cell the degraded patriarch could no longer resume the innocence and security of a private monk. The past he regretted, he was discontented with the present, and the future he had reason to dread: the Oriental bishops successively disengaged their cause from his unpopular name, and each day decreased the number of the schismatics who revered Nestorius as the confessor of the faith. After a residence at Antioch of four years, the hand of Theodosius subscribed an edict which ranked him with Simon the magician, proscribed his opinions and followers, condemned his writings to the flames, and banished his person first to Petra in Arabia, and at length to Oasis, one of the *islands* of the Libyan desert. Secluded from the church and from the world, the exile was still pursued by the rage of bigotry and war. A wandering tribe of the Blemmyes or Nubians invaded his solitary prison: in their retreat they dismissed a

265

crowd of useless captives; but no sooner had Nestorius reached the banks of the Nile, than he would gladly have escaped from a Roman and orthodox city to the milder servitude of the savages. His flight was punished as a new crime: the soul of the patriarch inspired the civil and ecclesiastical powers of Egypt; the magistrates, the soldiers, the monks, devoutly tortured the enemy of Christ and St. Cyril; and, as far as the confines of Æthiopia, the heretic was alternately dragged and re-called, till his aged body was broken by the hardships and accidents of these reiterated journeys. Yet his mind was still independent and erect; the president of Thebais was awed by his pastoral letters; he survived the Catho-lic tyrant of Alexandria, and, after sixteen years' banish-ment, the synod of Chalcedon would perhaps have re-stored him to the honours, or at least to the communion, of the church. The death of Nestorius prevented his obedience to their welcome summons; and his disease might afford some colour to the scandalous report, that his tongue, the organ of blasphemy, had been eaten by the worms. He was buried in a city of Upper Egypt, known by the names of Chemnis, or Panopolis, or Akmim; but the immortal malice of the Jacobites has persevered for ages to cast stones against his sepulchre, and to propagate the foolish tradition that it was never watered by the rain of heaven, which equally descends on the righteous and the ungodly. Humanity may drop a tear on the fate of Nestorius; yet justice must observe that he suffered the persecution which he had approved and inflicted.

The death of the Alexandrian primate, after a reign of thirty-two years, abandoned the Catholics to the in-temperance of zeal and the abuse of victory. The *mono-physite* doctrine (one incarnate nature) was rigorously preached in the churches of Egypt and the monasteries of the East; the primitive creed of Apollinaris was pro-tected by the sanctity of Cyril; and the name of EUTY-CHES, his venerable friend, has been applied to the sect most adverse to the Syrian heresy of Nestorius. His rival Eutyches was the abbot, or archimandrite, or superior of three hundred monks; but the opinions of a simple and illiterate recluse might have expired in the cell where he had slept above seventy years if the resentment or indiscretion of Flavian, the Byzantine pontiff, had not exposed the scandal to the eyes of the Christian world. His domestic synod was instantly convened, their proceedings were sullied with clamour and artifice, and the aged heretic was surprised into a seeming confession that Christ had not derived his body from the substance of the Virgin Mary. From their partial decree Eutyches appealed to a general council; and his cause was vigorously asserted by his godson Chrysaphius, the reigning eunuch of the palace, and his accomplice Dioscorus, who had succeeded to the throne, the creed, the talents, and the vices of the nephew of Theophilus. By the special summons of Theodosius, the second synod of Ephesus was judiciously composed of ten metropolitans and ten bishops from each of the six dioceses of the Eastern empire: some exceptions of favour or merit enlarged the number to one hundred and thirty-five; and the Syrian Barsumas, as the chief and representative of the monks, was invited to sit and vote with the successors of the apostles. But the despotism of the Alexandrian patriarch again oppressed the freedom of debate: the same spiritual and carnal weapons were again drawn from the arsenals of Egypt; the Asiatic veterans, a band of archers, served under the orders of Dioscorus; and the more formidable monks, whose minds were inaccessible to reason or mercy, besieged the doors of the cathedral. The general and, as it should seem, the unconstrained voice of the fathers accepted the faith and even the anathemas of Cyril; and the heresy of the two natures was formally condemned in the persons and writings of the most learned Orientals. "May those who divide Christ be divided with the sword, may they be hewn in pieces, may they be burned alive!" were the charitable wishes of a Christian synod. The innocence and sanctity of Eutyches were acknowledged without hesitation; but the prelates, more especially those of Thrace and Asia, were unwilling to depose their patriarch for the use or even the abuse of his lawful jurisdiction. They embraced the knees of Dioscorus, as he stood with a threatening aspect on the footstool of his throne, and conjured him to forgive the offences and to respect the dignity of his brother. "Do you mean to raise a sedition?" exclaimed the relentless tyrant. "Where are the officers?" At these words a furious multitude of monks and soldiers, with stakes, and swords, and chains, burst into the church: the trembling bishops hid themselves behind the altar or under the benches; and as they were not inspired with the zeal of martyrdom, they successively subscribed a blank paper, which was afterwards filled with the condemnation of the Byzantine pontiff. Flavian was instantly delivered to the wild beasts of this spiritual amphitheatre: the monks were stimulated by the voice and example of Barsumas to avenge the injuries of Christ: it is said that the patriarch of Alexandria reviled, and buffeted, and kicked, and trampled his brother of Constantinople: it is certain that the victim, before he could reach the place of his exile, expired on the third day of the wounds and bruises which he had received at Ephesus. This second synod has been justly branded as a gang of robbers and assassins; yet the accusers of Dioscorus would magnify his violence, to alleviate the cowardice and inconstancy of their own behaviour.

The faith of Egypt had prevailed: but the vanquished party was supported by the same pope who encountered without fear the hostile rage of Attila and Genseric. The theology of Leo, his famous *tome* or epistle on the mystery of the incarnation, had been disregarded by the synod of Ephesus: his authority, and that of the Latin church, was insulted in his legates, who escaped from slavery and death to relate the melancholy tale of the tyranny of Dioscorus and the martyrdom of Flavian. His provincial synod annulled the irregular proceedings of Ephesus; but as this step was itself irregular, he solicited the convocation of a general council in the free and orthodox provinces of Italy. From his independent throne the Roman bishop spoke and acted without danger as the head of the Christians, and his dictates were obsequiously transcribed by Placidia and her son

Valentinian,[8] who addressed their Eastern colleague to restore the peace and unity of the church. But the pageant of Oriental royalty was moved with equal dexterity by the hand of the eunuch; and Theodosius could pronounce, without hesitation, that the church was already peaceful and triumphant, and that the recent flame had been extinguished by the just punishment of the Nestorians. Perhaps the Greeks would be still involved in the heresy of the Monophysites, if the emperor's horse had not fortunately stumbled; Theodosius expired; his orthodox sister, Pulcheria, with a nominal husband, succeeded to the throne; Chrysaphius was burnt, Dioscorus was disgraced, the exiles were recalled, and the *tome* of Leo was subscribed by the Oriental bishops. Yet the pope was disappointed in his favourite project of a Latin council: he disdained to preside in the Greek synod which was speedily assembled at Nice in Bithynia; his legates required in a peremptory tone the presence of the emperor; and the weary fathers were transported to Chalcedon under the immediate eye of Marcian and the senate of Constantinople. A quarter of a mile from the Thracian Bosphorus the church of St. Euphemia was built on the summit of a gentle though lofty ascent: the triple structure was celebrated as a prodigy of art, and the boundless prospect of the land and sea might have raised the mind of a sectary to the contemplation of the God of the universe. Six hundred and thirty bishops were ranged in order in the nave of the church; but the patriarchs of the East were preceded by the legates, of whom the third was a simple priest; and the place of honour was reserved for twenty laymen of consular or senatorian rank. The gospel was ostentatiously displayed in the centre, but the rule of faith was defined by the papal and imperial ministers, who moderated the thirteen sessions of the council of Chalcedon. Their partial interposition silenced the intemperate shouts and execrations which degraded the episcopal gravity; but on the formal accusation of the

---

8 [Placidia, daughter of Theodosius the Great, ruled the Western Empire in the name of her son Valentinian III from 425 till her death in 450. *Ed.*]

legates, Dioscorus was compelled to descend from his throne to the rank of a criminal, already condemned in the opinion of his judges. The Orientals, less adverse to Nestorius than to Cyril, accepted the Romans as their deliverers: Thrace, and Pontus, and Asia, were exasperated against the murderer of Flavian, and the new patriarchs of Constantinople and Antioch secured their places by the sacrifice of their benefactor. The bishops of Palestine, Macedonia, and Greece were attached to the faith of Cyril; but in the face of the synod, in the heat of the battle, the leaders, with their obsequious train, passed from the right to the left wing, and decided the victory by this seasonable desertion. Of the seventeen suffragans who sailed from Alexandria, four were tempted from their allegiance, and the thirteen, falling prostrate on the ground, implored the mercy of the council, with sighs and tears, and a pathetic declaration, that, if they yielded, they should be massacred, on their return to Egypt, by the indignant people. A tardy repentance was allowed to expiate the guilt or error of the accomplices of Dioscorus: but their sins were accumulated on his head; he neither asked nor hoped for pardon, and the moderation of those who pleaded for a general amnesty was drowned in the prevailing cry of victory and revenge. To save the reputation of his late adherents, some *personal* offences were skilfully detected; his rash and illegal excommunication of the pope, and his contumacious refusal (while he was detained a prisoner) to attend the summons of the synod. Witnesses were introduced to prove the special facts of his pride, avarice, and cruelty; and the fathers heard with abhorrence that the alms of the church were lavished on the female dancers, that his palace, and even his bath, was open to the prostitutes of Alexandria, and that the infamous Pansophia, or Irene, was publicly entertained as the concubine of the patriarch.

For these scandalous offences Dioscorus was deposed by the synod and banished by the emperor; but the purity of his faith was declared in the presence, and with the tacit approbation, of the fathers. Their prudence supposed rather than pronounced the heresy of

Eutyches, who was never summoned before their tribunal; and they sat silent and abashed when a bold Monophysite, casting at their feet a volume of Cyril, challenged them to anathematise in his person the doctrine of the saint. If we fairly peruse the acts of Chalcedon as they are recorded by the orthodox party, we shall find that a great majority of the bishops embraced the simple unity of Christ; and the ambiguous concession that he was formed OF or FROM two natures might imply either their previous existence, or their subsequent confusion, or some dangerous interval between the conception of the man and the assumption of the God. The Roman theology, more positive and precise, adopted the term most offensive to the ears of the Egyptians, that Christ existed IN two natures; and this momentous particle (which the memory, rather than the understanding, must retain) had almost produced a schism among the Catholic bishops. The *tome* of Leo had been respectfully, perhaps sincerely, subscribed; but they protested, in two successive debates, that it was neither expedient nor lawful to transgress the sacred landmarks which had been fixed at Nice, Constantinople, and Ephesus, according to the rule of Scripture and tradition. At length they yielded to the importunities of their masters, but their infallible decree, after it had been ratified with deliberate votes and vehement acclamations, was overturned in the next session by the opposition of the legates and their Oriental friends. It was in vain that a multitude of episcopal voices repeated in chorus, "The definition of the fathers is orthodox and immutable! The heretics are now discovered! Anathema to the Nestorians! Let them depart from the synod! Let them repair to Rome." The legates threatened, the emperor was absolute, and a committee of eighteen bishops prepared a new decree, which was imposed on the reluctant assembly. In the name of the fourth general council, the Christ in one person, but *in* two natures, was announced to the Catholic world: an invisible line was drawn between the heresy of Apollinaris and the faith of St. Cyril; and the road to paradise, a bridge as sharp as a razor, was suspended over the abyss by the master-hand of the theological artist. During ten centuries of blindness and servitude Europe received her religious opinions from the oracle of the Vatican; and the same doctrine, already varnished with the rust of antiquity, was admitted without dispute into the creed of the reformers, who disclaimed the supremacy of the Roman pontiff. The synod of Chalcedon still triumphs in the Protestant churches: but the ferment of controversy has subsided, and the most pious Christians of the present day are ignorant, or careless, of their own belief concerning the mystery of the incarnation.

9. The End of the Western Empire

[Meanwhile the Western Empire was slowly crumbling under the blows of the barbarians. By the middle of the fifth century the Goths were partly romanised and Christianised (through Arian); but the Vandals, who conquered Africa, were barbarians and the Saxons, who invaded England, and the Huns, who overran Gaul, were heathen as well. In its last days, the Western Empire was a barbarian protectorate, and in 476 its protector, Odoacer, "resolved to abolish the useless and expensive office" of Emperor. Having forced the abdication of its last holder, Romulus Augustulus, he made himself King of Italy. At this point (chapter XXXVIII) Gibbon inserted his "General Observations on the Fall of the Roman Empire in the West."]

The Greeks, after their country had been reduced into a province, imputed the triumphs of Rome, not to the merit, but to the FORTUNE, of the republic. The inconstant goddess, who so blindly distributes and resumes her favours, had *now* consented (such was the language of envious flattery) to resign her wings, to descend from her globe, and to fix her firm and immutable throne on the banks of the Tiber. A wiser Greek, who has composed, with a philosophic spirit, the memorable history of his own times, deprived his countrymen of this vain and delusive comfort, by opening to their view the deep foundations of the greatness of Rome. The fidelity of the citizens to each other and to the state was confirmed by the habits of education and the prejudices of religion.

273

Honour, as well as virtue, was the principle of the republic; the ambitious citizens laboured to deserve the solemn glories of a triumph; and the ardour of the Roman youth was kindled into active emulation as often as they beheld the domestic images of their ancestors. The temperate struggles of the patricians and plebeians had finally established the firm and equal balance of the constitution, which united the freedom of popular assemblies with the authority and wisdom of a senate and the executive powers of a regal magistrate. When the consul displayed the standard of the republic, each citizen bound himself, by the obligation of an oath, to draw his sword in the cause of his country till he had discharged the sacred duty by a military service of ten years. This wise institution continually poured into the field the rising generations of freemen and soldiers; and their numbers were reinforced by the warlike and populous states of Italy, who, after a brave resistance, had yielded to the valour and embraced the alliance of the Romans. The sage historian, who excited the virtue of the younger Scipio and beheld the ruin of Carthage, has accurately described their military system; their levies, arms, exercises, subordination, marches, encampments; and the invincible legion, superior in active strength to the Macedonian phalanx of Philip and Alexander. From these institutions of peace and war Polybius has deduced the spirit and success of a people incapable of fear and impatient of repose. The ambitious design of conquest, which might have been defeated by the seasonable conspiracy of mankind, was attempted and achieved; and the perpetual violation of justice was maintained by the political virtues of prudence and courage. The arms of the republic, sometimes vanquished in battle, always victorious in war, advanced with rapid steps to the Euphrates, the Danube, the Rhine, and the Ocean; and the images of gold, or silver, or brass, that might serve to represent the nations and their kings, were successively broken by the *iron* monarchy of Rome.

The rise of a city, which swelled into an empire, may deserve, as a singular prodigy, the reflection of a philosophic mind. But the decline of Rome was the natural and inevitable effect of immoderate greatness. Prosperity ripened the principle of decay; the causes of destruction multiplied with the extent of conquest; and as soon as time or accident had removed the artificial supports, the stupendous fabric yielded to the pressure of its own weight. The story of its ruin is simple and obvious; and instead of inquiring *why* the Roman empire was destroyed, we should rather be surprised that it had subsisted so long. The victorious legions, who, in distant wars, acquired the vices of strangers and mercenaries, first oppressed the freedom of the republic, and afterwards violated the majesty of the purple. The emperors, anxious for their personal safety and the public peace, were reduced to the base expedient of corrupting the discipline which rendered them alike formidable to their sovereign and to the enemy; the vigour of the military government was relaxed and finally dissolved by the partial institutions of Constantine; and the Roman world was overwhelmed by a deluge of barbarians.

The decay of Rome has been frequently ascribed to the translation of the seat of empire; but this history has already shown that the powers of government were *divided* rather than *removed*. The throne of Constantinople was erected in the East; while the West was still possessed by a series of emperors who held their residence in Italy, and claimed their equal inheritance of the legions and provinces. This dangerous novelty impaired the strength and fomented the vices of a double reign: the instruments of an oppressive and arbitrary system were multiplied; and a vain emulation of luxury, not of merit, was introduced and supported between the degenerate successors of Theodosius. Extreme distress, which unites the virtue of a free people, embitters the factions of a declining monarchy. The hostile favourites of Arcadius and Honorius betrayed the republic to its common enemies; and the Byzantine court beheld with indifference, perhaps with pleasure, the disgrace of Rome, the misfortunes of Italy, and the loss of the West. Under the succeeding reigns the alliance of the two empires was restored; but the aid of the Oriental Romans was tardy, doubtful, and ineffectual; and the national schism of the

275

Greeks and Latins was enlarged by the perpetual difference of language and manners, of interests, and even of religion. Yet the salutary event approved in some measure the judgement of Constantine. During a long period of decay his impregnable city repelled the victorious armies of barbarians, protected the wealth of Asia, and commanded, both in peace and war, the important straits which connect the Euxine and Mediterranean seas. The foundation of Constantinople more essentially contributed to the preservation of the East than to the ruin of the West.

As the happiness of a *future* life is the great object of religion, we may hear without surprise or scandal that the introduction, or at least the abuse of Christianity, had some influence on the decline and fall of the Roman empire. The clergy successfully preached the doctrines of patience and pusillanimity; the active virtues of society were discouraged; and the last remains of military spirit were buried in the cloister: a large portion of public and private wealth was consecrated to the specious demands of charity and devotion; and the soldiers' pay was lavished on the useless multitudes of both sexes who could only plead the merits of abstinence and chastity. Faith, zeal, curiosity, and the more earthly passions of malice and ambition, kindled the flame of theological discord; the church, and even the state, were distracted by religious factions, whose conflicts were sometimes bloody and always implacable; the attention of the emperors was diverted from camps to synods; the Roman world was oppressed by a new species of tyranny; and the persecuted sects became the secret enemies of their country. Yet party-spirit, however pernicious or absurd, is a principle of union as well as of dissension. The bishops, from eighteen hundred pulpits, inculcated the duty of passive obedience to a lawful and orthodox sovereign; their frequent assemblies and perpetual correspondence maintained the communion of distant churches; and the benevolent temper of the Gospel was strengthened, though confined, by the spiritual alliance of the catholics. The sacred indolence of the monks was devoutly embraced by a servile and effeminate age; but if superstition had not afforded a decent retreat, the same vices would have tempted the unworthy Romans to desert, from baser motives, the standard of the republic. Religious precepts are easily obeyed which indulge and sanctify the natural inclinations of their votaries; but the pure and genuine influence of Christianity may be traced in its beneficial, though imperfect, effects on the barbarian proselytes of the North. If the decline of the Roman empire was hastened by the conversion of Constantine, his victorious religion broke the violence of the fall, and mollified the ferocious temper of the conquerors.

This awful revolution may be usefully applied to the instruction of the present age. It is the duty of a patriot to prefer and promote the exclusive interest and glory of his native country: but a philosopher may be permitted to enlarge his views, and to consider Europe as one great republic, whose various inhabitants have attained almost the same level of politeness and cultivation. The balance of power will continue to fluctuate, and the prosperity of our own or the neighbouring kingdoms may be alternately exalted or depressed; but these partial events cannot essentially injure our general state of happiness, the system of arts, and laws, and manners, which so advantageously distinguish, above the rest of mankind, the Europeans and their colonies. The savage nations of the globe are the common enemies of civilised society; and we may inquire, with anxious curiosity, whether Europe is still threatened with a repetition of those calamities which formerly oppressed the arms and institutions of Rome. Perhaps the same reflections will illustrate the fall of that mighty empire, and explain the probable causes of our actual security.

I. The Romans were ignorant of the extent of their danger and the number of their enemies. Beyond the Rhine and Danube the northern countries of Europe and Asia were filled with innumerable tribes of hunters and shepherds, poor, voracious, and turbulent; bold in arms, and impatient to ravish the fruits of industry. The barbarian world was agitated by the rapid impulse of war; and the peace of Gaul or Italy was shaken by the distant revolutions of China. The Huns, who fled before a vic-

torious enemy, directed their march towards the West;
and the torrent was swelled by the gradual accession of
captives and allies. The flying tribes who yielded to the
Huns assumed in *their* turn the spirit of conquest; the
endless column of barbarians pressed on the Roman empire with accumulated weight; and, if the foremost were
destroyed, the vacant space was instantly replenished by
new assailants. Such formidable emigrations no longer
issue from the North; and the long repose, which has
been imputed to the decrease of population, is the happy
consequence of the progress of arts and agriculture. Instead of some rude villages thinly scattered among its
woods and morasses, Germany now produces a list of
two thousand three hundred walled towns: the Christian kingdoms of Denmark, Sweden, and Poland have
been successively established; and the Hanse merchants,
with the Teutonic knights, have extended their colonies
along the coast of the Baltic as far as the Gulf of Finland. From the Gulf of Finland to the Eastern Ocean,
Russia now assumes the form of a powerful and civilised
empire. The plough, the loom, and the forge are introduced on the banks of the Volga, the Oby, and the
Lena; and the fiercest of the Tartar hordes have been
taught to tremble and obey. The reign of independent
barbarism is now contracted to a narrow span; and the
remnant of Calmucks or Uzbecks, whose forces may be
almost numbered, cannot seriously excite the apprehensions of the great republic of Europe. Yet this apparent
security should not tempt us to forget that new enemies
and unknown dangers may *possibly* arise from some
obscure people, scarcely visible in the map of the world.
The Arabs or Saracens, who spread their conquests from
India to Spain, had languished in poverty and contempt
till Mahomet breathed into those savage bodies the soul
of enthusiasm.

II. The empire of Rome was firmly established by the
singular and perfect coalition of its members. The subject nations, resigning the hope and even the wish of
independence, embraced the character of Roman citizens; and the provinces of the West were reluctantly
torn by the barbarians from the bosom of their mother

country. But this union was purchased by the loss of national freedom and military spirit; and the servile provinces, destitute of life and motion, expected their safety from the mercenary troops and governors who were directed by the orders of a distant court. The happiness of an hundred millions depended on the personal merit of one or two men, perhaps children, whose minds were corrupted by education, luxury, and despotic power. The deepest wounds were inflicted on the empire during the minorities of the sons and grandsons of Theodosius; and, after those incapable princes seemed to attain the age of manhood, they abandoned the church to the bishops, the state to the eunuchs, and the provinces to the barbarians. Europe is now divided into twelve powerful, though unequal kingdoms, three respectable commonwealths, and a variety of smaller, though independent states: the chances of royal and ministerial talents are multiplied, at least, with the number of its rulers; and a Julian, or Semiramis, may reign in the North, while Arcadius and Honorius again slumber on the thrones of the South. The abuses of tyranny are restrained by the mutual influence of fear and shame; republics have acquired order and stability; monarchies have imbibed the principles of freedom, or, at least, of moderation; and some sense of honour and justice is introduced into the most defective constitutions by the general manners of the times. In peace, the progress of knowledge and industry is accelerated by the emulation of so many active rivals: in war, the European forces are exercised by temperate and undecisive contests. If a savage conqueror should issue from the deserts of Tartary, he must repeatedly vanquish the robust peasants of Russia, the numerous armies of Germany, the gallant nobles of France, and the intrepid freemen of Britain; who, perhaps, might confederate for their common defence. Should the victorious barbarians carry slavery and desolation as far as the Atlantic Ocean, ten thousand vessels would transport beyond their pursuit the remains of civilised society; and Europe would revive and flourish in the American world, which is already filled with her colonies and institutions.

III. Cold, poverty, and a life of danger and fatigue fortify the strength and courage of barbarians. In every age they have oppressed the polite and peaceful nations of China, India, and Persia, who neglected, and still neglect, to counterbalance these natural powers by the resources of military art. The warlike states of antiquity, Greece, Macedonia, and Rome, educated a race of soldiers; exercised their bodies, disciplined their courage, multiplied their forces by regular evolutions, and converted the iron which they possessed into strong and serviceable weapons. But this superiority insensibly declined with their laws and manners: and the feeble policy of Constantine and his successors armed and instructed, for the ruin of the empire, the rude valour of the barbarian mercenaries. The military art has been changed by the invention of gunpowder; which enables man to command the two most powerful agents of nature, air and fire. Mathematics, chemistry, mechanics, architecture, have been applied to the service of war; and the adverse parties oppose to each other the most elaborate modes of attack and of defence. Historians may indignantly observe that the preparations of a siege would found and maintain a flourishing colony; yet we cannot be displeased that the subversion of a city should be a work of cost and difficulty; or that an industrious people should be protected by those arts which survive and supply the decay of military virtue. Cannon and fortifications now form an impregnable barrier against the Tartar horse; and Europe is secure from any future eruption of barbarians; since, before they can conquer, they must cease to be barbarous. Their gradual advances in the science of war would always be accompanied, as we may learn from the example of Russia, with a proportionable improvement in the arts of peace and civil policy; and they themselves must deserve a place among the polished nations whom they subdue.

Should these speculations be found doubtful or fallacious, there still remains a more humble source of comfort and hope. The discoveries of ancient and modern navigators, and the domestic history or tradition of the most enlightened nations, represent the *human savage* naked both in mind and body, and destitute of laws, of arts, of ideas, and almost of language. From this abject condition, perhaps the primitive and universal state of man, he has gradually arisen to command the animals, to fertilise the earth, to traverse the ocean, and to measure the heavens. His progress in the improvement and exercise of his mental and corporeal faculties has been irregular and various; infinitely slow in the beginning, and increasing by degrees with redoubled velocity: ages of laborious ascent have been followed by a moment of rapid downfall; and the several climates of the globe have felt the vicissitudes of light and darkness. Yet the experience of four thousand years should enlarge our hopes and diminish our apprehensions: we cannot determine to what height the human species may aspire in their advances towards perfection; but it may safely be presumed that no people, unless the face of nature is changed, will relapse into their original barbarism. The improvements of society may be viewed under a threefold aspect. 1. The poet or philosopher illustrates his age and country by the efforts of a *single* mind; but these superior powers of reason or fancy are rare and spontaneous productions; and the genius of Homer, or Cicero, or Newton, would excite less admiration if they could be created by the will of a prince or the lessons of a preceptor. 2. The benefits of law and policy, of trade and manufactures, of arts and sciences, are more solid and permanent; and *many* individuals may be qualified, by education and discipline, to promote, in their respective stations, the interest of the community. But this general order is the effect of skill and labour; and the complex machinery may be decayed by time, or injured by violence. 3. Fortunately for mankind, the more useful, or, at least, more necessary arts, can be performed without superior talents or national subordination; without the powers of *one*, or the union of *many*. Each village, each family, each individual, must always possess both ability and inclination to perpetuate the use of fire and of metals; the propagation and service of domestic animals; the methods of hunting and fishing; the rudiments of navigation; the imperfect cultivation of corn or other

281

nutritive grain; and the simple practice of the mechanic trades. Private genius and public industry may be extirpated; but these hardy plants survive the tempest, and strike an everlasting root into the most unfavourable soil. The splendid days of Augustus and Trajan were eclipsed by a cloud of ignorance; and the barbarians subverted the laws and palaces of Rome. But the scythe, the invention or emblem of Saturn, still continued annually to mow the harvests of Italy; and the human feasts of the Læstrigons have never been renewed on the coast of Campania.

Since the first discovery of the arts, war, commerce, and religious zeal have diffused among the savages of the Old and New World these inestimable gifts: they have been successively propagated; they can never be lost. We may therefore acquiesce in the pleasing conclusion that every age of the world has increased and still increases the real wealth, the happiness, the knowledge, and perhaps the virtue, of the human race.[1]

---

[1] The merit of discovery has too often been stained with avarice, cruelty, and fanaticism; and the intercourse of nations has produced the communication of disease and prejudice. A singular exception is due to the virtue of our own times and country. The five great voyages, successively undertaken by the command of his present Majesty, were inspired by the pure and generous love of science and of mankind. The same prince, adapting his benefactions to the different stages of society, has founded a school of painting in his capital, and has introduced into the islands of the South Sea the vegetables and animals most useful to human life.

10. The Gothic Kingdom of Italy

[*The Western Empire might have collapsed, but the Dark Age had not yet begun; for the barbarian successor-states retained and cherished much of the old structure. In Italy, Theodoric the Ostrogoth, having destroyed Odoacer, established himself in the old imperial capital of Ravenna and reigned for 26 years (493-526 A.D.), under the nominal sovereignty of Constantinople. This stable Gothic kingdom of Italy, which Gibbon describes in chapter XXXIX, continued Roman institutions after the end of the Western Empire. Theodoric himself is described by Gibbon as a "rare and meritorious example of a barbarian who sheathed his sword in the pride of victory and the vigour of his age," "a Gothic king who might have deserved a statue among the best and bravest of the ancient Romans." The most famous of his ministers was the senator Boethius, whose* Consolation of Philosophy *was afterwards translated into Anglo-Saxon by King Alfred, and became a favourite book of the Middle Ages.*]

The union of the Goths and Romans might have fixed for ages the transient happiness of Italy; and the first of nations, a new people of free subjects and enlightened soldiers, might have gradually arisen from the mutual emulation of their respective virtues. But the sublime merit of guiding or seconding such a revolution was not reserved for the reign of Theodoric: he wanted either the genius or the opportunities of a legislator; and while he indulged the Goths in the enjoyment of rude liberty, he servilely copied the institutions, and even the abuses, of the political system which had been framed by Constantine and his successors. From a tender regard to the expiring prejudices of Rome, the barbarian declined the name, the purple, and the diadem of the emperors; but he assumed, under the hereditary title of king, the whole substance and plenitude of Imperial prerogative. His addresses to the Eastern throne were respectful and ambiguous: he celebrated in pompous style the harmony of the two republics, applauded his own government as the perfect similitude of a sole and undivided empire, and claimed above the kings of the earth the same preeminence which he modestly allowed to the person or rank of Anastasius. The alliance of the East and West was annually declared by the unanimous choice of two consuls; but it should seem that the Italian candidate, who was named by Theodoric, accepted a formal confirmation from the sovereign of Constantinople. The Gothic palace of Ravenna reflected the image of the court of Theodosius or Valentinian. The Prætorian præfect, the præfect of Rome, the quæstor, the master of the offices, with the public and patrimonial treasurers, whose functions are painted in gaudy colours by the rhetoric of Cassiodorus, still continued to act as the ministers of state. And the subordinate care of justice and the revenue was delegated to seven consulars, three correctors, and five presidents, who governed the fifteen *regions* of Italy according to the principles, and even the forms, of Roman jurisprudence. The violence of the conquerors was abated or eluded by the slow artifice of judicial proceedings; the civil administration, with its honours and emoluments, was confined to the Italians; and the people still preserved their dress and language, their laws and customs, their personal freedom, and two-thirds of their landed property. It had been the object of Augustus to conceal the introduction of monarchy; it was the policy of Theodoric to disguise the reign of a barbarian. If his subjects were sometimes awakened from this pleasing vision of a Roman government, they derived more substantial comfort from the character of a Gothic prince who had penetration to discern, and firmness to pursue, his own and the public interest. Theodoric loved the virtues which he possessed, and the talents of which he was destitute. Liberius was promoted to the office of Prætorian præfect for his unshaken fidelity to the unfortunate cause of Odoacer. The ministers of Theodoric, Cassiodorus, and Boethius, have reflected on his reign the lustre of their genius and learning. More prudent or more fortunate than his colleague, Cassiodorus preserved his own esteem without forfeiting the royal favour; and after passing thirty years in the honours of the world, he was blessed with an equal term of repose in the devout and studious solitude of Squillace.

As the patron of the republic, it was the interest and duty of the Gothic king to cultivate the affections of the senate and people. The nobles of Rome were flattered by sonorous epithets and formal professions of respect, which had been more justly applied to the merit and authority of their ancestors. The people enjoyed, without fear or danger, the three blessings of a capital, order, plenty, and public amusements. A visible diminution of their numbers may be found even in the measure of liberality; yet Apulia, Calabria, and Sicily poured their tribute of corn into the granaries of Rome; an allowance of bread and meat was distributed to the indigent citizens; and every office was deemed honourable which was consecrated to the care of their health and happiness. The public games, such as a Greek ambassador might politely applaud, exhibited a faint and feeble copy of the magnificence of the Cæsars: yet the musical, the gymnastic, and the pantomime arts, had not totally sunk in oblivion; the wild beasts of Africa still exercised in the amphitheatre the courage and dexterity of the hunters; and the indulgent Goth either patiently tolerated or gently restrained the blue and green factions, whose contests so often filled the circus with clamour, and even with blood. In the seventh year of his peaceful reign, Theodoric visited the old capital of the world; the senate and people advanced in solemn procession to salute a second Trajan, a new Valentinian; and he nobly supported that character, by the assurance of a just and legal government, in a discourse which he was

285

not afraid to pronounce in public and to inscribe on a tablet of brass. Rome, in this august ceremony, shot a last ray of declining glory; and a saint, the spectator of this pompous scene, could only hope, in his pious fancy, that it was excelled by the celestial splendour of the New Jerusalem. During a residence of six months, the fame, the person, and the courteous demeanour of the Gothic king excited the admiration of the Romans, and he contemplated, with equal curiosity and surprise, the monuments that remained of their ancient greatness. He imprinted the footsteps of a conqueror on the Capitoline hill, and frankly confessed that each day he viewed with fresh wonder the forum of Trajan and his lofty column. The theatre of Pompey appeared, even in its decay, as a huge mountain, artificially hollowed and polished, and adorned by human industry; and he vaguely computed that a river of gold must have been drained to erect the colossal amphitheatre of Titus. From the mouths of fourteen aqueducts a pure and copious stream was diffused into every part of the city; among these the Claudian water, which arose at the distance of thirty-eight miles in the Sabine mountains, was conveyed along a gentle though constant declivity of solid arches, till it descended on the summit of the Aventine hill. The long and spacious vaults which had been constructed for the purpose of common sewers subsisted after twelve centuries in their pristine strength; and these subterraneous channels have been preferred to all the visible wonders of Rome. The Gothic kings, so injuriously accused of the ruin of antiquity, were anxious to preserve the monuments of the nation whom they had subdued. The royal edicts were framed to prevent the abuses, the neglect, or the depredations of the citizens themselves; and a professed architect, the annual sum of two hundred pounds of gold, twenty-five thousand tiles, and the receipt of customs from the Lucrine port, were assigned for the ordinary repairs of the walls and public edifices. A similar care was extended to the statues of metal or marble of men or animals. The spirit of the horses which have given a modern name to the Quirinal was applauded by the barbarians; the brazen elephants of the *Via sacra* were diligently restored; the famous heifer of Myron deceived the cattle, as they were driven through the forum of peace; and an officer was created to protect those works of art, which Theodoric considered as the noblest ornament of his kingdom.

After the example of the last emperors, Theodoric preferred the residence of Ravenna, where he cultivated an orchard with his own hands. As often as the peace of his kingdom was threatened (for it was never invaded) by the barbarians, he removed his court to Verona on the northern frontier, and the image of his palace, still extant on a coin, represents the oldest and most authentic model of Gothic architecture. These two capitals, as well as Pavia, Spoleto, Naples, and the rest of the Italian cities, acquired under his reign the useful or splendid decorations of churches, aqueducts, baths, porticoes, and palaces. But the happiness of the subject was more truly conspicuous in the busy scene of labour and luxury, in the rapid increase and bold enjoyment of national wealth. From the shades of Tibur and Præneste, the Roman senators still retired in the winter season to the warm sun and salubrious springs of Baiæ; and their villas, which advanced on solid moles into the bay of Naples, commanded the various prospect of the sky, the earth, and the water. On the eastern side of the Hadriatic a new Campania was formed in the fair and fruitful province of Istria, which communicated with the palace of Ravenna by an easy navigation of one hundred miles. The rich productions of Lucania and the adjacent provinces were exchanged at the Marcilian fountain, in a populous fair annually dedicated to trade, intemperance, and superstition. In the solitude of Comum, which had once been animated by the mild genius of Pliny, a transparent basin above sixty miles in length still reflected the rural seats which encompassed the margin of the Larian lake; and the gradual ascent of the hills was covered by a triple plantation of olives, of vines, and of chestnut-trees. Agriculture revived under the shadow of peace, and the number of husbandmen was multiplied by the redemption of captives. The iron-mines of Dalmatia, a gold-mine in Bruttium, were carefully explored,

287

and the Pomptine marshes, as well as those of Spoleto, were drained and cultivated by private undertakers, whose distant reward must depend on the continuance of the public prosperity. Whenever the seasons were less propitious, the doubtful precautions of forming magazines of corn, fixing the price, and prohibiting the exportation, attested at least the benevolence of the state; but such was the extraordinary plenty which an industrious people produced from a grateful soil, that a gallon of wine was sometimes sold in Italy for less than three farthings, and a quarter of wheat at about five shillings and sixpence. A country possessed of so many valuable objects of exchange soon attracted the merchants of the world, whose beneficial traffic was encouraged and protected by the liberal spirit of Theodoric. The free intercourse of the provinces by land and water was restored and extended; the city gates were never shut either by day or by night; and the common saying, that a purse of gold might be safely left in the fields, was expressive of the conscious security of the inhabitants.

A difference of religion is always pernicious and often fatal to the harmony of the prince and people: the Gothic conqueror had been educated in the profession of Arianism, and Italy was devoutly attached to the Nicene faith. But the persuasion of Theodoric was not infected by zeal: and he piously adhered to the heresy of his fathers, without condescending to balance the subtile arguments of theological metaphysics. Satisfied with the private toleration of his Arian sectaries, he justly conceived himself to be the guardian of the public worship, and his external reverence for a superstition which he despised may have nourished in his mind the salutary indifference of a statesman or philosopher. The catholics of his dominions acknowledged, perhaps with reluctance, the peace of the church; their clergy, according to the degrees of rank or merit, were honourably entertained in the palace of Theodoric; he esteemed the living sanctity of Cæsarius and Epiphanius, the orthodox bishops of Arles and Pavia; and presented a decent offering on the tomb of St. Peter, without any scrupulous inquiry into the creed of the apostle. His favourite Goths, and even his mother, were permitted to retain or embrace the Athanasian faith, and his long reign could not afford the example of an Italian catholic who, either from choice or compulsion, had deviated into the religion of the conqueror. The people, and the barbarians themselves, were edified by the pomp and order of religious worship; the magistrates were instructed to defend the just immunities of ecclesiastical persons and possessions; the bishops held their synods, the metropolitans exercised their jurisdiction, and the privileges of sanctuary were maintained or moderated according to the spirit of the Roman jurisprudence. With the protection, Theodoric assumed the legal supremacy, of the church; and his firm administration restored or extended some useful prerogatives which had been neglected by the feeble emperors of the West. He was not ignorant of the dignity and importance of the Roman pontiff, to whom the venerable name of POPE was now appropriated. The peace or the revolt of Italy might depend on the character of a wealthy and popular bishop, who claimed such ample dominion both in heaven and earth; who had been declared in a numerous synod to be pure from all sin, and exempt from all judgment. When the chair of St. Peter was disputed by Symmachus and Laurence, they appeared at his summons before the tribunal of an Arian monarch, and he confirmed the election of the most worthy or the most obsequious candidate. At the end of his life, in a moment of jealousy and resentment, he prevented the choice of the Romans, by nominating a pope in the palace of Ravenna. The danger and furious contests of a schism were mildly restrained, and the last decree of the senate was enacted to extinguish, if it were possible, the scandalous venality of the papal elections.

I have descanted with pleasure on the fortunate condition of Italy, but our fancy must not hastily conceive that the golden age of the poets, a race of men without vice or misery, was realised under the Gothic conquest. The fair prospect was sometimes overcast with clouds; the wisdom of Theodoric might be deceived, his power

289

might be resisted, and the declining age of the monarch was sullied with popular hatred and patrician blood. In the first insolence of victory he had been tempted to deprive the whole party of Odoacer of the civil and even the natural rights of society; a tax, unseasonably imposed after the calamities of war, would have crushed the rising agriculture of Liguria; a rigid pre-emption of corn, which was intended for the public relief, must have aggravated the distress of Campania. These dangerous projects were defeated by the virtue and eloquence of Epiphanius and Boethius, who, in the presence of Theodoric himself, successfully pleaded the cause of the people: but, if the royal ear was open to the voice of truth, a saint and a philosopher are not always to be found at the ear of kings. The privileges of rank, or office, or favour were too frequently abused by Italian fraud and Gothic violence, and the avarice of the king's nephew was publicly exposed, at first by the usurpation, and afterwards by the restitution, of the estates which he had unjustly extorted from his Tuscan neighbours. Two hundred thousand barbarians, formidable even to their master, were seated in the heart of Italy; they indignantly supported the restraints of peace and discipline; the disorders of their march were always felt and sometimes compensated; and where it was dangerous to punish, it might be prudent to dissemble, the sallies of their native fierceness. When the indulgence of Theodoric had remitted two-thirds of the Ligurian tribute, he condescended to explain the difficulties of his situation, and to lament the heavy though inevitable burdens which he imposed on his subjects for their own defence. These ungrateful subjects could never be cordially reconciled to the origin, the religion, or even the virtues of the Gothic conqueror; past calamities were forgotten, and the sense or suspicion of injuries was rendered still more exquisite by the present felicity of the times.

Even the religious toleration which Theodoric had the glory of introducing into the Christian world was painful and offensive to the orthodox zeal of the Italians. They respected the armed heresy of the Goths; but their pious rage was safely pointed against the rich and defenceless

Jews, who had formed their establishments at Naples, Rome, Ravenna, Milan, and Genoa, for the benefit of trade and under the sanction of the laws. Their persons were insulted, their effects were pillaged, and their synagogues were burnt by the mad populace of Ravenna and Rome, inflamed, as it should seem, by the most frivolous or extravagant pretences. The government which could neglect, would have deserved such an outrage. A legal inquiry was instantly directed; and, as the authors of the tumult had escaped in the crowd, the whole community was condemned to repair the damage, and the obstinate bigots, who refused their contributions, were whipped through the streets by the hand of the executioner. This simple act of justice exasperated the discontent of the catholics, who applauded the merit and patience of these holy confessors. Three hundred pulpits deplored the persecution of the church; and if the chapel of St. Stephen at Verona was demolished by the command of Theodoric, it is probable that some miracle hostile to his name and dignity had been performed on that sacred theatre. At the close of a glorious life, the king of Italy discovered that he had excited the hatred of a people whose happiness he had so assiduously laboured to promote; and his mind was soured by indignation, jealousy, and the bitterness of unrequited love. The Gothic conqueror condescended to disarm the unwarlike natives of Italy, interdicting all weapons of offence, and excepting only a small knife for domestic use. The deliverer of Rome was accused of conspiring with the vilest informers against the lives of senators whom he suspected of a secret and treasonable correspondence with the Byzantine court. After the death of Anastasius, the diadem had been placed on the head of a feeble old man, but the powers of government were assumed by his nephew Justinian, who already meditated the extirpation of heresy and the conquest of Italy and Africa. A rigorous law, which was published at Constantinople, to reduce the Arians, by the dread of punishment, within the pale of the church, awakened the just resentment of Theodoric, who claimed for his distressed brethren of the East the same indulgence which he had so long granted to the catholics of his dominions. At his stern command the Roman pontiff, with four *illustrious* senators, embarked on an embassy of which he must have alike dreaded the failure or the success. The singular veneration shown to the first pope who had visited Constantinople was punished as a crime by this jealous monarch; the artful or peremptory refusal of the Byzantine court might excuse an equal, and would provoke a larger, measure of retaliation; and a mandate was prepared in Italy to prohibit, after a stated day, the exercise of the catholic worship. By the bigotry of his subjects and enemies the most tolerant of princes was driven to the brink of persecution, and the life of Theodoric was too long, since he lived to condemn the virtue of Boethius and Symmachus.

The senator Boethius is the last of the Romans whom Cato or Tully could have acknowledged for their countryman. As a wealthy orphan, he inherited the patrimony and honours of the Anician family, a name ambitiously assumed by the kings and emperors of the age, and the appellation of Manlius asserted his genuine or fabulous descent from a race of consuls and dictators who had repulsed the Gauls from the Capitol, and sacrificed their sons to the discipline of the republic. In the youth of Boethius the studies of Rome were not totally abandoned; a Virgil is now extant corrected by the hand of a consul; and the professors of grammar, rhetoric, and jurisprudence were maintained in their privileges and pensions by the liberality of the Goths. But the erudition of the Latin language was insufficient to satiate his ardent curiosity; and Boethius is said to have employed eighteen laborious years in the schools of Athens, which were supported by the zeal, the learning, and the diligence of Proclus and his disciples. The reason and piety of their Roman pupil were fortunately saved from the contagion of mystery and magic which polluted the groves of the Academy; but he imbibed the spirit, and imitated the method, of his dead and living masters, who attempted to reconcile the strong and subtle sense of Aristotle with the devout contemplation and sublime fancy of Plato. After his return to Rome, and his marriage with the daughter of his friend the patrician Symmachus, Boethius still continued, in a palace of ivory and marble, to prosecute the same studies. The church was edified by his profound defence of the orthodox creed against the Arian, the Eutychian, and the Nestorian heresies; and the catholic unity was explained or exposed in a formal treatise by the *indifference* of three distinct though consubstantial persons. For the benefit of his Latin readers, his genius submitted to teach the first elements of the arts and sciences of Greece. The geometry of Euclid, the music of Pythagoras, the arithmetic of Nicomachus, the mechanics of Archimedes, the astronomy of Ptolemy, the theology of Plato, and the logic of Aristotle, with the commentary of Porphyry, were translated and illustrated by the indefatigable pen of the Roman senator. And he alone was esteemed capable of describing the wonders of art, a sundial, a water-clock, or a sphere which represented the motions of the planets. From these abstruse speculations Boethius stooped—or, to speak more truly, he rose—to the social duties of public and private life; the indigent were relieved by his liberality, and his eloquence, which flattery might compare to the voice of Demosthenes or Cicero, was uniformly exerted in the cause of innocence and humanity. Such conspicuous merit was felt and rewarded by a discerning prince: the dignity of Boethius was adorned with the titles of consul and patrician, and his talents were usefully employed in the important station of master of the offices. Notwithstanding the equal claims of the East and West, his two sons were created, in their tender youth, the consuls of the same year. On the memorable day of their inauguration they proceeded in solemn pomp from their palace to the forum amidst the applause of the senate and people; and their joyful father, the true consul of Rome, after pronouncing an oration in the praise of his royal benefactor, distributed a triumphal largess in the games of the circus. Prosperous in his fame and fortunes, in his public honours and private alliances, in the cultivation of science and the consciousness of virtue, Boethius might have been styled happy, if that precarious epithet could be safely applied before the last term of the life of man.

A philosopher, liberal of his wealth and parsimonious of his time, might be insensible to the common allurements of ambition, the thirst of gold and employment. And some credit may be due to the asseveration of Boethius, that he had reluctantly obeyed the divine Plato, who enjoins every virtuous citizen to rescue the state from the usurpation of vice and ignorance. For the integrity of his public conduct he appeals to the memory of his country. His authority had restrained the pride and oppression of the royal officers, and his eloquence had delivered Paulianus from the dogs of the palace. He had always pitied, and often relieved, the distress of the provincials, whose fortunes were exhausted by public and private rapine; and Boethius alone had courage to oppose the tyranny of the barbarians, elated by conquest, excited by avarice, and, as he complains, encouraged by impunity. In these honourable contests his spirit soared above the consideration of danger, and perhaps of prudence; and we may learn from the example of Cato that a character of pure and inflexible virtue is the most apt to be misled by prejudice, to be heated by enthusiasm, and to confound private enmities with public justice. The disciple of Plato might exaggerate the infirmities of nature and the imperfections of society; and the mildest form of a Gothic kingdom, even the weight of allegiance and gratitude, must be insupportable to the free spirit of a Roman patriot. But the favour and fidelity of Boethius declined in just proportion with the public happiness, and an unworthy colleague was imposed to divide and control the power of the master of the offices. In the last gloomy season of Theodoric he indignantly felt that he was a slave; but as his master had only power over his life, he stood, without arms and without fear, against the face of an angry barbarian, who had been provoked to believe that the safety of the senate was incompatible with his own. The senator Albinus was accused and already convicted on the presumption of *hoping*, as it was said, the liberty of Rome. "If Albinus be criminal," exclaimed the orator, "the senate and myself are all guilty of the same crime. If we are innocent, Albinus is equally entitled to the protection of the laws." These laws might not have punished the simple and barren wish of an unattainable blessing; but they would have shown less indulgence to the rash confession of Boethius, that, had he known of a conspiracy, the tyrant never should. The advocate of Albinus was soon involved in the danger and perhaps the guilt of his client; their signature (which they denied as a forgery) was affixed to the original address inviting the emperor to deliver Italy from the Goths; and three witnesses of honourable rank, perhaps of infamous reputation, attested the treasonable designs of the Roman patrician. Yet his innocence must be presumed, since he was deprived by Theodoric of the means of justification, and rigorously confined in the tower of Pavia, while the senate, at the distance of five hundred miles, pronounced a sentence of confiscation and death against the most illustrious of its members. At the command of the barbarians, the occult science of a philosopher was stigmatised with the names of sacrilege and magic. A devout and dutiful attachment to the senate was condemned as criminal by the trembling voices of the senators themselves; and their ingratitude deserved the wish or prediction of Boethius, that, after him, none should be found guilty of the same offence.

While Boethius, oppressed with fetters, expected each moment the sentence of the stroke of death, he composed in the tower of Pavia the *Consolation of Philosophy;* a golden volume not unworthy of the leisure of Plato or Tully, but which claims incomparable merit from the barbarism of the times and the situation of the author. The celestial guide whom he had so long invoked at Rome and Athens now condescended to illumine his dungeon, to revive his courage, and to pour into his wounds her salutary balm. She taught him to compare his long prosperity and his recent distress, and to conceive new hopes from the inconstancy of fortune. Reason had informed him of the precarious condition of her gifts; experience had satisfied him of their real value; he had enjoyed them without guilt, he might resign them without a sigh, and calmly disdain the impotent malice of his enemies, who had left him happiness, since they had left him virtue. From the earth Boethius ascended to heaven in search of the SUPREME GOOD; explored the metaphysical labyrinth of chance and destiny, of prescience and free-will, of time and eternity; and generously attempted to reconcile the perfect attributes of the Deity with the apparent disorders of his moral and physical government. Such topics of consolation, so obvious, so vague, or so abstruse, are ineffectual to subdue the feelings of human nature. Yet the sense of misfortune may be diverted by the labour of thought; and the sage who could artfully combine in the same work the various riches of philosophy, poetry, and eloquence, must already have possessed the intrepid calmness which he affected to seek. Suspense, the worst of evils, was at length determined by the ministers of death, who executed, and perhaps exceeded, the inhuman mandate of Theodoric. A strong cord was fastened round the head of Boethius, and forcibly tightened till his eyes almost started from their sockets; and some mercy may be discovered in the milder torture of beating him with clubs till he expired. But his genius survived to diffuse a ray of knowledge over the darkest ages of the Latin world; the writings of the philosopher were translated by the most glorious of the English kings, and the third emperor of the name of Otho removed to a more honourable tomb the bones of a catholic saint who, from his Arian persecutors, had acquired the honours of martyrdom and the fame of miracles. In the last hours of Boethius he derived some comfort from the safety of his two sons, of his wife, and of his father-in-law, the venerable Symmachus. But the grief of Symmachus was indiscreet, and perhaps disrespectful: he had presumed to lament, he might dare to revenge, the death of an injured friend. He was dragged in chains from Rome to the palace of Ravenna, and the suspicions of Theodoric could only be appeased by the blood of an innocent and aged senator.

Humanity will be disposed to encourage any report which testifies the jurisdiction of conscience and the remorse of kings; and philosophy is not ignorant that the most horrid spectres are sometimes created by the powers of a disordered fancy, and the weakness of a distempered body. After a life of virtue and glory, Theodoric was now descending with shame and guilt into the grave: his mind was humbled by the contrast of the past, and justly alarmed by the invisible terrors of futurity. One evening, as it is related, when the head of a large fish was served on the royal table, he suddenly exclaimed that he beheld the angry countenance of Symmachus, his eyes glaring fury and revenge, and his mouth armed with long sharp teeth, which threatened to devour him. The monarch instantly retired to his chamber, and, as he lay trembling with aguish cold under a weight of bed-clothes, he expressed in broken murmurs to his physician Elpidius his deep repentance for the murders of Boethius and Symmachus. His malady increased, and, after a dysentery which continued three days, he expired in the palace of Ravenna, in the thirty-third, or, if we compute from the invasion of Italy, in the thirty-seventh year of his reign. Conscious of his approaching end, he divided his treasures and provinces between his two grandsons, and fixed the Rhône as their common boundary. Amalaric was restored to the throne of Spain. Italy, with all the conquests of the Ostrogoths, was bequeathed to Athalaric, whose age did not exceed ten years, but who was cherished as the last male offspring of the line of Amali, by the short-lived marriage of his mother Amalasuntha with a royal fugitive of the same blood. In the presence of the dying monarch the Gothic chiefs and Italian magistrates mutually engaged their faith and loyalty to the young prince and to his guardian mother; and received, in the same awful moment, his last salutary advice to maintain the laws, to love the senate and people of Rome, and to cultivate with decent reverence the friendship of the emperor. The monument of Theodoric was erected by his daughter Amalasuntha in a conspicuous situation, which commanded the city of Ravenna, the harbour, and the adjacent coast. A chapel of a circular form, thirty feet in diameter, is crowned by a dome of one entire piece of granite: from the centre of the dome four columns arose, which supported in a vase of porphyry the remains of the Gothic king, surrounded by the brazen statues of the twelve apostles. His spirit, after some previous expiation, might have been permitted to mingle with the benefactors of mankind, if an Italian hermit had not been witness in a vision to the damnation of Theodoric, whose soul was plunged by the ministers of divine vengeance into the volcano of Lipari, one of the flaming mouths of the infernal world.

11. Justinian

[*The Gothic kingdom of Italy was the twilight
after the end of the Western Empire. It barely
survived the death of Theodoric. Already, in his
last years, Constantinople was in the power of its
most famous ruler, Justinian. Justinian ruled in
effect under his uncle, the self-made usurper Justin, from 518; on Justin's death, in 527, he became legal emperor; in his long reign (he died in
565), thanks to his generals Belisarius and Narses,
he conquered the Vandals in Africa, the Visigoths
in Spain and the Ostrogoths in Italy, and so restored, to some extent, the old unity of the Empire. It was a brief and costly restoration; the
Dark Age of Italy begins with the Byzantine-
Gothic war. Meanwhile Justinian, aided by his
less orthodox empress Theodora, was refashioning
the institutions and the aspect of Constantinople.
He codified the law, built or rebuilt numerous
churches (including Santa Sophia), and studded
the restored empire with fortresses. In chapter XL
Gibbon describes some of the events and achievements of this long, magnificent, expensive reign.*]

From his elevation to his death, Justinian governed the
Roman empire thirty-eight years, seven months, and thirteen days. The events of his reign, which excite our
curious attention by their number, variety, and importance, are diligently related by the secretary of Belisarius,
a rhetorician, whom eloquence had promoted to the rank
of senator and præfect of Constantinople. According to
the vicissitudes of courage or servitude, of favour or
disgrace, Procopius successively composed the *history*, the

panegyric, and the *satire* of his own times. . . . From
these various materials I shall now proceed to describe
the reign of Justinian, which will deserve and occupy
an ample space. The present chapter will explain the
elevation and character of Theodora, the factions of the
circus, and the peaceful administration of the sovereign
of the East. In the three succeeding chapters I shall relate the wars of Justinian, which achieved the conquest
of Africa and Italy; and I shall follow the victories of
Belisarius and Narses, without disguising the vanity of
their triumphs, or the hostile virtue of the Persian and
Gothic heroes. The series of this volume will embrace the
jurisprudence and theology of the emperor; the controversies and sects which still divide the Oriental church;
the reformation of the Roman law which is obeyed or
respected by the nations of modern Europe.

In the exercise of supreme power, the first act of Justinian was to divide it with the woman whom he loved,
the famous Theodora, whose strange elevation cannot be
applauded as the triumph of female virtue. Under the
reign of Anastasius, the care of the wild beasts maintained by the green faction at Constantinople was intrusted to Acacius, a native of the isle of Cyprus, who,
from his employment, was surnamed the master of the
bears. This honourable office was given after his death
to another candidate, notwithstanding the diligence of
his widow, who had already provided a husband and a
successor. Acacius had left three daughters, Comito,
THEODORA, and Anastasia, the eldest of whom did not
then exceed the age of seven years. On a solemn festival,
these helpless orphans were sent by their distressed and
indignant mother, in the garb of suppliants, into the
midst of the theatre: the green faction received them
with contempt, the blues with compassion; and this difference, which sunk deep into the mind of Theodora,
was felt long afterwards in the administration of the
empire. As they improved in age and beauty, the three
sisters were successively devoted to the public and private
pleasures of the Byzantine people; and Theodora, after
following Comito on the stage, in the dress of a slave,

with a stool on her head, was at length permitted to exercise her independent talents. She neither danced, nor sung, nor played on the flute; her skill was confined to the pantomime arts; she excelled in buffoon characters; and as often as the comedian swelled her cheeks, and complained with a ridiculous tone and gesture of the blows that were inflicted, the whole theatre of Constantinople resounded with laughter and applause. The beauty of Theodora was the subject of more flattering praise, and the source of more exquisite delight. Her features were delicate and regular; her complexion, though somewhat pale, was tinged with a natural colour; every sensation was instantly expressed by the vivacity of her eyes; her easy motions displayed the graces of a small but elegant figure; and either love or adulation might proclaim that painting and poetry were incapable of delineating the matchless excellence of her form. But this form was degraded by the facility with which it was exposed to the public eye, and prostituted to licentious desire. Her venal charms were abandoned to a promiscuous crowd of citizens and strangers, of every rank and of every profession: the fortunate lover who had been promised a night of enjoyment was often driven from her bed by a stronger or more wealthy favourite; and when she passed through the streets, her presence was avoided by all who wished to escape either the scandal or the temptation. The satirical historian has not blushed to describe the naked scenes which Theodora was not ashamed to exhibit in the theatre. After exhausting the arts of sensual pleasure, she most ungratefully murmured against the parsimony of Nature;[1] but her murmurs, her pleasures, and her arts, must be veiled in the obscurity of a learned language. After reigning for some time the delight and contempt of the capital, she condescended to accompany Ecebolus, a native of Tyre, who had obtained the government of the African Pentapolis. But this union was frail and transient: Ecebolus soon rejected an expensive or faithless concubine; she was reduced at Alexandria to extreme distress; and in her

---

[1] She wished for a *fourth* altar on which she might pour libations to the god of love.

laborious return to Constantinople, every city of the East admired and enjoyed the fair Cyprian, whose merit appeared to justify her descent from the peculiar island of Venus. The vague commerce of Theodora, and the most detestable precautions, preserved her from the danger which she feared; yet once, and once only, she became a mother. The infant was saved and educated in Arabia by his father, who imparted to him on his death-bed that he was the son of an empress. Filled with ambitious hopes, the unsuspecting youth immediately hastened to the palace of Constantinople, and was admitted to the presence of his mother. As he was never more seen, even after the decease of Theodora, she deserves the foul imputation of extinguishing with his life a secret so offensive to her imperial virtue.

In the most abject state of her fortune and reputation, some vision, either of sleep or of fancy, had whispered to Theodora the pleasing assurance that she was destined to become the spouse of a potent monarch. Conscious of her approaching greatness, she returned from Paphlagonia to Constantinople; assumed, like a skilful actress, a more decent character; relieved her poverty by the laudable industry of spinning wool; and affected a life of chastity and solitude in a small house, which she afterwards changed into a magnificent temple. Her beauty, assisted by art or accident, soon attracted, captivated, and fixed, the patrician Justinian, who already reigned with absolute sway under the name of his uncle. Perhaps she contrived to enhance the value of a gift which she had so often lavished on the meanest of mankind; perhaps she inflamed, at first by modest delays, and at last by sensual allurements, the desires of a lover who, from nature or devotion, was addicted to long vigils and abstemious diet. When his first transports had subsided, she still maintained the same ascendant over his mind by the more solid merit of temper and understanding. Justinian delighted to ennoble and enrich the object of his affection: the treasures of the East were poured at her feet, and the nephew of Justin was determined, perhaps by religious scruples, to bestow on his concubine the sacred and legal character of a wife. But the laws of Rome expressly prohibited the marriage of a senator with any female who had been dishonoured by a servile origin or theatrical profession: the empress Lupicina or Euphemia, a barbarian of rustic manners, but of irreproachable virtue, refused to accept a prostitute for her niece; and even Vigilantia, the superstitious mother of Justinian, though she acknowledged the wit and beauty of Theodora, was seriously apprehensive lest the levity and arrogance of that artful paramour might corrupt the piety and happiness of her son. These obstacles were removed by the inflexible constancy of Justinian. He patiently expected the death of the empress; he despised the tears of his mother, who soon sunk under the weight of her affliction; and a law was promulgated, in the name of the emperor Justin, which abolished the rigid jurisprudence of antiquity. A glorious repentance (the words of the edict) was left open for the unhappy females who had prostituted their persons on the theatre, and they were permitted to contract a legal union with the most illustrious of the Romans. This indulgence was speedily followed by the solemn nuptials of Justinian and Theodora; her dignity was gradually exalted with that of her lover; and, as soon as Justin had invested his nephew with the purple, the patriarch of Constantinople placed the diadem on the heads of the emperor and empress of the East. But the usual honours which the severity of Roman manners had allowed to the wives of princes could not satisfy either the ambition of Theodora or the fondness of Justinian. He seated her on the throne as an equal and independent colleague in the sovereignty of the empire, and an oath of allegiance was imposed on the governors of the provinces in the joint names of Justinian and Theodora. The Eastern world fell prostrate before the genius and fortune of the daughter of Acacius. The prostitute who, in the presence of innumerable spectators, had polluted the theatre of Constantinople, was adored as a queen in the same city, by grave magistrates, orthodox bishops, victorious generals, and captive monarchs.

Those who believe that the female mind is totally depraved by the loss of chastity will eagerly listen to all the

303

invectives of private envy or popular resentment, which have dissembled the virtues of Theodora, exaggerated her vices, and condemned with rigour the venal or voluntary sins of the youthful harlot. From a motive of shame or contempt, she often declined the servile homage of the multitude, escaped from the odious light of the capital, and passed the greatest part of the year in the palaces and gardens which were pleasantly seated on the sea-coast of the Propontis and the Bosphorus. Her private hours were devoted to the prudent as well as grateful care of her beauty, the luxury of the bath and table, and the long slumber of the evening and the morning. Her secret apartments were occupied by the favourite women and eunuchs, whose interests and passions she indulged at the expense of justice: the most illustrious personages of the state were crowded into a dark and sultry ante-chamber; and when at last, after tedious attendance, they were admitted to kiss the feet of Theodora, they ex-perienced, as her humour might suggest, the silent ar-rogance of an empress or the capricious levity of a comedian. Her rapacious avarice to accumulate an im-mense treasure may be excused by the apprehension of her husband's death, which could leave no alternative between ruin and the throne; and fear as well as ambi-tion might exasperate Theodora against two generals who, during a malady of the emperor, had rashly de-clared that they were not disposed to acquiesce in the choice of the capital. But the reproach of cruelty, so re-pugnant even to her softer vices, has left an indelible stain on the memory of Theodora. Her numerous spies observed and zealously reported every action, or word, or look, injurious to their royal mistress. Whomsoever they accused were cast into her peculiar prisons, inaccessible to the inquiries of justice; and it was rumoured that the torture of the rack or scourge had been inflicted in the presence of a female tyrant, insensible to the voice of prayer or of pity. Some of these unhappy victims per-ished in deep unwholesome dungeons, while others were permitted, after the loss of their limbs, their reason, or their fortune, to appear in the world, the living monu-ments of her vengeance, which was commonly extended to the children of those whom she had suspected or injured. The senator or bishop whose death or exile Theodora had pronounced, was delivered to a trusty messenger, and his diligence was quickened by a menace from her own mouth. "If you fail in the execution of my commands, I swear by him who liveth for ever that your skin shall be flayed from your body."

If the creed of Theodora had not been tainted with heresy, her exemplary devotion might have atoned, in the opinion of her contemporaries, for pride, avarice, and cruelty; but if she employed her influence to assuage the intolerant fury of the emperor, the present age will allow some merit to her religion, and much indulgence to her speculative errors. The name of Theodora was introduced, with equal honour, in all the pious and charitable foundations of Justinian; and the most benevolent institution of his reign may be ascribed to the sympathy of the empress for her less fortunate sisters, who had been seduced or compelled to embrace the trade of prostitution. A palace, on the Asiatic side of the Bosphorus, was converted into a stately and spacious monastery, and a liberal maintenance was assigned to five hundred women who had been collected from the streets and brothels of Constantinople. In this safe and holy retreat they were devoted to perpetual confinement; and the despair of some, who threw themselves headlong into the sea, was lost in the gratitude of the penitents who had been delivered from sin and misery by their generous benefactress. The prudence of Theodora is celebrated by Justinian himself; and his laws are attributed to the sage counsels of his most reverend wife, whom he had received as the gift of the Deity. Her courage was displayed amidst the tumult of the people and the terrors of the court. Her chastity, from the moment of her union with Justinian, is founded on the silence of her implacable enemies; and although the daughter of Acacius might be satiated with love, yet some applause is due to the firmness of a mind which could sacrifice pleasure and habit to the stronger sense either of duty or interest. The wishes and prayers of Theodora could never obtain the blessing of a lawful son, and she buried an infant daughter, the sole offspring of her marriage. Notwithstanding this disappointment, her dominion was permanent and absolute; she preserved, by art or merit, the affections of Justinian; and their seeming dissensions were always fatal to the courtiers who believed them to be sincere. Perhaps her health had been impaired by the licentiousness of her youth; but it was always delicate, and she was directed by her physicians to use the Pythian warmbaths. In this journey the empress was followed by the Prætorian præfect, the great treasurer, several counts and patricians, and a splendid train of four thousand attendants: the highways were repaired at her approach; a palace was erected for her reception; and as she passed through Bithynia she distributed liberal alms to the churches, the monasteries, and the hospitals, that they might implore Heaven for the restoration of her health. At length, in the twenty-fourth year of her marriage, and the twenty-second of her reign, she was consumed by a cancer; and the irreparable loss was deplored by her husband, who, in the room of a theatrical prostitute, might have selected the purest and most noble virgin of the East.

A material difference may be observed in the games of antiquity: the most eminent of the Greeks were actors, the Romans were merely spectators. The Olympic stadium was open to wealth, merit, and ambition; and if the candidates could depend on their personal skill and activity, they might pursue the footsteps of Diomede and Menelaus, and conduct their own horses in the rapid career. Ten, twenty, forty chariots, were allowed to start at the same instant; a crown of leaves was the reward of the victor, and his fame, with that of his family and country, was chanted in lyric strains more durable than monuments of brass and marble. But a senator, or even a citizen, conscious of his dignity, would have blushed to expose his person or his horses in the circus of Rome. The games were exhibited at the expense of the republic, the magistrates, or the emperors; but the reins were abandoned to servile hands; and if the profits of a favourite charioteer sometimes exceeded those of an advocate, they must be considered as the effects of popular extravagance, and the high wages of a disgraceful profession. The race, in its first institution, was a simple contest of two chariots, whose drivers were distinguished by *white* and *red* liveries: two additional colours, a light *green* and a cærulean *blue,* were afterwards introduced; and, as the races were repeated twenty-five times, one hundred chariots contributed in the same day to the pomp of the circus. The four *factions* soon acquired a legal establishment and a mysterious origin, and their fanciful colours were derived from the various appearances of nature in the four seasons of the year; the red dog-star of summer, the snows of winter, the deep shades of autumn, and the cheerful verdure of the spring. Another interpretation preferred the elements to the seasons, and the struggle of the green and blue was supposed to represent the conflict of the earth and sea. Their respective victories announced either a plentiful harvest or a prosperous navigation, and the hostility of the husbandmen and mariners was somewhat less absurd than the blind ardour of the Roman people, who devoted their lives and fortunes to the colour which they had espoused. Such folly was disdained and indulged by the wisest princes; but the names of Caligula, Nero, Vitellius, Verus, Commodus, Caracalla, and Elagabalus, were enrolled in the blue or green factions of the circus: they frequented their stables, applauded their favourites, chastised their antagonists, and deserved the esteem of the populace by the natural or affected imitation of their manners. The bloody and tumultuous contest continued to disturb the public festivity till the last age of the spectacles of Rome; and Theodoric, from a motive of justice or affection, interposed his authority to protect the greens against the violence of a consul and a patrician who were passionately addicted to the blue faction of the circus.

Constantinople adopted the follies, though not the virtues, of ancient Rome; and the same factions which had agitated the circus raged with redoubled fury in the hippodrome. Under the reign of Anastasius, this popular frenzy was inflamed by religious zeal; and the greens, who had treacherously concealed stones and daggers un-

der baskets of fruit, massacred at a solemn festival three
thousand of their blue adversaries. From the capital this
pestilence was diffused into the provinces and cities of
the East, and the sportive distinction of two colours produced two strong and irreconcilable factions, which shook
the foundations of a feeble government. The popular dissensions, founded on the most serious interest or holy
pretence, have scarcely equalled the obstinacy of this
wanton discord, which invaded the peace of families,
divided friends and brothers, and tempted the female sex,
though seldom seen in the circus, to espouse the inclinations of their lovers, or to contradict the wishes of their
husbands. Every law, either human or divine, was trampled under foot; and as long as the party was successful, its deluded followers appeared careless of private distress or public calamity. The licence, without the freedom, of democracy, was revived at Antioch and Constantinople, and the support of a faction became necessary to every candidate for civil or ecclesiastical honours.
A secret attachment to the family or sect of Anastasius
was imputed to the greens; the blues were zealously devoted to the cause of orthodoxy and Justinian, and their
grateful patron protected, above five years, the disorders
of a faction whose seasonable tumults overawed the
palace, the senate, and the capitals of the East. Insolent
with royal favour, the blues affected to strike terror by a
peculiar and barbaric dress—the long hair of the Huns,
their close sleeves and ample garments, a lofty step, and
a sonorous voice. In the day they concealed their two-
edged poniards, but in the night they boldly assembled
in arms and in numerous bands, prepared for every act
of violence and rapine. Their adversaries of the green
faction, or even inoffensive citizens, were stripped and
often murdered by these nocturnal robbers, and it became dangerous to wear any gold buttons or girdles, or
to appear at a late hour in the streets of a peaceful
capital. . . . The despair of the greens, who were persecuted by their enemies and deserted by the magistrate, assumed the privilege of defence, perhaps of retaliation; but
those who survived the combat were dragged to execution, and the unhappy fugitives, escaping to woods and

caverns, preyed without mercy on the society from whence they were expelled. Those ministers of justice who had courage to punish the crimes and to brave the resentment of the blues became the victims of their indiscreet zeal: a præfect of Constantinople fled for refuge to the holy sepulchre, a count of the East was ignominiously whipped, and a governor of Cilicia was hanged, by the order of Theodora, on the tomb of two assassins whom he had condemned for the murder of his groom, and a daring attack upon his own life. An aspiring candidate may be tempted to build his greatness on the public confusion, but it is the interest as well as duty of a sovereign to maintain the authority of the laws. The first edict of Justinian, which was often repeated and sometimes executed, announced his firm resolution to support the innocent, and to chastise the guilty, of every denomination and *colour*. Yet the balance of justice was still inclined in favour of the blue faction, by the secret affection, the habits, and the fears of the emperor; his equity, after an apparent struggle, submitted without reluctance to the implacable passions of Theodora, and the empress never forgot or forgave the injuries of the comedian. At the accession of the younger Justin, the proclamation of equal and rigorous justice indirectly condemned the partiality of the former reign. "Ye blues, Justinian is no more! ye greens, he is still alive."

A sedition, which almost laid Constantinople in ashes, was excited by the mutual hatred and momentary reconciliation of the two factions. In the fifth year of his reign Justinian celebrated the festival of the ides of January: the games were incessantly disturbed by the clamorous discontent of the greens; till the twenty-second race the emperor maintained his silent gravity; at length, yielding to his impatience, he condescended to hold, in abrupt sentences, and by the voice of a crier, the most singular dialogue that ever passed between a prince and his subjects. Their first complaints were respectful and modest; they accused the subordinate ministers of oppression, and proclaimed their wishes for the long life and victory of the emperor. "Be patient and attentive, ye insolent railers!" exclaimed Justinian; "be mute, ye Jews, Samari-

tans, and Manichæans!" The greens still attempted to
awaken his compassion. "We are poor, we are innocent,
we are injured, we dare not pass through the streets: a
general persecution is exercised against our name and
colour. Let us die, O emperor! but let us die by your
command, and for your service!" But the repetition of
partial and passionate invectives degraded, in their eyes,
the majesty of the purple; they renounced allegiance to
the prince who refused justice to his people, lamented
that the father of Justinian had been born, and branded
his son with the opprobrious names of a homicide, an
ass, and a perjured tyrant. "Do you despise your lives?"
cried the indignant monarch. The blues rose with fury
from their seats, their hostile clamours thundered in
the hippodrome, and their adversaries, deserting the unequal contest, spread terror and despair through the
streets of Constantinople. At this dangerous moment,
seven notorious assassins of both factions, who had been
condemned by the præfect, were carried round the city,
and afterwards transported to the place of execution in
the suburb of Pera. Four were immediately beheaded; a
fifth was hanged; but, when the same punishment was
inflicted on the remaining two, the rope broke, they fell
alive to the ground, the populace applauded their escape,
and the monks of St. Conon, issuing from the neighbouring convent, conveyed them in a boat to the sanctuary of the church. As one of these criminals was of the
blue, and the other of the green, livery, the two factions
were equally provoked by the cruelty of their oppressor
or the ingratitude of their patron, and a short truce was
concluded till they had delivered their prisoners and
satisfied their revenge. The palace of the præfect, who
withstood the seditious torrent, was instantly burnt, his
officers and guards were massacred, the prisons were
forced open, and freedom was restored to those who
could only use it for the public destruction. A military
force which had been despatched to the aid of the civil
magistrate was fiercely encountered by an armed multitude, whose numbers and boldness continually increased:
and the Heruli, the wildest barbarians in the service of
empire, overturned the priests and their relics, which,

from a pious motive, had been rashly interposed to separate the bloody conflict. The tumult was exasperated by this sacrilege; the people fought with enthusiasm in the cause of God; the women, from the roofs and windows, showered stones on the heads of the soldiers, who darted firebrands against the houses; and the various flames, which had been kindled by the hands of citizens and strangers, spread without control over the face of the city. The conflagration involved the cathedral of St. Sophia, the baths of Zeuxippus, a part of the palace from the first entrance to the altar of Mars, and the long portico from the palace to the forum of Constantine: a large hospital, with the sick patients, was consumed; many churches and stately edifices were destroyed; and an immense treasure of gold and silver was either melted or lost. From such scenes of horror and distress the wise and wealthy citizens escaped over the Bosphorus to the Asiatic side, and during five days Constantinople was abandoned to the factions, whose watchword, NIKA, *vanquish!* has given a name to this memorable sedition.

As long as the factions were divided, the triumphant blues and desponding greens appeared to behold with the same indifference the disorders of the state. They agreed to censure the corrupt management of justice and the finance; and the two responsible ministers, the artful Tribonian and the rapacious John of Cappadocia, were loudly arraigned as the authors of the public misery. The peaceful murmurs of the people would have been disregarded: they were heard with respect when the city was in flames; the quæstor and the præfect were instantly removed, and their offices were filled by two senators of blameless integrity. After this popular concession Justinian proceeded to the hippodrome to confess his own errors, and to accept the repentance of his grateful subjects; but they distrusted his assurances, though solemnly pronounced in the presence of the holy gospels; and the emperor, alarmed by their distrust, retreated with precipitation to the strong fortress of the palace. The obstinacy of the tumult was now imputed to a secret and ambitious conspiracy, and a suspicion was entertained that the insurgents, more especially the green faction, had been supplied with arms and money by Hypatius and Pompey, two patricians who could neither forget with honour, nor remember with safety, that they were the nephews of the emperor Anastasius. Capriciously trusted, disgraced, and pardoned by the jealous levity of the monarch, they had appeared as loyal servants before the throne, and, during five days of the tumult, they were detained as important hostages; till at length, the fears of Justinian prevailing over his prudence, he viewed the two brothers in the light of spies, perhaps of assassins, and sternly commanded them to depart from the palace. After a fruitless representation that obedience might lead to involuntary treason, they retired to their houses, and in the morning of the sixth day Hypatius was surrounded and seized by the people, who, regardless of his virtuous resistance and the tears of his wife, transported their favourite to the forum of Constantine, and, instead of a diadem, placed a rich collar on his head. If the usurper, who afterwards pleaded the merit of his delay, had complied with the advice of his senate, and urged the fury of the multitude, their first irresistible effort might have oppressed or expelled his trembling competitor. The Byzantine palace enjoyed a free communication with the sea, vessels lay ready at the garden-stairs, and a secret resolution was already formed to convey the emperor with his family and treasures to a safe retreat at some distance from the capital.

Justinian was lost, if the prostitute whom he raised from the theatre had not renounced the timidity as well as the virtues of her sex. In the midst of a council where Belisarius was present, Theodora alone displayed the spirit of a hero, and she alone, without apprehending his future hatred, could save the emperor from the imminent danger and his unworthy fears. "If flight," said the consort of Justinian, "were the only means of safety, yet I should disdain to fly. Death is the condition of our birth, but they who have reigned should never survive the loss of dignity and dominion. I implore Heaven that I may never be seen, not a day, without my diadem and purple; that I may no longer behold the light when I cease to be saluted with the name of queen. If you resolve, O Cæsar! to fly, you have treasures; I behold the sea, you have ships; but tremble lest the desire of life should expose you to wretched exile and ignominious death. For my own part, I adhere to the maxim of antiquity, that the throne is a glorious sepulchre." The firmness of a woman restored the courage to deliberate and act, and courage soon discovers the resources of the most desperate situation. It was an easy and a decisive measure to revive the animosity of the factions; the blues were astonished at their own guilt and folly, that a trifling injury should provoke them to conspire with their implacable enemies against a gracious and liberal benefactor; they again proclaimed the majesty of Justinian; and the greens, with their upstart emperor, were left alone in the hippodrome. The fidelity of the guards was doubtful; but the military force of Justinian consisted in three thousand veterans, who had been trained to valour and discipline in the Persian and Illyrian wars. Under the command of Belisarius and Mundus, they silently marched in two divisions from the palace, forced their obscure way through narrow passages, expiring flames, and falling edifices, and burst open at the same moment the two opposite gates of the hippodrome. In this narrow space the disorderly and affrighted crowd was incapable of resisting on either side a firm and regular attack; the blues signalised the fury of their repentance, and it is computed that above thirty thousand persons were slain in the merciless and promiscuous carnage of the day. Hypatius was dragged from his throne, and conducted with his brother Pompey to the feet of the emperor; they implored his clemency, but their crime was manifest, their innocence uncertain, and Justinian had been too much terrified to forgive. The next morning the two nephews of Anastasius, with eighteen *illustrious* accomplices, of patrician or consular rank, were privately executed by the soldiers, their bodies were thrown into the sea, their palaces razed, and their fortunes confiscated. The hippodrome itself was condemned, during several years, to a mournful silence; with the restoration of the games the same disorders revived, and the blue and green factions continued to afflict the reign of

313

Justinian, and to disturb the tranquillity of the Eastern empire.

That empire, after Rome was barbarous, still embraced the nations whom she had conquered beyond the Hadriatic, and as far as the frontiers of Ethiopia and Persia. Justinian reigned over sixty-four provinces and nine hundred and thirty-five cities; his dominions were blessed by nature with the advantages of soil, situation, and climate, and the improvements of human art had been perpetually diffused along the coast of the Mediterranean and the banks of the Nile from ancient Troy to the Egyptian Thebes. Abraham had been relieved by the well-known plenty of Egypt; the same country, a small and populous tract, was still capable of exporting each year two hundred and sixty thousand quarters of wheat for the use of Constantinople; and the capital of Justinian was supplied with the manufactures of Sidon fifteen centuries after they had been celebrated in the poems of Homer. The annual powers of vegetation, instead of being exhausted by two thousand harvests, were renewed and invigorated by skilful husbandry, rich manure, and seasonable repose. The breed of domestic animals was infinitely multiplied. Plantations, buildings, and the instruments of labour and luxury, which are more durable than the term of human life, were accumulated by the care of successive generations. Tradition preserved, and experience simplified, the humble practice of the arts; society was enriched by the division of labour and the facility of exchange; and every Roman was lodged, clothed, and subsisted by the industry of a thousand hands. The invention of the loom and distaff has been piously ascribed to the gods. In every age a variety of animal and vegetable productions, hair, skins, wool, flax, cotton, and at length *silk,* have been skilfully manufactured to hide or adorn the human body; they were stained with an infusion of permanent colours, and the pencil was successfully employed to improve the labours of the loom. In the choice of those colours which imitate the beauties of nature, the freedom of taste and fashion was indulged; but the deep purple which the Phœnicians extracted from a shell-fish was restrained to the sacred person and palace of the emperor, and the penalties of treason were denounced against the ambitious subjects who dared to usurp the prerogative of the throne.

I need not explain that *silk* is originally spun from the bowels of a caterpillar, and that it composes the golden tomb from whence a worm emerges in the form of a butterfly. Till the reign of Justinian, the silkworms who feed on the leaves of the white mulberry-tree were confined to China; those of the pine, the oak, and the ash were common in the forests both of Asia and Europe; but as their education is more difficult, and their produce more uncertain, they were generally neglected. . . . Whatever suspicions may be raised by the garments of the Medes and Assyrians, Virgil is the most ancient writer who expressly mentions the soft wool which was combed from the trees of the Seres or Chinese; and this natural error, less marvellous than the truth, was slowly corrected by the knowledge of a valuable insect, the first artificer of the luxury of nations. That rare and elegant luxury was censured, in the reign of Tiberius, by the gravest of the Romans; and Pliny, in affected though forcible language, has condemned the thirst of gain, which explored the last confines of the earth for the pernicious purpose of exposing to the public eye naked draperies and transparent matrons. A dress which showed the turn of the limbs and colour of the skin might gratify vanity or provoke desire; the silks which had been closely woven in China were sometimes unravelled by the Phœnician women, and the precious materials were multiplied by a looser texture, and the intermixture of linen threads. Two hundred years after the age of Pliny the use of pure or even of mixed silks was confined to the female sex, till the opulent citizens of Rome and the provinces were insensibly familiarised with the example of Elagabalus, the first who, by this effeminate habit, had sullied the dignity of an emperor and a man. Aurelian complained that a pound of silk was sold at Rome for twelve ounces of gold; but the supply increased with the demand, and the price diminished with the supply. If accident or monopoly sometimes raised the value even above the standard of

Aurelian, the manufacturers of Tyre and Berytus were sometimes compelled, by the operation of the same causes, to content themselves with a ninth part of that extravagant rate. A law was thought necessary to discriminate the dress of comedians from that of senators, and of the silk exported from its native country the far greater part was consumed by the subjects of Justinian. They were still more intimately acquainted with a shell-fish of the Mediterranean, surnamed the silkworm of the sea: the fine wool or hair by which the mother-of-pearl affixes itself to the rock is now manufactured for curiosity rather than use; and a robe obtained from the same singular materials was the gift of the Roman emperor to the satraps of Armenia.[2]

A valuable merchandise of small bulk is capable of defraying the expense of land-carriage, and the caravans traversed the whole latitude of Asia in two hundred and forty-three days from the Chinese ocean to the sea-coast of Syria. Silk was immediately delivered to the Romans by the Persian merchants, who frequented the fairs of Armenia and Nisibis; but this trade, which in the intervals of truce was oppressed by avarice and jealousy, was totally interrupted by the long wars of the rival monarchies. The Great King might proudly number Sogdiana, and even *Serica,* among the provinces of his empire, but his real dominion was bounded by the Oxus, and his useful intercourse with the Sogdoites, beyond the river, depended on the pleasure of their conquerors, the white Huns and the Turks, who successively reigned over that industrious people. Yet the most savage dominion has not extirpated the seeds of agriculture and commerce in a region which is celebrated as one of the four gardens of Asia; the cities of Samarcand and Bochara are advantageously seated for the exchange of its various productions, and their merchants purchased from the Chinese the raw or manufactured silk which they transported into Persia for the use of the Roman empire. In the vain capital of China the Sogdian caravans were entertained

[2] These *pinnes de mer* are found near Smyrna, Sicily, Corsica, and Minorca; and a pair of gloves of their silk was presented to Pope Benedict XIV.

as the suppliant embassies of tributary kingdoms, and, if they returned in safety, the bold adventure was rewarded with exorbitant gain. But the difficult and perilous march from Samarcand to the first town of Shensi could not be performed in less than sixty, eighty, or one hundred days; as soon as they had passed the Jaxartes they entered the desert, and the wandering hordes, unless they are restrained by armies and garrisons, have always considered the citizen and the traveller as the objects of lawful rapine. To escape the Tartar robbers and the tyrants of Persia, the silk-caravans explored a more southern road: they traversed the mountains of Thibet, descended the streams of the Ganges or the Indus, and patiently expected, in the ports of Guzerat and Malabar, the annual fleets of the West. But the dangers of the desert were found less intolerable than toil, hunger, and the loss of time; the attempt was seldom renewed, and the only European who has passed that unfrequented way applauds his own diligence that, in nine months after his departure from Pekin, he reached the mouth of the Indus. The ocean, however, was open to the free communication of mankind. From the great river to the tropic of Cancer the provinces of China were subdued and civilised by the emperors of the North; they were filled about the time of the Christian era with cities and men, mulberry-trees and their precious inhabitants; and if the Chinese, with the knowledge of the compass, had possessed the genius of the Greeks or Phœnicians, they might have spread their discoveries over the southern hemisphere. I am not qualified to examine, and I am not disposed to believe, their distant voyages to the Persian Gulf or the Cape of Good Hope; but their ancestors might equal the labours and success of the present race, and the sphere of their navigation might extend from the isles of Japan to the straits of Malacca, the Pillars, if we may apply that name, of an Oriental Hercules. Without losing sight of land, they might sail along the coast to the extreme promontory of Achin, which is annually visited by ten or twelve ships laden with the productions, the manufactures, and even the artificers of China; the island of Sumatra and the opposite peninsula are faintly delineated as the regions of gold and silver, and the trading cities named in the geography of Ptolemy may indicate that this wealth was not solely derived from the mines. The direct interval between Sumatra and Ceylon is about three hundred leagues; the Chinese and Indian navigators were conducted by the flight of birds and periodical winds, and the ocean might be securely traversed in square-built ships, which, instead of iron, were sewed together with the strong thread of the cocoanut. Ceylon, Serendib, or Taprobana was divided between two hostile princes, one of whom possessed the mountains, the elephants, and the luminous carbuncle, and the other enjoyed the more solid riches of domestic industry, foreign trade, and the capacious harbour of Trinquemale, which received and dismissed the fleets of the East and West. In this hospitable isle, at an equal distance (as it was computed) from their respective countries, the silk-merchants of China, who had collected in their voyages aloes, cloves, nutmeg, and sandal-wood, maintained a free and beneficial commerce with the inhabitants of the Persian Gulf. The subjects of the Great King exalted, without a rival, his power and magnificence; and the Roman, who confounded their vanity by comparing his paltry coin with a gold medal of the emperor Anastasius, had sailed to Ceylon, in an Æthiopian ship, as a simple passenger.

As silk became of indispensable use, the emperor Justinian saw with concern that the Persians had occupied by land and sea the monopoly of this important supply, and that the wealth of his subjects was continually drained by a nation of enemies and idolators. An active government would have restored the trade of Egypt and the navigation of the Red Sea, which had decayed with the prosperity of the empire; and the Roman vessels might have sailed for the purchase of silk to the ports of Ceylon, of Malacca, or even of China. Justinian embraced a more humble expedient, and solicited the aid of his Christian allies, the Æthiopians of Abyssinia, who had recently acquired the arts of navigation, the spirit of trade, and the seaport of Adulis, still decorated with the trophies of a Grecian conqueror. Along the African coast they penetrated to the equator in search of gold, emeralds, and aromatics; but they wisely declined an unequal competition, in which they must be always prevented by the vicinity of the Persians to the markets of India: and the emperor submitted to the disappointment till his wishes were gratified by an unexpected event. The Gospel had been preached to the Indians: a bishop already governed the Christians of St. Thomas on the pepper-coast of Malabar; a church was planted in Ceylon, and the missionaries pursued the footsteps of commerce to the extremities of Asia. Two Persian monks had long resided in China, perhaps in the royal city of Nankin, the seat of a monarch addicted to foreign superstitions, and who actually received an embassy from the isle of Ceylon. Amidst their pious occupations they viewed with a curious eye the common dress of the Chinese, the manufactures of silk, and the myriads of silkworms, whose education (either on trees or in houses) had once been considered as the labour of queens. They soon discovered that it was impracticable to transport the short-lived insect, but that in the eggs a numerous progeny might be preserved and multiplied in a distant climate. Religion or interest had more power over the Persian monks than the love of their country: after a long journey they arrived at Constantinople, imparted their project to the emperor, and were liberally encouraged by the gifts and promises of Justinian. To the historians of that prince a campaign at the foot of Mount Caucasus has seemed — more deserving of a minute relation than the labours of these missionaries of commerce, who again entered China, deceived a jealous people by concealing the eggs of the silkworm in a hollow cane, and returned in triumph with the spoils of the East. Under their direction the eggs were hatched at the proper season by the artificial heat of dung; the worms were fed with mulberry-leaves; they lived and laboured in a foreign climate; a sufficient number of butterflies was saved to propagate the race, and trees were planted to supply the nourishment of the rising generations. Experience and reflection corrected the errors of a new attempt, and the Sogdoite ambassadors acknowledged in the succeeding reign

319

that the Romans were not inferior to the natives of China in the education of the insects and the manufactures of silk, in which both China and Constantinople have been surpassed by the industry of modern Europe. I am not insensible of the benefits of elegant luxury; yet I reflect with some pain that if the importers of silk had introduced the art of printing, already practised by the Chinese, the comedies of Menander and the entire decads of Livy would have been perpetuated in the editions of the sixth century. A larger view of the globe might at least have promoted the improvement of speculative science; but the Christian geography was forcibly extracted from texts of Scripture, and the study of nature was the surest symptom of an unbelieving mind. The orthodox faith confined the habitable world to *one* temperate zone, and represented the earth as an oblong surface, four hundred days' journey in length, two hundred in breadth, encompassed by the ocean and covered by the solid crystal of the firmament.

The subjects of Justinian were dissatisfied with the times and with the government. Europe was overrun by the barbarians and Asia by the monks: the poverty of the West discouraged the trade and manufactures of the East: the produce of labour was consumed by the unprofitable servants of the church, the state, and the army; and a rapid decrease was felt in the fixed and circulating capitals which constitute the national wealth. The public distress had been alleviated by the economy of Anastasius, and that prudent emperor accumulated an immense treasure while he delivered his people from the most odious or oppressive taxes. . . . His example was neglected, and his treasure was abused, by the nephew of Justin. The riches of Justinian were speedily exhausted by alms and buildings, by ambitious wars and ignominious treaties. His revenues were found inadequate to his expenses. Every art was tried to extort from the people the gold and silver which he scattered with a lavish hand from Persia to France: his reign was marked by the vicissitudes, or rather by the combat, of rapaciousness and avarice, of splendour and poverty; he lived with the reputation of hidden treasures, and bequeathed to his successor the payment of his debts.

[*After describing the heavy cost, in taxes, of Justinian's rule, Gibbon goes on to describe his equally costly buildings.*]

The *edifices* of Justinian were cemented with the blood and treasure of his people; but those stately structures appeared to announce the prosperity of the empire, and actually displayed the skill of their architects. Both the theory and practice of the arts which depend on mathematical science and mechanical power were cultivated under the patronage of the emperors; the fame of Archimedes was rivalled by Proclus and Anthemius; and if their *miracles* had been related by intelligent spectators, they might now enlarge the speculations, instead of exciting the distrust, of philosophers. A tradition has prevailed that the Roman fleet was reduced to ashes in the port of Syracuse by the burning-glasses of Archimedes; and it is asserted that a similar expedient was employed by Proclus to destroy the Gothic vessels in the harbour of Constantinople, and to protect his benefactor Anastasius against the bold enterprise of Vitalian. A machine was fixed on the walls of the city, consisting of a hexagon mirror of polished brass, with many smaller and movable polygons to receive and reflect the rays of the meridian sun; and a consuming flame was darted to the distance, perhaps, of two hundred feet. The truth of these two extraordinary facts is invalidated by the silence of the most authentic historians; and the use of burning-glasses was never adopted in the attack or defence of places. Yet the admirable experiments of a French philosopher have demonstrated the possibility of such a mirror; and, since it is possible, I am more disposed to attribute the art to the greatest mathematicians of antiquity, than to give the merit of the fiction to the idle fancy of a monk or a sophist. According to another story, Proclus applied sulphur to the destruction of the Gothic fleet; in a modern imagination, the name of sulphur is instantly connected with the suspicion of gunpowder, and that suspicion is propagated by the secret arts of his disciple Anthemius. A citizen of Tralles in Asia had five sons, who were all distinguished in their respective professions by merit and success. Olympius excelled in the knowledge and practice of the Roman jurisprudence. Dioscorus and Alexander became learned physicians; but the skill of the former was exercised for the benefit of his fellow-citizens, while his more ambitious brother acquired wealth and reputation at Rome. The fame of Metrodorus the grammarian, and of Anthemius the mathematician and architect, reached the ears of the emperor Justinian, who invited them to Constantinople; and while the one instructed the rising generation in the schools of eloquence, the other filled the capital and provinces with more lasting monuments of his art. . . . The genius of Anthemius, and his colleague Isidore the Milesian, was excited and employed by a prince whose taste for architecture had degenerated into a mischievous and costly passion. His favourite architects submitted their designs and difficulties to Justinian, and discreetly confessed how much their laborious meditations were surpassed by the intuitive knowledge or celestial inspiration of an emperor whose views were always directed to the benefit of his people, the glory of his reign, and the salvation of his soul.

The principal church, which was dedicated by the founder of Constantinople to Saint Sophia, or the eternal wisdom, had been twice destroyed by fire; after the exile of John Chrysostom and during the *Nika* of the blue and green factions. No sooner did the tumult subside than the Christian populace deplored their sacrilegious rashness; but they might have rejoiced in the calamity, had they foreseen the glory of the new temple, which at the end of forty days was strenuously undertaken by the piety of Justinian. The ruins were cleared away, a more spacious plan was described, and, as it required the consent of some proprietors of ground, they obtained the most exorbitant terms from the eager desires and timorous conscience of the monarch. Anthemius formed the design, and his genius directed the hands of ten thousand workmen, whose payment in pieces of fine silver was never delayed beyond the evening. The emperor himself, clad in a linen tunic, surveyed each day their rapid progress, and encouraged their diligence by his familiarity, his zeal, and his rewards. The new cathedral of St. Sophia was consecrated by the patriarch, five years, eleven months, and ten days from the first foundation; and in the midst of the solemn festival Justinian exclaimed with devout vanity, "Glory be to God, who hath thought me worthy to accomplish so great a work; I have vanquished thee, O Solomon!" But the pride of the Roman Solomon, before twenty years had elapsed, was humbled by an earthquake, which overthrew the eastern part of the dome. Its splendour was again restored by the perseverance of the same prince; and in the thirty-sixth year of his reign Justinian celebrated the second dedication of a temple which remains, after twelve centuries, a stately monument of his fame. The architecture of St. Sophia, which is now converted into the principal mosque, has been imitated by the Turkish sultans, and that venerable pile continues to excite the fond admiration of the Greeks, and the more rational curiosity of European travellers. The eye of the spectator is disappointed by an irregular prospect of half-domes and shelving roofs: the western front, the principal approach, is destitute of simplicity and magnificence; and the scale of dimensions has been much surpassed by several of the Latin cathedrals. But the architect who first erected an *aërial* cupola is entitled to the praise of bold design and skilful execution. The dome of St. Sophia, illuminated by four-and-twenty windows, is formed with so small a curve, that the depth is equal only to one-sixth of its diameter; the measure of that diameter is one hundred and fifteen feet, and the lofty centre, where a crescent has supplanted the cross, rises to the perpendicular height of one hundred and eighty feet above the pavement. The circle which encompasses the dome lightly reposes on four strong arches, and their weight is firmly supported by four massy piles, whose strength is assisted on the northern and southern sides by four columns of Egyptian granite. A Greek cross, inscribed in a quadrangle, represents the form of the edifice; the exact breadth is two hundred and forty-

323

three feet, and two hundred and sixty-nine may be assigned for the extreme length, from the sanctuary in the east to the nine western doors which open into the vestibule, and from thence into the *narthex* or exterior portico. That portico was the humble station of the penitents. The nave or body of the church was filled by the congregation of the faithful; but the two sexes were prudently distinguished, and the upper and lower galleries were allotted for the more private devotion of the women. Beyond the northern and southern piles, a balustrade, terminated on either side by the thrones of the emperor and the patriarch, divided the nave from the choir; and the space, as far as the steps of the altar, was occupied by the clergy and singers. The altar itself, a name which insensibly became familiar to Christian ears, was placed in the eastern recess, artificially built in the form of a demicylinder; and this sanctuary communicated by several doors with the sacristy, the vestry, the baptistery, and the contiguous buildings, subservient either to the pomp of worship, or the private use of the ecclesiastical ministers. The memory of past calamities inspired Justinian with a wise resolution that no wood, except for the doors, should be admitted into the new edifice; and the choice of the materials was applied to the strength, the lightness, or the splendour of the respective parts. The solid piles which sustained the cupola were composed of huge blocks of freestone, hewn into squares and triangles, fortified by circles of iron, and firmly cemented by the infusion of lead and quicklime; but the weight of the cupola was diminished by the levity of its substance, which consists either of pumice-stone that floats in the water, or of bricks, from the isle of Rhodes, five times less ponderous than the ordinary sort. The whole frame of the edifice was constructed of brick; but those base materials were concealed by a crust of marble; and the inside of St. Sophia, the cupola, the two larger and the six smaller semidomes, the walls, the hundred columns, and the pavement, delight even the eyes of barbarians with a rich and variegated picture.

A poet, who beheld the primitive lustre of St. Sophia, enumerates the colours, the shades, and the spots of ten or twelve marbles, jaspers, and porphyries, which nature had profusely diversified, and which were blended and contrasted as it were by a skilful painter. The triumph of Christ was adorned with the last spoils of Paganism, but the greater part of these costly stones was extracted from the quarries of Asia Minor, the isles and continent of Greece, Egypt, Africa, and Gaul. Eight columns of porphyry, which Aurelian had placed in the Temple of the Sun, were offered by the piety of a Roman matron; eight others of green marble were presented by the ambitious zeal of the magistrates of Ephesus: both are admirable by their size and beauty, but every order of architecture disclaims their fantastic capitals. A variety of ornaments and figures was curiously expressed in mosaic; and the images of Christ, of the Virgin, of saints, and of angels, which have been defaced by Turkish fanaticism, were dangerously exposed to the superstition of the Greeks. According to the sanctity of each object, the precious metals were distributed in thin leaves or in solid masses. The balustrade of the choir, the capitals of the pillars, the ornaments of the doors and galleries, were of gilt bronze. The spectator was dazzled by the glittering aspect of the cupola. The sanctuary contained forty thousand pound weight of silver, and the holy vases and vestments of the altar were of the purest gold, enriched with inestimable gems. Before the structure of the church had arisen two cubits above the ground, forty-five thousand two hundred pounds were already consumed, and the whole expense amounted to three hundred and twenty thousand. Each reader, according to the measure of his belief, may estimate their value either in gold or silver; but the sum of one million sterling is the result of the lowest computation. A magnificent temple is a laudable monument of national taste and religion, and the enthusiast who entered the dome of St. Sophia might be tempted to suppose that it was the residence, or even the workmanship, of the Deity. Yet how dull is the artifice, how insignificant is the labour, if it be compared with the formation of the vilest insect that crawls upon the surface of the temple!

So minute a description of an edifice which time has

respected may attest the truth and excuse the relation of the innumerable works, both in the capital and provinces, which Justinian constructed on a smaller scale and less durable foundations. In Constantinople alone, and the adjacent suburbs, he dedicated twenty-five churches to the honour of Christ, the Virgin, and the saints. Most of these churches were decorated with marble and gold; and their various situation was skilfully chosen in a populous square or a pleasant grove, on the margin of the seashore or on some lofty eminence which overlooked the continents of Europe and Asia. The church of the Holy Apostles at Constantinople, and that of St. John at Ephesus, appear to have been framed on the same model: their domes aspired to imitate the cupolas of St. Sophia, but the altar was more judiciously placed under the centre of the dome, at the junction of four stately porticoes, which more accurately expressed the figure of the Greek cross. The Virgin of Jerusalem might exult in the temple erected by her imperial votary on a most ungrateful spot, which afforded neither ground nor materials to the architect. A level was formed by raising part of a deep valley to the height of the mountain. The stones of a neighbouring quarry were hewn into regular forms; each block was fixed on a peculiar carriage drawn by forty of the strongest oxen, and the roads were widened for the passage of such enormous weights. Lebanon furnished her loftiest cedars for the timbers of the church; and the seasonable discovery of a vein of red marble supplied its beautiful columns, two of which, the supporters of the exterior portico, were esteemed the largest in the world. The pious munificence of the emperor was diffused over the Holy Land; and if reason should condemn the monasteries of both sexes which were built or restored by Justinian, yet charity must applaud the wells which he sunk, and the hospitals which he founded, for the relief of the weary pilgrims. The schismatical temper of Egypt was ill entitled to the royal bounty; but in Syria and Africa some remedies were applied to the disasters of wars and earthquakes, and both Carthage and Antioch, emerging from their ruins, might revere the name of their gracious benefactor. Almost every saint in the calendar acquired the honours of a temple—almost every city of the empire obtained the solid advantages of bridges, hospitals, and aqueducts; but the severe liberality of the monarch disdained to indulge his subjects in the popular luxury of baths and theatres. While Justinian laboured for the public service, he was not unmindful of his own dignity and ease. The Byzantine palace, which had been damaged by the conflagration, was restored with new magnificence; and some notion may be conceived of the whole edifice by the vestibule or hall, which, from the doors perhaps, or the roof, was surnamed *chalce*, or the brazen. The dome of a spacious quadrangle was supported by massy pillars; the pavement and walls were incrusted with many-coloured marbles—the emerald green of Laconia, the fiery red, and the white Phrygian stone, intersected with veins of a sea-green hue. The mosaic paintings of the dome and sides represented the glories of the African and Italian triumphs. On the Asiatic shore of the Propontis, at a small distance to the east of Chalcedon, the costly palace and gardens of Heræum were prepared for the summer residence of Justinian, and more especially of Theodora. The poets of the age have celebrated the rare alliance of nature and art, the harmony of the nymphs of the groves, the fountains and the waves; yet the crowd of attendants who followed the court complained of their inconvenient lodgings, and the nymphs were too often alarmed by the famous Porphyrio, a whale of ten cubits in breadth and thirty in length, who was stranded at the mouth of the river Sangaris after he had infested more than half a century the seas of Constantinople.

The fortifications of Europe and Asia were multiplied by Justinian; but the repetition of those timid and fruitless precautions exposes, to a philosophic eye, the debility of the empire.[2] From Belgrade to the Euxine, from the conflux of the Save to the mouth of the Danube, a chain of above fourscore fortified places was extended along the banks of the great river. Single watch-towers

---

2 Montesquieu observes that Justinian's empire was like France in the time of the Norman inroads—never so weak as when every village was fortified.

were changed into spacious citadels; vacant walls, which the engineers contracted or enlarged according to the nature of the ground, were filled with colonies or garrisons; a strong fortress defended the ruins of Trajan's bridge; and several military stations affected to spread beyond the Danube the pride of the Roman name. But that name was divested of its terrors; the barbarians, in their annual inroads, passed and contemptuously repassed before these useless bulwarks; and the inhabitants of the frontier, instead of reposing under the shadow of the general defence, were compelled to guard with incessant vigilance their separate habitations. The solitude of ancient cities was replenished; the new foundations of Justinian acquired, perhaps too hastily, the epithets of impregnable and populous; and the auspicious place of his own nativity attracted the grateful reverence of the vainest of princes. Under the name of *Justiniana prima,* the obscure village of Tauresium became the seat of an archbishop and a præfect, whose jurisdiction extended over seven warlike provinces of Illyricum; and the corrupt appellation of *Giustendil* still indicates, about twenty miles to the south of Sophia, the residence of a Turkish sanjak. For the use of the emperor's countrymen, a cathedral, a palace, and an aqueduct were speedily constructed; the public and private edifices were adapted to the greatness of a royal city; and the strength of the walls resisted, during the lifetime of Justinian, the unskilful assaults of the Huns and Sclavonians. Their progress was sometimes retarded, and their hopes of rapine were disappointed, by the innumerable castles which, in the provinces of Dacia, Epirus, Thessaly, Macedonia, and Thrace, appeared to cover the whole face of the country. Six hundred of these forts were built or repaired by the emperor; but it seems reasonable to believe that the far greater part consisted only of a stone or brick tower in the midst of a square or circular area, which was surrounded by a wall and ditch, and afforded in a moment of danger some protection to the peasants and cattle of the neighbouring villages. Yet these military works, which exhausted the public treasure, could not remove the just apprehensions of Justinian and his European subjects.

The warm-baths of Anchialus, in Thrace, were rendered as safe as they were salutary; but the rich pastures of Thessalonica were foraged by the Scythian cavalry; the delicious vale of Tempe, three hundred miles from the Danube, was continually alarmed by the sound of war; and no unfortified spot, however distant or solitary, could securely enjoy the blessings of peace. The straits of Thermopylæ, which seemed to protect, but which had so often betrayed, the safety of Greece, were diligently strengthened by the labours of Justinian. From the edge of the sea-shore, through the forests and valleys, and as far as the summit of the Thessalian mountains, a strong wall was continued which occupied every practicable entrance. Instead of a hasty crowd of peasants, a garrison of two thousand soldiers was stationed along the rampart, granaries of corn and reservoirs of water were provided for their use, and, by a precaution that inspired the cowardice which it foresaw, convenient fortresses were erected for their retreat. The walls of Corinth, overthrown by an earthquake, and the mouldering bulwarks of Athens and Platæa, were carefully restored; the barbarians were discouraged by the prospect of successive and painful sieges, and the naked cities of Peloponnesus were covered by the fortifications of the isthmus of Corinth. At the extremity of Europe, another peninsula, the Thracian Chersonesus, runs three days' journey into the sea, to form, with the adjacent shores of Asia, the straits of the Hellespont. The intervals between eleven populous towns were filled by lofty woods, fair pastures, and arable lands; and the isthmus, of thirty-seven stadia or furlongs, had been fortified by a Spartan general nine hundred years before the reign of Justinian. In an age of freedom and valour the slightest rampart may prevent a surprise; and Procopius appears insensible of the superiority of ancient times, while he praises the solid construction and double parapet of a wall whose long arms stretched on either side into the sea, but whose strength was deemed insufficient to guard the Chersonesus, if each city, and particularly Gallipoli and Sestus, had not been secured by their peculiar fortifications. . . .

[After describing the fortifications with which Justinian sought to protect the eastern frontier, from the Crimea to the borders of Abyssinia, Gibbon concludes the chapter with the destruction of two ancient institutions, the most distinctive institutions of independent Greece and republican Rome.]

Justinian suppressed the schools of Athens and the consulship of Rome, which had given so many sages and heroes to mankind. Both these institutions had long since degenerated from their primitive glory, yet some reproach may be justly inflicted on the avarice and jealousy of a prince by whose hand such venerable ruins were destroyed.

Athens, after her Persian triumphs, adopted the philosophy of Ionia and the rhetoric of Sicily; and these studies became the patrimony of a city whose inhabitants, about thirty thousand males, condensed, within the period of a single life, the genius of ages and millions. Our sense of the dignity of human nature is exalted by the simple recollection that Isocrates was the companion of Plato and Xenophon; that he assisted, perhaps with the historian Thucydides, at the first representations of the Œdipus of Sophocles and the Iphigenia of Euripides; and that his pupils Æschines and Demosthenes contended for the crown of patriotism in the presence of Aristotle, the master of Theophrastus, who taught at Athens with the founders of the Stoic and Epicurean sects. The ingenuous youth of Attica enjoyed the benefits of their domestic education, which was communicated without envy to the rival cities. Two thousand disciples heard the lessons of Theophrastus; the schools of rhetoric must have been still more populous than those of philosophy; and a rapid succession of students diffused the fame of their teachers as far as the utmost limits of the Grecian language and name. Those limits were enlarged by the victories of Alexander; the arts of Athens survived her freedom and dominion; and the Greek colonies which the Macedonians planted in Egypt, and scattered over Asia, undertook long and frequent pilgrimages to worship the Muses in their favourite temple on the banks of the Ilissus. The

Latin conquerors respectfully listened to the instructions of their subjects and captives; the names of Cicero and Horace were enrolled in the schools of Athens; and after the perfect settlement of the Roman empire, the natives of Italy, of Africa, and of Britain, conversed in the groves of the Academy with their fellow-students of the East. The studies of philosophy and eloquence are congenial to a popular state, which encourages the freedom of inquiry, and submits only to the force of persuasion. In the republics of Greece and Rome the art of speaking was the powerful engine of patriotism or ambition; and the schools of rhetoric poured forth a colony of statesmen and legislators. When the liberty of public debate was suppressed, the orator, in the honourable profession of an advocate, might plead the cause of innocence and justice; he might abuse his talents in the more profitable trade of panegyric; and the same precepts continued to dictate the fanciful declamations of the sophist, and the chaster beauties of historical composition. The systems which professed to unfold the nature of God, of man, and of the universe, entertained the curiosity of the philosophic student; and according to the temper of his mind, he might doubt with the Sceptics, or decide with the Stoics, sublimely speculate with Plato, or severely argue with Aristotle. The pride of the adverse sects had fixed an unattainable term of moral happiness and perfection: but the race was glorious and salutary; the disciples of Zeno, and even those of Epicurus, were taught both to act and to suffer; and the death of Petronius was not less effectual than that of Seneca to humble a tyrant by the discovery of his impotence. The light of science could not indeed be confined within the walls of Athens. Her incomparable writers address themselves to the human race; the living masters emigrated to Italy and Asia; Berytus, in later times, was devoted to the study of the law; astronomy and physic were cultivated in the museum of Alexandria; but the Attic schools of rhetoric and philosophy maintained their superior reputation from the Peloponnesian war to the reign of Justinian. Athens, though situate in a barren soil, possessed a pure air, a free navigation, and the monuments of ancient art. That sacred retirement was seldom disturbed by the business of trade or government; and the last of the Athenians were distinguished by their lively wit, the purity of their taste and language, their social manners, and some traces, at least in discourse, of the magnanimity of their fathers. In the suburbs of the city, the *Academy* of the Platonists, the *Lyceum* of the Peripatetics, the *Portico* of the Stoics, and the *Garden* of the Epicureans, were planted with trees and decorated with statues; and the philosophers, instead of being immured in a cloister, delivered their instructions in spacious and pleasant walks, which at different hours were consecrated to the exercises of the mind and body. The genius of the founders still lived in those venerable seats; the ambition of succeeding to the masters of human reason excited a generous emulation; and the merit of the candidates was determined, on each vacancy, by the free voices of an enlightened people. The Athenian professors were paid by their disciples: according to their mutual wants and abilities, the price appears to have varied from a mina to a talent; and Isocrates himself, who derides the avarice of the sophists, required, in his school of rhetoric, about thirty pounds from each of his hundred pupils. The wages of industry are just and honourable, yet the same Isocrates shed tears at the first receipt of a stipend: the Stoic might blush when he was hired to preach the contempt of money; and I should be sorry to discover that Aristotle or Plato so far degenerated from the example of Socrates as to exchange knowledge for gold. But some property of lands and houses was settled, by the permission of the laws, and the legacies of deceased friends, on the philosophic chairs of Athens. Epicurus bequeathed to his disciples the gardens which he had purchased for eighty minæ or two hundred and fifty pounds, with a fund sufficient for their frugal subsistence and monthly festivals; and the patrimony of Plato afforded an annual rent, which, in eight centuries, was gradually increased from three to one thousand pieces of gold. The schools of Athens were protected by the wisest and most virtuous of the Roman princes. The library, which Hadrian founded, was placed in a portico adorned with pictures, statues, and a roof of alabaster, and supported by one hundred columns of Phrygian marble. The public salaries were assigned by the generous spirit of the Antonines; and each professor, of politics, of rhetoric, of the Platonic, the Peripatetic, the Stoic, and the Epicurean philosophy, received an annual stipend of ten thousand drachmæ, or more than three hundred pounds sterling. After the death of Marcus, these liberal donations, and the privileges attached to the *thrones* of science, were abolished and revived, diminished and enlarged; but some vestige of royal bounty may be found under the successors of Constantine; and their arbitrary choice of an unworthy candidate might tempt the philosophers of Athens to regret the days of independence and poverty. It is remarkable that the impartial favour of the Antonines was bestowed on the four adverse sects of philosophy, which they considered as equally useful, or at least as equally innocent. Socrates had formerly been the glory and the reproach of his country; and the first lessons of Epicurus so strangely scandalised the pious ears of the Athenians, that by his exile, and that of his antagonists, they silenced all vain disputes concerning the nature of the gods. But in the ensuing year they recalled the hasty decree, restored the liberty of the schools, and were convinced by the experience of ages that the moral character of philosophers is not affected by the diversity of their theological speculations.

The Gothic arms were less fatal to the schools of Athens than the establishment of a new religion, whose ministers superseded the exercise of reason, resolved every question by an article of faith, and condemned the infidel or sceptic to eternal flames. In many a volume of laborious controversy they exposed the weakness of the understanding and the corruption of the heart, insulted human nature in the sages of antiquity, and proscribed the spirit of philosophical inquiry, so repugnant to the doctrine, or at least to the temper, of a humble believer. The surviving sect of the Platonists, whom Plato would have blushed to acknowledge, extravagantly mingled a sublime theory with the practice of superstition and magic; and as they remained alone in the midst of a Christian world, they indulged a secret rancour against the government of the church and state, whose severity was still suspended over their heads. About a century after the reign of Julian, Proclus was permitted to teach in the philosophic chair of the Academy; and such was his industry, that he frequently, in the same day, pronounced five lessons, and composed seven hundred lines. His sagacious mind explored the deepest questions of morals and metaphysics, and he ventured to urge eighteen arguments against the Christian doctrine of the creation of the world. But in the intervals of study he *personally* conversed with Pan, Æsculapius, and Minerva, in whose mysteries he was secretly initiated, and whose prostrate statues he adored; in the devout persuasion that the philosopher, who is a citizen of the universe, should be the priest of its various deities. An eclipse of the sun announced his approaching end; and his Life, with that of his scholar Isidore, compiled by two of their most learned disciples, exhibits a deplorable picture of the second childhood of human reason. Yet the golden chain, as it was fondly styled, of the Platonic succession, continued forty-four years from the death of Proclus to the edict of Justinian, which imposed a perpetual silence on the schools of Athens, and excited the grief and indignation of the few remaining votaries of Grecian science and superstition. Seven friends and philosophers, Diogenes and Hermias, Eulalius and Priscian, Damascius, Isidore, and Simplicius, who dissented from the religion of their sovereign, embraced the resolution of seeking in a foreign land the freedom which was denied in their native country. They had heard, and they credulously believed, that the republic of Plato was realised in the despotic government of Persia, and that a patriot king reigned over the happiest and most virtuous of nations. They were soon astonished by the natural discovery that Persia resembled the other countries of the globe; that Chosroes, who affected the name of a philosopher, was vain, cruel, and ambitious; that bigotry, and a spirit of intolerance, prevailed among the Magi; that the nobles were haughty, the courtiers servile, and the magistrates unjust; that the guilty sometimes escaped, and that the innocent were often oppressed. The disappointment of the philosophers provoked them to overlook the real virtues of the Persians; and they were scandalised, more deeply perhaps than became their profession, with the plurality of wives and concubines, the incestuous marriages, and the custom of exposing dead bodies to the dogs and vultures, instead of hiding them in the earth, or consuming them with fire. Their repentance was expressed by a precipitate return, and they loudly declared that they had rather die on the borders of the empire than enjoy the wealth and favour of the barbarian. From this journey, however, they derived a benefit which reflects the purest lustre on the character of Chosroes. He required that the seven sages who had visited the court of Persia should be exempted from the penal laws which Justinian enacted against his Pagan subjects; and this privilege, expressly stipulated in a treaty of peace, was guarded by the vigilance of a powerful mediator. Simplicius and his companions ended their lives in peace and obscurity; and as they left no disciples, they terminate the long list of Grecian philosophers, who may be justly praised, notwithstanding their defects, as the wisest and most virtuous of their contemporaries. The writings of Simplicius are now extant. His physical and metaphysical commentaries on Aristotle have passed away with the fashion of the times; but his moral interpretation of Epictetus is preserved in the library of nations, as a classic book, most excellently adapted to direct the will, to purify the heart, and to confirm the understanding, by a just confidence in the nature both of God and man.

About the same time that Pythagoras first invented the appellation of philosopher, liberty and the consulship were founded at Rome by the elder Brutus. The revolutions of the consular office, which may be viewed in the successive lights of a substance, a shadow, and a name, have been occasionally mentioned in the present history. The first magistrates of the republic had been chosen by the people, to exercise, in the senate and in the camp, the powers of peace and war, which were afterwards translated to the emperors. But the tradition of ancient dignity was long revered by the Romans and barbarians. A Gothic historian applauds the consulship of Theodoric as the height of all temporal glory and greatness; the king of Italy himself congratulates those annual favourites of fortune who, without the cares, enjoyed the splendour of the throne; and at the end of a thousand years two consuls were created by the sovereigns of Rome and Constantinople for the sole purpose of giving a date to the year and a festival to the people. But the expenses of this festival, in which the wealthy and the vain aspired to surpass their predecessors, insensibly arose to the enormous sum of fourscore thousand pounds; the wisest senators declined a useless honour which involved the certain ruin of their families, and to this reluctance I should impute the frequent chasms in the last age of the consular *Fasti*. The predecessors of Justinian had assisted from the public treasures the dignity of the less opulent candidates; the avarice of that prince preferred the cheaper and more convenient method of advice and regulation. Seven *processions* or spectacles were the number to which his edict confined the horse and chariot races, the athletic sports, the music and pantomimes of the theatre, and the hunting of wild beasts; and small pieces of silver were discreetly substituted to the gold medals, which had always excited tumult and drunkenness when they were scattered with a profuse hand among the populace. Notwithstanding these precautions and his own example, the succession of consuls finally ceased in the thirteenth year of Justinian, whose despotic temper might be gratified by the silent extinction of a title which admonished the Romans of their ancient freedom. Yet the annual consulship still lived in the minds of the people; they fondly expected its speedy restoration; they applauded the gracious condescension of successive princes, by which it was assumed in the first year of their reign; and three centuries elapsed, after the death of Justinian, before that obsolete dignity, which had been suppressed by custom, could be abolished by law. The imperfect mode of distinguishing each year by the name of a magistrate was usefully supplied by the date of a permanent era: the creation of the world, according to the Septuagint version, was adopted by the Greeks; and the Latins, since the age of Charlemagne, have computed their time from the birth of Christ.

12. The New Byzantine Empire

[By the end of his fourth volume Gibbon had carried his narrative down to the reign, in Constantinople, of Heraclius (610-641). He might have
been content to stop there: the best modern historians regard the reign of Heraclius as the real
end of the Roman empire; for it was then that
the Mohammedan revolution, rolling out from
Arabia, destroyed the known landmarks of Antiquity. With the ruin of the Persian Empire and
the destruction of Mediterranean unity, the old
Roman empire lost its balance and its base; the
triumphs of Justinian seemed, in retrospect, a
belated anachronism; and from now on the Eastern
Empire was not Roman but Greco-Asiatic, looking
east. Nevertheless, this "Byzantine" empire, diminished in extent, but reorganised in form, lasted,
through many vicissitudes, for another 800 years,
and Gibbon, captivated by his story, decided to
cover these 800 years, even if it meant quickening
his pace. In chapter XLVIII, the first chapter of
his fifth volume, he explained the plan of the last
two volumes.]

I have now deduced from Trajan to Constantine, from
Constantine to Heraclius, the regular series of the Roman emperors; and faithfully exposed the prosperous and
adverse fortunes of their reigns. Five centuries of the
decline and fall of the empire have already elapsed; but
a period of more than eight hundred years still separates
me from the term of my labours, the taking of Constantinople by the Turks. Should I persevere in the same
course, should I observe the same measure, a prolix and

slender thread would be spun through many a volume, nor would the patient reader find an adequate reward of instruction or amusement. At every step, as we sink deeper in the decline and fall of the Eastern empire, the annals of each succeeding reign would impose a more ungrateful and melancholy task. These annals must continue to repeat a tedious and uniform tale of weakness and misery; the natural connection of causes and events would be broken by frequent and hasty transitions, and a minute accumulation of circumstances must destroy the light and effect of those general pictures which compose the use and ornament of a remote history. From the time of Heraclius the Byzantine theatre is contracted and darkened: the line of empire, which had been defined by the laws of Justinian and the arms of Belisarius, recedes on all sides from our view; the Roman name, the proper subject of our inquiries, is reduced to a narrow corner of Europe, to the lonely suburbs of Constantinople; and the fate of the Greek empire has been compared to that of the Rhine, which loses itself in the sands before its waters can mingle with the ocean. The scale of dominion is diminished to our view by the distance of time and place; nor is the loss of external splendour compensated by the nobler gifts of virtue and genius. In the last moments of her decay Constantinople was doubtless more opulent and populous than Athens at her most flourishing era, when a scanty sum of six thousand talents, or twelve hundred thousand pounds sterling, was possessed by twenty-one thousand male citizens of an adult age. But each of these citizens was a freeman who dared to assert the liberty of his thoughts, words, and actions; whose person and property were guarded by equal law; and who exercised his independent vote in the government of the republic. Their numbers seem to be multiplied by the strong and various discriminations of character; under the shield of freedom, on the wings of emulation and vanity, each Athenian aspired to the level of the national dignity; from this commanding eminence some chosen spirits soared beyond the reach of a vulgar eye; and the chances of superior merit in a great and populous kingdom, as they are proved by experience, would excuse the computation of

imaginary millions. The territories of Athens, Sparta, and
their allies, do not exceed a moderate province of France
or England; but after the trophies of Salamis and Platæa, they expand in our fancy to the gigantic size of Asia,
which had been trampled under the feet of the victorious
Greeks. But the subjects of the Byzantine empire, who
assume and dishonour the names both of Greeks and
Romans, present a dead uniformity of abject vices, which
are neither softened by the weakness of humanity nor
animated by the vigour of memorable crimes. The freemen of antiquity might repeat with generous enthusiasm
the sentence of Homer, "that on the first day of his servitude the captive is deprived of one half of his manly
virtue." But the poet had only seen the effects of civil
or domestic slavery, nor could he foretell that the second
moiety of manhood must be annihilated by the spiritual
despotism, which shackles not only the actions but even
the thoughts of the prostrate votary. By this double yoke
the Greeks were oppressed under the successors of Heraclius; the tyrant, a law of eternal justice, was degraded
by the vices of his subjects; and on the throne, in the
camp, in the schools, we search, perhaps with fruitless
diligence, the names and characters that may deserve
to be rescued from oblivion. Nor are the defects of the
subject compensated by the skill and variety of the painters. Of a space of eight hundred years, the four first
centuries are overspread with a cloud interrupted by some
faint and broken rays of historic light: in the lives of
the emperors, from Maurice to Alexius, Basil the Macedonian has alone been the theme of a separate work; and
the absence, or loss, or imperfection of contemporary evidence, must be poorly supplied by the doubtful authority
of more recent compilers. The four last centuries are
exempt from the reproach of penury; and with the Comnenian family the historic muse of Constantinople again
revives, but her apparel is gaudy, her motions are without elegance or grace. A succession of priests, or courtiers, treads in each other's footsteps in the same path of
servitude and superstition: their views are narrow, their
judgment is feeble or corrupt: and we close the volume of
copious barrenness, still ignorant of the causes of events,

the characters of the actors, and the manners of the times, which they celebrate or deplore. The observation which has been applied to a man may be extended to a whole people, that the energy of the sword is communicated to the pen; and it will be found by experience that the tone of history will rise or fall with the spirit of the age.

From these considerations I should have abandoned without regret the Greek slaves and their servile historians, had I not reflected the fate of the Byzantine monarchy is *passively* connected with the most splendid and important revolutions which have changed the state of the world. The space of the lost provinces was immediately replenished with new colonies and rising kingdoms: the active virtues of peace and war deserted from the vanquished to the victorious nations; and it is in their origin and conquests, in their religion and government, that we must explore the causes and effects of the decline and fall of the Eastern empire. Nor will this scope of narrative, the riches and variety of these materials, be incompatible with the unity of design and composition. As, in his daily prayers, the Musulman of Fez or Delhi still turns his face towards the temple of Mecca, the historian's eye shall be always fixed on the city of Constantinople. The excursive line may embrace the wilds of Arabia and Tartary, but the circle will be ultimately reduced to the decreasing limit of the Roman monarchy.

On this principle I shall now establish the plan of the last two volumes of the present work. The first chapter will contain, in a regular series, the emperors who reigned at Constantinople during a period of six hundred years, from the days of Heraclius to the Latin conquest: a rapid abstract, which may be supported by a *general* appeal to the order and text of the original historians. In this introduction I shall confine myself to the revolutions of the throne, the succession of families, the personal characters of the Greek princes, the mode of their life and death, the maxims and influence of their domestic government, and the tendency of their reign to accelerate or suspend the downfall of the Eastern empire. Such a chronological review will serve to illustrate the various

341

argument of the subsequent chapters; and each circumstance of the eventful story of the barbarians will adapt itself in a proper place to the Byzantine annals. The internal state of the empire, and the dangerous heresy of the Paulicians, which shook the East and enlightened the West, will be the subject of two separate chapters; but these inquiries must be postponed till our farther progress shall have opened the view of the world in the ninth and tenth centuries of the Christian era. After this foundation of Byzantine history, the following nations will pass before our eyes, and each will occupy the space to which it may be entitled by greatness or merit, or the degree of connection with the Roman world and the present age. I. The FRANKS; a general appellation which includes all the barbarians of France, Italy, and Germany, who were united by the sword and sceptre of Charlemagne. The persecution of images and their votaries separated Rome and Italy from the Byzantine throne, and prepared the restoration of the Roman empire in the West. II. The ARABS or SARACENS. Three ample chapters will be devoted to this curious and interesting object. In the first, after a picture of the country and its inhabitants, I shall investigate the character of Mohammed; the character, religion, and success of the prophet. In the second I shall lead the Arabs to the conquest of Syria, Egypt, and Africa, the provinces of the Roman empire; nor can I check their victorious career till they have overthrown the monarchies of Persia and Spain. In the third I shall inquire how Constantinople and Europe were saved by the luxury and arts, the division and decay, of the empire of the caliphs. A single chapter will include, III. The BULGARIANS, IV. HUNGARIANS, and V. RUSSIANS, who assaulted by sea or by land the provinces and the capital; but the last of these, so important in their present greatness, will excite some curiosity in their origin and infancy. VI. The NORMANS; or rather the private adventurers of that warlike people, who founded a powerful kingdom in Apulia and Sicily, shook the throne of Constantinople, displayed the trophies of chivalry, and almost realised the wonders of romance. VII. The LATINS; the subjects of the pope, the nations of the West, who enlisted under the banner of the cross for the recovery or relief of the holy sepulchre. The Greek emperors were terrified and preserved by the myriads of pilgrims who marched to Jerusalem with Godfrey of Bouillon and the peers of Christendom. The second and third crusades trod in the footsteps of the first: Asia and Europe were mingled in a sacred war of two hundred years; and the Christian powers were bravely resisted and finally expelled by Saladin and the Mamalukes of Egypt. In these memorable crusades a fleet and army of French and Venetians were diverted from Syria to the Thracian Bosphorus: they assaulted the capital, they subverted the Greek monarchy: and a dynasty of Latin princes was seated near threescore years on the throne of Constantine. VIII. The GREEKS themselves, during this period of captivity and exile, must be considered as a foreign nation; the enemies, and again the sovereigns of Constantinople. Misfortune had rekindled a spark of national virtue; and the Imperial series may be continued with some dignity from their restoration to the Turkish conquest. IX. The MOGULS and TARTARS. By the arms of Zingis and his descendants the globe was shaken from China to Poland and Greece: the sultans were overthrown: the caliphs fell, and the Cæsars trembled on their throne. The victories of Timour suspended above fifty years the final ruin of the Byzantine empire. X. I have already noticed the first appearance of the TURKS; and the names of the fathers, of *Seljuk* and *Othman,* discriminate the two successive dynasties of the nation which emerged in the eleventh century from the Scythian wilderness. The former established a potent and splendid kingdom from the banks of the Oxus to Antioch and Nice; and the first crusade was provoked by the violation of Jerusalem and the danger of Constantinople. From a humble origin the *Ottomans* arose the scourge and terror of Christendom. Constantinople was besieged and taken by Mohammed II., and his triumph annihilates the remnant, the image, the title, of the Roman empire in the East. The schism of the Greeks will be connected with their last calamities and the restoration of learning

343

in the Western world. I shall return from the captivity of the new to the ruins of ancient ROME; and the venerable name, the interesting theme, will shed a ray of glory on the conclusion of my labours.

13. Byzantine Enlightenment, Roman Darkness

[After the Arab conquests, which deprived Constantinople not only of the conquests of Justinian but also of the ancient Roman provinces of Syria, Egypt and North Africa, both Rome and Constantinople passed through years of crisis. Their relations with each other also deteriorated. After the death of Charlemagne (814) the Byzantine emperors declined to recognise his successors as emperors of the West. As the bishops of Rome and Constantinople were both at the mercy of the lay rulers, spiritual relations naturally deteriorated with secular. In 858, the Byzantine emperor appointed a learned layman, Photius, as Patriarch. This was not relished at Rome and the schism of the two churches began (or at least was thought in retrospect to have begun) with the reign of "the execrable Photius." After this "the darkness and corruption of the tenth century suspended the intercourse, without reconciling the minds, of the two nations." How difficult such reconciliation was is shown by a comparison of the two societies. In the ninth century Byzantium emerged from the years of crisis and, under the "Macedonian" dynasty, which reigned from 867 to 1081, enjoyed a prosperity and a culture whose extent and limitations Gibbon describes in chapter LIII.]

In the ninth century we trace the first dawnings of the restoration of science. After the fanaticism of the Arabs had subsided, the caliphs aspired to conquer the arts,

345

rather than the provinces, of the empire: their liberal curiosity rekindled the emulation of the Greeks, brushed away the dust from their ancient libraries, and taught them to know and reward the philosophers, whose labours had been hitherto repaid by the pleasure of study and the pursuit of truth. The Cæsar Bardas, the uncle of Michael the Third, was the generous protector of letters, a title which alone has preserved his memory and excused his ambition. A particle of the treasures of his nephew was sometimes diverted from the indulgence of vice and folly; a school was opened in the palace of Magnaura, and the presence of Bardas excited the emulation of the masters and students. At their head was the philosopher Leo, archbishop of Thessalonica; his profound skill in astronomy and the mathematics was admired by the strangers of the East, and this occult science was magnified by vulgar credulity, which modestly supposes that all knowledge superior to its own must be the effect of inspiration or magic. At the pressing entreaty of the Cæsar, his friend, the celebrated Photius, renounced the freedom of a secular and studious life, ascended the patriarchal throne, and was alternately excommunicated and absolved by the synods of the East and West. By the confession even of priestly hatred, no art or science, except poetry, was foreign to this universal scholar, who was deep in thought, indefatigable in reading, and eloquent in diction. Whilst he exercised the office of protospathaire, or captain of the guards, Photius was sent ambassador to the caliph of Bagdad. The tedious hours of exile, perhaps of confinement, were beguiled by the hasty composition of his *Library*, a living monument of erudition and criticism. Two hundred and fourscore writers, historians, orators, philosophers, theologians, are reviewed without any regular method; he abridges their narrative or doctrine, appreciates their style and character, and judges even the fathers of the church with a discreet freedom which often breaks through the superstition of the times. The emperor Basil, who lamented the defects of his own education, intrusted to the care of Photius his son and successor Leo the Philosopher, and the reign of that prince and of his son

Constantine Porphyrogenitus forms one of the most prosperous eras of the Byzantine literature. By their munificence the treasures of antiquity were deposited in the Imperial library; by their pens, or those of their associates, they were imparted in such extracts and abridgments as might amuse the curiosity, without oppressing the indolence, of the public. Besides the *Basilics*, or code of laws, the arts of husbandry and war, of feeding or destroying the human species, were propagated with equal diligence; and the history of Greece and Rome was digested into fifty-three heads or titles, of which two only (of embassies, and of virtues and vices) have escaped the injuries of time. In every station the reader might contemplate the image of the past world, apply the lesson or warning of each page, and learn to admire, perhaps to imitate, the examples of a brighter period. I shall not expatiate on the works of the Byzantine Greeks, who, by the assiduous study of the ancients, have deserved, in some measure, the remembrance and gratitude of the moderns. The scholars of the present age may still enjoy the benefit of the philosophical commonplace-book of Stobæus, the grammatical and historic lexicon of Suidas, the Chiliads of Tzetzes, which comprise six hundred narratives in twelve thousand verses, and the commentaries on Homer of Eustathius archbishop of Thessalonica, who, from his horn of plenty, has poured the names and authorities of four hundred writers. From these originals, and from the numerous tribe of scholiasts and critics, some estimate may be formed of the literary wealth of the twelfth century. Constantinople was enlightened by the genius of Homer and Demosthenes, of Aristotle and Plato; and in the enjoyment or neglect of our present riches we must envy the generation that could still peruse the history of Theopompus, the orations of Hyperides, the comedies of Menander, and the odes of Alcæus and Sappho. The frequent labour of illustration attests not only the existence but the popularity of the Grecian classics; the general knowledge of the age may be deduced from the example of two learned females, the empress Eudocia and the princess Anna Comnena, who cultivated, in the purple, the arts of rhetoric and philosophy. The vulgar dialect of the city was gross and barbarous: a more correct and elaborate style distinguished the discourse, or at least the compositions, of the church and palace, which sometimes affected to copy the purity of the Attic models.

In our modern education, the painful though necessary attainment of two languages which are no longer living may consume the time and damp the ardour of the youthful student. The poets and orators were long imprisoned in the barbarous dialects of our Western ancestors, devoid of harmony or grace; and their genius, without precept or example, was abandoned to the rude and native powers of their judgment and fancy. But the Greeks of Constantinople, after purging away the impurities of their vulgar speech, acquired the free use of their ancient language, the most happy composition of human art, and a familiar knowledge of the sublime masters who had pleased or instructed the first of nations. But these advantages only tend to aggravate the reproach and shame of a degenerate people. They held in their lifeless hands the riches of their fathers, without inheriting the spirit which had created and improved that sacred patrimony: they read, they praised, they compiled, but their languid souls seemed alike incapable of thought and action. In the revolution of ten centuries, not a single discovery was made to exalt the dignity or promote the happiness of mankind. Not a single idea has been added to the speculative systems of antiquity, and a succession of patient disciples became in their turn the dogmatic teachers of the next servile generation. Not a single composition of history, philosophy, or literature, has been saved from oblivion by the intrinsic beauties of style or sentiment, of original fancy, or even of successful imitation. In prose, the least offensive of the Byzantine writers are absolved from censure by their naked and unpresuming simplicity: but the orators, most eloquent in their own conceit, are the farthest removed from the models whom they affect to emulate. In every page our taste and reason are wounded by the choice of gigantic and obsolete words, a stiff and intricate phraseology, the discord of images, the childish play of false or unseasonable ornament, and the painful attempt to elevate themselves, to astonish the reader, and to involve a trivial meaning in the smoke of obscurity and exaggeration. Their prose is soaring to the vicious affection of poetry: their poetry is sinking below the flatness and insipidity of prose. The tragic, epic, and lyric muses were silent and inglorious: the bards of Constantinople seldom rose above a riddle or epigram, a panegyric or tale; they forgot even the rules of prosody; and with the melody of Homer yet sounding in their ears, they confound all measure of feet and syllables in the impotent strains which have received the name of *political* or city verses. The minds of the Greeks were bound in the fetters of a base and imperious superstition, which extends her dominion round the circle of profane science. Their understandings were bewildered in metaphysical controversy: in the belief of visions and miracles they had lost all principles of moral evidence, and their taste was vitiated by the homilies of the monks, an absurd medley of declamation and Scripture. Even these contemptible studies were no longer dignified by the abuse of superior talents: the leaders of the Greek church were humbly content to admire and copy the oracles of antiquity, nor did the schools or pulpit produce any rivals of the fame of Athanasius and Chrysostom.

In all the pursuits of active and speculative life, the emulation of states and individuals is the most powerful spring of the efforts and improvements of mankind. The cities of ancient Greece were cast in the happy mixture of union and independence, which is repeated on a larger scale, but in a looser form, by the nations of modern Europe: the union of language, religion, and manners, which renders them the spectators and judges of each other's merit: the independence of government and interest, which asserts their separate freedom, and excites them to strive for pre-eminence in the career of glory. The situation of the Romans was less favourable; yet in the early ages of the republic, which fixed the national character, a similar emulation was kindled among the states of Latium and Italy; and in the arts and sciences they aspired to equal or surpass their Grecian masters. The empire of the Cæsars undoubtedly checked the activity and progress of the human mind: its magnitude might indeed allow some scope for domestic competition; but when it was gradually reduced, at first to the East, and at last to Greece and Constantinople, the Byzantine subjects were degraded to an abject and languid temper, the natural effect of their solitary and insulated state. From the North they were oppressed by nameless tribes of barbarians, to whom they scarcely imparted the appellation of men. The language and religion of the more polished Arabs were an insurmountable bar to all social intercourse. The conquerors of Europe were their brethren in the Christian faith; but the speech of the Franks or Latins was unknown, their manners were rude, and they were rarely connected, in peace or war, with the successors of Heraclius. Alone in the universe, the self-satisfied pride of the Greeks was not disturbed by the comparison of foreign merit; and it is no wonder if they fainted in the race, since they had neither competitors to urge their speed, nor judges to crown their victory. The nations of Europe and Asia were mingled by the expeditions to the Holy Land; and it is under the Comnenian dynasty that a faint emulation of knowledge and military virtue was rekindled in the Byzantine empire.

[*Such a society, so civilised, so insulated, so complacent, could afford to despise the barbarians of the West and their spiritual leaders. In chapter XLIX Gibbon gives a picture of the Popes whose learning and piety were outraged by the appointment of the accomplished and scholarly Photius.*]

These emperors, in the election of the popes, continued to exercise the powers which had been assumed by the Gothic and Grecian princes; and the importance of this prerogative increased with the temporal estate and spiritual jurisdiction of the Roman church. In the Christian aristocracy the principal members of the clergy still formed a senate to assist the administration, and to supply the vacancy, of the bishop. Rome was divided into twenty-eight parishes, and each parish was governed by a cardinal-priest, or presbyter—a title which, however common and modest in its origin, has aspired to emulate the purple of kings. Their number was enlarged by the association of the seven deacons of the most considerable hospitals, the seven palatine judges of the Lateran, and some dignitaries of the church. This ecclesiastical senate was directed by the seven cardinal-bishops of the Roman province, who were less occupied in the suburb dioceses of Ostia, Porto, Velitræ, Tusculum, Præneste, Tibur, and the Sabines, than by their weekly service in the Lateran, and their superior share in the honours and authority of the apostolic see. On the death of the pope these bishops recommended a successor to the suffrage of the college of cardinals, and their choice was ratified or rejected by the applause or clamour of the Roman people. But the election was imperfect; nor could the pontiff be legally consecrated till the emperor, the advocate of the church, had graciously signified his approbation and consent. The royal commissioner examined on the spot the form and freedom of the proceedings; nor was it till after a previous scrutiny into the qualifications of the candidates that he accepted an oath of fidelity, and confirmed the donations which had successively enriched the patrimony of St. Peter. In the frequent schisms the rival claims were submitted to the sentence of the emperor; and in a synod of bishops he presumed to judge, to condemn, and to punish the crimes of a guilty pontiff. Otho the First imposed a treaty on the senate and people, who engaged to prefer the candidate most acceptable to his majesty: his successors anticipated or prevented their choice: they bestowed the Roman benefice, like the bishoprics of Cologne or Bamberg, on their chancellors or preceptors; and whatever might be the merit of a Frank or Saxon, his name sufficiently attests the interposition of foreign power. These acts of prerogative were most speciously excused by the vices of a popular election. The competitor who had been excluded by the cardinals appealed to the passions or avarice of the multitude; the Vatican and the Lateran were stained with blood; and the most powerful senators, the marquises of Tuscany and the counts of Tusculum, held the apostolic see in a long and disgraceful servitude. The Roman pontiffs of the ninth and tenth centuries were insulted, imprisoned, and murdered by their tyrants; and such was their indigence, after the loss and usurpation of the ecclesiastical patrimonies, that they could neither support the state of a prince, nor exercise the charity of a priest. The influence of two sister prostitutes, Marozia and Theodora, was founded on their wealth and beauty, their political and amorous intrigues: the most strenuous of their lovers were rewarded with the Roman mitre, and their reign may have suggested to the darker ages[1] the fable of a female pope.[2] The bastard son, the grandson, and the great-grandson of Marozia, a rare genealogy, were seated in the chair of St. Peter; and it was at the age of nineteen years that the second of these became the head of the Latin church. His youth and manhood were of a suitable complexion; and the nations of pilgrims could bear testimony to the charges that were urged against him in a Roman synod, and in the presence of Otho the Great. As John XII had renounced the dress and decencies of his profession, the *soldier* may not perhaps be dishonoured by the wine which he drank, the blood that he spilt, the flames that he kindled, or the licentious pursuits of gaming and hunting. His open simony might be the consequence of distress; and his blasphemous invocation of Jupiter and

---

[1] The advocates for Pope Joan produce one hundred and fifty witnesses, or rather echoes, of the fourteenth, fifteenth, and sixteenth centuries. They bear testimony against themselves and the legend, by multiplying the proof that so curious a story *must* have been repeated by writers of every description to whom it was known. On those of the ninth and tenth centuries the recent event would have flashed with a double force. Would Photius have spared such a reproach? Could Liutprand have missed such scandal? It is scarcely worth while to discuss the various readings of Martinus Polonus, Sigebert of Gemblours, or even Marianus Scotus; but a most palpable forgery is the passage of Pope Joan which has been foisted into some MSS. and editions of the Roman Anastasius.

[2] Till the Reformation the tale was repeated and believed without offence: and Joan's female statue long occupied her place among the popes in the cathedral of Sienna. She has been annihilated by two learned Protestants, Blondel and Bayle: but their brethren were scandalised by this equitable and generous criticism. Spanheim and Lenfant attempt to save this poor engine of controversy; and even Mosheim condescends to cherish some doubt and suspicion.

Venus, if it be true, could not possibly be serious. But we read, with some surprise, that the worthy grandson of Marozia lived in public adultery with the matrons of Rome; that the Lateran palace was turned into a school for prostitution; and that his rapes of virgins and widows had deterred the female pilgrims from visiting the tomb of St. Peter, lest, in the devout act, they should be violated by his successor. The Protestants have dwelt with malicious pleasure on these characters of Antichrist; but to a philosophic eye the vices of the clergy are far less dangerous than their virtues. After a long series of scandal the apostolic see was reformed and exalted by the austerity and zeal of Gregory VII. That ambitious monk devoted his life to the execution of two projects. I. To fix in the college of cardinals the freedom and independence of election, and for ever to abolish the right of usurpation of the emperors and the Roman people. II. To bestow and resume the Western empire as a fief or benefice of the church, and to extend his temporal dominion over the kings and kingdoms of the earth. After a contest of fifty years the first of these designs was accomplished by the firm support of the ecclesiastical order, whose liberty was connected with that of their chief. But the second attempt, though it was crowned with some partial and apparent success, has been vigorously resisted by the secular power, and finally extinguished by the improvement of human reason.

14. The Crusades

[The distance between Rome and Byzantium was suddenly narrowed, at the end of the eleventh century, by the new conquests of the Seljuk Turks. In 1071 Byzantium, already threatened in the Balkans by barbarians from the North, lost the relics of Italy to the Normans. In the same year Alp Arslan, the Turkish leader, by the decisive victory of Manzikert, opened the way to Asia Minor, the source of the Byzantine armies; and his successors, from their new capital of Nice, only a hundred miles away, threatened Constantinople itself. At the same time the Turks overran Syria, and captured Jerusalem, where their intolerance of pilgrims (contrasting with the tolerance of their Arab predecessors) provoked the Christians of Western Europe. This double threat alarmed both East and West. The Byzantine emperor looked westward to the hitherto despised barbarians of Europe for allies to defend his capital; and he found an unexpectedly warm response. "A new spirit had arisen of religious chivalry and papal dominion; a nerve was touched of exquisite feeling; and the sensation vibrated to the heart of Europe." In chapter LVIII Gibbon describes the realisation of this new spirit in the first Crusade.]

About twenty years after the conquest of Jerusalem by the Turks, the holy sepulchre was visited by a hermit of the name of Peter, a native of Amiens, in the province of Picardy in France. His resentment and sympathy were excited by his own injuries and the oppression of the

354

Christian name; he mingled his tears with those of the patriarch, and earnestly inquired if no hopes of relief could be entertained from the Greek emperors of the East. The patriarch exposed the vices and weakness of the successors of Constantine. "I will rouse," exclaimed the hermit, "the martial nations of Europe in your cause;" and Europe was obedient to the call of the hermit. The astonished patriarch dismissed him with epistles of credit and complaint; and no sooner did he land at Bari than Peter hastened to kiss the feet of the Roman pontiff. His stature was small, his appearance contemptible; but his eye was keen and lively, and he possessed that vehemence of speech which seldom fails to impart the persuasion of the soul. He was born of a gentleman's family (for we must now adopt a modern idiom), and his military service was under the neighbouring counts of Boulogne, the heroes of the first crusade. But he soon relinquished the sword and the world; and if it be true that his wife, however noble, was aged and ugly, he might withdraw with the less reluctance from her bed to a convent, and at length to a hermitage. In this austere solitude his body was emaciated, his fancy was inflamed; whatever he wished, he believed; whatever he believed, he *saw* in dreams and revelations. From Jerusalem the pilgrim returned an accomplished fanatic; but as he excelled in the popular madness of the times, Pope Urban the Second received him as a prophet, applauded his glorious design, promised to support it in a general council, and encouraged him to proclaim the deliverance of the Holy Land. Invigorated by the approbation of the pontiff, his zealous missionary traversed, with speed and success, the provinces of Italy and France. His diet was abstemious, his prayers long and fervent, and the alms which he received with one hand, he distributed with the other: his head was bare, his feet naked, his meagre body was wrapped in a coarse garment; he bore and displayed a weighty crucifix; and the ass on which he rode was sanctified, in the public eye, by the service of the man of God. He preached to innumerable crowds in the churches, the streets, and the highways: the hermit entered with equal confidence the palace and the cottage; and the people,

355

for all was people, was impetuously moved by his call to repentance and arms. When he painted the sufferings of the natives and pilgrims of Palestine, every heart was melted to compassion; every breast glowed with indignation when he challenged the warriors of the age to defend their brethren, and rescue their Saviour: his ignorance of art and language was compensated by sighs, and tears, and ejaculations; and Peter supplied the deficiency of reason by loud and frequent appeals to Christ and his mother, to the saints and angels of paradise, with whom he had personally conversed. The most perfect orator of Athens might have envied the success of his eloquence: the rustic enthusiast inspired the passions which he felt, and Christendom expected with impatience the counsels and decrees of the supreme pontiff.

The magnanimous spirit of Gregory the Seventh had already embraced the design of arming Europe against Asia; the ardour of his zeal and ambition still breathes in his epistles; from either side of the Alps fifty thousand Catholics had enlisted under the banner of St. Peter; and his successor reveals *his* intention of marching at their head against the impious sectaries of Mohammed. But the glory or reproach of executing, though not in person, this holy enterprise, was reserved for Urban the Second, the most faithful of his disciples. He undertook the conquest of the East, whilst the larger portion of Rome was possessed and fortified by his rival Guibert of Ravenna, who contended with Urban for the name and honours of the pontificate. He attempted to unite the powers of the West, at a time when the princes were separated from the church, and the people from their princes, by the excommunication which himself and his predecessors had thundered against the emperor and the king of France. Philip the First of France supported with patience the censures which he had provoked by his scandalous life and adulterous marriage. Henry the Fourth of Germany asserted the right of investitures, the prerogative of confirming his bishops by the delivery of the ring and crosier. But the emperor's party was crushed in Italy by the arms of the Normans and the countess Mathilda; and the long quarrel had been recently envenomed by the revolt of his

356

son Conrad and the shame of his wife, who, in the synods of Constance and Placentia, confessed the manifold prostitutions to which she had been exposed by a husband regardless of her honour and his own. So popular was the cause of Urban, so weighty was his influence, that the council which he summoned at Placentia was composed of two hundred bishops of Italy, France, Burgundy, Swabia, and Bavaria. Four thousand of the clergy and thirty thousand of the laity attended this important meeting; and, as the most spacious cathedral would have been inadequate to the multitude, the session of seven days was held in a plain adjacent to the city. The ambassadors of the Greek emperor, Alexius Comnenus, were introduced to plead the distress of their sovereign, and the danger of Constantinople, which was divided only by a narrow sea from the victorious Turks, the common enemies of the Christian name. In their suppliant address they flattered the pride of the Latin princes; and, appealing at once to their policy and religion, exhorted them to repel the barbarians on the confines of Asia, rather than to expect them in the heart of Europe. At the sad tale of the misery and perils of their Eastern brethren the assembly burst into tears: the most eager champions declared their readiness to march; and the Greek ambassadors were dismissed with the assurance of a speedy and powerful succour. The relief of Constantinople was included in the larger and most distant project of the deliverance of Jerusalem; but the prudent Urban adjourned the final decision to a second synod, which he proposed to celebrate in some city of France in the autumn of the same year. The short delay would propagate the flame of enthusiasm; and his firmest hope was in a nation of soldiers still proud of the pre-eminence of their name, and ambitious to emulate their hero Charlemagne, who, in the popular romance of Turpin, had achieved the conquest of the Holy Land. A latent motive of affection or vanity might influence the choice of Urban: he was himself a native of France, a monk of Clugny, and the first of his countrymen who ascended the throne of St. Peter. The pope had illustrated his family and province; nor is there perhaps a more exquisite gratification than to revisit, in a conspicuous dignity, the humble and laborious scenes of our youth.

It may occasion some surprise that the Roman pontiff should erect, in the heart of France, the tribunal from whence he hurled his anathemas against the king; but our surprise will vanish so soon as we form a just estimate of a king of France of the eleventh century. Philip the First was the great-grandson of Hugh Capet, the founder of the present race, who, in the decline of Charlemagne's posterity, added the regal title to his patrimonial estates of Paris and Orleans. In this narrow compass he was possessed of wealth and jurisdiction; but in the rest of France Hugh and his first descendants were no more than the feudal lords of about sixty dukes and counts, of independent and hereditary power, who disdained the control of laws and legal assemblies, and whose disregard of their sovereign was revenged by the disobedience of their inferior vassals. At Clermont, in the territories of the count of Auvergne, the pope might brave with impunity the resentment of Philip; and the council which he convened in that city was not less numerous or respectable than the synod of Placentia. Besides his court and council of Roman cardinals, he was supported by thirteen archbishops and two hundred and twenty-five bishops; the number of mitred prelates was computed at four hundred; and the fathers of the church were blessed by the saints and enlightened by the doctors of the age. From the adjacent kingdoms a martial train of lords and knights of power and renown attended the council, in high expectation of its resolves; and such was the ardour of zeal and curiosity, that the city was filled, and many thousands, in the month of November, erected their tents or huts in the open field. A session of eight days produced some useful or edifying canons for the reformation of manners; a severe censure was pronounced against the licence of private war; the Truce of God was confirmed, a suspension of hostilities during four days of the week; women and priests were placed under the safeguard of the church; and a protection of three years was extended to husbandmen and merchants, the defenceless victims of military rapine. But a law, however venerable be the sanction, cannot suddenly transform the temper of the times; and the benevolent efforts of Urban deserve the less praise, since he laboured to appease some domestic quarrels that he might spread the flames of war from the Atlantic to the Euphrates. From the synod of Placentia the rumour of his great design had gone forth among the nations: the clergy on their return had preached in every diocese the merit and glory of the deliverance of the Holy Land; and when the pope ascended a lofty scaffold in the market-place of Clermont, his eloquence was addressed to a well-prepared and impatient audience. His topics were obvious, his exhortation was vehement, his success inevitable. The orator was interrupted by the shout of thousands, who with one voice, and in their rustic idiom, exclaimed aloud, "God wills it, God wills it!" "It is indeed the will of God," replied the pope; "and let this memorable word, the inspiration surely of the Holy Spirit, be for ever adopted as your cry of battle, to animate the devotion and courage of the champions of Christ. His cross is the symbol of your salvation; wear it, a red, a bloody cross, as an external mark, on your breasts or shoulders, as a pledge of your sacred and irrevocable engagement." The proposal was joyfully accepted; great numbers, both of the clergy and laity, impressed on their garments the sign of the cross, and solicited the pope to march at their head. This dangerous honour was declined by the more prudent successor of Gregory, who alleged the schism of the church, and the duties of his pastoral office, recommending to the faithful, who were disqualified by sex or profession, by age or infirmity, to aid with their prayers and alms the personal service of their robust brethren. The name and powers of his legate he devolved on Adhemar, bishop of Puy, the first who had received the cross at his hands. The foremost of the temporal chiefs was Raymond, count of Toulouse, whose ambassadors in the council excused the absence, and pledged the honour, of their master. After the confession and absolution of their sins, the champions of the cross were dismissed with a superfluous admonition to invite their countrymen and friends; and their departure for the Holy Land was fixed to the festival of the Assumption, the fifteenth of August, of the ensuing year.

So familiar, and as it were so natural to man, is the practice of violence, that our indulgence allows the slightest provocation, the most disputable right, as a sufficient ground of national hostility. But the name and nature of a *holy* war demands a more rigorous scrutiny; nor can we hastily believe that the servants of the Prince of Peace would unsheathe the sword of destruction unless the motive were pure, the quarrel legitimate, and the necessity inevitable. The policy of an action may be determined from the tardy lessons of experience; but before we act, our conscience should be satisfied of the justice and propriety of our enterprise. In the age of the crusades, the Christians, both of the East and West, were persuaded of their lawfulness and merit; their arguments are clouded by the perpetual abuse of Scripture and rhetoric; but they seem to insist on the right of natural and religious defence, their peculiar title to the Holy Land, and the impiety of their Pagan and Mohammedan foes.[1] I. The right of a just defence may fairly include our civil and spiritual allies: it depends on the existence of danger; and that danger must be estimated by the twofold consideration of the malice and the power of our enemies. A pernicious tenet has been imputed to the Mohammedans, the duty of *extirpating* all other religions by the sword. This charge of ignorance and bigotry is refuted by the Koran, by the history of the Musulman conquerors, and by their public and legal toleration of the Christian worship. But it cannot be denied that the Oriental churches are depressed under their iron yoke; that, in peace and war, they assert a divine and indefeasible claim of universal empire; and that, in their orthodox creed, the unbelieving nations are continually threatened with the loss of religion or liberty. In the eleventh century the victorious arms of the Turks presented a real and urgent apprehension of these losses. They had sub-

[1] If the reader will turn to the first scene of the First Part of Henry the Fourth, he will see in the text of Shakespeare the natural feelings of enthusiasm; and in the notes of Dr. Johnson the workings of a bigoted, though vigorous, mind, greedy of every pretence to hate and persecute those who dissent from his creed.

dued in less than thirty years the kingdoms of Asia, as far as Jerusalem and the Hellespont; and the Greek empire tottered on the verge of destruction. Besides an honest sympathy for their brethren, the Latins had a right and interest in the support of Constantinople, the most important barrier of the West; and the privilege of defence must reach to prevent, as well as to repel, an impending assault. But this salutary purpose might have been accomplished by a moderate succour; and our calmer reason must disclaim the innumerable hosts and remote operations which overwhelmed Asia and depopulated Europe. II. Palestine could add nothing to the strength or safety of the Latins; and fanaticism alone could pretend to justify the conquest of that distant and narrow province. The Christians affirmed that their inalienable title to the promised land had been sealed by the blood of their divine Saviour; it was their right and duty to rescue their inheritance from the unjust possessors, who profaned his sepulchre, and oppressed the pilgrimage of his disciples. Vainly would it be alleged that the pre-eminence of Jerusalem and the sanctity of Palestine have been abolished with the Mosaic law; that the God of the Christians is not a local deity, and that the recovery of Bethlehem or Calvary, his cradle or his tomb, will not atone for the violation of the moral precepts of the Gospel. Such arguments glance aside from the leaden shield of superstition; and the religious mind will not easily relinquish its hold on the sacred ground of mystery and miracle. III. But the holy wars which have been waged in every climate of the globe, from Egypt to Livonia, and from Peru to Hindostan, require the support of some more general and flexible tenet. It has been often supposed, and sometimes affirmed, that a difference of religion is a worthy cause of hostility; that obstinate unbelievers may be slain or subdued by the champions of the cross; and that grace is the sole fountain of dominion as well as of mercy. Above four hundred years before the first crusade, the eastern and western provinces of the Roman empire had been acquired about the same time, and in the same manner, by the barbarians of Germany and Arabia. Time and treaties had legitimated the conquests of the *Christian* Franks; but in the eyes of their subjects and neighbours the Mohammedan princes were still tyrants and usurpers, who, by the arms of war or rebellion, might be lawfully driven from their unlawful possession.

As the manners of the Christians were relaxed, their discipline of penance was enforced; and with the multiplication of sins the remedies were multiplied. In the primitive church a voluntary and open confession prepared the work of atonement. In the middle ages the bishops and priests interrogated the criminal, compelled him to account for his thoughts, words, and actions, and prescribed the terms of his reconciliation with God. But as this discretionary power might alternately be abused by indulgence and tyranny, a rule of discipline was framed to inform and regulate the spiritual judges. This mode of legislation was invented by the Greeks; their *penitentials* were translated, or imitated, in the Latin church; and in the time of Charlemagne the clergy of every diocese were provided with a code, which they prudently concealed from the knowledge of the vulgar. In this dangerous estimate of crimes and punishments each case was supposed, each difference was remarked, by the experience or penetration of the monks; some sins are enumerated which innocence could not have suspected, and others which reason cannot believe; and the more ordinary offences of fornication and adultery, of perjury and sacrilege, of rapine and murder, were expiated by a penance which, according to the various circumstances, was prolonged from forty days to seven years. During this term of mortification the patient was healed, the criminal was absolved, by a salutary regimen of fasts and prayers: the disorder of his dress was expressive of grief and remorse; and he humbly abstained from all the business and pleasure of social life. But the rigid execution of these laws would have depopulated the palace, the camp, and the city; the barbarians of the West believed and trembled; but nature often rebelled against principle; and the magistrate laboured without effect to enforce the jurisdiction of the priest. A literal accomplishment of penance was indeed impracticable:

the guilt of adultery was multiplied by daily repetition; that of homicide might involve the massacre of a whole people; each act was separately numbered; and, in those times of anarchy and vice, a modest sinner might easily incur a debt of three hundred years. His insolvency was relieved by a commutation or *indulgence:* a year of penance was appreciated at twenty-six *solidi* of silver, about four pounds sterling, for the rich; at three solidi, or nine shillings, for the indigent: and these alms were soon appropriated to the use of the church, which derived from the redemption of sins an inexhaustible source of opulence and dominion. A debt of three hundred years, or twelve hundred pounds, was enough to impoverish a plentiful fortune; the scarcity of gold and silver was supplied by the alienation of land; and the princely donations of Pepin and Charlemagne are expressly given for the *remedy* of their soul. It is a maxim of the civil law, that whosover cannot pay with his purse must pay with his body; and the practice of flagellation was adopted by the monks—a cheap though painful equivalent. By a fantastic arithmetic, a year of penance was taxed at three thousand lashes; and such was the skill and patience of a famous hermit, St. Dominic of the Iron Cuirass, that in six days he could discharge an entire century by a whipping of three hundred thousand stripes. His example was followed by many penitents of both sexes; and as a vicarious sacrifice was accepted, a sturdy disciplinarian might expiate on his own back the sins of his benefactors. These compensations of the purse and the person introduced, in the eleventh century, a more honourable mode of satisfaction. The merit of military service against the Saracens of Africa and Spain had been allowed by the predecessors of Urban the Second. In the council of Clermont, that pope proclaimed a *plenary indulgence* to those who should enlist under the banner of the cross; the absolution of *all* their sins, and a full receipt for *all* that might be due of canonical penance. The cold philosophy of modern times is incapable of feeling the impression that was made on a sinful and fanatic world. At the voice of their pastor, the robber, the incendiary, the homicide, arose by thousands to redeem their souls by repeating on the infidels the same deeds which they had exercised against their Christian brethren; and the terms of atonement were eagerly embraced by offenders of every rank and denomination. None were pure; none were exempt from the guilt and penalty of sin; and those who were the least amenable to the justice of God and the church were the best entitled to the temporal and eternal recompense of their pious courage. If they fell, the spirit of the Latin clergy did not hesitate to adorn their tomb with the crown of martyrdom; and should they survive, they could expect without impatience the delay and increase of their heavenly reward. They offered their blood to the Son of God, who had laid down his life for their salvation: they took up the cross, and entered with confidence into the way of the Lord. His providence would watch over their safety; perhaps his visible and miraculous power would smooth the difficulties of their holy enterprise. The cloud and pillar of Jehovah had marched before the Israelites into the promised land. Might not the Christians more reasonably hope that the rivers would open for their passage; that the walls of the strongest cities would fall at the sound of their trumpets; and that the sun would be arrested in his mid-career to allow them time for the destruction of the infidels?

Of the chiefs and soldiers who marched to the holy sepulchre, I will dare to affirm that *all* were prompted by the spirit of enthusiasm, the belief of merit, the hope of reward, and the assurance of divine aid. But I am equally persuaded that in *many* it was not the sole, that in *some* it was not the leading, principle of action. The use and abuse of religion are feeble to stem, they are strong and irresistible to impel, the stream of national manners. Against the private wars of the barbarians, their bloody tournaments, licentious loves, and judicial duels, the popes and synods might ineffectually thunder. It is a more easy task to provoke the metaphysical disputes of the Greeks, to drive into the cloister the victims of anarchy or despotism, to sanctify the patience of slaves and cowards, or to assume the merit of the humanity and benevolence of modern Christians. War and exercise were the reigning passions of the Franks or Latins; they were enjoined, as a penance, to gratify those passions, to visit distant lands, and to draw their swords against the nations of the East. Their victory, or even their attempt, would immortalise the names of the intrepid heroes of the cross; and the purest piety could not be insensible to the most splendid prospect of military glory. In the petty quarrels of Europe they shed the blood of their friends and countrymen for the acquisition, perhaps, of a castle or a village. They could march with alacrity against the distant and hostile nations who were devoted to their arms; their fancy already grasped the golden sceptres of Asia; and the conquest of Apulia and Sicily by the Normans might exalt to royalty the hopes of the most private adventurer. Christendom, in her rudest state, must have yielded to the climate and cultivation of the Mohammedan countries; and their natural and artificial wealth had been magnified by the tales of pilgrims and the gifts of an imperfect commerce. The vulgar, both the great and small, were taught to believe every wonder, of lands flowing with milk and honey, of mines and treasures, of gold and diamonds, of palaces of marble and jasper, and of odoriferous groves of cinnamon and frankincense. In this earthly paradise each warrior depended on his sword to carve a plenteous and honourable establishment, which he measured only by the extent of his wishes. Their vassals and soldiers trusted their fortunes to God and their master: the spoils of a Turkish emir might enrich the meanest follower of the camp; and the flavour of the wines, the beauty of the Grecian women, were temptations more adapted to the nature, than to the profession, of the champions of the cross. The love of freedom was a powerful incitement to the multitudes who were oppressed by feudal or ecclesiastical tyranny. Under this holy sign, the peasants and burghers, who were attached to the servitude of the glebe, might escape from a haughty lord, and transplant themselves and their families to a land of liberty. The monk might release himself from the discipline of his convent, the debtor might suspend the accumulation of usury and the pursuit of his creditors, and outlaws and malefactors of every cast might continue to brave the laws and elude the punishment of their crimes.

These motives were potent and numerous: when we have singly computed their weight on the mind of each individual, we must add the infinite series, the multiplying powers of example and fashion. The first proselytes became the warmest and most effectual missionaries of the cross: among their friends and countrymen they preached the duty, the merit, and the recompense of their holy vow, and the most reluctant hearers were insensibly drawn within the whirlpool of persuasion and authority. The martial youth were fired by the reproach or suspicion of cowardice; the opportunity of visiting with an army the sepulchre of Christ was embraced by the old and infirm, by women and children, who consulted rather their zeal than their strength; and those who in the evening had derided the folly of their companions were the most eager, the ensuing day, to tread in their footsteps. The ignorance which magnified the hopes, diminished the perils, of the enterprise. Since the Turkish conquest, the paths of pilgrimage were obliterated; the chiefs themselves had an imperfect notion of the length of the way and the state of their enemies; and such was the stupidity of the people, that, at the sight of the first city or castle beyond the limits of their knowledge, they were ready to ask whether that was not the Jerusalem, the term and object of their labours. Yet the more prudent of the crusaders, who were not sure that they should be fed from heaven with a shower of quails or manna, provided themselves with those precious metals which, in every country, are the representatives of every commodity. To defray, according to their rank, the expenses of the road, princes alienated their provinces, nobles their lands and castles, peasants their cattle and the instruments of husbandry. The value of property was depreciated by the eager competition of multitudes; while the price of arms and horses was raised to an exorbitant height by the wants and impatience of the buyers. Those who remained at home, with sense and money, were enriched by the epidemical disease: the sovereigns acquired at a cheap rate the domains of their vassals, and the ecclesiastical purchasers completed the payment by the assurance of their prayers. The cross, which was commonly sewed on the garment, in cloth or silk, was inscribed by some zealots on their skin: an hot iron, or indelible liquor, was applied to perpetuate the mark; and a crafty monk, who showed the miraculous impression on his breast, was repaid with the popular veneration and the richest benefices of Palestine.

The fifteenth of August had been fixed in the council of Clermont for the departure of the pilgrims; but the day was anticipated by the thoughtless and needy crowd of plebeians; and I shall briefly despatch the calamities which they inflicted and suffered before I enter on the more serious and successful enterprise of the chiefs. Early in the spring, from the confines of France and Lorraine, above sixty thousand of the populace of both sexes flocked round the first missionary of the crusade, and pressed him, with clamorous importunity, to lead them to the holy sepulchre. The hermit, assuming the character, without the talents or authority, of a general, impelled or obeyed the forward impulse of his votaries along the banks of the Rhine and Danube. Their wants and numbers soon compelled them to separate, and his lieutenant, Walter the Penniless, a valiant though needy soldier, conducted a vanguard of pilgrims, whose condition may be determined from the proportion of eight horsemen to fifteen thousand foot. The example and footsteps of Peter were closely pursued by another fanatic, the monk Godescal, whose sermons had swept away fifteen or twenty thousand peasants from the villages of Germany. Their rear was again pressed by a herd of two hundred thousand, the most stupid and savage refuse of the people, who mingled with their devotion a brutal licence of rapine, prostitution, and drunkenness. Some counts and gentlemen, at the head of three thousand horse, attended the motions of the multitude to partake in the spoil: but their genuine leaders (may we credit such folly?) were a goose and a goat, who were carried in the front, and to whom these worthy Christians ascribed an infusion of the divine spirit. Of these, and of other bands of enthusiasts, the first and most easy warfare was against the Jews, the murderers of the Son of God. In the trading cities of the Moselle and the Rhine their colonies were numerous and rich, and they enjoyed, under the protection of the emperor and the bishops, the free exercise of their religion. At Verdun, Treves, Mentz, Spires, Worms, many thousands of that unhappy people were pillaged and massacred, nor had they felt a more bloody stroke since the persecution of Hadrian. A remnant was saved by the firmness of their bishops, who accepted a feigned and transient conversion; but the more obstinate Jews opposed their fanaticism to the fanaticism of the Christians, barricaded their houses, and, precipitating themselves, their families, and their wealth into the rivers or the flames, disappointed the malice, or at least the avarice, of their implacable foes.

Between the frontiers of Austria and the seat of the Byzantine monarchy the crusaders were compelled to traverse an interval of six hundred miles, the wild and desolate countries of Hungary and Bulgaria. The soil is fruitful, and intersected with rivers; but it was then covered with morasses and forests, which spread to a boundless extent whenever man has ceased to exercise his dominion over the earth. Both nations had imbibed the rudiments of Christianity: the Hungarians were ruled by their native princes, the Bulgarians by a lieutenant of the Greek emperor; but, on the slightest provocation, their ferocious nature was rekindled, and ample provocation was afforded by the disorders of the first pilgrims. Agriculture must have been unskilful and languid among a people whose cities were built of reeds and timber, which were deserted in the summer season for the tents of hunters and shepherds. A scanty supply of provisions was rudely demanded, forcibly seized, and greedily consumed, and on the first quarrel the crusaders gave a loose to indignation and revenge. But their ignorance of the country, of war, and of discipline exposed them to every snare. The Greek præfect of Bulgaria commanded a regular force; at the trumpet of the Hungarian king, the eighth or the tenth of his martial subjects bent their bows and mounted on horseback; their policy was insidious, and their retaliation on these pious robbers was unrelenting and bloody. About a third of the naked fugitives, and the hermit Peter was of the number, escaped to the Thracian mountains; and the emperor, who respected the pilgrimage and succour of the Latins, conducted them by secure and easy journeys to Constantinople, and advised them to await the arrival of their brethren. For a while they remembered their faults and losses, but no sooner were they revived by the hospitable entertainment, than their venom was again inflamed; they stung their benefactor, and neither gardens, nor palaces, nor churches, were safe from their depredations. For his own safety, Alexius allured them to pass over to the Asiatic side of the Bosphorus; but their blind impetuosity soon urged them to desert the station which he had assigned, and to rush headlong against the Turks, who occupied the road of Jerusalem. The hermit, conscious of his shame, had withdrawn from the camp to Constantinople; and his lieutenant, Walter the Penniless, who was worthy of a better command, attempted without success to introduce some order and prudence among the herd of savages. They separated in quest of prey, and themselves fell an easy prey to the arts of the sultan. By a rumour that their foremost companions were rioting in the spoils of his capital, Soliman tempted the main body to descend into the plain of Nice: they were overwhelmed by the Turkish arrows, and a pyramid of bones informed their companions of the place of their defeat. Of the first crusaders, three hundred thousand had already perished before a single city was rescued from the infidels, before their graver and more noble brethren had completed the preparations of their enterprise.

None of the great sovereigns of Europe embarked their persons in the first crusade. The emperor Henry the Fourth was not disposed to obey the summons of the pope; Philip the First of France was occupied by his pleasures; William Rufus of England by a recent conquest; the kings of Spain were engaged in a domestic war against the Moors; and the northern monarchs of Scotland, Denmark, Sweden, and Poland were yet strangers to the passions and interests of the South. The religious ardour was more strongly felt by the princes of the second order, who held an important place in the feudal system. Their situation will naturally cast under four distinct heads the review of their names and characters; but I may escape some needless repetition, by observing at once that courage and the exercise of arms are the common attribute of these Christian adventurers. I. The first rank both in war and council is justly due to Godfrey of Bouillon; and happy would it have been for the crusaders, if they had trusted themselves to the sole conduct of that accomplished hero, a worthy representative of Charlemagne, from whom he was descended in the female line. His father was of the noble race of the counts of Boulogne: Brabant, the lower province of Lorraine, was the inheritance of his mother; and by the emperor's bounty he was himself invested with that ducal title, which has been improperly transferred to his lordship of Bouillon in the Ardennes. In the service of Henry the Fourth he bore the great standard of the empire, and pierced with his lance the breast of Rodolph, the rebel king: Godfrey was the first who ascended the walls of Rome; and his sickness, his vow, perhaps his remorse for bearing arms against the pope, confirmed an early resolution of visiting the holy sepulchre, not as a pilgrim, but a deliverer. His valour was matured by prudence and moderation; his piety, though blind, was sincere; and, in the tumult of a camp, he practised the real and fictitious virtues of a convent. Superior to the private factions of the chiefs, he reserved his enmity for the enemies of Christ; and though he gained a kingdom by the attempt, his pure and disinterested zeal was acknowledged by his rivals. Godfrey of Bouillon was accompanied by his two brothers, by Eustace the elder, who had succeeded to the county of Boulogne, and by the younger, Baldwin, a character of more ambiguous virtue. The duke of Lorraine was alike celebrated on either side of the Rhine: from his birth and education, he was equally conversant with the French and Teutonic languages: the barons of France, Germany, and Lorraine assembled their vassals; and the confederate force that marched under his banner was composed of fourscore thousand

foot and about ten thousand horse. II. In the parliament
that was held at Paris, in the king's presence, about two
months after the council of Clermont, Hugh, count of
Vermandois, was the most conspicuous of the princes
who assumed the cross. But the appellation of *the Great*
was applied, not so much to his merit or possessions
(though neither were contemptible), as to the royal
birth of the brother of the king of France. Robert, duke
of Normandy, was the eldest son of William the Conqueror; but on his father's death he was deprived of the
kingdom of England, by his own indolence and the activity of his brother Rufus. The worth of Robert was degraded by an excessive levity and easiness of temper: his
cheerfulness seduced him to the indulgence of pleasure;
his profuse liberality impoverished the prince and people; his indiscriminate clemency multiplied the number
of offenders; and the amiable qualities of a private man
became the essential defects of a sovereign. For the
trifling sum of ten thousand marks he mortgaged Normandy during his absence to the English usurper; but
his engagement and behaviour in the holy war announced in Robert a reformation of manners, and restored him in some degree to the public esteem. Another
Robert was count of Flanders, a royal province, which,
in this century, gave three queens to the thrones of
France, England, and Denmark: he was surnamed the
Sword and Lance of the Christians; but in the exploits
of a soldier he sometimes forgot the duties of a general.
Stephen, count of Chartres, of Blois, and of Troyes, was
one of the richest princes of the age; and the number
of his castles has been compared to the three hundred
and sixty-five days of the year. His mind was improved
by literature; and, in the council of the chiefs, the eloquent Stephen was chosen to discharge the office of their
president. These four were the principal leaders of the
French, the Normans, and the pilgrims of the British
isles: but the list of the barons who were possessed
of three or four towns would exceed, says a contemporary,
the catalogue of the Trojan war. III. In the south of
France the command was assumed by Adhemar, bishop
of Puy, the pope's legate, and by Raymond count of St.

Giles and Toulouse, who added the prouder titles of duke
of Narbonne and marquis of Provence. The former was
a respectable prelate, alike qualified for this world and
the next. The latter was a veteran warrior, who had
fought against the Saracens of Spain, and who consecrated his declining age, not only to the deliverance, but
to the perpetual service, of the holy sepulchre. His experience and riches gave him a strong ascendant in the
Christian camp, whose distress he was often able, and
sometimes willing, to relieve. But it was easier for him
to extort the praise of the Infidels than to preserve the
love of his subjects and associates. His eminent qualities
were clouded by a temper, haughty, envious, and obstinate; and, though he resigned an ample patrimony
for the cause of God, his piety, in the public opinion, was
not exempt from avarice and ambition. A mercantile,
rather than a martial, spirit prevailed among his *provincials*, a common name, which included the natives of
Auvergne and Languedoc, the vassals of the kingdom
of Burgundy or Arles. From the adjacent frontier of
Spain he drew a band of hardy adventurers; as he
marched through Lombardy, a crowd of Italians flocked
to his standard, and his united force consisted of one
hundred thousand horse and foot. If Raymond was the
first to enlist and the last to depart, the delay may be
excused by the greatness of his preparation and the
promise of an everlasting farewell. IV. The name of Bohemond, the son of Robert Guiscard, was already famous
by his double victory over the Greek emperor: but his
father's will had reduced him to the principality of Taren-
tum, and the remembrance of his Eastern trophies, till
he was awakened by the rumour and passage of the
French pilgrims. It is in the person of this Norman chief
that we may seek for the coolest policy and ambition,
with a small alloy of religious fanaticism. His conduct
may justify a belief that he had secretly directed the design of the pope, which he affected to second with astonishment and zeal: at the siege of Amalphi his example
and discourse inflamed the passions of a confederate
army; he instantly tore his garment to supply crosses for
the numerous candidates, and prepared to visit Con-

stantinople and Asia at the head of ten thousand horse and twenty thousand foot. Several princes of the Norman race accompanied this veteran general; and his cousin Tancred was the partner, rather than the servant, of the war. In the accomplished character of Tancred we discover all the virtues of a perfect knight, the true spirit of chivalry, which inspired the generous sentiments and social offices of man far better than the base philosophy, or the baser religion, of the times. . . .

Such were the troops, and such the leaders, who assumed the cross for the deliverance of the holy sepulchre. As soon as they were relieved by the absence of the plebeian multitude, they encouraged each other, by interviews and messages, to accomplish their vow, and hasten their departure. Their wives and sisters were desirous of partaking the danger and merit of the pilgrimage: their portable treasures were conveyed in bars of silver and gold; and the princes and barons were attended by their equipage of hounds and hawks to amuse their leisure and to supply their table. The difficulty of procuring subsistence for so many myriads of men and horses engaged them to separate their forces: their choice or situation determined the road; and it was agreed to meet in the neighbourhood of Constantinople, and from thence to begin their operations against the Turks. From the banks of the Meuse and the Moselle, Godfrey of Bouillon followed the direct way of Germany, Hungary, and Bulgaria; and, as long as he exercised the sole command, every step afforded some proof of his prudence and virtue. On the confines of Hungary he was stopped three weeks by a Christian people, to whom the name, or at least the abuse, of the cross was justly odious. The Hungarians still smarted with the wounds which they had received from the first pilgrims: in their turn they had abused the right of defence and retaliation; and they had reason to apprehend a severe revenge from a hero of the same nation, and who was engaged in the same cause. But, after weighing the motives and the events, the virtuous duke was content to pity the crimes and misfortunes of his worthless brethren; and his twelve deputies, the messengers of peace, requested in his name a free passage and an equal market. To remove their suspicions, Godfrey trusted himself, and afterwards his brother, to the faith of Carloman, king of Hungary, who treated them with a simple but hospitable entertainment: the treaty was sanctified by their common Gospel; and a proclamation, under pain of death, restrained the animosity and licence of the Latin soldiers. From Austria to Belgrade, they traversed the plains of Hungary, without enduring or offering an injury; and the proximity of Carloman, who hovered on their flanks with his numerous cavalry, was a precaution not less useful for their safety than for his own. They reached the banks of the Save; and no sooner had they passed the river than the king of Hungary restored the hostages, and saluted their departure with the fairest wishes for the success of their enterprise. With the same conduct and discipline Godfrey pervaded the woods of Bulgaria and the frontiers of Thrace; and might congratulate himself that he had almost reached the first term of his pilgrimage without drawing his sword against a Christian adversary. After an easy and pleasant journey through Lombardy, from Turin to Aquileia, Raymond and his provincials marched forty days through the savage country of Dalmatia and Sclavonia. The weather was a perpetual fog; the land was mountainous and desolate; the natives were either fugitive or hostile: loose in their religion and government, they refused to furnish provisions or guides; murdered the stragglers; and exercised by night and day the vigilance of the count, who derived more security from the punishment of some captive robbers than from his interview and treaty with the prince of Scodra. His march between Durazzo and Constantinople was harassed, without being stopped, by the peasants and soldiers of the Greek emperor; and the same faint and ambiguous hostility was prepared for the remaining chiefs, who passed the Adriatic from the coast of Italy. Bohemond had arms and vessels, and foresight and discipline; and his name was not forgotten in the provinces of Epirus and Thessaly. Whatever obstacles he encountered were surmounted by his military conduct and the valour of Tancred; and if the Norman prince affected to spare the Greeks, he gorged his soldiers with the full plunder of an heretical castle. The nobles of France pressed forwards with the vain and thoughtless ardour of which their nation has been sometimes accused. From the Alps to Apulia the march of Hugh the Great, of the two Roberts, and of Stephen of Chartres, through a wealthy country, and amidst the applauding Catholics, was a devout or triumphant progress: they kissed the feet of the Roman pontiff; and the golden standard of St. Peter was delivered to the brother of the French monarch. But in this visit of piety and pleasure they neglected to secure the season and the means of their embarkation: the winter was insensibly lost: their troops were scattered and corrupted in the towns of Italy. They separately accomplished their passage, regardless of safety or dignity; and within nine months from the feast of the Assumption, the day appointed by Urban, all the Latin princes had reached Constantinople. But the count of Vermandois was produced as a captive; his foremost vessels were scattered by a tempest; and his person, against the law of nations, was detained by the lieutenants of Alexius. Yet the arrival of Hugh had been announced by four-and-twenty knights in golden armour, who commanded the emperor to revere the general of the Latin Christians, the brother of the king of kings.

In some Oriental tale I have read the fable of a shepherd who was ruined by the accomplishment of his own wishes: he had prayed for water; the Ganges was turned into his grounds, and his flock and cottage were swept away by the inundation. Such was the fortune, or at least the apprehension, of the Greek emperor Alexius Comnenus, whose name has already appeared in this history, and whose conduct is so differently represented by his daughter Anna, and by the Latin writers.[2] In the council of Placentia his ambassadors had solicited a moderate succour, perhaps of ten thousand soldiers; but he was astonished by the approach of so many potent chiefs

---

[2] In their views of the character and conduct of Alexius, Maimbourg has favoured the *Catholic* Franks, and Voltaire has been partial to the *schismatic* Greeks. The prejudice of a philosopher is less excusable than that of a Jesuit.

and fanatic nations. The emperor fluctuated between hope and fear, between timidity and courage; but in the crooked policy which he mistook for wisdom, I cannot believe, I cannot discern, that he maliciously conspired against the life or honour of the French heroes. The promiscuous multitudes of Peter the Hermit were savage beasts, alike destitute of humanity and reason: nor was it possible for Alexius to prevent or deplore their destruction. The troops of Godfrey and his peers were less contemptible, but not less suspicious, to the Greek emperor. Their motives *might* be pure and pious; but he was equally alarmed by his knowledge of the ambitious Bohemond, and his ignorance of the Transalpine chiefs: the courage of the French was blind and headstrong; they might be tempted by the luxury and wealth of Greece, and elated by the view and opinion of their invincible strength; and Jerusalem might be forgotten in the prospect of Constantinople. After a long march and painful abstinence, the troops of Godfrey encamped in the plains of Thrace; they heard with indignation that their brother, the count of Vermandois, was imprisoned by the Greeks; and their reluctant duke was compelled to indulge them in some freedom of retaliation and rapine. They were appeased by the submission of Alexius: he promised to supply their camp; and as they refused, in the midst of winter, to pass the Bosphorus, their quarters were assigned among the gardens and palaces on the shores of that narrow sea. But an incurable jealousy still rankled in the minds of the two nations, who despised each other as slaves and barbarians. Ignorance is the ground of suspicion, and suspicion was inflamed into daily provocations: prejudice is blind, hunger is deaf; and Alexius is accused of a design to starve or assault the Latins in a dangerous post, on all sides encompassed with the waters. Godfrey sounded his trumpets, burst the net, overspread the plain, and insulted the suburbs: but the gates of Constantinople were strongly fortified; the ramparts were lined with archers; and after a doubtful conflict, both parties listened to the voice of peace and religion. The gifts and promises of the emperor insensibly soothed the fierce spirit of the Western strangers; as a Christian warrior, he rekindled their zeal for the prosecution of their holy enterprise, which he engaged to second with his troops and treasures. On the return of spring, Godfrey was persuaded to occupy a pleasant and plentiful camp in Asia; and no sooner had he passed the Bosphorus than the Greek vessels were suddenly recalled to the opposite shore. The same policy was repeated with the succeeding chiefs, who were swayed by the example, and weakened by the departure, of their foremost companions. By his skill and diligence Alexius prevented the union of any two of the confederate armies at the same moment under the walls of Constantinople; and before the feast of the Pentecost not a Latin pilgrim was left on the coast of Europe.

The same arms which threatened Europe might deliver Asia, and repel the Turks from the neighbouring shores of the Bosphorus and Hellespont. The fair provinces from Nice to Antioch were the recent patrimony of the Roman emperor; and his ancient and perpetual claim still embraced the kingdoms of Syria and Egypt. In his enthusiasm, Alexius indulged, or affected, the ambitious hope of leading his new allies to subvert the thrones of the East; but the calmer dictates of reason and temper dissuaded him from exposing his royal person to the faith of unknown and lawless barbarians. His prudence, or his pride, was content with extorting from the French princes an oath of homage and fidelity, and a solemn promise that they would either restore, or hold, their Asiatic conquests, as the humble and loyal vassals of the Roman empire. Their independent spirit was fired at the mention of this foreign and voluntary servitude: they successively yielded to the dexterous application of gifts and flattery; and the first proselytes became the most eloquent and effectual missionaries to multiply the companions of their shame. The pride of Hugh of Vermandois was soothed by the honours of his captivity; and in the brother of the French king the example of submission was prevalent and weighty. In the mind of Godfrey of Bouillon every human consideration was

377

subordinate to the glory of God and the success of the crusade. He had firmly resisted the temptations of Bohemond and Raymond, who urged the attack and conquest of Constantinople. Alexius esteemed his virtues, deservedly named him the champion of the empire, and dignified his homage with the filial name and the rights of adoption. The hateful Bohemond was received as a true and ancient ally; and if the emperor reminded him of former hostilities, it was only to praise the valour that he had displayed, and the glory that he had acquired, in the fields of Durazzo and Larissa. . . . The two Roberts, the son of the conqueror of England, and the kinsman of three queens, bowed in their turn before the Byzantine throne. A private letter of Stephen of Chartres attests his admiration of the emperor, the most excellent and liberal of men, who taught him to believe that he was a favourite, and promised to educate and establish his youngest son. In his southern province, the count of St. Giles and Toulouse faintly recognised the supremacy of the king of France, a prince of a foreign nation and language. At the head of a hundred thousand men, he declared that he was the soldier and servant of Christ alone, and that the Greek might be satisfied with an equal treaty of alliance and friendship. His obstinate resistance enhanced the value and the price of his submission; and he shone, says the princess Anna, among the barbarians, as the sun amidst the stars of heaven. His disgust of the noise and insolence of the French, his suspicions of the designs of Bohemond, the emperor imparted to his faithful Raymond; and that aged statesman might clearly discern, that, however false in friendship, he was sincere in his enmity. The spirit of chivalry was last subdued in the person of Tancred; and none could deem themselves dishonoured by the imitation of that gallant knight. He disdained the gold and flattery of the Greek monarch; assaulted in his presence an insolent patrician; escaped to Asia in the habit of a private soldier; and yielded with a sigh to the authority of Bohemond, and the interest of the Christian cause. The best and most ostensible reason was the impossibility of passing the sea and accomplishing their vow without the licence and the vessels of Alexius; but they cherished a secret hope, that, as soon as they trod the continent of Asia, their swords would obliterate their shame, and dissolve the engagement, which on his side might not be very faithfully performed. The ceremony of their homage was grateful to a people who had long since considered pride as the substitute of power. High on his throne the emperor sat mute and immovable: his majesty was adored by the Latin princes; and they submitted to kiss either his feet or his knees, an indignity which their own writers are ashamed to confess, and unable to deny. . . .

The conquest of Asia was undertaken and achieved by Alexander, with thirty-five thousand Macedonians and Greeks; and his best hope was in the strength and discipline of his phalanx of infantry. The principal force of the crusaders consisted in their cavalry; and when that force was mustered in the plains of Bithynia, the knights and their martial attendants on horseback amounted to one hundred thousand fighting men, completely armed with the helmet and coat of mail. The value of these soldiers deserved a strict and authentic account; and the flower of European chivalry might furnish, in a first effort, this formidable body of heavy horse. A part of the infantry might be enrolled for the service of scouts, pioneers, and archers; but the promiscuous crowd were lost in their own disorder; and we depend not on the eyes or knowledge, but on the belief and fancy, of a chaplain of Count Baldwin, in the estimate of six hundred thousand pilgrims able to bear arms, besides the priests and monks, the women and children, of the Latin camp. The reader starts; and before he is recovered from his surprise I shall add, on the same testimony, that, if all who took the cross had accomplished their vow, above SIX MILLIONS would have migrated from Europe to Asia. Under this oppression of faith I derive some relief from a more sagacious and thinking writer, who, after the same review of the cavalry, accuses the credulity of the priest of Chartres, and even doubts whether the *Cisalpine* regions (in the geography of a Frenchman) were sufficient to produce and pour forth such incredible multitudes. The coolest scepticism will remember that of these religious volunteers great numbers never beheld Constantinople and Nice. Of enthusiasm the influence is irregular and transient: many were detained at home by reason or cowardice, by poverty or weakness; and many were repulsed by the obstacles of the way, the more insuperable as they were unforeseen to these ignorant fanatics. The savage countries of Hungary and Bulgaria were whitened with their bones: their vanguard was cut in pieces by the Turkish sultan; and the loss of the first adventure, by the sword, or climate, or fatigue, has already been stated at three hundred thousand men. Yet the myriads that survived, that marched, that pressed forwards on the holy pilgrimage, were a subject of astonishment to themselves and to the Greeks. The copious energy of her language sinks under the efforts of the princess Anna: the images of locusts, of leaves and flowers, of the sands of the sea, or the stars of heaven, imperfectly represent what she had seen and heard; and the daughter of Alexius exclaims that Europe was loosened from its foundations, and hurled against Asia. The ancient hosts of Darius and Xerxes labour under the same doubt of a vague and indefinite magnitude; but I am inclined to believe that a larger number has never been contained within the lines of a single camp than at the siege of Nice, the first operation of the Latin princes. Their motives, their characters, and their arms, have been already displayed. Of their troops, the most numerous portion were natives of France: the Low Countries, the banks of the Rhine, and Apulia sent a powerful reinforcement: some bands of adventurers were drawn from Spain, Lombardy, and England; and from the distant bogs and mountains of Ireland and Scotland issued some naked and savage fanatics, ferocious at home, but unwarlike abroad. Had not superstition condemned the sacrilegious prudence of depriving the poorest or weakest Christian of the merit of the pilgrimage, the useless crowd, with mouths but without hands, might have been stationed in the Greek empire till their companions had opened and secured the way of the Lord. A small remnant of the pilgrims, who passed the Bosphorus, was permitted to visit the holy sepulchre. Their northern constitution was scorched by the rays, and infected by the vapours, of a Syrian sun. They consumed, with heedless prodigality, their stores of water and provision: their numbers exhausted the inland country: the sea was remote, the Greeks were unfriendly, and the Christians of every sect fled before the voracious and cruel rapine of their brethren. In the dire necessity of famine, they sometimes roasted and devoured the flesh of their infant or adult captives. Among the Turks and Saracens, the idolaters of Europe were rendered more odious by the name and reputation of cannibals; the spies, who introduced themselves into the kitchen of Bohemond, were shown several human bodies turning on the spit: and the artful Norman encouraged a report which increased at the same time the abhorrence and the terror of the infidels.

I have expatiated with pleasure on the first steps of the crusaders, as they paint the manners and character of Europe: but I shall abridge the tedious and uniform narrative of their blind achievements, which were performed by strength and are described by ignorance. From their first station in the neighbourhood of Nicomedia, they advanced in successive divisions; passed the contracted limit of the Greek empire; opened a road through the hills; and commenced, by the siege of his capital, their pious warfare against the Turkish sultan.

[*The crusaders captured the Turkish capital, and so gave permanent relief to Byzantium; they then went on and established the Latin Kingdom of Jerusalem under Godfrey de Bouillon. At first the new Christian kingdom was cramped and precarious; but later . . .*]

By the arms of Godfrey himself, and of the two Baldwins, his brother and cousin, who succeeded to the throne, the Latins breathed with more ease and safety; and at length they equalled, in the extent of their dominions, though not in the millions of their subjects, the ancient princes of Judah and Israel. After the reduction of the maritime cities of Laodicea, Tripoli, Tyre, and Ascalon, which were powerfully assisted by the fleets of Venice, Genoa, and Pisa, and even of Flanders and Norway, the range of sea-coast from Scanderoon to the borders of Egypt was possessed by the Christian pilgrims. If the prince of Antioch disclaimed his supremacy, the counts of Edessa and Tripoli owned themselves the vassals of the king of Jerusalem: the Latins reigned beyond the Euphrates; and the four cities of Hems, Hamah, Damascus, and Aleppo were the only relics of the Mohammedan conquests in Syria. The laws and language, the manners and titles, of the French nation and Latin church, were introduced into these transmarine colonies. According to the feudal jurisprudence, the principal states and subordinate baronies descended in the line of male and female succession: but the children of the first conquerors, a motley and degenerate race, were dissolved by the luxury of the climate; the arrival of new crusaders from Europe was a doubtful hope and a casual event. The service of the feudal tenures was performed by six hundred and sixty-six knights, who might expect the aid of two hundred more under the banner of the count of Tripoli; and each knight was attended to the field by four squires or archers on horseback. Five thousand and seventy-five *serjeants*, most probably foot-soldiers, were supplied by the churches and cities; and the whole legal militia of the kingdom could not exceed eleven thousand men, a slender defence against the surrounding myriads of Saracens and Turks. But the firmest bulwark of Jerusalem was founded on the knights of the Hospital of St. John, and of the temple of Solomon; on the strange association of a monastic and military life, which fanaticism might suggest, but which policy must approve. The flower of the nobility of Europe aspired to wear the cross, and to profess the vows, of these respectable orders; their spirit and discipline were immortal; and the speedy donation of twenty-eight thousand farms, or manors, enabled them

to support a regular force of cavalry and infantry for
the defence of Palestine. The austerity of the convent
soon evaporated in the exercise of arms: the world was
scandalised by the pride, avarice, and corruption of these
Christian soldiers; their claims of immunity and jurisdiction disturbed the harmony of the church and state;
and the public peace was endangered by their jealous
emulation. But in their most dissolute period the knights
of the hospital and temple maintained their fearless and
fanatic character: they neglected to live, but they were
prepared to die, in the service of Christ; and the spirit
of chivalry, the parent and offspring of the crusades, has
been transplanted by this institution from the holy sepulchre to the isle of Malta.

[*The Crusades were more fatal to Constantinople than
to the Moslems. They introduced the "Franks" of Western
Europe to the East and sharpened their appetite not only
against their enemies, the "infidel" Turks, but also against
their allies, the Christian but "schismatic" Greeks. If the
first Crusade established the Latin Kingdom of Jerusalem,
it also increased the distrust between Franks and Greeks,
and the fourth Crusade, diverted by the Venetians from
Egypt to Constantinople, ended in 1204 with the sack
of the city, the division of the Empire between Frankish
feudatories and Venetian capitalists, and the conversion
of its shrunken heart into the Latin Empire of the East.
To all appearances, the historic Byzantine Empire ended
with the conquest of 1204: the revenge of the West for
the conquest and ruin of Rome by Justinian.*

*In fact it was not so. From their base in Nice or
Nicæa, the seat of the first General Council of the Church
and the temporary capital of the Seljuk Turks, the Greeks,
led by the able "emperor of Nicæa" John Vatatzes, skilfully undermined the Latin empire of Constantinople
just as the Mamelukes of Egypt undermined the Latin
Kingdom of Jerusalem. In 1261 the last Latin Emperor
was driven out and the capital recovered by Vatatzes'
general and successor, John Palæologus. In 1291 the last
relics of the Kingdom of Jerusalem fell to the Mamelukes.
Thus by the end of the thirteenth century the Crusades*

had failed and, in Gibbon's words, "a mournful and soli-
tary silence prevailed along the coast which had so long
resounded with the WORLD'S DEBATE." In chapter LXI
Gibbon summarises the results of the whole movement.]

After this narrative of the expeditions of the Latins to
Palestine and Constantinople, I cannot dismiss the subject without revolving the general consequences on the
countries that were the scene, and on the nations that
were the actors, of these memorable crusades. As soon
as the arms of the Franks were withdrawn, the impression, though not the memory, was erased in the Mohammedan realms of Egypt and Syria. The faithful disciples
of the prophet were never tempted by a profane desire
to study the laws or language of the idolaters; nor did
the simplicity of their primitive manners receive the
slightest alteration from their intercourse in peace and
war with the unknown strangers of the West. The Greeks,
who thought themselves proud, but who were only vain,
showed a disposition somewhat less inflexible. In the
efforts for the recovery of their empire they emulated the
valour, discipline, and tactics of their antagonists. The
modern literature of the West they might justly despise;
but its free spirit would instruct them in the rights of
man; and some institutions of public and private life
were adopted from the French. The correspondence of
Constantinople and Italy diffused the knowledge of the
Latin tongue; and several of the fathers and classics were
at length honoured with a Greek version. But the national and religious prejudices of the Orientals were inflamed by persecution; and the reign of the Latins confirmed the separation of the two churches.

If we compare, at the era of the crusades, the Latins of
Europe with the Greeks and Arabians, their respective
degrees of knowledge, industry, and art, our rude ancestors must be content with the third rank in the scale of
nations. Their successive improvement and present superiority may be ascribed to a peculiar energy of character,
to an active and imitative spirit, unknown to their more
polished rivals, who at that time were in a stationary
or retrograde state. With such a disposition the Latins

should have derived the most early and essential benefits from a series of events which opened to their eyes the prospect of the world, and introduced them to a long and frequent intercourse with the more cultivated regions of the East. The first and most obvious progress was in trade and manufactures, in the arts which are strongly prompted by the thirst of wealth, the calls of necessity, and the gratification of the sense or vanity. Among the crowd of unthinking fanatics a captive or a pilgrim might sometimes observe the superior refinements of Cairo and Constantinople: the first importer of windmills[3] was the benefactor of nations; and if such blessings are enjoyed without any grateful remembrance, history has condescended to notice the more apparent luxuries of silk and sugar, which were transported into Italy from Greece and Egypt. But the intellectual wants of the Latins were more slowly felt and supplied; the ardour of studious curiosity was awakened in Europe by different causes and more recent events; and, in the age of the crusades, they viewed with careless indifference the literature of the Greeks and Arabians. Some rudiments of mathematical and medicinal knowledge might be imparted in practice and in figures; necessity might produce some interpreters for the grosser business of merchants and soldiers; but the commerce of the Orientals had not diffused the study and knowledge of their languages in the schools of Europe. If a similar principle of religion repulsed the idiom of the Koran, it should have excited their patience and curiosity to understand the original text of the Gospel; and the same grammar would have unfolded the sense of Plato and the beauties of Homer. Yet, in a reign of sixty years, the Latins of Constantinople disdained the speech and learning of their subjects; and the manuscripts were the only treasures which the natives might enjoy without rapine or envy. Aristotle was indeed the oracle of the Western universities, but it was a barbarous Aristotle; and, instead of ascending to the fountain head, his Latin votaries humbly accepted a corrupt and remote version from the Jews and Moors of Andalusia.

3 Windmills, first invented in the dry country of Asia Minor, were used in Normandy as early as the year 1105.

The principle of the crusades was a savage fanaticism; and the most important effects were analogous to the cause. Each pilgrim was ambitious to return with his sacred spoils, the relics of Greece and Palestine;[4] and each relic was preceded and followed by a train of miracles and visions. The belief of the Catholics was corrupted by new legends, their practice by new superstitions; and the establishment of the inquisition, the mendicant orders of monks and friars, the last abuse of indulgences, and the final progress of idolatry, flowed from the baleful fountain of the holy war. The active spirit of the Latins preyed on the vitals of their reason and religion; and if the ninth and tenth centuries were the times of darkness, the thirteenth and fourteenth were the age of absurdity and fable.

In the profession of Christianity, in the cultivation of a fertile land, the northern conquerors of the Roman empire insensibly mingled with the provincials and rekindled the embers of the arts of antiquity. Their settlements about the age of Charlemagne had acquired some degree of order and stability, when they were overwhelmed by new swarms of invaders, the Normans, Saracens, and Hungarians, who replunged the western countries of Europe into their former state of anarchy and barbarism. About the eleventh century the second tempest had subsided by the expulsion or conversion of the enemies of Christendom: the tide of civilisation, which had so long ebbed, began to flow with a steady and accelerated course; and a fairer prospect was opened to the hopes and efforts of the rising generations. Great was the increase, and rapid the progress, during the two hundred years of the crusades; and some philosophers have applauded the propitious influence of these holy wars, which appear to me to have checked rather than forwarded the maturity of Europe.[5] The lives and labours of millions which were

---

4 Such was the opinion of the great Leibnitz, a master of the history of the middle ages. I shall only instance the pedigree of the Carmelites and the flight of the house of Loretto, which were both derived from Palestine.

5 On this interesting subject, the progress of society in Europe, a strong ray of philosophic light has broke from Scotland in our

buried in the East would have been more profitably employed in the improvement of their native country: the accumulated stock of industry and wealth would have overflowed in navigation and trade; and the Latins would have been enriched and enlightened by a pure and friendly correspondence with the climates of the East. In one respect I can indeed perceive the accidental operation of the crusades, not so much in producing a benefit as in removing an evil. The larger portion of the inhabitants of Europe was chained to the soil, without freedom, or property, or knowledge; and the two orders of ecclesiastics and nobles, whose numbers were comparatively small, alone deserved the name of citizens and men. This oppressive system was supported by the arts of the clergy and the swords of the barons. The authority of the priests operated in the darker ages as a salutary antidote: they prevented the total extinction of letters, mitigated the fierceness of the times, sheltered the poor and defenceless, and preserved or revived the peace and order of civil society. But the independence, rapine, and discord of the feudal lords were unmixed with any semblance of good; and every hope of industry and improvement was crushed by the iron weight of the martial aristocracy. Among the causes that undermined that Gothic edifice, a conspicuous place must be allowed to the crusades. The estates of the barons were dissipated, and their race was often extinguished in these costly and perilous expeditions. Their poverty extorted from their pride those charters of freedom which unlocked the fetters of the slave, secured the farm of the peasant and the shop of the artificer, and gradually restored a substance and a soul to the most numerous and useful part of the community. The conflagration which destroyed the tall and barren trees of the forest gave air and scope to the vegetation of the smaller and nutritive plants of the soil.

---

own times; and it is with private, as well as public regard, that I repeat the names of Hume, Robertson, and Adam Smith.

15. The Fall of Constantinople

[With the failure of the crusades, Constantinople
resumed its old position as the capital of a Greek
empire. Indeed, under its last dynasty of the Pa-
læologi—the last and longest in its whole history
—it was more Greek than ever; for all the non-
Greek provinces were lost. But it was also weaker
than ever. It emerged from its troubles as little
more than a protectorate, first, of rival Italian
cities, then of successive Turkish sultans.

For meanwhile the last enemy was closing in.
Where the Franks of the West had failed, the
Ottoman Turks of the East, the conquerors and
successors of the Seljuks, would succeed. Since
the thirteenth century they had been slowly pressing forward. By the second half of the fourteenth
century they were established in Europe, with
their capital at Adrianople. Successive emperors
sought to buy Western support, even by submit-
ting to the religion of Rome, and in 1439, the
emperor John Palæologus actually subscribed an
Act of Union at the Council of Florence; but the
support thus obtained was always illusory and the
religious concessions were invariably repudiated
by the Greek people. Even the meteoric conquests
of the Mongols under Timur (or Tamerlane) only
gave a temporary respite. In 1402, Timur totally
defeated and captured the Turkish sultan Bayezid
at Ankara; but after Timur's death, Bayezid's successors reconstituted his state and resumed its
pressure on Europe. By 1451, when Mohammed II
became sultan, Constantinople was already sur-

rounded and the end was in sight. Mohammed re-
solved to hasten it. In chapter LXVIII Gibbon de-
scribes the final conquest and the death of the last
Christian emperor, Constantine Palæologus.]

The siege of Constantinople by the Turks attracts our
first attention to the person and character of the great
destroyer. Mohammed the Second was the son of the
second Amurath; and though his mother has been decorated with the titles of Christian and princess, she is more
probably confounded with the numerous concubines who
peopled from every climate the harem of the sultan. His
first education and sentiments were those of a devout
Musulman; and as often as he conversed with an infidel
he purified his hands and face by the legal rites of ablu-
tion. Age and empire appear to have relaxed this narrow
bigotry: his aspiring genius disdained to acknowledge
a power above his own; and in his looser hours he presumed (it is said) to brand the prophet of Mecca as a
robber and impostor. Yet the sultan persevered in a decent reverence for the doctrine and discipline of the
Koran: his private indiscretion must have been sacred
from the vulgar ear; and we should suspect the credulity
of strangers and sectaries, so prone to believe that a mind
which is hardened against truth must be armed with
superior contempt for absurdity and error. Under the tuition of the most skilful masters Mohammed advanced
with an early and rapid progress in the paths of knowledge; and besides his native tongue it is affirmed that he
spoke or understood five languages. . . .

The history and geography of the world were familiar
to his memory: the lives of the heroes of the East, perhaps of the West, excited his emulation: his skill in
astrology is excused by the folly of the times, and supposes some rudiments of mathematical science; and a
profane taste for the arts is betrayed in his liberal invitation and reward of the painters of Italy. But the influence
of religion and learning were employed without effect
on his savage and licentious nature. I will not transcribe,
nor do I firmly believe, the stories of his fourteen pages
whose bellies were ripped open in search of a stolen

melon, or of the beauteous slave whose head he severed from her body to convince the Janizaries that their master was not the votary of love. His sobriety is attested by the silence of the Turkish annals, which accuse three, and three only, of the Ottoman line of the vice of drunkenness. But it cannot be denied that his passions were at once furious and inexorable; that in the palace, as in the field, a torrent of blood was spilt on the slightest provocation; and that the noblest of the captive youth were often dishonoured by his unnatural lust. In the Albanian war he studied the lessons, and soon surpassed the example, of his father; and the conquest of two empires, twelve kingdoms, and two hundred cities, a vain and flattering account, is ascribed to his invincible sword. He was doubtless a soldier, and possibly a general; Constantinople has sealed his glory; but if we compare the means, the obstacles, and the achievements, Mohammed the Second must blush to sustain a parallel with Alexander or Timur. Under his command the Ottoman forces were always more numerous than their enemies, yet their progress was bounded by the Euphrates and the Adriatic, and his arms were checked by Huniades and Scanderbeg, by the Rhodian knights, and by the Persian king.

In the reign of Amurath he twice tasted of royalty, and twice descended from the throne: his tender age was incapable of opposing his father's restoration, but never could he forgive the vizirs who had recommended that salutary measure. His nuptials were celebrated with the daughter of a Turkman emir; and, after a festival of two months, he departed from Adrianople with his bride to reside in the government of Magnesia. Before the end of six weeks he was recalled by a sudden message from the divan which announced the decease of Amurath and the mutinous spirit of the Janizaries. His speed and vigour commanded their obedience: he passed the Hellespont with a chosen guard: and at the distance of a mile from Adrianople the vizirs and emirs, the imams and cadhis, the soldiers and the people, fell prostrate before the new sultan. They affected to weep, they affected to rejoice: he ascended the throne at the age of twenty-one years, and removed the cause of sedition by the death, the inevitable death, of his infant brothers. The ambassadors of Europe and Asia soon appeared to congratulate his accession and solicit his friendship, and to all he spoke the language of moderation and peace. The confidence of the Greek emperor was revived by the solemn oaths and fair assurances with which he sealed the ratification of the treaty: and a rich domain on the banks of the Strymon was assigned for the annual payment of three hundred thousand aspers, the pension of an Ottoman prince who was detained at his request in the Byzantine court. Yet the neighbours of Mohammed might tremble at the severity with which a youthful monarch reformed the pomp of his father's household: the expenses of luxury were applied to those of ambition, and a useless train of seven thousand falconers was either dismissed from his service or enlisted in his troops. In the first summer of his reign he visited with an army the Asiatic provinces; but after humbling the pride Mohammed accepted the submission of the Caramanian, that he might not be diverted by the smallest obstacle from the execution of his great design.

The Mohammedan, and more especially the Turkish casuists, have pronounced that no promise can bind the faithful against the interest and duty of their religion, and that the sultan may abrogate his own treaties and those of his predecessors. The justice and magnanimity of Amurath had scorned this immoral privilege; but his son, though the proudest of men, could stoop from ambition to the basest arts of dissimulation and deceit. Peace was on his lips while war was in his heart: he incessantly sighed for the possession of Constantinople; and the Greeks, by their own indiscretion, afforded the first pretence of the fatal rupture. Instead of labouring to be forgotten, their ambassadors pursued his camp to demand the payment, and even the increase, of their annual stipend: the divan was importuned by their complaints; and the vizir, a secret friend of the Christians, was constrained to deliver the sense of his brethren. "Ye foolish and miserable Romans," said Calil, "we know your devices, and ye are ignorant of your own danger! the scrupulous Amurath is no more; his throne is occu-

pied by a young conqueror whom no laws can bind, and
no obstacles can resist: and if you escape from his hands,
give praise to the divine clemency, which yet delays the
chastisement of your sins. Why do ye seek to affright us
by vain and indirect menaces? Release the fugitive
Orchan, crown him sultan of Romania, call the Hungarians from beyond the Danube, arm against us the
nations of the West, and be assured that you will only
provoke and precipitate your ruin." But if the fears of
the ambassadors were alarmed by the stern language of
the vizir, they were soothed by the courteous audience
and friendly speeches of the Ottoman prince; and Mohammed assured them that on his return to Adrianople he
would redress the grievances, and consult the true interests of the Greeks. No sooner had he repassed the
Hellespont than he issued a mandate to suppress their
pension, and to expel their officers from the banks of the
Strymon: in this measure he betrayed a hostile mind;
and the second order announced, and in some degree
commenced, the siege of Constantinople. In the narrow
pass of the Bosphorus an Asiatic fortress had formerly
been raised by his grandfather; in the opposite situation,
on the European side, he resolved to erect a more formidable castle, and a thousand masons were commanded
to assemble in the spring on a spot named Asomaton,
about five miles from the Greek metropolis.[1] Persuasion
is the resource of the feeble; and the feeble can seldom
persuade: the ambassadors of the emperor attempted,
without success, to divert Mohammed from the execution
of his design. They represented that his grandfather had
solicited the permission of Manuel to build a castle on
his own territories; but that this double fortification,
which would command the strait, could only tend to
violate the alliance of the nations, to intercept the Latins
who traded in the Black Sea, and perhaps to annihilate
the subsistence of the city. "I form no enterprise," replied
the perfidious sultan, "against the city; but the empire of
Constantinople is measured by her walls. Have you forgot
the distress to which my father was reduced when you
formed a league with the Hungarians, when they invaded

---

[1] [This is the great fortress of Rumeli Hisar, still standing. *Ed.*]

our country by land, and the Hellespont was occupied by the French galleys? Amurath was compelled to force the passage of the Bosphorus; and your strength was not equal to your malevolence. I was then a child at Adrianople; the Moslems trembled, and for a while the *Gabours* insulted our disgrace. But when my father had triumphed in the field of Varna, he vowed to erect a fort on the western shore, and that vow it is my duty to accomplish. Have ye the right, have ye the power, to control my actions on my own ground? For that ground *is* my own: as far as the shores of the Bosphorus Asia is inhabited by the Turks, and Europe is deserted by the Romans. Return, and inform your king that the present Ottoman is far different from his predecessors, that *his* resolutions surpass *their* wishes, and that *he* performs more than *they* could resolve. Return in safety; but the next who delivers a similar message may expect to be flayed alive." After this declaration, Constantine, the first of the Greeks in spirit as in rank, had determined to unsheathe the sword, and to resist the approach and establishment of the Turks on the Bosphorus. He was disarmed by the advice of his civil and ecclesiastical ministers, who recommended a system less generous, and even less prudent, than his own, to approve their patience and long-suffering, to brand the Ottoman with the name and guilt of an aggressor, and to depend on chance and time for their own safety, and the destruction of a fort which could not long be maintained in the neighbourhood of a great and populous city. Amidst hope and fear, the fears of the wise and the hopes of the credulous, the winter rolled away; the proper business of each man and each hour was postponed; and the Greeks shut their eyes against the impending danger, till the arrival of the spring and the sultan decided the assurance of their ruin.

Of a master who never forgives, the orders are seldom disobeyed. On the twenty-sixth of March the appointed spot of Asomaton was covered with an active swarm of Turkish artificers; and the materials by sea and land were diligently transported from Europe and Asia. The lime had been burnt in Cataphrygia, the timber was cut down in the woods of Heraclea and Nicomedia, and the stones were dug from the Anatolian quarries. Each of the thousand masons was assisted by two workmen; and a measure of two cubits was marked for their daily task. The fortress was built in a triangular form; each angle was flanked by a strong and massy tower, one on the declivity of the hill, two along the sea-shore; a thickness of twenty-two feet was assigned for the walls, thirty for the towers; and the whole building was covered with a solid platform of lead. Mohammed himself pressed and directed the work with indefatigable ardour: his three vizirs claimed the honour of finishing their respective towers; the zeal of the cadhis emulated that of the Janizaries; the meanest labour was ennobled by the service of God and the sultan; and the diligence of the multitude was quickened by the eye of a despot whose smile was the hope of fortune, and whose frown was the messenger of death. The Greek emperor beheld with terror the irresistible progress of the work, and vainly strove by flattery and gifts to assuage an implacable foe, who sought, and secretly fomented, the slightest occasion of a quarrel. Such occasions must soon and inevitably be found. The ruins of stately churches, and even the marble columns which had been consecrated to Saint Michael the archangel, were employed without scruple by the profane and rapacious Moslems; and some Christians, who presumed to oppose the removal, received from their hands the crown of martyrdom. Constantine had solicited a Turkish guard to protect the fields and harvests of his subjects: the guard was fixed; but their first order was to allow free pasture to the mules and horses of the camp, and to defend their brethren if they should be molested by the natives. The retinue of an Ottoman chief had left their horses to pass the night among the ripe corn; the damage was felt, the insult was resented, and several of both nations were slain in a tumultuous conflict. Mohammed listened with joy to the complaint; and a detachment was commanded to exterminate the guilty village: the guilty had fled; but forty innocent and unsuspecting reapers were massacred by the soldiers. Till this provocation Constantinople had been open to the visits of commerce and curiosity: on the first alarm the gates were shut; but the emperor, still anxious for peace, released on the third day his Turkish captives, and expressed, in a last message, the firm resignation of a Christian and a soldier. "Since neither oaths, nor treaty, nor submission can secure peace; pursue," said he to Mohammed, "your impious warfare. My trust is in God alone: if it should please him to mollify your heart, I shall rejoice in the happy change; if he delivers the city into your hands, I submit without a murmur to his holy will. But until the Judge of the earth shall pronounce between us, it is my duty to live and die in the defence of my people." The sultan's answer was hostile and decisive: his fortifications were completed; and before his departure for Adrianople he stationed a vigilant Aga and four hundred Janizaries to levy a tribute on the ships of every nation that should pass within the reach of their cannon. A Venetian vessel, refusing obedience to the new lords of the Bosphorus, was sunk with a single bullet. The master and thirty sailors escaped in the boat; but they were dragged in chains to the *Porte:* the chief was impaled, his companions were beheaded; and the historian Ducas beheld, at Demotica, their bodies exposed to the wild beasts. The siege of Constantinople was deferred till the ensuing spring; but an Ottoman army marched into the Morea to divert the force of the brothers of Constantine. At this era of calamity one of these princes, the despot Thomas, was blessed or afflicted with the birth of a son—"the last heir," says the plaintive Phranza, "of the last spark of the Roman empire."

The Greeks and the Turks passed an anxious and sleepless winter: the former were kept awake by their fears, the latter by their hopes; both by the preparations of defence and attack; and the two emperors, who had the most to lose or to gain, were the most deeply affected by the national sentiment. In Mohammed that sentiment was inflamed by the ardour of his youth and temper: he amused his leisure with building at Adrianople the lofty palace of Jehan Numa (the watch-tower of the world); but his serious thoughts were irrevocably bent on the conquest of the city of Cæsar.

[*Mohammed made a particular study of "the recent and tremendous discovery of the Latins," gunpowder, and found a renegade Christian gunfounder, Urban, who made for him "a piece of brass ordnance of stupendous and almost incredible magnitude," which was carried 150 miles on "a frame or carriage of thirty waggons linked together and drawn along by a team of sixty oxen."*]

While Mohammed threatened the capital of the East, the Greek emperor implored with fervent prayers the assistance of earth and Heaven. But the invisible powers were deaf to his supplications; and Christendom beheld with indifference the fall of Constantinople, while she derived at least some promise of supply from the jealous and temporal policy of the sultan of Egypt. Some states were too weak, and others too remote; by some the danger was considered as imaginary, by others as inevitable: the Western princes were involved in their endless and domestic quarrels; and the Roman pontiff was exasperated by the falsehood or obstinacy of the Greeks. Instead of employing in their favour the arms and treasures of Italy, Nicholas the Fifth had foretold their approaching ruin; and his honour was engaged in the accomplishment of his prophecy. Perhaps he was softened by the last extremity of their distress; but his compassion was tardy; his efforts were faint and unavailing; and Constantinople had fallen before the squadrons of Genoa and Venice could sail from their harbours. Even the princes of the Morea and of the Greek islands affected a cold neutrality: the Genoese colony of Galata negotiated a private treaty; and the sultan indulged them in the delusive hope that by his clemency they might survive the ruin of the empire. A plebeian crowd and some Byzantine nobles basely withdrew from the danger of their country; and the avarice of the rich denied the emperor, and reserved for the Turks, the secret treasures which might have raised in their defence whole armies of mercenaries. The indigent and solitary prince prepared however to sustain his formidable adversary; but if his courage were equal to the peril, his strength was inadequate to the contest. In the beginning of the spring the Turkish vanguard swept the towns and villages as far as the gates of Constantinople: submission was spared and protected; whatever presumed to resist was exterminated with fire and sword. The Greek places on the Black Sea, Mesembria, Acheloum, and Bizon, surrendered on the first summons; Selymbria alone deserved the honours of a siege or blockade; and the bold inhabitants, while they were invested by land, launched their boats, pillaged the opposite coast of Cyzicus, and sold their captives in the public market. But on the approach of Mohammed himself all was silent and prostrate: he first halted at the distance of five miles; and, from thence advancing in battle array, planted before the gate of St. Romanus the Imperial standard; and on the sixth day of April formed the memorable siege of Constantinople.

The troops of Asia and Europe extended on the right and left from the Propontis to the harbour; the Janizaries in the front were stationed before the sultan's tent; the Ottoman line was covered by a deep intrenchment; and a subordinate army enclosed the suburb of Galata, and watched the doubtful faith of the Genoese. . . . The whole mass of the Turkish powers is magnified by Ducas, Chalcocondyles, and Leonard of Chios, to the amount of three or four hundred thousand men; but Phranza was a less remote and more accurate judge; and his precise definition of two hundred and fifty-eight thousand does not exceed the measure of experience and probability. The navy of the besiegers was less formidable: the Propontis was overspread with three hundred and twenty sail; but of these no more than eighteen could be rated as galleys of war; and the far greater part must be degraded to the condition of store-ships and transports, which poured into the camp fresh supplies of men, ammunition, and provisions. In her last decay Constantinople was still peopled with more than a hundred thousand inhabitants; but these numbers are found in the accounts, not of war, but of captivity; and they mostly consisted of mechanics, of priests, of women, and of men devoid of that spirit which even women have sometimes exerted for the common safety. I can suppose, I could almost excuse, the reluctance of subjects to serve

397

on a distant frontier, at the will of a tyrant; but the man who dares not expose his life in the defence of his children and his property has lost in society the first and most active energies of nature. By the emperor's command a particular inquiry had been made through the streets and houses, how many of the citizens, or even of the monks, were able and willing to bear arms for their country. The lists were intrusted to Phranza, and after a diligent addition he informed his master, with grief and surprise, that the national defence was reduced to four thousand nine hundred and seventy *Romans*. Between Constantine and his faithful minister this comfortless secret was preserved; and a sufficient proportion of shields, cross-bows, and muskets, was distributed from the arsenal to the city bands. They derived some accession from a body of two thousand strangers, under the command of John Justiniani, a noble Genoese; a liberal donative was advanced to these auxiliaries; and a princely recompense, the isle of Lemnos, was promised to the valour and victory of their chief. A strong chain was drawn across the mouth of the harbour: it was supported by some Greek and Italian vessels of war and merchandise; and the ships of every Christian nation, that successively arrived from Candia and the Black Sea, were detained for the public service. Against the powers of the Ottoman empire, a city of the extent of thirteen, perhaps of sixteen, miles was defended by a scanty garrison of seven or eight thousand soldiers. Europe and Asia were open to the besiegers; but the strength and provisions of the Greeks must sustain a daily decrease; nor could they indulge the expectation of any foreign succour or supply.

The primitive Romans would have drawn their swords in the resolution of death or conquest. The primitive Christians might have embraced each other, and awaited in patience and charity the stroke of martyrdom. But the Greeks of Constantinople were animated only by the spirit of religion, and that spirit was productive only of animosity and discord. Before his death the emperor John Palæologus had renounced the unpopular measure of a union with the Latins; nor was the idea revived till the distress of his brother Constantine imposed a last trial of flattery and dissimulation. With the demand of temporal aid his ambassadors were instructed to mingle the assurance of spiritual obedience: his neglect of the church was excused by the urgent cares of the state; and his orthodox wishes solicited the presence of a Roman legate. The Vatican had been too often deluded; yet the signs of repentance could not decently be overlooked; a legate was more easily granted than an army; and about six months before the final destruction, the cardinal Isidore of Russia appeared in that character with a retinue of priests and soldiers. The emperor saluted him as a friend and father; respectfully listened to his public and private sermons; and with the most obsequious of the clergy and laymen subscribed the act of union, as it had been ratified in the council of Florence. On the twelfth of December the two nations, in the church of St. Sophia, joined in the communion of sacrifice and prayer; and the names of the two pontiffs were solemnly commemorated; the names of Nicholas the Fifth, the vicar of Christ, and of the patriarch Gregory, who had been driven into exile by a rebellious people.

But the dress and language of the Latin priest who officiated at the altar were an object of scandal; and it was observed with horror that he consecrated a cake or wafer of *unleavened* bread, and poured cold water into the cup of the sacrament. A national historian acknowledges with a blush that none of his countrymen, not the emperor himself, were sincere in this occasional conformity. Their hasty and unconditional submission was palliated by a promise of future revisal; but the best, or the worst, of their excuses was the confession of their own perjury. When they were pressed by the reproaches of their honest brethren, "Have patience," they whispered, "have patience till God shall have delivered the city from the great dragon who seeks to devour us. You shall then perceive whether we are truly reconciled with the Azymites."[2] But patience is not the attribute of zeal; nor can the arts of a court be adapted to the freedom and violence of popular enthusiasm. From the dome of St.

---

[2] [Users of unleavened bread: a Greek term for the 'schismatic' Catholics. *Ed.*]

Sophia the inhabitants of either sex, and of every degree, rushed in crowds to the cell of the monk Gennadius, to consult the oracle of the church. The holy man was invisible; entranced as it should seem, in deep meditation, or divine rapture: but he had exposed on the door of his cell a speaking tablet; and they successively withdrew, after reading these tremendous words: "O miserable Romans, why will ye abandon the truth; and why, instead of confiding in God, will ye put your trust in the Italians? In losing your faith you will lose your city. Have mercy on me, O Lord! I protest in thy presence that I am innocent of the crime. O miserable Romans, consider, pause, and repent. At the same moment that you renounce the religion of your fathers, by embracing impiety, you submit to a foreign servitude." According to the advice of Gennadius, the religious virgins, as pure as angels, and as proud as demons, rejected the act of union, and abjured all communion with the present and future associates of the Latins; and their example was applauded and imitated by the greatest part of the clergy and people. From the monastery the devout Greeks dispersed themselves in the taverns; drank confusion to the slaves of the pope; emptied their glasses in honour of the image of the holy Virgin; and besought her to defend against Mohammed the city which she had formerly saved from Chosroes and the Chagan. In the double intoxication of zeal and wine, they valiantly exclaimed, "What occasion have we for succour, or union, or Latins? far from us be the worship of the Azymites!" During the winter that preceded the Turkish conquest the nation was distracted by this epidemical frenzy; and the season of Lent, the approach of Easter, instead of breathing charity and love, served only to fortify the obstinacy and influence of the zealots. The confessors scrutinised and alarmed the conscience of their votaries, and a rigorous penance was imposed on those who had received the communion from a priest who had given an express or tacit consent to the union. His service at the altar propagated the infection to the mute and simple spectators of the ceremony: they forfeited, by the impure spectacle, the virtue of the sacerdotal character; nor was it lawful, even in danger of sudden death, to invoke the assistance of their prayers or absolution. No sooner had the church of St. Sophia been polluted by the Latin sacrifice than it was deserted as a Jewish synagogue, or a heathen temple, by the clergy and people; and a vast and gloomy silence prevailed in that venerable dome, which had so often smoked with a cloud of incense, blazed with innumerable lights, and resounded with the voice of prayer and thanksgiving. The Latins were the most odious of heretics and infidels; and the first minister of the empire, the great duke, was heard to declare that he had rather behold in Constantinople the turban of Mohammed than the pope's tiara or a cardinal's hat. A sentiment so unworthy of Christians and patriots was familiar and fatal to the Greeks: the emperor was deprived of the affection and support of his subjects; and their native cowardice was sanctified by resignation to the divine decree or the visionary hope of a miraculous deliverance.

Of the triangle which composes the figure of Constantinople the two sides along the sea were made inaccessible to an enemy; the Propontis by nature, and the harbour by art. Between the two waters, the basis of the triangle, the land side was protected by a double wall and a deep ditch of the depth of one hundred feet. Against this line of fortification, which Phranza, an eye-witness, prolongs to the measure of six miles, the Ottomans directed their principal attack; and the emperor, after distributing the service and command of the most perilous stations, undertook the defence of the external wall. In the first days of the siege the Greek soldiers descended into the ditch, or sallied into the field; but they soon discovered that, in the proportion of their numbers, one Christian was of more value than twenty Turks; and, after these bold preludes, they were prudently content to maintain the rampart with their missile weapons. Nor should this prudence be accused of pusillanimity. The nation was indeed pusillanimous and base; but the last Constantine deserves the name of a hero: his noble band of volunteers was inspired with Roman virtue; and the foreign auxiliaries supported the honour of the Western chivalry. The incessant volleys of lances and arrows were accompanied with the smoke, the sound, and the fire of their musketry and cannon. Their small arms discharged at the same time either five, or even ten, balls of lead, of the size of a walnut; and, according to the closeness of the ranks and the force of the powder, several breast-plates and bodies were transpierced by the same shot. But the Turkish approaches were soon sunk in trenches or covered with ruins. Each day added to the science of the Christians; but their inadequate stock of gunpowder was wasted in the operations of each day. Their ordnance was not powerful either in size or number; and if they possessed some heavy cannon, they feared to plant them on the walls, lest the aged structure should be shaken and overthrown by the explosion. The same destructive secret had been revealed to the Moslems; by whom it was employed with the superior energy of zeal, riches, and despotism. The great cannon of Mohammed has been separately noticed: an important and visible object in the history of the times; but that enormous engine was flanked by two fellows almost of equal magnitude: the long order of the Turkish artillery was pointed against the walls; fourteen batteries thundered at once on the most accessible places; and of one of these it is ambiguously expressed that it was mounted with one hundred and thirty guns, or that it discharged one hundred and thirty bullets. Yet in the power and activity of the sultan we may discern the infancy of the new science. Under a master who counted the moments the great cannon could be loaded and fired no more than seven times in one day. The heated metal unfortunately burst; several workmen were destroyed, and the skill of an artist was admired who bethought himself of preventing the danger and the accident, by pouring oil, after each explosion, into the mouth of the cannon.

The first random shots were productive of more sound than effect; and it was by the advice of a Christian that the engineers were taught to level their aim against the two opposite sides of the salient angles of a bastion. However imperfect, the weight and repetition of the fire made some impression on the walls; and the Turks, pushing their approaches to the edge of the ditch, attempted to fill the enormous chasm and to build a road to the assault. Innumerable fascines, and hogsheads, and trunks of trees, were heaped on each other; and such was the impetuosity of the throng, that the foremost and the weakest were pushed headlong down the precipice and instantly buried under the accumulated mass. To fill the ditch was the toil of the besiegers; to clear away the rubbish was the safety of the besieged; and, after a long and bloody conflict, the web that had been woven in the day was still unravelled in the night. The next resource of Mohammed was the practice of mines; but the soil was rocky; in every attempt he was stopped and undermined by the Christian engineers; nor had the art been yet invented of replenishing those subterraneous passages with gunpowder and blowing whole towers and cities into the air. A circumstance that distinguishes the siege of Constantinople is the reunion of the ancient and modern artillery. The cannon were intermingled with the mechanical engines for casting stones and darts; the bullet and the battering-ram were directed against the same walls; nor had the discovery of gunpowder superseded the use of the liquid and unextinguishable fire. A wooden turret of the largest size was advanced on rollers: this portable magazine of ammunition and fascines was protected by a threefold covering of bulls' hides; incessant volleys were securely discharged from the loopholes; in the front three doors were contrived for the alternate sally and retreat of the soldiers and workmen. They ascended by a staircase to the upper platform, and, as high as the level of that platform, a scaling-ladder could be raised by pulleys to form a bridge and grapple with the adverse rampart. By these various arts of annoyance, some as new as they were pernicious to the Greeks, the tower of St. Romanus was at length overturned: after a severe struggle the Turks were repulsed from the breach and interrupted by darkness; but they trusted that with the return of light they should renew the attack with fresh vigour and decisive success. Of this pause of action, this interval of hope, each moment was improved by the activity of the emperor and Justiniani, who passed the night on the spot, and urged the labours which involved the safety of the church and city. At the dawn of day the impatient sultan perceived, with astonishment and grief, that his wooden turret had been reduced to ashes: the ditch was cleared and restored, and the tower of St. Romanus was again strong and entire. He deplored the failure of his design, and uttered a profane exclamation, that the word of the thirty-seven thousand prophets should not have compelled him to believe that such a work, in so short a time, could have been accomplished by the infidels.

The generosity of the Christian princes was cold and tardy; but in the first apprehension of a siege Constantine had negotiated, in the isles of the Archipelago, the Morea, and Sicily, the most indispensable supplies. As early as the beginning of April, five great ships, equipped for merchandise and war, would have sailed from the harbour of Chios, had not the wind blown obstinately from the north. One of these ships bore the Imperial flag; the remaining four belonged to the Genoese; and they were laden with wheat and barley, with wine, oil, and vegetables, and, above all, with soldiers and mariners, for the service of the capital. After a tedious delay a gentle breeze, and on the second day a strong gale from the south, carried them through the Hellespont and the Propontis; but the city was already invested by sea and land, and the Turkish fleet, at the entrance of the Bosphorus, was stretched from shore to shore, in the form of a crescent, to intercept, or at least to repel, these bold auxiliaries. The reader who has present to his mind the geographical picture of Constantinople will conceive and admire the greatness of the spectacle. The five Christian ships continued to advance with joyful shouts, and a full press both of sails and oars, against the hostile fleet of three hundred vessels; and the rampart, the camp, the coasts of Europe and Asia, were lined with innumerable spectators, who anxiously awaited the event of this momentous succour. At the first view that event could not appear doubtful; the superiority of the Moslems was beyond all measure or account, and, in a calm, their numbers and valour must inevitably have prevailed. But their hasty and imperfect navy had been created, not by the genius of the people, but by the will of the sultan: in the height of their prosperity the Turks have acknowledged that, if God had given them the earth, he had left the sea to the infidels; and a series of defeats, a rapid progress of decay, has established the truth of their modest confession. Except eighteen galleys of some force, the rest of their fleet consisted of open boats, rudely constructed and awkwardly managed, crowded with troops, and destitute of cannon; and since courage arises in a great measure from the consciousness of strength, the bravest of the Janizaries might tremble on a new element. In the Christian squadron five stout and lofty ships were guided by skilful pilots, and manned with the veterans of Italy and Greece, long practised in the arts and perils of the sea. Their weight was directed to sink or scatter the weak obstacles that impeded their passage: their artillery swept the waters; their liquid fire was poured on the heads of the adversaries, who, with the design of boarding, presumed to approach them; and the winds and waves are always on the side of the ablest navigators. In this conflict the Imperial vessel, which had been almost overpowered, was rescued by the Genoese; but the Turks, in a distant and a closer attack, were twice repulsed with considerable loss. Mohammed himself sat on horseback on the beach, to encourage their valour by his voice and presence, by the promise of reward, and by fear more potent than the fear of the enemy. The passions of his soul, and even the gestures of his body, seemed to imitate the actions of the combatants; and, as if he had been the lord of nature, he spurred his horse with a fearless and impotent effort into the sea. His loud reproaches, and the clamours of the camp, urged the Ottomans to a third attack, more fatal and bloody than the two former; and I must repeat, though I cannot credit, the evidence of Phranza, who affirms, from their own mouth, that they lost above twelve thousand men in the slaughter of the day. They fled in disorder to the shores of Europe and Asia, while the Christian squadron, triumphant and unhurt, steered along the Bosphorus, and securely anchored within the chain of the harbour. The introduction of this supply revived the hopes of the Greeks, and accused the supineness of their Western allies. Amidst the deserts of Anatolia and the rocks of Palestine, the millions of the crusades had buried themselves in a voluntary and inevitable grave; but the situation of the Imperial city was strong against her enemies, and accessible to her friends; and a rational and moderate armament of the maritime states might have saved the relics of the Roman name, and maintained a Christian fortress in the heart of the Ottoman empire. Yet this was the sole and feeble attempt for the deliverance of Constantinople: the more distant powers were insensible of its danger; and the ambassador of Hungary, or at least of Huniades,[3] resided in the Turkish camp, to remove the fears and to direct the operations of the sultan.

It was difficult for the Greeks to penetrate the secret of the divan; yet the Greeks are persuaded that a resistance so obstinate and surprising had fatigued the perseverance of Mohammed. He began to meditate a retreat; and the siege would have been speedily raised, if the ambition and jealousy of the second vizir had not opposed the perfidious advice of Calil Bashaw, who still maintained a secret correspondence with the Byzantine court. The reduction of the city appeared to be hopeless, unless a double attack could be made from the harbour as well as from the land; but the harbour was inaccessible: an impenetrable chain was now defended by eight large ships, more than twenty of a smaller size, with several galleys and sloops; and, instead of forcing this barrier, the Turks might apprehend a naval sally and a second encounter in the open sea. In this perplexity the genius of Mohammed conceived and executed a plan of a bold and marvellous cast, of transporting by land his lighter vessels and military stores from the Bosphorus into the higher part of the harbour. The distance is about ten miles; the ground is uneven, and was overspread with thickets; and, as the road must be opened behind the suburb of Galata, their free passage or total destruction must depend on the option of the Genoese. But these

---

[3] [John Hunyadi, King of Hungary. *Ed.*]

selfish merchants were ambitious of the favour of being the last devoured, and the deficiency of art was supplied by the strength of obedient myriads. A level way was covered with a broad platform of strong and solid planks; and to render them more slippery and smooth, they were anointed with the fat of sheep and oxen. Fourscore light galleys and brigantines of fifty and thirty oars were disembarked on the Bosphorus shore, arranged successively on rollers, and drawn forwards by the power of men and pulleys. Two guides or pilots were stationed at the helm and the prow of each vessel: the sails were unfurled to the winds, and the labour was cheered by song and acclamation. In the course of a single night this Turkish fleet painfully climbed the hill, steered over the plain, and was launched from the declivity into the shallow waters of the harbour, far above the molestation of the deeper vessels of the Greeks. The real importance of this operation was magnified by the consternation and confidence which it inspired; but the notorious, unquestionable fact was displayed before the eyes, and is recorded by the pens, of the two nations. A similar stratagem had been repeatedly practised by the ancients; the Ottoman galleys (I must again repeat) should be considered as large boats; and, if we compare the magnitude and the distance, the obstacles and the means, the boasted miracle has perhaps been equalled by the industry of our times.[4] As soon as Mohammed had occupied the upper harbour with a fleet and army, he constructed in the narrowest part a bridge, or rather mole, of fifty cubits in breadth and one hundred in length: it was formed of casks and hogsheads, joined with rafters, linked with iron, and covered with a solid floor. On this floating battery he planted one of his largest cannon, while the fourscore galleys, with troops and scaling-ladders, approached the most accessible side, which had formerly been stormed by the Latin conquerors. The indolence of the Christians has been accused for not destroying these unfinished works; but their fire, by a superior fire, was

---

[4] I particularly allude to our own embarkations on the lakes of Canada in the years 1776 and 1777, so great in the labour, so fruitless in the event.

controlled and silenced; nor were they wanting in a
nocturnal attempt to burn the vessels as well as the
bridge of the sultan. His vigilance prevented their approach: their foremost galliots were sunk or taken; forty
youths, the bravest of Italy and Greece, were inhumanly
massacred at his command; nor could the emperor's
grief be assuaged by the just though cruel retaliation of
exposing from the walls the heads of two hundred and
sixty Musulman captives. After a siege of forty days the
fate of Constantinople could no longer be averted.
The diminutive garrison was exhausted by a double attack: the fortifications, which had stood for ages against
hostile violence, were dismantled on all sides by the
Ottoman cannon; many breaches were opened, and near
the gate of St. Romanus four towers had been levelled
with the ground. For the payment of his feeble and
mutinous troops, Constantine was compelled to despoil
the churches with the promise of a fourfold restitution;
and his sacrilege offered a new reproach to the enemies
of the union. A spirit of discord impaired the remnant
of the Christian strength: the Genoese and Venetian
auxiliaries asserted the pre-eminence of their respective
service; and Justiniani and the great duke, whose ambition was not extinguished by the common danger, accused each other of treachery and cowardice.

During the siege of Constantinople the words of peace
and capitulation had been sometimes pronounced; and
several embassies had passed between the camp and the
city. The Greek emperor was humbled by adversity; and
would have yielded to any terms compatible with religion
and royalty. The Turkish sultan was desirious of sparing
the blood of his soldiers; still more desirous of securing
for his own use the Byzantine treasures; and he accomplished a sacred duty in presenting to the *Gabours* the
choice of circumcision, of tribute, or of death. The avarice of Mohammed might have been satisfied with an
annual sum of one hundred thousand ducats; but his
ambition grasped the capital of the East: to the prince
he offered a rich equivalent, to the people a free toleration, or a safe departure: but after some fruitless treaty,
he declared his resolution of finding either a throne or

a grave under the walls of Constantinople. A sense of honour, and the fear of universal reproach, forbade Palæologus to resign the city into the hands of the Ottomans; and he determined to abide the last extremities of war. Several days were employed by the sultan in the preparations of the assault; and a respite was granted by his favourite science of astrology, which had fixed on the twenty-ninth of May as the fortunate and fatal hour. On the evening of the twenty-seventh he issued his final orders; assembled in his presence the military chiefs; and dispersed his heralds through the camp to proclaim the duty and the motives of the perilous enterprise. Fear is the first principle of a despotic government; and his menaces were expressed in the Oriental style, that the fugitives and deserters, had they the wings of a bird, should not escape from his inexorable justice. The greatest part of his bashaws and Janizaries were the offspring of Christian parents: but the glories of the Turkish name were perpetuated by successive adoption; and in the gradual change of individuals, the spirit of a legion, a regiment, or an *oda*, is kept alive by imitation and discipline. In this holy warfare the Moslems were exhorted to purify their minds with prayer, their bodies with seven ablutions; and to abstain from food till the close of the ensuing day. A crowd of dervishes visited the tents, to instil the desire of martyrdom, and the assurance of spending an immortal youth amidst the rivers and gardens of paradise, and in the embraces of the black-eyed virgins. Yet Mohammed principally trusted to the efficacy of temporal and visible rewards. A double pay was promised to the victorious troops: "The city and the buildings," said Mohammed, "are mine; but I resign to your valour the captives and the spoil, the treasures of gold and beauty; be rich and be happy. Many are the provinces of my empire: the intrepid soldier who first ascends the walls of Constantinople shall be rewarded with the government of the fairest and most wealthy; and my gratitude shall accumulate his honours and fortunes above the measure of his own hopes." Such various and potent motives diffused among the Turks a general ardour, regardless of life and impatient for action:

409

the camp re-echoed with the Moslem shouts of "God is God: there is but one God, and Mohammed is the apostle of God;" and the sea and land, from Galata to the seven towers, were illuminated by the blaze of their nocturnal fires.

Far different was the state of the Christians; who, with loud and impotent complaints, deplored the guilt, or the punishment, of their sins. The celestial image of the Virgin had been exposed in solemn procession; but their divine patroness was deaf to their entreaties: they accused the obstinacy of the emperor for refusing a timely surrender; anticipated the horrors of their fate; and sighed for the repose and security of Turkish servitude. The noblest of the Greeks, and the bravest of the allies, were summoned to the palace, to prepare them, on the evening of the twenty-eighth, for the duties and dangers of the general assault. The last speech of Palæologus was the funeral oration of the Roman empire: he promised, he conjured, and he vainly attempted to infuse the hope which was extinguished in his own mind. In this world all was comfortless and gloomy; and neither the Gospel nor the church have proposed any conspicuous recompense to the heroes who fall in the service of their country. But the example of their prince, and the confinement of a siege, had armed these warriors with the courage of despair; and the pathetic scene is described by the feelings of the historian Phranza, who was himself present at this mournful assembly. They wept, they embraced: regardless of their families and fortunes, they devoted their lives; and each commander, departing to his station, maintained all night a vigilant and anxious watch on the rampart. The emperor, and some faithful companions, entered the dome of St. Sophia, which in a few hours was to be converted into a mosque; and devoutly received, with tears and prayers, the sacrament of the holy communion. He reposed some moments in the palace, which resounded with cries and lamentations; solicited the pardon of all whom he might have injured; and mounted on horseback to visit the guards, and explore the motions of the enemy. The distress and fall of the last Constantine are more glorious than the long prosperity of the Byzantine Cæsars.

In the confusion of darkness an assailant may sometimes succeed; but in this great and general attack, the military judgment and astrological knowledge of Mohammed advised him to expect the morning, the memorable twenty-ninth of May, in the fourteen hundred and fifty-third year of the Christian era. The preceding night had been strenuously employed: the troops, the cannon, and the fascines were advanced to the edge of the ditch, which in many parts presented a smooth and level passage to the breach; and his fourscore galleys almost touched, with the prows and their scaling ladders, the less defensible walls of the harbour. Under pain of death, silence was enjoined; but the physical laws of motion and sound are not obedient to discipline or fear: each individual might suppress his voice and measure his footsteps; but the march and labour of thousands must inevitably produce a strange confusion of dissonant clamours, which reached the ears of the watchmen of the towers. At daybreak, without the customary signal of the morning gun, the Turks assaulted the city by sea and land; and the similitude of a twined or twisted thread has been applied to the closeness and continuity of their line of attack. The foremost ranks consisted of the refuse of the host, a voluntary crowd who fought without order or command; of the feebleness of age or childhood, of peasants and vagrants, and of all who had joined the camp in the blind hope of plunder and martyrdom. The common impulse drove them onwards to the wall; the most audacious to climb were instantly precipitated; and not a dart, not a bullet, of the Christians, was idly wasted on the accumulated throng. But their strength and ammunition were exhausted in this laborious defence: the ditch was filled with the bodies of the slain; they supported the footsteps of their companions; and of this devoted vanguard the death was more serviceable than the life. Under their respective bashaws and sanjaks, the troops of Anatolia and Romania were successively led to the charge: their progress was various and doubtful; but, after a conflict of two hours, the Greeks

411

still maintained and improved their advantage; and the voice of the emperor was heard, encouraging his soldiers to achieve, by a last effort, the deliverance of their country. In that fatal moment the Janizaries arose, fresh, vigorous, and invincible. The sultan himself on horseback, with an iron mace in his hand, was the spectator and judge of their valour; he was surrounded by ten thousand of his domestic troops, whom he reserved for the decisive occasion; and the tide of battle was directed and impelled by his voice and eye. His numerous ministers of justice were posted behind the line, to urge, to restrain, and to punish; and if danger was in the front, shame and inevitable death were in the rear, of the fugitives. The cries of fear and of pain were drowned in the martial music of drums, trumpets, and attaballs; and experience has proved that the mechanical operation of sounds, by quickening the circulation of the blood and spirits, will act on the human machine more forcibly than the eloquence of reason and honour. From the lines, the galleys, and the bridge, the Ottoman artillery thundered on all sides; and the camp and city, the Greeks and the Turks, were involved in a cloud of smoke, which could only be dispelled by the final deliverance or destruction of the Roman empire. The single combats of the heroes of history or fable amuse our fancy and engage our affections: the skilful evolutions of war may inform the mind, and improve a necessary, though pernicious, science. But in the uniform and odious pictures of a general assault, all is blood, and horror, and confusion; nor shall I strive, at the distance of three centuries and a thousand miles, to delineate a scene of which there could be no spectators, and of which the actors themselves were incapable of forming any just or adequate idea.

The immediate loss of Constantinople may be ascribed to the bullet, or arrow, which pierced the gauntlet of John Justiniani. The sight of his blood, and the exquisite pain, appalled the courage of the chief, whose arms and counsels were the firmest rampart of the city. As he withdrew from his station in quest of a surgeon, his flight was perceived and stopped by the indefatigable emperor. "Your wound," exclaimed Palæologus, "is slight; the danger is pressing: your presence is necessary; and whither will you retire?"—"I will retire," said the trembling Genoese, "by the same road which God has opened to the Turks," and at these words he hastily passed through one of the breaches of the inner wall. By this pusillanimous act he stained the honours of a military life; and the few days which he survived in Galata, or the isle of Chios, were embittered by his own and the public reproach. His example was imitated by the greatest part of the Latin auxiliaries, and the defence began to slacken when the attack was pressed with redoubled vigour. The number of the Ottomans was fifty, perhaps a hundred, times superior to that of the Christians; the double walls were reduced by the cannon to a heap of ruins: in a circuit of several miles some places must be found more easy of access, or more feebly guarded; and if the besiegers could penetrate in a single point, the whole city was irrecoverably lost. The first who deserved the sultan's reward was Hassan the Janizary, of gigantic stature and strength. With his scimitar in one hand and his buckler in the other, he ascended the outward fortification: of the thirty Janizaries who were emulous of his valour, eighteen perished in the bold adventure. Hassan and his twelve companions had reached the summit: the giant was precipitated from the rampart: he rose on one knee, and was again oppressed by a shower of darts and stones. But his success had proved that the achievement was possible: the walls and towers were instantly covered with a swarm of Turks; and the Greeks, now driven from the vantage ground, were overwhelmed by increasing multitudes. Amidst these multitudes, the emperor, who accomplished all the duties of a general and a soldier, was long seen and finally lost. The nobles, who fought round his person, sustained, till their last breath, the honourable names of Palæologus and Cantacuzene: his mournful exclamation was heard, "Cannot there be found a Christian to cut off my head?" and his last fear was that of falling alive into the hands of the infidels. The prudent despair of Constantine cast away the purple: amidst the tumult he fell by an unknown hand, and his body was buried under a mountain of the slain. After his death resistance and order were no more: the Greeks fled towards the city; and many were pressed and stifled in the narrow pass of the gate of St. Romanus. The victorious Turks rushed through the breaches of the inner wall; and as they advanced into the streets, they were soon joined by their brethren, who had forced the gate Phenar on the side of the harbour. In the first heat of the pursuit about two thousand Christians were put to the sword; but avarice soon prevailed over cruelty; and the victors acknowledged that they should immediately have given quarter, if the valour of the emperor and his chosen bands had not prepared them for a similar opposition in every part of the capital. It was thus, after a siege of fifty-three days, that Constantinople, which had defied the power of Chosroes, the Chagan, and the caliphs, was irretrievably subdued by the arms of Mohammed the Second. Her empire only had been subverted by the Latins: her religion was trampled in the dust by the Moslem conquerors.

The tidings of misfortune fly with a rapid wing; yet such was the extent of Constantinople, that the more distant quarters might prolong, some moments, the happy ignorance of their ruin. But in the general consternation, in the feelings of selfish or social anxiety, in the tumult and thunder of the assault, a *sleepless* night and morning must have elapsed; nor can I believe that many Grecian ladies were awakened by the Janizaries from a sound and tranquil slumber. On the assurance of the public calamity, the houses and convents were instantly deserted; and the trembling inhabitants flocked together in the streets, like a herd of timid animals, as if accumulated weakness could be productive of strength, or in the vain hope that amid the crowd each individual might be safe and invisible. From every part of the capital they flowed into the church of St. Sophia: in the space of an hour, the sanctuary, the choir, the nave, the upper and lower galleries, were filled with the multitudes of fathers and husbands, of women and children, of priests, monks, and religious virgins: the doors were barred on the inside, and they sought protection from the sacred dome which they had so lately abhorred as a profane and polluted edifice. Their confidence was founded on the prophecy of an enthusiast or impostor, that one day the Turks would enter Constantinople, and pursue the Romans as far as the column of Constantine in the square before St. Sophia: but that this would be the term of their calamities; that an angel would descend from heaven with a sword in his hand, and would deliver the empire, with that celestial weapon, to a poor man seated at the foot of the column. "Take this sword," would he say, "and avenge the people of the Lord." At these animating words the Turks would instantly fly, and the victorious Romans would drive them from the West, and from all Anatolia, as far as the frontiers of Persia. It is on this occasion that Ducas, with some fancy and much truth, upbraids the discord and obstinacy of the Greeks. "Had that angel appeared," exclaims the historian, "had he offered to exterminate your foes if you would consent to the union of the church, even then, in that fatal moment, you would have rejected your safety, or have deceived your God."

While they expected the descent of the tardy angel, the doors were broken with axes; and as the Turks encountered no resistance, their bloodless hands were employed in selecting and securing the multitude of their prisoners. Youth, beauty, and the appearance of wealth, attracted their choice; and the right of property was decided among themselves by a prior seizure, by personal strength, and by the authority of command. In the space of an hour the male captives were bound with cords, the females with their veils and girdles. The senators were linked with their slaves; the prelates with the porters of the church; and young men of a plebeian class with noble maids whose faces had been invisible to the sun and their nearest kindred. In this common captivity the ranks of society were confounded; the ties of nature were cut asunder; and the inexorable soldier was careless of the father's groans, the tears of the mother, and the lamentations of the children. The loudest in their wailings were the nuns, who were torn from the altar with naked bosoms, outstretched hands, and dishevelled hair;

415

and we should piously believe that few could be tempted
to prefer the vigils of the harem to those of the monastery. Of these unfortunate Greeks, of these domestic
animals, whole strings were rudely driven through the
streets; and as the conquerors were eager to return for
more prey, their trembling pace was quickened with
menaces and blows. At the same hour a similar rapine
was exercised in all the churches and monasteries, in
all the palaces and habitations, of the capital; nor could
any place, however sacred or sequestered, protect the
persons or the property of the Greeks. Above sixty thousand of this devoted people were transported from the
city to the camp and fleet; exchanged or sold according
to the caprice or interest of their masters, and dispersed
in remote servitude through the provinces of the Ottoman
empire. Among these we may notice some remarkable
characters. The historian Phranza, first chamberlain and
principal secretary, was involved with his family in the
common lot. After suffering four months the hardships
of slavery, he recovered his freedom: in the ensuing winter he ventured to Adrianople, and ransomed his wife
from the *mir bashi*, or master of the horse; but his two
children, in the flower of youth and beauty, had been
seized for the use of Mohammed himself. The daughter
of Phranza died in the seraglio, perhaps a virgin: his
son, in the fifteenth year of his age, preferred death to
infamy, and was stabbed by the hand of the royal lover.
A deed thus inhuman cannot surely be expiated by the
taste and liberality with which he released a Grecian
matron and her two daughters, on receiving a Latin ode
from Philelphus, who had chosen a wife in that noble
family. The pride or cruelty of Mohammed would have
been most sensibly gratified by the capture of a Roman
legate; but the dexterity of Cardinal Isidore eluded the
search, and he escaped from Galata in a plebeian habit.
The chain and entrance of the outward harbour was still
occupied by the Italian ships of merchandise and war.
They had signalised their valour in the siege: they embraced the moment of retreat, while the Turkish mariners
were dissipated in the pillage of the city. When they
hoisted sail, the beach was covered with a suppliant and

lamentable crowd; but the means of transportation were scanty; the Venetians and Genoese selected their countrymen; and, notwithstanding the fairest promises of the sultan, the inhabitants of Galata evacuated their houses, and embarked with their most precious effects.

In the fall and the sack of great cities an historian is condemned to repeat the tale of uniform calamity: the same effects must be produced by the same passions; and when those passions may be indulged without control, small, alas! is the difference between civilised and savage man. Amidst the vague exclamations of bigotry and hatred, the Turks are not accused of a wanton or immoderate effusion of Christian blood: but according to their maxims (the maxims of antiquity), the lives of the vanquished were forfeited; and the legitimate reward of the conqueror was derived from the service, the sale, or the ransom of his captives of both sexes. The wealth of Constantinople had been granted by the sultan to his victorious troops; and the rapine of an hour is more productive than the industry of years. But as no regular division was attempted of the spoil, the respective shares were not determined by merit; and the rewards of valour were stolen away by the followers of the camp, who had declined the toil and danger of the battle. The narrative of their depredations could not afford either amusement or instruction: the total amount, in the last poverty of the empire, has been valued at four millions of ducats; and of this sum a small part was the property of the Venetians, the Genoese, the Florentines, and the merchants of Ancona. Of these foreigners the stock was improved in quick and perpetual circulation: but the riches of the Greeks were displayed in the idle ostentation of palaces and wardrobes, or deeply buried in treasures of ingots and old coin, lest it should be demanded at their hands for the defence of their country. The profanation and plunder of the monasteries and churches excited the most tragic complaints. The dome of St. Sophia itself, the earthly heaven, the second firmament, the vehicle of the cherubim, the throne of the glory of God, was despoiled of the oblations of ages; and the gold and silver, the pearls and jewels, the vases and sacerdotal ornaments, were most wickedly converted to the service of mankind. After the divine images had been stripped of all that could be valuable to a profane eye, the canvas, or the wood, was torn, or broken, or burnt, or trod under foot, or applied, in the stables or the kitchen, to the vilest uses. The example of sacrilege was imitated, however, from the Latin conquerors of Constantinople; and the treatment which Christ, the Virgin, and the saints had sustained from the guilty Catholic, might be inflicted by the zealous Musulman on the monuments of idolatry. Perhaps, instead of joining the public clamour, a philosopher will observe that in the decline of the arts the workmanship could not be more valuable than the work, and that a fresh supply of visions and miracles would speedily be renewed by the craft of the priest and the credulity of the people. He will more seriously deplore the loss of the Byzantine libraries, which were destroyed or scattered in the general confusion: one hundred and twenty thousand manuscripts are said to have disappeared; ten volumes might be purchased for a single ducat; and the same ignominious price, too high perhaps for a shelf of theology, included the whole works of Aristotle and Homer, the noblest productions of the science and literature of ancient Greece. We may reflect with pleasure that an inestimable portion of our classic treasures was safely deposited in Italy; and that the mechanics of a German town had invented an art which derides the havoc of time and barbarism.

From the first hour of the memorable twenty-ninth of May, disorder and rapine prevailed in Constantinople till the eighth hour of the same day, when the sultan himself passed in triumph through the gate of St. Romanus. He was attended by his vizirs, bashaws, and guards, each of whom (says a Byzantine historian) was robust as Hercules, dexterous as Apollo, and equal in battle to any ten of the race of ordinary mortals. The conqueror gazed with satisfaction and wonder on the strange though splendid appearance of the domes and palaces, so dissimilar from the style of Oriental architecture. In the hippodrome, or *atmeidan*, his eye was attracted by the twisted column of the three serpents; and, as a trial of his strength, he shattered with his iron mace or battle-axe the under jaw of one of these monsters, which in the eyes of the Turks were the idols or talismans of the city. At the principal door of St. Sophia he alighted from his horse and entered the dome; and such was his jealous regard for that monument of his glory, that, on observing a zealous Musulman in the act of breaking the marble pavement, he admonished him with his scimitar that, if the spoil and captives were granted to the soldiers, the public and private buildings had been reserved for the prince. By his command the metropolis of the Eastern church was transformed into a mosque: the rich and portable instruments of superstition had been removed; the crosses were thrown down; and the walls, which were covered with images and mosaics, were washed and purified, and restored to a state of naked simplicity. On the same day, or on the ensuing Friday, the *muezin*, or crier, ascended the most lofty turret, and proclaimed the *ezan*, or public invitation, in the name of God and his prophet; the imam preached; and Mohammed the Second performed the *namaz* of prayer and thanksgiving on the great altar, where the Christian mysteries had so lately been celebrated before the last of the Cæsars. From St. Sophia he proceeded to the august but desolate mansion of a hundred successors of the great Constantine, but which in a few hours had been stripped of the pomp of royalty. A melancholy reflection on the vicissitudes of human greatness forced itself on his mind, and he repeated an elegant distich of Persian poetry: "The spider has wove his web in the Imperial palace, and the owl hath sung her watch-song on the towers of Afrasiab."

Yet his mind was not satisfied, nor did the victory seem complete, till he was informed of the fate of Constantine—whether he had escaped, or been made prisoner, or had fallen in the battle. Two Janizaries claimed the honour and reward of his death: the body, under a heap of slain, was discovered by the golden eagles embroidered on his shoes; the Greeks acknowledged with tears the head of their late emperor; and, after exposing the bloody trophy, Mohammed bestowed on his rival the honours of a decent funeral. . . . On the eighteenth of June the victorious sultan returned to Adrianople, and smiled at the base and hollow embassies of the Christian princes, who viewed their approaching ruin in the fall of the Eastern empire.

16. Medieval Rome

[While New Rome was being transformed into the capital of Islam, Old Rome was resuming its position as the capital of Christendom. It had to resume it because in the fourteenth century it was nearly lost. In 1309, the Popes, like the Emperors a thousand years before, had abandoned the turbulent city which, even at the height of their world-power, they had never been able to control, and established themselves under French protection at Avignon. But Rome did not accept its fallen status lightly, and in the abandoned and impoverished city the mood of resentment was dignified, in the middle of the century, by the classical revivalism of Petrarch (himself a Tuscan who lived at Avignon) and the political romanticism of his plebeian hero, the Roman Cola Rienzi. In 1347, Rienzi made himself popular dictator, or "tribune," of Rome; but his rule was short-lived, and thereafter Petrarch contented himself with urging the return to the city of its old masters, the Popes. Ultimately, in 1378, an Italian pope, Urban VI, was elected; but the French cardinals, who had been intimidated into electing him, were determined to keep the papacy in France. They were "attached to the language, manners and climate of Avignon; to their stately palaces; above all, to the wines of Burgundy"; and so they escaped from Rome and elected a French Pope, who remained at Avignon and was recognised by France, Spain and their client states. Thus the seventy years of "Babylonish captivity" *in Avignon were merely followed by the forty years of "the Great Schism," which lasted until the Council of Constance (1414-1418) deposed all Popes (there were now three of them) and procured the election of Martin V. In chapter LXX Gibbon describes the Great Schism and its end.]*

From the banks of the Tiber and the Rhône the hostile pontiffs encountered each other with the pen and the sword: the civil and ecclesiastical order of society was disturbed; and the Romans had their full share of the mischiefs of which they may be arraigned as the primary authors. They had vainly flattered themselves with the hope of restoring the seat of the ecclesiastical monarchy, and of relieving their poverty with the tributes and offerings of the nations; but the separation of France and Spain diverted the stream of lucrative devotion; nor could the loss be compensated by the two jubilees which were crowded into the space of ten years. By the avocations of the schism, by foreign arms, and popular tumults, Urban the Sixth and his three successors were often compelled to interrupt their residence in the Vatican. The Colonna and Ursini still exercised their deadly feuds: the bannerets of Rome asserted and abused the privileges of a republic: the vicars of Christ, who had levied a military force, chastised their rebellion with the gibbet, the sword, and the dagger; and, in a friendly conference, eleven deputies of the people were perfidiously murdered and cast into the street. Since the invasion of Robert the Norman, the Romans had pursued their domestic quarrels without the dangerous interposition of a stranger. But in the disorders of the schism, an aspiring neighbour, Ladislaus king of Naples, alternately supported and betrayed the pope and the people; by the former he was declared *gonfalonier,* or general, of the church, while the latter submitted to his choice the nomination of their magistrates. Besieging Rome by land and water, he thrice entered the gates as a barbarian conqueror; profaned the altars, violated the virgins, pillaged the merchants, performed his devotions at St. Peter's, and left a garrison in the castle of St. Angelo. His arms were sometimes unfortunate, and to a delay of three days he was indebted for his life and crown: but Ladislaus triumphed in his turn; and it was only his premature death that could save the metropolis and the ecclesiastical state from the ambitious conqueror, who had assumed the title, or at least the powers, of King of Rome.

I have not undertaken the ecclesiastical history of the schism; but Rome, the object of these last chapters, is deeply interested in the disputed succession of her sovereigns. The first counsels for the peace and union of Christendom arose from the university of Paris, from the faculty of the Sorbonne, whose doctors were esteemed, at least in the Gallican church, as the most consummate masters of theological science. Prudently waiving all invidious inquiry into the origin and merits of the dispute, they proposed, as a healing measure, that the two pretenders of Rome and Avignon should abdicate at the same time, after qualifying the cardinals of the adverse factions to join in a legitimate election; and that the nations should *subtract* their obedience, if either of the competitors preferred his own interest to that of the public. At each vacancy these physicians of the church deprecated the mischiefs of a hasty choice; but the policy of the conclave and the ambition of its members were deaf to reason and entreaties; and whatsoever promises were made, the pope could never be bound by the oaths of the cardinal. During fifteen years the pacific designs of the university were eluded by the arts of the rival pontiffs, the scruples or passions of their adherents, and the vicissitudes of French factions, that ruled the insanity of Charles the Sixth. At length a vigorous resolution was embraced; and a solemn embassy, of the titular patriarch of Alexandria, two archbishops, five bishops, five abbots, three knights, and twenty doctors, was sent to the courts of Avignon and Rome, to require, in the name of the church and king, the abdication of the two pretenders, of Peter de Luna, who styled himself Benedict the Thirteenth, and of Angelo Corrario, who assumed the name of Gregory the Twelfth. For the ancient honour of Rome, and the success of their commission, the ambassadors solicited a conference with the magistrates of the city, whom they gratified by a positive declaration that the most Christian king did not entertain a wish of transporting the holy see from the Vatican, which he considered as the genuine and proper seat of the successor of St. Peter. In the name of the senate and people, an eloquent Roman asserted their desire to co-operate in the union of the church, deplored the temporal and spiritual calamities of the long schism, and requested the protection of France against the arms of the king of Naples. The answers of Benedict and Gregory were alike edifying and alike deceitful; and, in evading the demand of their abdication, the two rivals were animated by a common spirit. They agreed on the necessity of a previous interview; but the time, the place, and the manner, could never be ascertained by mutual consent. "If the one advances," says a servant of Gregory, "the other retreats; the one appears an animal fearful of the land, the other a creature apprehensive of the water. And thus, for a short remnant of life and power, will these aged priests endanger the peace and salvation of the Christian world."

The Christian world was at length provoked by their obstinacy and fraud: they were deserted by their cardinals, who embraced each other as friends and colleagues; and their revolt was supported by a numerous assembly of prelates and ambassadors. With equal justice, the council of Pisa deposed the popes of Rome and Avignon; the conclave was unanimous in the choice of Alexander the Fifth, and his vacant seat was soon filled by a similar election of John the Twenty-third, the most profligate of mankind. But instead of extinguishing the schism, the rashness of the French and Italians had given a third pretender to the chair of St. Peter. Such new claims of the synod and conclave were disputed; three kings, of Germany, Hungary, and Naples, adhered to the cause of Gregory the Twelfth: and Benedict the Thirteenth, himself a Spaniard, was acknowledged by the devotion and patriotism of that powerful nation. The rash proceedings of Pisa were corrected by the council of Constance; the emperor Sigismond acted a conspicuous part as the advocate or protector of the Catholic church; and the number and weight of civil and ecclesiastical members might seem to constitute the states-general of Europe. Of the three popes, John the Twenty-third was the first victim: he fled and was brought back a prisoner: the most scandalous charges were suppressed; the vicar of Christ was only accused of piracy, murder, rape, sodomy, and incest; and after subscribing his own condemnation, he expiated in prison the imprudence of trusting his person to a free city beyond the Alps. Gregory the Twelfth, whose obedience was reduced to the narrow precincts of Rimini, descended with more honour from the throne; and his ambassador convened the session in which he renounced the title and authority of lawful pope. To vanquish the obstinacy of Benedict the Thirteenth or his adherents, the emperor in person undertook a journey from Constance to Perpignan. The kings of Castile, Arragon, Navarre, and Scotland, obtained an equal and honourable treaty: with the concurrence of the Spaniards, Benedict was deposed by the council; but the harmless old man was left in a solitary castle to excommunicate twice each day the rebel kingdoms which had deserted his cause. After thus eradicating the remains of the schism, the synod of Constance proceeded with slow and cautious steps to elect the sovereign of Rome and the head of the church. On this momentous occasion the college of twenty-three cardinals was fortified with thirty deputies; six of whom were chosen in each of the five great nations of Christendom—the Italian, the German, the French, the Spanish, and the English; the interference of strangers was softened by their generous preference of an Italian and a Roman; and the hereditary, as well as personal, merit of Otho Colonna recommended him to the conclave. Rome accepted with joy and obedience the noblest of her sons; the ecclesiastical state was defended by his powerful family; and the elevation of Martin the Fifth is the era of the restoration and establishment of the popes in the Vatican.

The royal prerogative of coining money, which had been exercised near three hundred years by the senate, was *first* resumed by Martin the Fifth, and his image and superscription introduce the series of the papal medals.

Of his two immediate successors, Eugenius the Fourth was the *last* pope expelled by the tumults of the Roman people, and Nicholas the Fifth, the *last* who was importuned by the presence of a Roman emperor.

[*Restored to unity and to Rome, the Popes soon recovered and increased their authority. With the aid of an impregnable citadel, a standing army and the novelty of gunpowder, they subdued, as never before, the turbulent populace and nobility, and the city gradually acquired a new character*.]

The long habits of obedience and education subdued the turbulent spirit of the nobles and commons of Rome. The barons forgot the arms and factions of their ancestors, and insensibly became the servants of luxury and government. Instead of maintaining a crowd of tenants and followers, the produce of their estates was consumed in the private expenses which multiply the pleasures and diminish the power of the lord. The Colonna and Ursini vied with each other in the decoration of their palaces and chapels; and their antique splendour was rivalled or surpassed by the sudden opulence of the papal families. In Rome the voice of freedom and discord is no longer heard; and, instead of the foaming torrent, a smooth and stagnant lake reflects the image of idleness and servitude.

A Christian, a philosopher, and a patriot, will be equally scandalised by the temporal kingdom of the clergy; and the local majesty of Rome, the remembrance of her consuls and triumphs, may seem to embitter the sense and aggravate the shame of her slavery. If we calmly weigh the merits and defects of the ecclesiastical government, it may be praised in its present state as a mild, decent, and tranquil system, exempt from the dangers of a minority, the sallies of youth, the expenses of luxury, and the calamities of war. But these advantages are overbalanced by a frequent, perhaps a septennial, election of a sovereign, who is seldom a native of the country: the reign of a *young* statesman of threescore, in the decline of his life and abilities, without hope to accomplish, and without children to inherit, the labours of his transitory reign. The successful candidate is drawn from the church, and even the convent—from the mode of education and life the most adverse to reason, humanity, and freedom. In the trammels of servile faith he has learned to believe because it is absurd, to revere all that is contemptible, and to despise whatever might deserve the esteem of a rational being; to punish error as a crime, to reward mortification and celibacy as the first of virtues; to place the saints of the calendar above the heroes of Rome and the sages of Athens; and to consider the missal, or the crucifix, as more useful instruments than the plough or the loom. In the office of nuncio, or the rank of cardinal, he may acquire some knowledge of the world; but the primitive stain will adhere to his mind and manners: from study and experience he may suspect the mystery of his profession; but the sacerdotal artist will imbibe some portion of the bigotry which he inculcates. The genius of Sixtus the Fifth burst from the gloom of a Franciscan cloister. In a reign of five years he exterminated the outlaws and banditti, abolished the *profane* sanctuaries of Rome, formed a naval and military force, restored and emulated the monuments of antiquity, and, after a liberal use and large increase of the revenue, left five millions of crowns in the castle of St. Angelo. But his justice was sullied with cruelty, his activity was prompted by the ambition of conquest: after his decease the abuses revived; the treasury was dissipated; he entailed on posterity thirty-five new taxes and the venality of offices; and, after his death, his statue was demolished by an ungrateful or an injured people. The wild and original character of Sixtus the Fifth stands alone in the series of the pontiffs: the maxims and effects of their temporal government may be collected from the positive and comparative view of the arts and philosophy, the agriculture and trade, the wealth and population, of the ecclesiastical state. For myself, it is my wish to depart in charity with all mankind, nor am I willing, in these last moments, to offend even the pope and clergy of Rome.

[*In the new peace of the Popes and the classical revival which Petrarch had inaugurated, the Romans began to study the relics of ancient greatness around them. In his last chapter Gibbon describes the ruinous state of Rome at the close of the Middle Ages and analyses the causes of its decay in the 1300 years of his* History. *He ascribes it to four main causes:*]

I. The injuries of time and nature. II. The hostile attacks of the barbarians and Christians. III. The use and abuse of the materials. And, IV. The domestic quarrels of the Romans.

I. The art of man is able to construct monuments far more permanent than the narrow span of his own existence: yet these monuments, like himself, are perishable and frail; and in the boundless annals of time his life and his labours must equally be measured as a fleeting moment. Of a simple and solid edifice it is not easy however to circumscribe the duration. As the wonders of ancient days, the pyramids attracted the curiosity of the ancients: a hundred generations, the leaves of autumn, have dropped into the grave; and after the fall of the Pharaohs and Ptolemies, the Cæsars and caliphs, the same pyramids stand erect and unshaken above the floods of the Nile. A complex figure of various and minute parts is more accessible to injury and decay; and the silent lapse of time is often accelerated by hurricanes and earthquakes, by fires and inundations. The air and earth have doubtless been shaken; and the lofty turrets of Rome have tottered from their foundations; but the seven hills do not appear to be placed on the great cavities of the globe; nor has the city, in any age, been exposed to the convulsions of nature, which, in the climate of Antioch, Lisbon, or Lima, have crumbled in a few moments the works of ages into dust. Fire is the most powerful agent of life and death: the rapid mischief may be kindled and propagated by the industry or negligence of mankind; and every period of the Roman annals is marked by the repetition of similar calamities. A memorable conflagration, the guilt or misfortune of Nero's reign, continued, though with unequal fury, either six or nine days. Innumerable buildings, crowded in close and crooked streets, supplied perpetual fuel for the flames; and when they ceased, four only of the fourteen regions were left entire; three were totally destroyed, and seven were deformed by the relics of smoking and lacerated edifices. In the full meridian of empire the metropolis arose with fresh beauty from her ashes; yet the memory of the old deplored their irreparable losses, the arts of Greece, the trophies of victory, the monuments of primitive or fabulous antiquity. In the days of distress and anarchy every wound is mortal, every fall irretrievable; nor can the damage be restored either by the public care of government, or the activity of private interest. Yet two causes may be alleged which render the calamity of fire more destructive to a flourishing than a decayed city. 1. The more combustible materials of brick, timber, and metals, are first melted or consumed; but the flames may play without injury or effect on the naked walls and massy arches that have been despoiled of their ornaments. 2. It is among the common and plebeian habitations that a mischievous spark is most easily blown to a conflagration; but as soon as they are devoured, the greater edifices which have resisted or escaped are left as so many islands in a state of solitude and safety. From her situation, Rome is exposed to the danger of frequent inundations. Without excepting the Tiber, the rivers that descend from either side of the Apennine have a short and irregular course; a shallow stream in the summer heats; an impetuous torrent when it is swelled in the spring or winter, by the fall of rain and the melting of the snows. When the current is repelled from the sea by adverse winds, when the ordinary bed is inadequate to the weight of waters, they rise above the banks, and overspread, without limits or control, the plains and cities of the adjacent country. Soon after the triumph of the first Punic war the Tiber was increased by unusual rains; and the inundation, surpassing all former measure of time and place, destroyed all the buildings that were situate below the hills of Rome. According to the variety of ground, the same mischief was produced by different means: and the edifices were either swept away by the sudden impulse, or dissolved and undermined by the long

429

continuance, of the flood. Under the reign of Augustus the same calamity was renewed: the lawless river overturned the palaces and temples on its banks; and, after the labours of the emperor in cleansing and widening the bed that was encumbered with ruins, the vigilance of his successors was exercised by similar dangers and designs. The project of diverting into new channels the Tiber itself, or some of the dependent streams, was long opposed by superstition and local interests; nor did the use compensate the toil and cost of the tardy and imperfect execution. The servitude of rivers is the noblest and most important victory which man has obtained over the licentiousness of nature;[1] and if such were the ravages of the Tiber under a firm and active government, what could oppose, or who can enumerate, the injuries of the city after the fall of the Western empire? A remedy was at length produced by the evil itself: the accumulation of rubbish and the earth that has been washed down from the hills is supposed to have elevated the plain of Rome fourteen or fifteen feet, perhaps, above the ancient level; and the modern city is less accessible to the attacks of the river.

II. The crowd of writers of every nation, who impute the destruction of the Roman monuments to the Goths and the Christians, have neglected to inquire how far they were animated by a hostile principle, and how far they possessed the means and the leisure to satiate their enmity. In the preceding volumes of this History I have described the triumph of barbarism and religion; and I can only resume, in a few words, their real or imaginary connection with the ruin of ancient Rome. Our fancy may create, or adopt, a pleasing romance, that the Goths and Vandals sallied from Scandinavia, ardent to avenge the flight of Odin; to break the chains, and to chastise the oppressors, of mankind; that they wished to burn the records of classic literature, and to found their national architecture on the broken members of the Tuscan

---

[1] See the *Epoques de la Nature* of the eloquent and philosophic Buffon. His picture of Guyana, in South America, is that of a new and savage land, in which the waters are abandoned to themselves, without being regulated by human industry.

and Corinthian orders. But in simple truth, the northern conquerors were neither sufficiently savage, nor sufficiently refined, to entertain such aspiring ideas of destruction and revenge. The shepherds of Scythia and Germany had been educated in the armies of the empire, whose discipline they acquired, and whose weakness they invaded: with the familiar use of the Latin tongue they had learned to reverence the name and titles of Rome; and, though incapable of emulating, they were more inclined to admire than to abolish the arts and studies of a brighter period. In the transient possession of a rich and unresisting capital, the soldiers of Alaric and Genseric were stimulated by the passions of a victorious army; amidst the wanton indulgence of lust or cruelty, portable wealth was the object of their search: nor could they derive either pride or pleasure from the unprofitable reflection that they had battered to the ground the works of the consuls and Cæsars. Their moments were indeed precious: the Goths evacuated Rome on the sixth, the Vandals on the fifteenth day; and, though it be far more difficult to build than to destroy, their hasty assault would have made a slight impression on the solid piles of antiquity. We may remember that both Alaric and Genseric affected to spare the buildings of the city; that they subsisted in strength and beauty under the auspicious government of Theodoric; and that the momentary resentment of Totila was disarmed by his own temper and the advice of his friends and enemies. From these innocent barbarians the reproach may be transferred to the Catholics of Rome. The statues, altars, and houses of the dæmons were an abomination in their eyes; and in the absolute command of the city, they might labour with zeal and perseverance to erase the idolatry of their ancestors. The demolition of the temples in the East affords to *them* an example of conduct, and to *us* an argument of belief; and it is probable that a portion of guilt or merit may be imputed with justice to the Roman proselytes. Yet their abhorrence was confined to the monuments of heathen superstition; and the civil structures that were dedicated to the business or pleasure of society might be preserved without injury or scandal. The change of religion was

431

accomplished, not by a popular tumult, but by the decrees of the emperors, of the senate, and of time. Of the Christian hierarchy, the bishops of Rome were commonly the most prudent and least fanatic; nor can any positive charge be opposed to the meritorious act of saving and converting the majestic structure of the Pantheon.

III. The value of any object that supplies the wants or pleasures of mankind is compounded of its substance and its form, of the materials and the manufacture. Its price must depend on the number of persons by whom it may be acquired and used; on the extent of the market; and consequently on the ease or difficulty of remote exportation, according to the nature of the commodity, its local situation, and the temporary circumstances of the world. The barbarian conquerors of Rome usurped in a moment the toil and treasure of successive ages; but, except the luxuries of immediate consumption, they must view without desire all that could not be removed from the city in the Gothic waggons or the fleet of the Vandals. Gold and silver were the first objects of their avarice; as in every country, and in the smallest compass, they represent the most ample command of the industry and possessions of mankind. A vase or a statue of those precious metals might tempt the vanity of some barbarian chief; but the grosser multitude, regardless of the form, was tenacious only of the substance; and the melted ingots might be readily divided and stamped into the current coin of the empire. The less active or less fortunate robbers were reduced to the baser plunder of brass, lead, iron, and copper: whatever had escaped the Goths and Vandals was pillaged by the Greek tyrants; and the emperor Constans, in his rapacious visit, stripped the bronze tiles from the roof of the Pantheon. The edifices of Rome might be considered as a vast and various mine; the first labour of extracting the materials was already performed; the metals were purified and cast; the marbles were hewn and polished; and after foreign and domestic rapine had been satiated, the remains of the city, could a purchaser have been found, were still venal. The monuments of antiquity had been left naked of their precious ornaments; but the Romans would demolish with their own hands the arches and walls, if the hope of profit could surpass the cost of the labour and exportation. If Charlemagne had fixed in Italy the seat of the Western empire, his genius would have aspired to restore, rather than to violate, the works of the Cæsars; but policy confined the French monarch to the forests of Germany; his taste could be gratified only by destruction; and the new palace of Aix-la-Chapelle was decorated with the marbles of Ravenna and Rome. Five hundred years after Charlemagne, a king of Sicily, Robert, the wisest and most liberal sovereign of the age, was supplied with the same materials by the easy navigation of the Tiber and the sea; and Petrach sighs an indignant complaint, that the ancient capital of the world should adorn from her own bowels the slothful luxury of Naples. But these examples of plunder or purchase were rare in the darker ages; and the Romans, alone and unenvied, might have applied to their private or public use the remaining structures of antiquity, if in their present form and situation they had not been useless in a great measure to the city and its inhabitants. The walls still described the old circumference, but the city had descended from the seven hills into the Campus Martius; and some of the noblest monuments which had braved the injuries of time were left in a desert far remote from the habitations of mankind. The palaces of the senators were no longer adapted to the manners or fortunes of their indigent successors: the use of baths[2] and porticoes was forgotten: in the sixth century the games of the theatre, amphitheatre, and circus had been interrupted: some temples were devoted to the prevailing worship; but the Christian churches preferred the holy figure of the cross; and fashion, or reason, had distributed after a peculiar model the cells and offices of the cloister. Under the ecclesiastical reign the number of these pious foundations was enormously multiplied; and the city was crowded with forty monasteries of men, twenty of women, and sixty chapters and colleges of canons and priests, who aggravated, instead

---

2 Yet Charlemagne washed and swam at Aix-la-Chapelle with a hundred of his courtiers; and Muratori describes, as late as the year 814, the public baths which were built at Spoleto in Italy.

of relieving, the depopulation of the tenth century. But if the forms of ancient architecture were disregarded by a people insensible of their use and beauty, the plentiful materials were applied to every call of necessity or superstition; till the fairest columns of the Ionic and Corinthian orders, the richest marbles of Paros and Numidia, were degraded, perhaps to the support of a convent or a stable. The daily havoc which is perpetrated by the Turks in the cities of Greece and Asia may afford a melancholy example; and in the gradual destruction of the monuments of Rome, Sixtus the Fifth may alone be excused for employing the stones of the Septizonium in the glorious edifice of St. Peter's. A fragment, a ruin, howsoever mangled or profaned, may be viewed with pleasure and regret; but the greater part of the marble was deprived of substance, as well as of place and proportion; it was burnt to lime for the purpose of cement. Since the arrival of Poggius the temple of Concord and many capital structures had vanished from his eyes; and an epigram of the same age expresses a just and pious fear that the continuance of this practice would finally annihilate all the monuments of antiquity. The smallness of their numbers was the sole check on the demands and depredations of the Romans. The imagination of Petrarch might create the presence of a mighty people; and I hesitate to believe that, even in the fourteenth century, they could be reduced to a contemptible list of thirty-three thousand inhabitants. From that period to the reign of Leo the Tenth, if they multiplied to the amount of eighty-five thousand, the increase of citizens was in some degree pernicious to the ancient city.

IV. I have reserved for the last the most potent and forcible cause of destruction, the domestic hostilities of the Romans themselves. Under the dominion of the Greek and French emperors the peace of the city was disturbed by accidental, though frequent, seditions: it is from the decline of the latter, from the beginning of the tenth century, that we may date the licentiousness of private war, which violated with impunity the laws of the Code and the Gospel, without respecting the majesty of the absent sovereign, or the presence and person of the vicar of Christ. In a dark period of five hundred years Rome was perpetually afflicted by the sanguinary quarrels of the nobles and the people, the Guelphs and Ghibelines, the Colonna and Ursini; and if much has escaped the knowledge, and much is unworthy of the notice, of history, I have exposed in the two preceding chapters the causes and effects of the public disorders. At such a time, when every quarrel was decided by the sword, and none could trust their lives or properties to the impotence of law, the powerful citizens were armed for safety, or offence, against the domestic enemies whom they feared or hated. Except Venice alone, the same dangers and designs were common to all the free republics of Italy; and the nobles usurped the prerogative of fortifying their houses, and erecting strong towers that were capable of resisting a sudden attack. The cities were filled with these hostile edifices; and the example of Lucca, which contained three hundred towers, her law, which confined their height to the measure of fourscore feet, may be extended with suitable latitude to the more opulent and populous states. The first step of the senator Brancaleone in the establishment of peace and justice was to demolish (as we have already seen) one hundred and forty of the towers of Rome; and, in the last days of anarchy and discord, as late as the reign of Martin the Fifth, forty-four still stood in one of the thirteen or fourteen regions of the city. To this mischievous purpose the remains of antiquity were most readily adapted: the temples and arches afforded a broad and solid basis for the new structures of brick and stone; and we can name the modern turrets that were raised on the triumphal monuments of Julius Cæsar, Titus, and the Antonines. With some slight alterations, a theatre, an amphitheatre, a mausoleum, was transformed into a strong and spacious citadel. I need not repeat that the mole of Hadrian has assumed the title and form of the castle of St. Angelo; the Septizonium of Severus was capable of standing against a royal army; the sepulchre of Metella has sunk under its outworks; the theatres of Pompey and Marcellus were occupied by the Savelli and Ursini families; and the rough fortress has been gradually softened to the splendour and elegance of an Italian palace. Even the churches were encompassed with arms and bulwarks, and the military engines on the roof of St. Peter's were the terror of the Vatican and the scandal of the Christian world. Whatever is fortified will be attacked; and whatever is attacked may be destroyed. Could the Romans have wrested from the popes the castle of St. Angelo, they had resolved by a public decree to annihilate that monument of servitude. Every building of defence was exposed to a siege; and in every siege the arts and engines of destruction were laboriously employed. After the death of Nicholas the Fourth, Rome, without a sovereign or a senate, was abandoned six months to the fury of civil war. "The houses," says a cardinal and poet of the times, "were crushed by the weight and velocity of enormous stones; the walls were perforated by the strokes of the battering-ram; the towers were involved in fire and smoke; and the assailants were stimulated by rapine and revenge." The work was consummated by the tyranny of the laws; and the factions of Italy alternately exercised a blind and thoughtless vengeance on their adversaries, whose houses and castles they razed to the ground. In comparing the *days* of foreign with the *ages* of domestic hostility, we must pronounce that the latter have been far more ruinous to the city; and our opinion is confirmed by the evidence of Petrarch. "Behold," says the laureate, "the relics of Rome, the image of her pristine greatness! neither time nor the barbarian can boast the merit of this stupendous destruction: it was perpetrated by her own citizens, by the most illustrious of her sons; and your ancestors (he writes to a noble Annibaldi) have done with battering-ram what the Punic hero could not accomplish with the sword." The influence of the two last principles of decay must in some degree be multiplied by each other; since the houses and towers which were subverted by civil war required a new and perpetual supply from the monuments of antiquity.

[*As a particular example, Gibbon gives the history of the Coliseum, whose fabric survived the Dark and Middle Ages almost intact.*]

The inside was damaged; but in the middle of the sixteenth century, an era of taste and learning, the exterior circumference of one thousand six hundred and twelve feet was still entire and inviolate: a triple elevation of fourscore arches, which rose to the height of one hundred and eight feet. Of the present ruin the nephews of Paul the Third are the guilty agents; and every traveller who views the Farnese palace may curse the sacrilege and luxury of these upstart princes. A similar reproach is applied to the Barberini; and the repetition of injury might be dreaded from every reign, till the Coliseum was placed under the safeguard of religion by the most liberal of the pontiffs, Benedict the Fourteenth, who consecrated a spot which persecution and fable had stained with the blood of so many Christian martyrs.

When Petrarch first gratified his eyes with a view of those monuments whose scattered fragments so far surpass the most eloquent descriptions, he was astonished at the supine indifference of the Romans themselves; he was humbled rather than elated by the discovery that, except his friend Rienzi, and one of the Colonna, a stranger of the Rhône was more conversant with these antiquities than the nobles and natives of the metropolis. . . .

But the clouds of barbarism were gradually dispelled; and the peaceful authority of Martin the Fifth and his successors restored the ornaments of the city as well as the order of the ecclesiastical state. The improvements of Rome, since the fifteenth century, have not been the spontaneous produce of freedom and industry. The first and most natural root of a great city is the labour and populousness of the adjacent country, which supplies the materials of subsistence, of manufactures, and of foreign trade. But the greater part of the Campagna of Rome is reduced to a dreary and desolate wilderness: the overgrown estates of the princes and the clergy are cultivated by the lazy hands of indigent and hopeless vassals; and the scanty harvests are confined or exported for the benefit of a monopoly. A second and more artificial cause of the growth of a metropolis is the residence of a monarch, the expense of a luxurious court, and the tributes of dependent provinces. Those provinces and tributes had been lost in the fall of the empire; and if some streams of the silver of Peru and the gold of Brazil have been attracted by the Vatican, the revenues of the cardinals, the fees of office, the oblations of pilgrims and clients, and the remnant of ecclesiastical taxes, afford a poor and precarious supply, which maintains, however, the idleness of the court and city. The population of Rome, far below the measure of the great capitals of Europe, does not exceed one hundred and seventy thousand inhabitants; and within the spacious enclosure of the walls, the largest portion of the seven hills is overspread with vineyards and ruins. The beauty and splendour of the modern city may be ascribed to the abuses of the government, to the influence of superstition. Each reign (the exceptions are rare) has been marked by the rapid elevation of a new family, enriched by the childless pontiff at the expense of the church and country. The palaces of these fortunate nephews are the most costly monuments of elegance and servitude: the perfect arts of architecture, painting, and sculpture, have been prostituted in their service; and their galleries and gardens are decorated with the most precious works of antiquity, which taste or vanity has prompted them to collect. The ecclesiastical revenues were more decently employed by the popes themselves in the pomp of the Catholic worship; but it is superfluous to enumerate their pious foundations of altars, chapels, and churches, since these lesser stars are eclipsed by the sun of the Vatican, by the dome of St. Peter, the most glorious structure that ever has been applied to the use of religion. The fame of Julius the Second, Leo the Tenth, and Sixtus the Fifth, is accompanied by the superior merit of Bramante and Fontana, of Raphael and Michæl Angelo; and the same munificence which had been displayed in palaces and temples was directed with equal zeal to revive and emulate the labours of antiquity. Prostrate obelisks were raised from the ground, and erected in the most conspicuous places; of the eleven aqueducts of the Cæsars and consuls, three were restored; the artificial rivers were conducted over a long series of old or of new arches, to discharge into marble basins a flood of salubrious and refreshing waters: and the spectator, impatient to ascend the steps of St. Peter's, is detained by a column of Egyptian granite, which rises between two lofty and perpetual fountains to the height of one hundred and twenty feet. The map, the description, the monuments of ancient Rome, have been elucidated by the diligence of the antiquarian and the student; and the footsteps of heroes, the relics, not of superstition, but of empire, are devoutly visited by a new race of pilgrims from the remote and once savage countries of the North.

Of these pilgrims, and of every reader, the attention will be excited by a History of the Decline and Fall of the Roman Empire; the greatest, perhaps, and most awful scene in the history of mankind. The various causes and progressive effects are connected with many of the events most interesting in human annals: the artful policy of the Cæsars, who long maintained the name and image of a free republic; the disorders of military despotism; the rise, establishment, and sects of Christianity; the foundation of Constantinople; the division of the monarchy; the invasion and settlements of the barbarians of Germany and Scythia; the institutions of the civil law; the character and religion of Mohammed; the temporal sovereignty of the popes; the restoration and decay of the Western empire of Charlemagne; the crusades of the Latins in the East; the conquests of the Saracens and Turks; the ruin of the Greek empire; the state and revolutions of Rome in the middle age. The historian may applaud the importance and variety of his subject; but, while he is conscious of his own imperfections, he must often accuse the deficiency of his materials. It was among the ruins of the Capitol that I first conceived the idea of a work which has amused and exercised near twenty years of my life, and which, however inadequate to my own wishes, I finally deliver to the curiosity and candour of the public.

LAUSANNE, *June 27, 1787.*

PART III
The Vindication

[*The circumstances in which Gibbon wrote his*
Vindication of Some Passages in the Fifteenth and
Sixteenth Chapters of the History of the Decline
and Fall of the Roman Empire *have been described
in his* Autobiography *(see above pp. 45-48) and
in the Introduction to this volume. In substance,
the* Vindication *is a technical work: an examination of disputed questions—the military service
of the first Christians, the reliability of their early
historians, the character of Eusebius, etc.—by
reference to the evidence. As such, it is conclusive:
the judgments in the* Decline and Fall, *however
casually expressed, were shown to be solidly based.
In so decisive an encounter it is unnecessary to re-
examine the evidence, but a short extract will
serve to illustrate the style of the work. For one
of his critics, Richard Watson, a learned and liberal Cambridge clergyman who afterwards became
a bishop, Gibbon showed respect; to his Oxford
opponents, as they were less learned and entirely
illiberal, he showed none.*]

When Dr. Watson gave to the public his Apology for
Christianity, in a Series of Letters, he addressed them
to the Author of the Decline and Fall of the Roman Empire, with a just confidence that he had considered this
important object in a manner not unworthy of his antagonist or of himself. Dr. Watson's mode of thinking
bears a liberal and a philosophic cast; his thoughts are
expressed with spirit, and that spirit is always tempered
by politeness and moderation. Such is the man whom I

440

should be happy to call my friend, and whom I should not blush to call my antagonist. . . .

There is, however, one passage, and one passage only, which must not pass without some explanation; and I shall the more eagerly embrace this occasion to illustrate what I had said, as the misconstruction of my true meaning seems to have made an involuntary, but unfavourable impression on the liberal mind of Dr. Watson. As I endeavour *not* to palliate the severity, but to discover the motives, of the Roman magistrates, I had remarked, "it was in vain that the oppressed believer asserted the unalienable rights of conscience and private judgment. Though his situation might excite the pity, his arguments could never reach the understanding, either of the philosophic or of the believing part of the Pagan world." The humanity of Dr. Watson takes fire on the supposed provocation, and he asks me with unusual quickness, "How, Sir, are the arguments for liberty of conscience so exceedingly inconclusive, that you think them incapable of reaching the understanding even of philosophers?" He continues to observe, that a captious adversary would embrace with avidity the opportunity this passage *affords,* of blotting my character with the odious stain of being a persecutor; a stain which no learning can wipe out, which no genius or ability can render amiable; and though he himself does not entertain such an opinion of my principles, his ingenuity tries in vain to provide me with the means of escape.

I must lament that I have not been successful in the explanation of a very simple notion of the spirit both of Philosophy and of Polytheism, which I have repeatedly inculcated. The arguments which assert the rights of conscience are not inconclusive in themselves, but the understanding of the Greeks and Romans was fortified against their evidence by an invincible prejudice. When we listen to the voice of Bayle, of Locke, and of genuine reason, in favour of religious toleration, we shall easily perceive that our most forcible appeal is made to our mutual feelings. If the Jew were allowed to argue with the Inquisitor, he would request that for a moment they might exchange their different situations, and might

441

safely ask his Catholic Tyrant, whether the fear of death would compel *him* to enter the synagogue, to receive the mark of circumcision, and to partake of the paschal lamb. As soon as the case of persecution was brought home to the breast of the Inquisitor, he must have found some difficulty in suppressing the dictates of natural equity, which would insinuate to his conscience, that he could have no right to inflict those punishments which under similar circumstances, he would esteem it as his duty to encounter. But this argument could not reach the understanding of a Polytheist, or of an ancient Philosopher. The former was ready, whenever he was summoned, or indeed without being summoned, to fall prostrate before the altars of any Gods who were adored in any part of the world, and to admit a vague persuasion of the *truth* and divinity of the most different modes of religion. The philosopher, who considered them, at least in their literal sense, as equally *false* and absurd, was not ashamed to disguise his sentiments, and to frame his actions according to the laws of his country, which imposed the same obligation on the philosophers and the people. When Pliny declared, that whatever was the opinion of the Christians, their obstinacy deserved punishment, the absurd cruelty of Pliny was excused in his own eye, by the consciousness that, in the situation of the Christians, he would not have refused the religious compliance which he exacted. I shall not repeat, that the Pagan worship was a matter, not of *opinion,* but of *custom;* that the toleration of the Romans was confined to nations or families who followed the practice of their ancestors; and that in the first ages of Christianity their persecution of the individuals who departed from the established religion was neither moderated by pure reason, nor inflamed by exclusive zeal. But I only desire to appeal, from the hasty apprehension, to the more deliberate judgment, of Dr. Watson himself. Should there still remain any difference of opinion between us, I shall be satisfied, if he will consider me as a sincere though perhaps unsuccessful lover of truth and as a firm friend to civil and ecclesiastical freedom.

Far be it from me, or from any faithful historian,

to impute to respectable societies the faults of some individual members. Our two Universities most undoubtedly contain the same mixture, and most probably the same
proportions, of zeal and moderation, of reason and superstition. Yet there is much less difference between the
smoothness of the Ionic, and the roughness of the Doric
dialect, than may be found between the polished style of
Dr. Watson, and the coarse language of Mr. Davis, Dr.
Chelsum, or Dr. Randolph. The second of these critics,
Dr. Chelsum of Christ Church, is unwilling that the
world should forget that *he* was the first who sounded to
arms, that *he* was the first who furnished the antidote to
the poison, and who, as early as the month of October
of the year 1776, published his *Strictures* on the two last
Chapters of Mr. Gibbon's History. The success of a pamphlet, which he modestly styles imperfect and ill-digested,
encouraged him to resume the controversy. In the beginning of the present year, his Remarks made their
second appearance, with some alteration of form, and a
large increase of bulk; and the author who seems to
fight under the protection of two episcopal banners, has
prefixed, in the front of his volume, his name and titles,
which in the former edition he had less honourably suppressed. His confidence is fortified by the alliance and
communications of a *distinguished* writer, Dr. Randolph,
&c. who, on a proper occasion, would, no doubt, be ready
to bear as honourable testimony to the merit and reputation of Dr. Chelsum. The two friends are indeed so
happily united by art and nature, that if the author of
the Remarks had not pointed out the valuable communications of the Margaret Professor, it would have been
impossible to separate their respective property. Writers
who possess any freedom of mind, may be known from
each other by the peculiar character of their style and
sentiments; but the champions who are enlisted in the
service of Authority, commonly wear the uniform of the
regiment. Oppressed with the same yoke, covered with the
same trappings, they heavily move along, perhaps not
with an equal pace, in the same beaten track of prejudice and preferment. Yet I should expose my own injustice, were I absolutely to confound with Mr. Davis

the two Doctors in Divinity, who are joined in one volume. The three critics appear to be animated by the same implacable resentment against the historian of the Roman Empire; they are alike disposed to support the same opinions by the same arts; and if in the language of the two latter, the disregard of politeness is somewhat less gross and indecent, the difference is not of such a magnitude as to excite in my breast any lively sensations of gratitude. It was the misfortune of Mr. Davis that he undertook to *write* before he had *read.* He set out with the stock of authorities which he found in my quotations, and boldly ventured to play his reputation against mine. Perhaps he may now repent of a loss which is not easily recovered; but if I had not surmounted my almost insuperable reluctance to a public dispute, many a reader might still be dazzled by the vehemence of his assertions, and might still believe that Mr. Davis had detected several wilful and important misrepresentations in my two last chapters. But the confederate doctors appear to be scholars of a higher form and longer experience; they enjoy a certain rank in their academical world; and as their zeal is enlightened by some rays of knowledge, so their desire to ruin the credit of their adversary is occasionally checked by the apprehension of injuring their own. These restraints, to which Mr. Davis was a stranger, have confined them to a very narrow and humble path of historical criticism; and if I were to correct, according to their wishes, all the particular facts against which they have advanced any objections, these corrections, admitted in their fullest extent, would hardly furnish materials for a decent list of *errata.*

The *dogmatical* part of their work, which in every sense of the word deserves that appellation, is ill adapted to engage my attention. I had declined the consideration of theological arguments, when they were managed by a candid and liberal adversary; and it would be inconsistent enough, if I should have refused to draw my sword in honourable combat against the keen and well-tempered weapon of Dr. Watson, for the sole purpose of encountering the rustic cudgel of two staunch and sturdy polemics.

[The following is the conclusion of Gibbon's demonstration, against "the confederate doctors," that the early Christians refused military service under the pagan emperors.]

Notwithstanding the plainest evidence, Dr. Chelsum will not believe that either Origen in theory, or Marcellus in practice, could seriously object to the use of arms; "because it is well known, that, far from declining the business of war altogether, whole legions of Christians served in the Imperial armies." I have not yet discovered, in the author or authors of the Remarks, many traces of a clear and enlightened understanding, yet I cannot suppose them so destitute of every reasoning principle, as to imagine that they here allude to the conduct of the Christians who embraced the profession of arms after their religion had obtained a public establishment. Whole legions of Christians served under the banners of Constantine and Justinian, as whole regiments of Christians are now enlisted in the service of France or England. The representation which I had given, was confined to the principles and practice of the church of which Origen and Marcellus were members, before the sense of public and private interest had reduced the lofty standard of evangelical perfection to the ordinary level of human nature. In those primitive times, where are the Christian legions that served in the imperial armies? Our ecclesiastical Pompeys may stamp with their foot, but no armed men will arise out of the earth, except the ghosts of the Thundering and the Thebæan legions; the former renowned for a miracle, and the latter for a martyrdom.[1] Either the two Protestant Doctors must acquiesce under some imputations which are better understood than expressed, or they must prepare, in the full light and freedom of the eighteenth century, to undertake the defence of two obsolete legions, the least absurd of which staggered the well-disciplined credulity of a Franciscan Friar. (See Pagi *Critic. ad Annal. Baronii*, A.D. 174. tom. i. p. 168.) Very different was the spirit and taste of the

---

[1] [For the pious legend of the Thebæan Legion see above p. 176 *Ed.*]

learned and ingenuous Dr. Jortin, who, after treating the
silly story of the Thundering legion with the contempt
it deserved, continues in the following words: "Moyle
wishes no greater penance to the believers of the Thundering Legion, than that they may also believe the Martyrdom of the Thebæan Legion (Moyle's *Works*, vol. ii. p.
103)": to which good wish, I say with Le Clerc (*Bibliothèque* A. et M. tom. xxvii. p. 193.) AMEN.

ABOUT THE EDITOR

Hugh R. Trevor-Roper, general editor of *The Great
Historians Series,* is the distinguished Regius Professor of Modern History at Oxford University. He
is probably most well-known to American readers
for his book, *The Last Days of Hitler,* which is a
classic in the field of modern German History and
was the result of official investigations carried out
by Professor Trevor-Roper at the behest of British
Intelligence in an attempt to unshroud the mystery surrounding the dictator's fate. The book has
already been translated into nineteen foreign languages. Professor Trevor-Roper is a specialist in
sixteenth and seventeenth-century history and has
published several other notable works: *Archbishop
Laud, Man and Events.* He has contributed numerous articles on political and historical subjects to
the journals and is familiar to American readers
of *The New York Times Magazine* and *Horizon.*

YOUR RECEIPT
THANK YOU

29 JAN 70

$000.10
TOTL $000.10

YOUR RECEIPT
THANK YOU

29 JAN 70

$000.10
TOTL $000.10

YOUR RECEIPT
THANK YOU

29 JAN 70

$000.90
$000.04
TOTL $000.94

YOUR RECEIPT
THANK YOU

29 JAN 70

$000.10 — GEN
2262 $000.10 TOTL 4

YOUR RECEIPT
THANK YOU

29 JAN 70

$000.10 — GEN
2263 $000.10 TOTL 4

YOUR RECEIPT
THANK YOU

29 JAN 70

$000.90 — TAXBKS
$000.04 —
2264 $000.94 TOTL 4

Index

INDEX

452